D0983363

WITHDRAWN

INTERNATIONAL POLITICAL ECONOMY SERIES

General Editor: Timothy M. Shaw, Professor of Political Science and International Development Studies, and Director of the Centre for Foreign Policy Studies, Dalhousie University, Nova Scotia, Canada

Recent titles include:

Pradeep Agrawal, Subir V. Gokarn, Veena Mishra, Kirit S. Parikh and Kunal Sen
ECONOMIC RESTRUCTURING IN EAST ASIA AND INDIA : Perspectives on Policy Reform

Solon L. Barraclough and Krishna B. Ghimire
FORESTS AND LIVELIHOODS: The Social Dynamics of Deforestation in Developing Countries

Jerker Carlsson, Gunnar Köhlin and Anders Ekbom
THE POLITICAL ECONOMY OF EVALUATION: International Aid Agencies and the Effectiveness of Aid

Steve Chan (*editor*)
FOREIGN DIRECT INVESTMENT IN A CHANGING GLOBAL POLITICAL ECONOMY

Edward A. Comor (*editor*)
THE GLOBAL POLITICAL ECONOMY OF COMMUNICATION

Paul Cook and Frederick Nixson (*editors*)
THE MOVE TO THE MARKET?: Trade and Industry Policy Reform in Transitional Economies

O. P. Dwivedi
DEVELOPMENT ADMINISTRATION: From Underdevelopment to Sustainable Development

John Healey and William Tordoff (*editors*)
VOTES AND BUDGETS: Comparative Studies in Accountable Governance in the South

Noeleen Heyzer, James V. Riker and Antonio B. Quizon (*editors*)
GOVERNMENT–NGO RELATIONS IN ASIA: Prospects and Challenges for People-Centred Development

George Kent
CHILDREN IN THE INTERNATIONAL POLITICAL ECONOMY

David Kowalewski
GLOBAL ESTABLISHMENT: The Political Economy of North/Asian Networks

Laura Macdonald
SUPPORTING CIVIL SOCIETY: The Political Role of Non-Governmental
Organizations in Central America

Gary McMahon (*editor*)
LESSONS IN ECONOMIC POLICY FOR EASTERN EUROPE FROM
LATIN AMERICA

Juan Antonio Morales and Gary McMahon (*editors*)
ECONOMIC POLICY AND THE TRANSITION TO DEMOCRACY:The Latin
American Experience

Paul J. Nelson
THE WORLD BANK AND NON-GOVERNMENTAL ORGANIZATIONS:
The Limits of Apolitical Development

Archibald R. M. Ritter and John M. Kirk (*editors*)
CUBA IN THE INTERNATIONAL SYSTEM: Normalization and Integration

Ann Seidman and Robert B. Seidman
STATE AND LAW IN THE DEVELOPMENT PROCESS: Problem-Solving and
Institutional Change in the Third World

Tor Skålnes
THE POLITICS OF ECONOMIC REFORM IN ZIMBABWE: Continuity and
Change in Development

John Sorenson (*editor*)
DISASTER AND DEVELOPMENT IN THE HORN OF AFRICA

Howard Stein (*editor*)
ASIAN INDUSTRIALIZATION AND AFRICA : Studies in Policy Alternatives
to Structural Adjustment

Deborah Stienstra
WOMEN'S MOVEMENTS AND INTERNATIONAL ORGANIZATIONS

Larry A. Swatuk and Timothy M. Shaw (*editors*)
THE SOUTH AT THE END OF THE TWENTIETH CENTURY: Rethinking the
Political Economy of Foreign Policy in Africa, Asia, the Caribbean and Latin
America

Sandra Whitworth
FEMINISM AND INTERNATIONAL RELATIONS

Southeast Asia in the New World Order

The Political Economy of a Dynamic Region

Edited by

David Wurfel
Professor of International Relations,
International Christian University, Tokyo, Japan
and Senior Research Associate
Joint Centre for Asia Pacific Studies
York University and University of Toronto, Canada

and

Bruce Burton
Associate Professor of Political Science
University of Windsor, Canada

St. Martin's Press
New York

SOUTHEAST ASIA IN THE NEW WORLD ORDER
Selection and editorial matter © David Wurfel and Bruce Burton 1996
Chapters 1–13 © Macmillan Press Ltd 1996
Chapter 14 © David Wurfel 1996
All rights reserved. No part of this book may be used or reproduced
in any manner whatsoever without written permission except in the
case of brief quotations embodied in critical articles or reviews.
For information, address:

St. Martin's Press, Scholarly and Reference Division,
175 Fifth Avenue, New York, N.Y. 10010

First published in the United States of America in 1996

Printed in Great Britain

ISBN 0–312–12834–7 (cloth)
ISBN 0–312–12835–5 (paper)

Library of Congress Cataloging-in-Publication Data
Southeast Asia in the New World Order : the political economy of a
dynamic region / edited by David Wurfel and Bruce Burton.
p.   cm. — (International political economy series)
Includes bibliographical references and index.
ISBN 0–312–12834–7 (cloth). — ISBN 0–312–12835–5 (paper)
1. Asia, Southeastern—Politics and government—1945– 2. Asia,
Southeastern—Foreign relations.   3. World politics—1989–
I. Wurfel, David.   II. Burton, Bruce.   III. Series.
DS518.1.S625   1996
320.959—dc20   95–14919
                                                            CIP

Contents

DS
518.1
.S625
1996

103096-4396Z

List of Tables	vii
List of Abbreviations	viii
Notes on the Contributors	xi
Editors' Preface	xv
Map of Southeast Asia	xx

PART I INTRODUCTION

1   Economic and Security Dimensions of the Emerging Order in the Asia Pacific
Paul M. Evans ... 3

PART II CHANGES IN THE REGIONAL ENVIRONMENT

2   ASEAN: New Modes of Economic Cooperation
Linda Y. C. Lim ... 19

3   New Political Roles for ASEAN
Donald Crone ... 36

4   The Emergence of Ecological Issues in Southeast Asia
James Clad and Aurora Medina Siy ... 52

5   Human Rights in Southeast Asia: Rhetoric and Reality
Geoffrey Robinson ... 74

PART III POLICIES OF EXTERNAL POWERS TOWARDS SOUTHEAST ASIA

6   US Policy Themes in Southeast Asia in the 1990s
Donald K. Emmerson ... 103

7   Soviet and Russian Policy towards Southeast Asia (1986–1995)
Vladimir Rakhmanin ... 128

8   China and Southeast Asia: The Challenge of Economic
    Competition
    Robert S. Ross   142

9   Japan and Southeast Asia: Facing an Uncertain Future
    Michael W. Donnelly and Richard Stubbs   165

10 Australian and Canadian Policy towards Southeast Asia
    Kim Richard Nossal   186

11 Western Europe and Southeast Asia
    Brian Bridges   204

PART IV REGIONAL POLICY CONFLICTS IN A
        'NEW WORLD ORDER'

12 The Evolution of Great Power Involvement in Cambodia
    Pierre Lizée   221

13 The Spratly Imbroglio in the Post-Cold War Era
    Mark J. Valencia   244

PART V CONCLUSION

14 The 'New World Order' in Southeast Asia: Some
    Analytical Explorations
    David Wurfel   273

Appendix: Tables   297
Index   307

List of Tables

4.1	Extent of forest areas in Southeast Asian countries, 1980 vs 1990	55
4.2	Major environmental problems of Southeast Asia	56–7
9.1	Japanese FDI in ASEAN countries	171
9.2	Japan–ASEAN trade	173
10.1	Australian and Canadian trade with ASEAN, 1970–1990	194

Appendices

AI	Basic demographic and economic indicators in Southeast Asia	299
A2	Basic social indicators in Southeast Asia	300
A3	Military and social expenditures in Southeast Asia	301
A4	Southeast Asian long-term debt	302
A5	Direction of Southeast Asian trade	303
A6	Official Development Assistance in Southeast Asia	305

List of Abbreviations

ADB	Asian Development Bank
AFTA	ASEAN Free Trade Area
AIC	ASEAN Industrial Complementation
AIJV	ASEAN Industrial Joint Venture
AIP	ASEAN Industrial Products
ANGOC	Asian Non-Governmental Organization Coalition
APEC	Asia-Pacific Economic Cooperation
ASEAN-CCI	Chambers of Commerce and Industry
BAe	British Aerospace
CGDK	Coalition Government of Democratic Kampuchea
CGI	Consultative Group on Indonesia
CIA	Central Intelligence Agency (US)
CIDA	Canadian International Development Agency
COMECON	Council for Mutual Economic Cooperation (East Europe)
CPC	China Petroleum Corporation
CPI	Communist Party of Indonesia
CSCA	Conference on Security and Cooperation in Asia
CSCE	Conference on Security and Cooperation in Europe
DOD	Department of Defense (US)
DPI	Democratic Pluralism Initiative
EAEC	East Asia Economic Caucus
EAEG	East Asia Economic Grouping
EASI	East Asia Security Initiative (US DOD)
EC	European Community
EDSA	Epifanio de los Santos Avenue (Philippines)
EEZ	Exclusive Economic Zone
EU	European Union
EFTA	European Free Trade Area
FDI	Foreign Direct Investment
FLAG	Free Legal Assistance Group (Philippines)
FPDA	Five-Power Defence Arrangement
FUNCINPEC	*Front Uni National Pour un Cambodge Indépendant, Neutre, Pacifique et Coopératif*
GATT	General Agreement on Tariffs and Trade
GDP	Gross Domestic Product

GSP	Generalized System of Preferences
ICCPR	International Covenant on Civil and Political Rights
ICSC	International Commission of Supervision and Control
IFIs	International Financial Institutions
IGGI	Intergovernmental Group on Indonesia
IMET	International Military Education and Training (US DOD)
IMF	International Monetary Fund
INGOs	International Non-Governmental Organizations
IRRI	International Rice Research Institute (Philippines)
KPNLF	Khmer People's National Liberation Front
LBH	Lembaga Bantuan Hukum (Indonesia)
LDP	Liberal Democratic Party (Japan)
MCP	Malayan Communist Party
MFN	Most Favoured Nation
MIA	Missing in Action
MITI	Ministry of International Trade and Industry (Japan)
MNLF	Moro National Liberation Front (Philippines)
NAFTA	North American Free Trade Agreement
NAM	Non-Aligned Movement
NICs	Newly Industrialized Countries
NIEs	Newly Industrialized Economies
NGO	Non-Governmental Organization
NPA	New People's Army (Philippines)
ODA	Official Development Assistance
OECD	Organization for Economic Cooperation and Development
OECF	Overseas Economic Cooperation Fund (Japan)
PECC	Pacific Economic Cooperation Council
PKO	Peace Keeping Operation (UN)
PLA–N	People's Liberation Army–Navy (China)
PMC	Post-Ministerial Conference (ASEAN)
PNG	Papua New Guinea
PRK	People's Republic of Kampuchea
PTA	Preferential Trading Arrangements
SEATO	South East Asia Treaty Organization
SLORC	State Law and Order Restoration Council (Burma/Myanmar)
SMA	Spratly Management Authority
SNC	Supreme National Council (Cambodia)
SOC	State of Cambodia
SOM	Senior Officials Meeting (ASEAN)

UDHR	Universal Declaration of Human Rights
UN	United Nations
UNAMIC	UN Advance Mission in Cambodia
UNCED	UN Conference on Environment and Development
UNDP	UN Development Programme
UNCHR	UN Commission on Human Rights
UNHCR	UN High Commission on Refugees
UNTAC	UN Transitional Authority in Cambodia
USAID	US Agency for International Development
USTR	US Trade Representative
WTO	World Trade Organization
ZOPFAN	Zone of Peace, Freedom, and Neutrality (ASEAN)

Notes on the Contributors

Brian Bridges is currently University Senior Lecturer in the Department of Social Sciences, Lingnan College, Hong Kong. He was previously Associate Fellow and Head of the East Asia Programme of the Royal Institute of International Affairs, London. He has written widely on British and European relations with the Asia Pacific and on international relations within the region. His latest book is *Japan and Korea in the 1990s: From Antagonism to Adjustment* (1993) and he co-authored with Japanese and Malaysian scholars *Pacific Asia in the 1990s* (1991).

Bruce Burton was educated at Oxford and The Hague, is an Associate Professor of Political Science and Co-ordinator of the International Relations Programme at the University of Windsor, and previously taught international relations at the Institute of Social Studies in The Hague. He is the author of numerous scholarly articles on Asian and international affairs and has travelled extensively in the region. He co-edited with David Wurfel *The Political Economy of Foreign Policy in Southeast Asia* (1990).

James Clad is currently Senior Associate with the Asia Pacific Policy Center in Washington, DC, and Professor of Southeast Asian Studies, Georgetown University. He has also previously been a Senior Associate with the Carnegie Endowment, a Senior Fellow at St. Antony's College, Oxford, and Bureau Chief for the *Far Eastern Economic Review* in Manila and Kuala Lumpur. He has contributed articles to *Foreign Affairs*, *Washington Quarterly* and other journals. He is the author of *Southeast Asia* (1987) and *Behind the Myth: Business, Money and Power in Southeast Asia* (1991), and co-author of *After the Crusade: American Foreign Policy for the Post-Superpower Age* (1995).

Donald Crone is Dean of the Faculty, Associate Professor and Chair of International Relations at Scripps College, Claremont, California. He is the author of *The ASEAN States: Coping with Dependence* (1983) and of numerous scholarly articles and book chapters on ASEAN, Pacific cooperation, and Southeast Asian politics. He is currently preparing a book on *Politics and Social Justice in Southeast Asia*.

Michael W. Donnelly is Associate Professor of Political Science and Associate Dean of the Faculty of Arts and Sciences, University of Toronto. He has written extensively on the contemporary Japanese political economy, including US–Japan trade negotiations, and is now completing a study of the development of nuclear power in Japan.

Donald K. Emmerson, Professor of Political Science at the University of Wisconsin, Madison, and Chair of the Council on Southeast Asia and Oceania of the Asia Society, has lectured widely in Asia and Europe. He is author, among numerous books and articles, of *ASEAN under Pressure* (1988) and *Indonesia's Elite: Political Culture and Cultural Politics* (1976). His commentaries on American policy in Southeast Asia have appeared in *Los Angeles Times*, *Asian Wall Street Journal*, *New York Times*, and *Christian Science Monitor*.

Paul M. Evans is Associate Professor of Political Science and Director of the Joint Centre for Asia Pacific Studies at York University, Toronto. He has published widely on the international political economy of the Asia Pacific region and is the author of *John Fairbank and the American Understanding of Modern China* (1988) and co-editor and contributor to *Reluctant Adversaries: Canada and the People's Republic of China, 1949–1970* (1991).

Linda Y. C. Lim is an economist from Singapore who teaches international business and Asian studies at the University of Michigan and runs its Southeast Asia Business Program. Her extensive publications focus on foreign investment, export manufacturing and the political economy of development. She is co-author of *Foreign Direct Investment and Industrialisation in Malaysia, Singapore, Taiwan and Thailand* (1991) and *Trade, Employment and Industrialisation in Singapore* (1986).

Pierre Lizée is currently Visiting Scholar at the Institute of East Asian Studies, University of California at Berkeley and a PhD candidate in political science at York University, Toronto. He is co-editor of *Cambodia – the 1989 Paris Peace Conference: Background, Analysis and Documents* (1991).

Kim Richard Nosssal is Professor and Head of Political Science at McMaster University, Hamilton, Ontario, and a specialist on Canadian foreign policy and Canadian relations with Asia. Among many articles and books, he is the author of *The Politics of Canadian Foreign Policy* (1989) and *Rain Dancing: Sanctions in Canadian and Australian Foreign Policy* (1994) and co-author of *Relocating Middle Powers: Australia and Canada in a Changing World Order* (1993).

Vladimir Rakhmanin is political counsellor of the Russian Embassy in Washington, DC. He and served previously in the Soviet Embassy in Beijing. In 1986 he worked as special assistant to Soviet Deputy Foreign Minister Rogachev, who was responsible for the Asia Pacific region. In that position he was closely involved in the process of negotiations on resolution of the Cambodian conflict, and establishment of the official dialogue with ASEAN.

Geoffrey Robinson, who recently completed a PhD in Government and Southeast Asian Studies at Cornell University, is Southeast Asian Research Director for Amnesty International in London, currently on leave as a Killam Post-Doctoral Fellow at the University of British Columbia. He is a specialist on Indonesia.

Robert S. Ross is Associate Professor of Political Science at Boston College. He has published numerous scholarly articles on Chinese foreign policy and is the author of *The Indochina Tangle: China's Vietnam Policy, 1975–1979* (1988) and of *China, the United States and the Soviet Union: Tripolarity and Policymaking in the Cold War* (1993).

Aurora Medina Siy is a PhD candidate at the School of Advanced International Studies, The John Hopkins University. She was formerly Senior Economic Development Specialist at the National Economic and Development Authority (Philippines).

Richard Stubbs is Associate Professor of Political Science at McMaster University, Hamilton, Ontario. He has served as Associate Director of the Joint Centre for Asia Pacific Studies in Toronto. He has published widely on Southeast Asian politics and the international commodity trade, and is the author of *Hearts and Minds in Guerrilla Warfare: The Malayan Emergency 1948–60* (1989) and co-editor of *Political Economy and the Changing Global Order* (1994).

Mark J. Valencia is currently Project Leader and Research Associate with the Institute of Economic Development and Policy, East–West Center, Honolulu and was previously Associate Professor with the

Department of Oceanography, University of Hawaii. Among his numerous publications are *Malaysia and the Law of the Sea: The Foreign Policy Issues, the Options and their Implications* (1991), *Pacific Ocean Boundary Problems: Status and Solutions* (1991, co-authored with Douglas Johnston) and *Southeast Asian Seas: Oil Under Troubled Waters* (1985).

David Wurfel, who was trained in the Southeast Asia Program and received his PhD in Government at Cornell University, was Professor of Political Science at the University of Windsor from 1969 to 1993, having taught previously at the Universities of Michigan, Missouri and Singapore. In 1995 he completed a two-year appointment as Professor of International Relations at the International Christian University in Tokyo, and is now Senior Research Associate at the Joint Centre for Asia Pacific Studies, Toronto. He is the author of *Filipino Politics: Development and Decay* (1988) and has contributed to, among others, *Governments and Politics in Southeast Asia* (1959), *Southeast Asia: Problems of US Policy* (1963), *The US and the Philippines* (1966), *Government and Rebellions in Southeast Asia* (1985), *Reinventing Socialism in Vietnam* (1993), and authored numerous journal articles on Asian politics and international affairs. He co-edited with Bruce Burton *The Political Economy of Foreign Policy in Southeast Asia* (1990).

Editors' Preface

The nature, origins and consequences of the dynamic changes that have been reshaping the international system since the mid-1980s are the subject of a rapidly growing literature and have been probed from a wide range of perspectives and at different levels of analysis (see References). Some authors have concentrated on the global level, others on a regional level. Several books, such as James Hsiung (ed.), *Asia Pacific in the New World Politics*, Sheldon Simon (ed.), *East Asian Security in the Post-Cold War Era*, Norman Palmer, *The New Regionalism in Asia and the Pacific* and Richard Higgott, Richard Leaver and John Ravenhill (eds), *Pacific Economic Relations in the 1990s: Conflict or Cooperation?*, have explored the international dimensions of the changes occurring in the Asia Pacific or East Asia. Ours is the first such book to focus on Southeast Asia.

There are certain advantages to employing the narrower focus. Unlike the Asia Pacific, whose boundaries are 'still fluid' (Stubbs and Underhill, p. 366), Southeast Asia is a clearly defined region and widely accepted as such.[1] Despite ethnic and cultural diversity, a strong regional organization, the Association of South East Asian Nations (ASEAN), has fostered close political–diplomatic cooperation and a network of 'complex interdependence' (Keohane and Nye) among its six member states. The growing sense of regional identity should be enhanced as membership is gradually extended from Vietnam, to Laos, Cambodia and Burma (Myanmar)[2] and the ASEANization of Southeast Asia is completed.

As we made clear on a previous occasion, we do not align ourselves with any particular theoretical orientation towards 'political economy'. (Wurfel and Burton, p. 1). We would concur with Geoffrey Underhill that the relationship between the political and economic domains is the 'central question' for international political economy and that the two domains 'cannot be separated in any meaningful sense'. The dynamics of economic and strategic issues are indeed 'intimately bound up with each other'. We have some reservations, however, about his second premise that 'economic structures and processes are the results of political interactions' and not of 'the spontaneous interaction of individual economic agents'. (Stubbs and Underhill, p. 18). While this is sometimes the case, it is not always so. In Southeast Asia and elsewhere market systems are not inevitably the outcome of political action. The balance between markets and states can vary in time and place.

We believe that an emphasis on the interplay between economic and political variables is a more valid approach than one which advocates the primacy of either politics or economics in international relations. It seems unlikely that 'geoeconomics will replace geopolitics in the global strategic-balance-of-power game' (Hsiung, p. 5), even though we recognize there has been a growing concern with 'economic security' in recent years. We would also note that our approach to political economy is inclusive rather than exclusive and recognizes the relevance of other variables besides the narrowly economic or political. Social, cultural and religious factors can clearly exert strong influences on political economy. In fact, if the concern is 'security', we would embrace 'comprehensive security' as the most meaningful concept.

We have chosen to place 'New World Order' in quotation marks not only because we wish to dissociate ourselves from President Bush's appropriation of the term in 1991 to legitimize his administration's attempt to preserve American hegemony; we believe the term to be more appropriate than 'post-Cold War' because many of the changes that became apparent at both global and regional levels with the ending of the Cold War were in fact under way before the momentous developments in Eastern Europe in 1989. Until then attention had been diverted from the major redistribution of power that was beginning to take place in the global political economy and from the emergence of an embryonic global civil society.

Japan was moving with relentless pace through the 1980s towards unquestioned economic superpower status and several Third World countries, including at least two from Southeast Asia – Malaysia and Thailand – were entering the ranks of the NICs. China's economic reforms and its transition to a market-style economy began in 1978, and by the mid-1980s, when Gorbachev was only just coming to power in the Soviet Union, its economy was booming, further undermining the bipolar system. Likewise, the foundations for the emergence in the 1990s of a form of global civil society date back to at least the 1970s, when modern grassroots organizations began to grow in many Third World states – including some in Southeast Asia – and developmental, human rights and environmental NGOs based in the First World began to expand in numbers and activities.

In sum, the origins of some important elements of the 'New World Order', in East and Southeast Asia as well as elsewhere, go back well before 1989. Granted that the collapse of the Soviet Union and the consequent Russian withdrawal from Southeast Asia had a significant and positive impact on ASEAN–Indochina relations and made possible a partial resolution of the Cambodian conflict and helped alter US-Philippine relations, an exclusively post-Cold War focus nevertheless directs attention away from the wider changes that were already in progress well before the dismantling of the Berlin Wall.

There are, of course, other legacies from the past besides Cold War-related ones influencing the international relations of Southeast Asia in the 'New World Order', such as the long-standing ethnic and territorial disputes. Thus while we count the *'New* World Order' as different from the old order, we recognize that there are significant elements of continuity. What is beyond question is that both old and new elements are now released from the constraints of bipolarity – with uncertain consequences for both regional and global systems.

Our book's analysis of Southeast Asia in the 'New World Order' begins with Paul Evans's survey of the economic and security dimensions of the emerging order in the Asia Pacific.[3] Since it refers to a number of themes developed by subsequent contributors, his chapter also serves as an introduction to those that follow.

In the next section, focusing on changes in the regional environment, two chapters are devoted to ASEAN. Linda Lim analyses New Modes of Economic Cooperation while Donald Crone looks at new political roles for one of the world's most successful regional organizations. Two sets of issues that have become increasingly significant in the international relations of Southeast Asia – ecological issues and human rights – are discussed in separate chapters by James Clad and Aurora Siy and by Geoffrey Robinson.

Then come four chapters examining the policies of the major external powers influencing the region: the United States (Donald Emmerson), Soviet Union/Russia (Vladimir Rakhmanin), Japan (Michael Donnelly and Richard Stubbs) and China (Robert Ross). Australian and Canadian interests are then discussed by Kim Richard Nossal and those of Western Europe by Brian Bridges.

The end of the Cold War and the proclamation of a 'New World Order' did not bring an end to conflict situations in the region, and the Cambodian power struggle and the Spratly imbroglio are analysed respectively by Pierre Lizée and Mark Valencia.

In his concluding chapter, David Wurfel places Southeast Asian dynamism in its broader Asia–Pacific and global settings. He applies concepts and issues such as region, multilateralism, market, democracy, and state as actor and as unit of analysis to Southeast Asia in the post-Cold War 'New World Order' in order to help throw new light on change within the region and to see how useful Southeast Asian experience is for testing global-level generalizations.

Most of the contributors to this volume presented initial versions of their chapters at a conference held at the University of Windsor in October 1992. The subsequent process of soliciting further contributions and of revision and exchange of drafts was an extended one. We are considerably indebted to all our contributors and to Macmillan, our publisher, for their patience and forbearance over the delays involved in bringing this multi-authored tricontinentally based project to a successful conclusion.

The Windsor conference was made possible by grants from the Social Science and Humanities Research Council of Canada, the Canada–ASEAN Centre, the University of Toronto–York University Joint Centre for Asia Pacific Studies and the President and the Deans of Arts and Social Sciences of the University of Windsor.

We are appreciative of the administrative and secretarial support we have received from the Political Science Department at the University of Windsor and the Division of International Studies at the International Christian University. We were fortunate in the high quality of the research assistance provided by Lisette Daignault and Vincent Halford, in Windsor, and Michael Croft and Arno Janssen, in Tokyo. We greatly benefitted from the scholarly comments and wise guidance of the series editor, Tim Shaw, though no one but editors and contributors should be held responsible for any shortcomings in the content of this volume.

Tokyo   DAVID WURFEL
Windsor   BRUCE BURTON

Notes

1. There is general agreement that the Southeast Asian region encompasses the following ten states: Brunei Darussalam, Indonesia, Malaysia, the Philippines, Singapore, Thailand, Burma (Myanmar), Cambodia, Laos and Vietnam. The first six together make up the current membership of ASEAN.
2. Both because the name is less well known and because it is a name adopted by a government that is widely regarded as illegitimate, we have preferred not to use Myanmar unless in a quotation or from a source which uses the term. Still, we have tried to respect contributors' preferences. In

any case, when Myanmar is used we have usually given Burma in parenthesis, and vice versa.
3. Asia Pacific (without a hyphen) is the form we employ when the term is used as a noun; when it is used adjectively, we include a hyphen.

References

Brecher, Jeremy, John Brown Childs and Jill Cutler (eds) (1993), *Global Visions: Beyond the New World Order* (Montreal and New York: Black Rose Books).

Bennis, Phylliss and Michael Moushabeck (eds) (1993) *Altered States: A Reader in the New World Order* (New York: Olive Branch Press).

Higgott, Richard, Richard Leaver and John Ravenhill (eds) (1993) *Pacific Economic Relations in the 1990s: Conflict or Cooperation?* (Boulder and London: Lynne Rienner).

Hogan, Michael (ed) (1992) *The End of the Cold War: Its Meaning and Implications* (Cambridge and New York: Cambridge University Press).

Hsiung, James (1993) *Asia Pacific in the New World Politics* (Boulder and London: Lynne Rienner).

Keohane, Robert and Joseph Nye (1977) *Power and Interdependence: World Politics in Transition* (Boston: Little, Brown).

Leaver, Richard and James Richardson (eds) (1993), *Charting the Post-Cold War Order* (Boulder: Westview Press).

Palmer, Norman (1991), *The New Regionalism in Asia and the Pacific* (Lexington: Lexington Books).

Simon, Sheldon (ed.) (1993) *East Asian Security in the Post-Cold War Era* (Armonk: M. E. Sharpe).

Stubbs, Richard and Geoffrey Underhill (eds) (1994) *Political Economy and the Changing Global Order* (Toronto: McClelland & Stewart).

Wurfel, David and Bruce Burton (eds) (1990) *The Political Economy of Foreign Policy in Southeast Asia* (Basingstoke: Macmillan; New York: St Martin's Press).

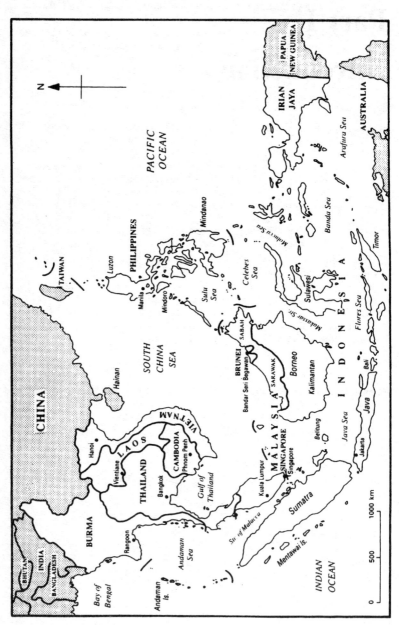

Southeast Asia

Part I
Introduction

1 Economic and Security Dimensions of the Emerging Order in the Asia Pacific

Paul M. Evans*

It comes as little surprise that the fourteen essays in this volume take very different positions on how to understand contemporary issues in Southeast Asia, how to locate Southeast Asia in a broader regional and global context, and how to link political economy with power politics. Contemporary academic and policy writing on Southeast Asia is marked by a healthy pluralism and diversity.

Yet the essays collected here do share two central assumptions. The first is that there have been recent and fundamental changes in the political and economic life of Southeast Asia. It is difficult to quarrel with the assertion by Michael Donnelly and Richard Stubbs that 'since 1989, Asia has become a dramatically different place'. Where the debate begins is in assessing the origins, dimensions and consequences of the forces that have produced this change. Some of the essays wish to go back to the founding of ASEAN in 1967. Two choose the Plaza Accord in 1985. And others look to the ending of the Cold War, a process which began to accelerate in 1989. Still others look to Asian and world system changes which began earlier than that. Periodization has its hazards.

The second starting point is that Southeast Asia can be treated as a coherent region. All of the essays begin with the premise that we can have a fruitful discussion of Southeast Asia without treating it merely as the sum of its independent national parts or by dividing it into smaller units such as ASEAN and Indochina. The analytical and political pull of 'One Southeast Asia', to borrow the phrase used in a series of meetings

* The author wishes to acknowledge the support of the Cooperative Security Competition Program of the Department of Foreign Affairs and International Trade, Ottawa, which helped enable completion of this chapter.

in Southeast Asia in 1993, now seems almost irresistible. The idea of 'Southeast Asia' is no longer being imposed by outside powers nor is it being undermined by national rivalries, ideological divides or great power conflict.

The phrase 'New World Order' selected by the editors is one way of conceptualizing the dynamics of contemporary international relations. Equally common in the mid-1990s is to use the idea of a 'post-Cold War' era. Though it is somewhat misleading in an Asian context – Soviet–American rivalry was never *the* defining element of Asian affairs and two Asian conflicts originating in the Cold War (in Cambodia and on the Korean peninsula) are far from concluded – it has the virtue of indicating that something fundamental has changed without clearly specifying the order that will replace it. Here I will take a different approach and conceive of the emerging 'world order' as a series of interconnected regional orders. The premise of my argument is that the dynamics of production and security are producing a 'world of regions', or less grandiosely what Donald Crone calls in his essay 'a more regionalized world order'. This is not to suggest that the twenty-first century will witness the inevitable rise of competing economic blocs or see civilizations clashing along continental lines. But it could very well be a world without a single overarching conflict or commonality.

In the mid-1900s the truly controversial issue is not whether Southeast Asia exists but how to locate it in a broader complex of social, economic and political forces. Academic analysts are acutely aware of the political and intellectual stakes in 'naming' the object of study (see Emmerson, 1984). And governments have very firm ideas about what kind of regional groupings and institutions they wish to see appear. They are expending considerable time and resources in presenting preferred options, as indicated by the ongoing rivalry between the proponents of Asia–Pacific Economic Cooperation (APEC) and an East Asia Economic Caucus (EAEC). Beyond competing over the composition of international organizations, very large sums of money are targeted at shaping social, political and educational programmes at home. Since 1967 the programme to create an 'ASEAN identity' in Southeast Asia has been vigorous but pales when compared to the funds spent in the United States, Canada and Australia since the mid-1980s to develop an 'Asia Pacific' focus.

The analytical contenders are several. One is to employ the concept of 'the Pacific', as Donald Crone does (see also Segal, 1990). Another is to place Southeast Asia in a Eurasian context, as Brian Bridges does, or as that part of 'Asia', south of China and east of India.[1] Most of the essays here use the much more recent formulation of 'Asia Pacific'. The concept is used in a variety of ways, but the common denominator is a rough geographical perimeter which includes East and Southeast Asia, North America and Australia. In an area of enormous size and diversity, the ties that bind are principally trade-related; the principal units of analysis are states. Some emphasize the trans-Pacific commonalities which bind the area together. North America and Australia thus do not just have interests in the region but are integrally *part* of it. Others place emphasis on the Asian part of the Pacific and understand others to be interacting with it (see Evans, 1994a).

The concept of 'Asia Pacific' and the thrust toward institution building originated outside Southeast Asia, principally in Japan and Australia. Several members of ASEAN initially opposed the idea on the grounds that it would undercut ASEAN. That opposition has now largely evaporated. It is seen as desirable to emphasize trans-Pacific connections, principally because of the abiding importance of the United States as a market for Southeast Asian goods and as the low-cost, low-risk provider of strategic stability around the Pacific.

SOUTHEAST ASIA IN AN EASTERN ASIAN CONTEXT

The recent economic changes in Southeast Asia have been astonishing in their speed and scope. In the space of a decade, the economies of Singapore, Thailand, Malaysia and Indonesia have not only been expanded but transformed. Southeast Asia's industrial revolution has been compressed into less than half a generation. Its consequences and achievements, pretty or not, can be seen in the skylines and street life of almost every major city in the region.

While it has been end markets in North America and Europe that have fuelled the successful strategies of export-oriented industrialization of Southeast Asia, it has been connections within Asia that have been fundamental to the transformation of industrial production and daily life. Southeast Asia has been connected to East Asia through trade for a thousand years but only in the past decade has it become an integral part of a broader regional production system which I have elsewhere labelled 'Eastern Asia' (see Evans, 1992). Eastern Asia is much larger than the Confucian or Chinese culture area (customarily but not universally referred to as 'East Asia') and encompasses a crescent arc running from Japan and China in the north to Indonesia in the south. Its component parts are less states and nations, though these are often convenient devices, than interconnected economic units which are located around the region.

As several recent studies reveal, regionalization in Eastern Asia has been multidimensional, including trade, investment, finance, developmental assistance flows, tourism and migration.[2] At the core of 'Eastern Asia' is what Linda Lim defines below as a 'regionally integrated production complex'. Behind the dynamic economic growth has been a fundamental restructuring of the economies and firms of the region. If a birth date for modern Eastern Asia can be pinpointed, it is the Plaza Agreement in 1985 between American and Japanese negotiators over the valuation of the dollar and yen. Combined with the welcome mat in Southeast Asia rolled out by a process of competitive deregulation among the ASEAN countries beginning in 1986, the ensuing wave of Japanese investment into Southeast Asia has produced a period of unprecedented economic activity. Not only was this investment unprecedented in volume (see the tables in Chapter 9, pp. 171 and 173), it was connected to production systems in several key industries which transformed basic industrial structures. Japan's trade with Southeast Asia has increasingly become intra-firm, intra-industry trade. Toyota, for example, has recently created integrated ASEAN operations involving production sites in Thailand, Malaysia, the Philippines and Indonesia. These are supplemented by inter-firm alliances. In its most advanced forms in electronics manufacturing, the company has become less important than the network, with firms producing component parts in production chains in geographically dispersed locations. The further appreciation of the yen in 1995 will only speed the process.

The Japanese connection remains paramount, but it has been supplemented by a rising level of investment from the United States and Europe and especially by a new wave of investment from the NICs of Northeast Asia, Hong Kong, Taiwan and South Korea. Between 1987 and 1992 Taiwanese companies invested about US$12 billion in Southeast Asian countries (Baum, 1993). In the past three years, this has been supplemented by a new flow of investment *among* Southeast Asian countries, a flow that has also extended into China. In 1993 the largest single investor in mainland China was a Thai firm, Chaeron Pokphand.

The integration of Southeast Asia into a larger Asian and Asia-Pacific context has several characteristics which differentiate it from the process of regional economic integration in Europe and North America. First, and most fundamentally, investment accelerated more rapidly than trade. Second, the principal players have not been governments (though they have played a vital role in creating the domestic arrangements necessary for economic growth) but private sector firms.

Third, the level of formal institutionalization has been low. Regulatory frameworks to facilitate cross-boundary transfers have been produced by tacit and unilateral policy adjustments rather than formal regional institutions or formal trade arrangements along the lines of formally negotiated free trade agreements. The only indigenous free trade area, the ASEAN Free Trade Area, created in 1991 is yet of only marginal importance to the overall economic flows of Asia Pacific. More importantly, its real motive is less to build intra-ASEAN co-operation than to encourage continued foreign investment flows into Southeast Asia.

Fourth, economic regionalization has not produced nor been supported by any common political aspirations to create an Asian commonwealth or supranational state. Economic integration has not been promoted as a path to other political objectives such as political unification or the eradication of war. Fifth, the division of labour within the region has been explicitly hierarchical. Very little effort has been made to harmonize economic and social conditions across the region or reduce regional disparities.

A sixth distinguishing characteristic of the Asia Pacific has been the recent and fast-paced development of trans-national economic sub-regions. They have developed as a response to still formidable barriers to the movement of goods, capital and labour across boundaries within Southeast Asia and throughout the broader Asia–Pacific region. The focus is not countries but adjacent areas within countries that have matching capabilities and resources. Two of these are in East and Northeast Asia: the South China Growth Triangle (involving south China, Hong Kong and Taiwan) and the Tumen River project. Planning is also under way for accelerated cooperation in and around the Sea of Japan and the Yellow Sea. Three are in Southeast Asia, including the southern growth triangle (involving Singapore, Johor province of Malaysia and the Riau province of Indonesia), the northern growth triangle (involving portions of Indonesia, Malaysia and Thailand) and the proposed eastern growth quadrangle (involving Mindanao in the Philippines, Sulawesi in Indonesia, East Malaysia and Brunei). Feasibility studies for a sixth, connecting East and Southeast Asia, centre on the Greater Mekong Region and involve six countries (China, Myanmar [Burma], Laos, Vietnam, Thailand and Cambodia).

This new and dynamic Asia–Pacific capitalism has produced some dramatic results. The most obvious is the high growth rates that much of Southeast Asia has enjoyed for almost a decade. It has been this growth that has created a vastly expanded middle class, a new group of successful capitalists and the growing self-confidence of states and leaders in the region.

The combination of these processes has not produced, however, any homogenization of strategies for social, political and economic management in Southeast Asia, much less a broader Eastern Asian or Asia–Pacific context. What they have done is to change the scope and intensity of economic activity and the interconnectedness of policy management on a regional basis.

Nor have they produced harmony. Undeniable components of the emerging order are unprecedented environmental degradation, political turbulence, a durable and hierarchical division of labour and a series of daunting new problems. As Linda Lim persuasively argues in her essay, there are few backward linkages in the production process and little local procurement by foreign multinationals. And Southeast Asian countries face growing trade deficits with Japan, continued dependence on US markets and Japanese technology, and increased vulnerability to the ongoing US trans-Pacific trade deficit (Bernard and Ravenhill, 1995).

SECURITY RELATIONS: AN UNCERTAIN TRANSITION

Contrary to the econophoric view that economic growth and integration make international conflict less likely, Southeast Asia and the broader Asia Pacific remain dangerous. The chance of direct military aggression is now remote and few governments face serious domestic insurgencies. Yet security relations in the broader Asia Pacific have entered a period of tremendous flux and uncertainty. The ending of the Cold War and the economic dynamism of the region are recasting regional arrangements. The system of bilateral security alliances and guarantees that have been the foundation of the regional security order since World War II are being replaced by a much more fluid set of arrangements. The United States remains a major stabilizing force in the Pacific but the gradual draw down of its military forces described by Donald Emmerson in his essay, the economic and military rise of several Asian states, and expanded economic interdependence are re-defining the American role. As Vladimir Rakhmanin stresses in his chapter, the Russian successor state is no longer a major military player in the Asia Pacific. For the first time in almost a century and a half, the future of the international order in the Western Pacific is largely in Asian hands.

The list of immediate and potential conflicts is lengthy. The boundary disputes over the Spratlys and Paracels are the most serious in Southeast Asia, but there are more than a dozen others often involving ethnic groups that spread across national boundaries. As Pierre Lizée capably demonstrates, the Cambodian conflict is now unlikely to provoke direct military confrontation between regional states but is far from resolved. The China–Taiwan division has direct implications for both Northeast and Southeast Asia. A military clash on the Korean peninsula would have major economic and political consequences around the Pacific. The production and transfer of increasingly sophisticated conventional weapons is a major concern as are the prospects of nuclear proliferation.

Added to this list of traditional security concerns is a longer one of new and 'unconventional' issues which affect the security and well-being of states and individuals in the region. These include environmental degradation, management of maritime resources, human rights violations, irregular migration of people across state boundaries, piracy, terrorism, illicit drugs and disease. Whether or not all of these issues can properly be called security issues is very much in debate, but it is clear that all of them are genuine problems in the region and have the potential to trigger the use of military force.

There have been two general reactions to the uncertainty and fluidity of regional security issues. One has been an increase in military spending by most of the countries of the region, especially in air and naval capacity. The motives for this increase are complex, involving a combination of (a) reaction to perceived threats; (b) availability of supply at attractive prices; and (c) enhanced capacity to pay. These do not add up to a classical arms race because the acquisitions are not specifically pegged in most instances to the actions of any other single state. But they do constitute the foundations of an arms build-up of major proportions in both scope and lethality (Ball, 1993).

A second has been a great deal of experimentation with new forms of cooperation and dialogue. There are hopeful signs as potential adversaries and former antagonists engage in cooperative ventures of tension reduction. Much of this has occurred at a bilateral level. China in particular has systematically improved its bilateral relations with almost all of its neighbours over the last several years – until recently.

Multilateralism in security matters is a comparatively new mode of international relations in the Asia Pacific, especially in Northeast Asia.

Most Asian countries have rejected the concept of a CSCE-like approach to creating a post-Cold War security order. On the other hand, at least eight countries have made concrete proposals for new diplomatic instruments to reduce regional tensions and prepare the way for a more stable order in future. The creation at a formal governmental level of the ASEAN Regional Forum and the proliferation of channels for non-governmental or 'track two'[3] dialogue on regional security do not amount to any kind of collective security regime for the Pacific. But they are important steps in laying the foundation for a security framework appropriate to the more complex, diffuse and integrated regional economy.

REACTIONS OF OUTSIDE POWERS

Michael Donnelly and Richard Stubbs make a compelling case for the view that Japanese decision makers are the practitioners of 'strategic coping' in dealing with Southeast Asia. The authors of the essays on the United States, Russia and China all come to strangely similar conclusions. None of the major powers has created a comprehensive and coherent policy for dealing with a Southeast Asia in rapid transition. Donald Emmerson argues that domestic inattention and conflict have undermined the efforts of recent American administrations to achieve the three professed aims of promoting security, prosperity and democracy in Southeast Asia. He, and others, feel the three goals to be contradictory, whatever the rhetorical and ideological gloss. While America's military capacity remains highly significant, bilateral economic tensions are increasing.

The case of Russia is almost the reverse. Rakhmanin indicates that Russia is developing an approach which, while sometimes weak in defining specific Russian interests, is acceptable in Southeast Asia. But Russia has little or no capacity to realize its objectives, especially in the commercial field.

China's 'smiling diplomacy', as Robert Ross argues, has been successful to a point. But the profession of good intentions meets two major obstacles. First, China's defence modernization programme is causing alarm in Southeast Asia even more than in Northeast Asia. In looking at future military threats to the region, it is China, not Russia, that figures most prominently in Southeast Asian minds – accentuated in 1995. China has also been conspicuously inept at reducing these suspicions and concerns by refusing transparency measures and by playing only a passive role in the regional dialogue process. Second, China is often perceived as a competitor to Southeast Asia, not just as a producer but also in attracting investment. An extra dimension here is the long-standing anxiety about the intentions of 'overseas Chinese' businesses in Southeast Asia.

European countries and the European Union have at best only been intermittent players in Southeast Asia in recent years, though this shows signs of changing, especially in commercial relations, as noted by Bridges.

Based on these assessments, curiously it is Japan that has probably been most effective in not just coping but also in playing a leadership role in Southeast Asia. Its economic ties with Southeast Asia are substantial (to say the least), complex, and growing. It is the dominant economy in Eastern Asia but has been able to deflect or manage discontent about its dominance. In security matters, through transparency measures and its quiet but supportive role in regional dialogue efforts, it has been able to reassure its southern neighbours about its intentions and capabilities. Considering the potential for suspicion, distrust and rancour, Japanese coping has been a notable success.

Kim Nossal's essay on Australian and Canadian engagement in Southeast Asia indicates the room for manoeuvre that has been afforded by the end of the Cold War and prompted by new economic opportunities. Some of the Canadian and Australian successes in the region result in part from their experience with multilateral institutions and processes. The comparative levels of Canadian and Australian involvement in the region are significantly different. Southeast Asia has emerged as top priority in Australian economic and security policy. Indeed, Australia is the only 'external' power to see itself as part of Southeast Asia and the most willing to change policy and domestic practices to integrate itself into the region.

FROM REGIONALIZATION TO REGIONALISM?

Until very recently, Southeast Asia's integration into a larger regional economy has not been associated with any pronounced forms of Asian regionalism. By regionalism I mean a conscious awareness of shared commonalities and the will to create institutions and processes to act upon those commonalities. ASEAN itself has of course tried to formulate a set of common norms and practices through such instruments as the Treaty of Amity and Cooperation and ideas like the Zone of Peace,

Freedom and Neutrality (ZOPFAN). But these were not extended northward into East Asia.

Nevertheless, one of the striking developments in East and Southeast Asia in the 1990s has been the effort to seek common perspectives on matters of regional concern. At the level of institution building in both the economic and security realms, most of this has been conducted on a trans-Pacific, Asia–Pacific basis.[4] But there has also been an Eastern Asian or Western Pacific effort to establish common positions on several sets of issues. The mechanism has not been through a dedicated regional organization but through a process of interactive adjustment of policy positions based on bilateral discussions and tacit understandings. One example has been the persistent effort of Japan and other countries in Eastern Asia to take a more positive view of the role and importance of state institutions in supporting economic growth (World Bank, 1993). The more visible, and incendiary, example concerns human rights.

Human rights issues have become much higher profile in the past five years for several reasons, noted in Geoffrey Robinson's chapter: the increasing permeability of Eastern Asia to international media; the expansion of NGO networks inside many Asian countries and on an international basis; the quickened base of political change in the wake of rapid economic development; and removal of Cold War constraints which encouraged some Western governments to downplay human rights abuses in favour of encouraging domestic stability against communist penetration. Human rights concerns are now indeed of 'critical importance in the international relations of Southeast Asian states'.

Throughout the 1990s most Asian countries have become more vociferous in challenging the imposition of standards of human rights and democratic development which they see to be the product of external pressure. The views of Asian elites are far from homogeneous but there are broad areas of consensus, as appeared at the Vienna Conference on Human Rights in 1993 and the Bangkok conference which preceded it. Few if any Asian nations supported the American effort to link human rights and MFN in the case of China or Canadian efforts to use aid conditionality as a way of punishing governments which violated human rights. And none openly supported sanctions against Indonesia after the Dili massacre in 1991.

It is possible to draw conclusions somewhat different from Robinson's and the Western NGO community. Many believe that external pressure in the form of economic sanctions and aid conditionality is not likely to improve the human rights situation. On the contrary, Asian resistance to external human rights pressure from the outside is growing rather than declining. Eastern Asian governments are more assertive, self-confident and organized in resisting what they see as outside efforts to impose standards and behaviour.

THE REQUIREMENTS OF LEADERSHIP

A central theme in the essays is that the era of single country dominance of Southeast Asia is now past. Viewed from the perspective of traditional balance of power politics, the situation in the Pacific is now one of an increasing multipolarity.[5] Viewed from a political economy perspective, the era of hegemonic leadership has ended. Durable alliances are giving way to more flexible coalitional arrangements. The relations among states more closely resemble a situation of complex interdependence, albeit one that is strongly hierarchical in nature. The key bilateral relationships, involving the United States, China and Japan, are all complex arrangements of competition and cooperation.

Some of the clues to what kind of non-hegemonic leadership style might emerge can be found within Southeast Asia. One of the most interesting features of the 1990s has been ASEAN's new role as a leader in the broader regional process of building economic and security institutions. While the United States remains by far the most powerful actor in bilateral economic negotiations and most of the multilateral financial institutions, it has not set the pace or direction of the process of regional institutionalization. In the economic organizations such as PECC and APEC, the ASEAN members have been pivotal both as accelerator and brake. If in the past, as Linda Lim argues, 'ASEAN organization's activities have always been dominated by the influence of external events', the ASEAN worm has turned and now plays a major role in determining the pace and direction of economic discussions well beyond the frontiers of Southeast Asia in such fora as APEC.

Southeast Asian leadership in security matters has been even more important. For example, with Canadian financial and technical support, Indonesia has been the principal player in convening an ongoing series of workshops on managing conflict in the South China Sea. The Asia–Pacific Roundtable in Kuala Lumpur is the largest annual gathering of security specialists. With the explicit support of Japan, the active encouragement of Australia, Canada and to a lesser extent South Korea, ASEAN has played the leading role in creating an Asia–Pacific-wide structure for security dialogue and consultation through the newly formed ASEAN Regional Forum. This is less a matter of Northeast Asian and American governments pushing ASEAN in a particular direction than a form of ASEAN-ization of East Asia and the broader Asia Pacific. The irony is unmistakable. As Donald Crone notes, 'That ASEAN, an organization that has assiduously avoided any semblance of a security organization since its initiation, should emerge as the primary organ for a wide-ranging Pacific security dialogue is a real measure of how much change a New World Order has induced.'

ASEAN's contemporary role has not just been to steer the multilateral institutional process but to play a leading part in generating the ideas which support new institutions and processes. It is thus a principal incubator as well as a building block for the new regional order. It has moved from the periphery to centre stage.

Notes

1. Others have trod the same path. Gerald Segal makes a case for 'Eurasia' in his essay 'Asia/Pacific Security Studies in Europe', in Paul M. Evans (ed.), *Studying Asia Pacific Security: The Future of Research, Training and Dialogue Activities* (Toronto: Joint Centre for Asia Pacific Studies, 1994). 'Asia' is provocatively rediscovered by Yoichi Funabashi in his 'The Asianization of Asia', *Foreign Affairs*, vol. 72, no. 5, (Nov/Dec 1993). For 'Euro-American Pacific' see Arif Dirlik, 'The Asia–Pacific Idea: Reality and Representation in the Invention of a Regional Structure', *Journal of World History*, vol. 3, no. 1 (1992).
2. The process and implications of economic regionalization have received a great deal of high-level attention in the past three years. Three major national studies are of note. The first, *East Asia: Regional Economic Integration and Implications for the United States*, was published by the United States International Trade Commission in May 1993. The second, *Economic Integration in the Asia-Pacific Region and the Options for Japan*, was published by the Ministry of Foreign Affairs in Tokyo in April 1993. The third, *Australia and North-East Asia in the 1990s: Accelerating Change*, was published by the East Asia Analytical Unit of the Australian Foreign Ministry in early 1992.
3. 'Track two' refers to the blended meetings of academics, journalists, etc. and officials (present in their personal and private capacities) which have become an Asia-Pacific speciality. There are now more than twenty ongoing 'track two' channels for multilateral discussion of regional security. In 1989 there were two. See Paul M. Evans, 'The Dialogue Process on Asia-Pacific Security Issues: Inventory and Analysis', in Evans (ed.), *Studying Asia Pacific Security*.
4. Recognizing the growing degree of economic interdependence among the economies of Eastern Asia and the need for a counterweight to perceived

bloc development in North America and Europe, Prime Minister Mahathir's concept of an 'East Asia Economic Caucus' can be seen as the highest profile attempt to create an all-Asian process. The EAEC concept is as much about identity and history as it is immediate economic interests and is thus a bell-wether for a more institutionalized expression of pan-Asianism.

5. Harry Harding has coined the phase 'multi-nodality' to express the idea that the contemporary Asia Pacific is composed of complex networks of competition and cooperation rather than entities that repel (Harding, 1991).

References

Abonyi, George and Bunyaraks Ninsananda (1991) *Global Change and Economic Restructuring in Southeast Asia: The Changing Context of Thai–Canada Relations* (Toronto: University of Toronto/York University Joint Centre for Asia Pacific Studies).

Australia, Ministry of Foreign Affairs (1992) *Australia and North-East Asia in the 1990s: Accelerating Change.*

Baum, Julian (1993) 'Taipei's Offshore Empire', *Far Eastern Economic Review* (18 March).

Ball, Desmond (1993) 'Arms and Affluence: Military Acquisitions in the Asia–Pacific Region', *International Security*, vol. 18, no. 3 (Winter, 1993–4), pp. 78–112.

Bernard, Mitchell (1994) *The Pattern and Implications of Transnational Production in Eastern Asia* (Toronto: University of Toronto/York University Joint Centre for Asia Pacific Studies).

Bernard, Mitchell and John Ravenhill (1995) 'Beyond Product Cycles and Flying Geese: Regionalization, Hierarchy and the Industrialization of East Asia', *World Politics* (January).

Emmerson, Donald (1984) 'Southeast Asia: What's in a Name?' *Journal of Southeast Asian Studies*, vol. 15, no. 1 (March).

Evans, Paul (1992), 'The Emergence of Eastern Asia and its Implications for Canada', *International Journal*, vol 47, no. 3.

Evans, Paul (1994a) 'Building Security: The Council for Security Cooperation in Asia Pacific (CSCAP)', *Pacific Affairs*, vol. 7, no. 2.

Evans, Paul (ed.) (1994b), *Studying Asia Pacific Security: The Future of Research, Training and Dialogue Activities* (Toronto: University of Toronto/York University Joint Centre for Asia Pacific Studies).

Dobson, Wendy (1993) *Japan in East Asia: Trading and Investment Strategies* (Singapore: Institute of Southeast Asian Studies).

Donnelly, Michael (1994) 'The Political Economy of Japanese Trade' in Richard Stubbs and Geoffrey Underhill (eds) *Political Economy and the Changing Global Order* (Toronto: McClelland & Stewart).

Funabashi, Yoichi (1993) 'The Asianization of Asia', *Foreign Affairs*, vol. 72, no. 5.

Harding, Harry (1991), 'New Era in the Asia Pacific Region: From Bipolarity to Multinodality', paper presented at Conference on International Relations Studies in China, Peking University (June).

Helleiner, Eric (1994) *Regionalization in the International Political Economy: A Comparative Perspective* (Toronto: University of Toronto/York University Joint Centre for Asia Pacific Studies).

Japan, Ministry of Foreign Affairs (1993) *Economic Integration in the Asia Pacific Region and the Options for Japan* (Tokyo).

Segal, Gerry (1990) *Rethinking the Pacific* (Oxford: Clarendon Press).

Stubbs, Richard (1995) *Regime Legitimacy and Economic Growth in Eastern Asia* (Toronto: University of Toronto/York University Joint Centre for Asia Pacific Studies).

United States, International Trade Commission (1993) *East Asia: Regional Economic Integration and Implications for the United States.*

World Bank (1993) *The East Asian Miracle: Economic Growth and Public Policy* (Oxford: Oxford University Press).

Part II

Changes in the Regional Environment

2 ASEAN: New Modes of Economic Cooperation

Linda Y. C. Lim

The Association of South East Asian Nations (ASEAN) has since its formation in 1967 been known for lack of progress in the field of regional economic integration. The reasons for this have been extensively discussed elsewhere (e.g. Kuntjoro-Jakti, 1987; Devan, 1987; Villegas, 1987; Chng, 1990; Lim, 1994) and need not concern us here. Rather, this Chapter will focus on why there now appear to be renewed and serious efforts at fostering regional economic integration within the ASEAN grouping; on whether these efforts constitute a new mode of regional cooperation; and on whether and why they are or are not likely to succeed where previous attempts at integration have failed.

EXTERNAL PRESSURES FOR ENHANCED REGIONAL ECONOMIC INTEGRATION

The ASEAN organization's activities have always been dominated by the influence of external events. Founded in 1967 at the height of the Vietnam War largely to promote regional peace and security, the association remained generally dormant until the US military defeat in Vietnam in 1975, when fear of Vietnamese communist expansionism spurred attempts at closer regional cooperation. Indeed, the ASEAN heads of government did not hold their first summit meeting until February 1976, in Bali, where it was decided that the ASEAN Economic Ministers should meet regularly to develop and implement economic cooperation proposals. Still, the importance of ASEAN's external economic partners was acknowledged when regular 'dialogues' with them were begun following the second ASEAN summit in Kuala Lumpur in August 1977. (After the annual ASEAN Ministerial Meeting, the six ASEAN foreign ministers meet with their counterparts from the US, Canada, Japan, Australia, New Zealand, the European Community (Union) and Korea; China and Russia have also asked to become ASEAN dialogue partners.) A third summit did not take place until 1987; held in Manila, it focused heavily on economic cooperation measures and relations with Japan, which by then had become the largest trade partner of and foreign investor in the grouping as a whole, as well as in most of its individual members.

The fourth ASEAN summit was held in Singapore in January 1992, twenty-five years after the association's inception. Only then was an agreement signed to establish an ASEAN Free Trade Area (AFTA), and only over a fifteen-year period. Regional economic cooperation schemes to date (Rieger, 1991) had been relatively insignificant in their scope and impact, and the renewed interest in closer cooperation once again reflected the dominant influence of external factors. The 'end of communism' in the West following the democratic revolutions in Eastern Europe from 1989, and culminating in the demise of the Soviet Union in 1991, practically overnight created potential new economic competitors, as these formerly socialist economies embraced market-oriented liberal economic reforms that both promised greater efficiency and wider participation in the world market, and increased their attractiveness to international direct investment also sought by the ASEAN countries. This added to the increased competition from other developing countries in Africa and Latin America resulting from World Bank/IMF-inspired structural adjustment policies of the 1980s, including liberalization and privatization.

At the same time, the European Economic Community was working toward single market integration by the end of 1992, while entering into a closer association with the European Free Trade Area (EFTA), and seriously entertaining requests from Poland, Hungary and Czechoslovakia to become associate members. Not to be outdone, the US, Canada and Mexico began negotiating a North American Free Trade Area (NAFTA) with possible extensions that would take in the entire hemisphere. ASEAN, like other Asian countries, feared that these new enlarged regional economic blocs could turn more protectionistic and inward-oriented, thereby threatening its traditional export markets as well as competing more effectively with ASEAN host countries for scarce international investment capital. Finally, a prolonged recession in the industrialized countries – eventually including Japan – was expected to begin hurting both export and foreign investment prospects for the outward-oriented ASEAN economies, though their growth continued to be sustained at levels much higher than those of their industrialized-country trade partners.

This external impetus for renewed efforts at ASEAN economic cooperation has been acknowledged in all official statements on the subject from the different member nations. At the ASEAN Foreign Ministers' Meeting in Manila in July 1992, the need to attract external (non-ASEAN) investments was cited as the major motivating force for the group's expressed commitment to AFTA. The belief here was that ASEAN now needed to provide the lure of a large integrated regional market to compete with newly-enlarged Western European and North American regional markets for international investments. Low costs were no longer sufficient as these were now similarly provided by many other countries around the world, especially Mexico and in Eastern Europe.

A more aggressive stance on this issue was taken by Prime Minister Dr Mahathir Mohammad of Malaysia, who in December 1990 proposed the formation of a pan-Asian regional economic bloc, which he called an East Asia Economic Grouping (EAEG). To include Japan, China, Korea, Taiwan and Hong Kong as well as the ASEAN countries, the proposed EAEG would function in unspecified ways as a 'counterweight' to the ongoing European and North American blocs. Unpopular with Japan and Indonesia, and drawing strong objections from the US with only a lukewarm response from other ASEAN neighbours besides Singapore, the concept of such a grouping was dropped in favour of a more modest East Asia Economic Caucus (EAEC) at the fourth ASEAN summit in Singapore in January 1992.

Controversial though it was, Mahathir's proposal in a sense reflected the new realities of ASEAN's international economic relations since the late 1980s. In that decade, Japan surpassed the US as the region's largest trade partner and aid donor, while investment flows from Korea, Taiwan, Hong Kong and Singapore collectively and in some cases individually dwarfed those of Japan and Western nations, especially the US (Merrill Lynch). Largely through 'market forces' – rising costs in land- and labour-scarce Northeast Asia causing industry to relocate to lower-cost, land- and labour-abundant Southeast Asia – the ASEAN economies became progressively more closely integrated with those of their other Asian neighbours. Fearing that its firms might be shut out of this large and fast-growing regional market, the US opposed a larger regional economic grouping as 'potentially protectionist', while supporting AFTA itself as a move toward freer world as well as regional trade. On the pan-Pacific level, the US favoured the Asia–Pacific Economic Cooperation (APEC) forum, which, in addition to proposed EAEC countries, includes itself, Canada, Australia, New Zealand, Papua New Guinea, Mexico, and Chile. Singapore was chosen as the site for the APEC secretariat.

As APEC gained momentum, with summits in Seattle in November 1993 and Bogor, Indonesia in November 1994, fear of being over-shadowed, or even pre-empted, by the larger grouping led to the announcement in April 1994 that AFTA would advance its date for achieving regional free trade from 2008 to 2003. By the time of the Bogor summit, all the ASEAN members had ratified the GATT Uruguay Round agreement, and at Bogor itself, APEC members agreed to accomplish pan-regional free trade by the year 2010 for its developed-country members (including Singapore) and 2020 for its developing country members.

DOMESTIC CONDITIONS FAVOURING ENHANCED REGIONAL INTEGRATION

Despite the external pressures and support for the formation of an ASEAN Free Trade Area, it is unlikely to have been agreed upon if domestic conditions in the ASEAN member nations were not conducive. Several factors contributed to this development, which is at odds with ASEAN's previously long-established reluctance to push for regional economic integration.

For one thing, liberal economic reforms in the 1980s and early 1990s (Ungku Aziz, 1990; Timberman, 1992; MacIntyre and Jayasuriya, 1992) already included unilateral universal trade liberalization measures in countries like the Philippines, Thailand and Indonesia. Average tariff levels and thus the protection received by domestic firms had been reduced without too much apparent economic or political disruption, and it is arguable that rapid growth – especially in manufactured exports – during this period both cushioned adjustment to increased competition and reduced domestic pressures for continued import protection. A prolonged period of economic success had also led to increased confidence on the part of both ASEAN governments and the local private business sectors in the ability of their countries and companies to compete in liberalized markets.

Domestic liberalization also included privatization, deregulation and a general – if still gradual and partial – reduction in the role of governments and state enterprises in the ASEAN national economies. Instead, the economic balance of power shifted toward private enterprise, which in ASEAN has always tended to favour regional integration more than governments. The latter are understandably reluctant to surrender the national sovereignty, bureaucratic control and public revenues which derive from trade restrictions and other regulations on private business activity. Many of the larger local private enterprises had grown, and learned much during two decades or more of infant industry protection so that they were now willing to relinquish it in exchange for freer access to their neighbours' markets. Having developed some internal firm competitive advantages, and in some cases having exhausted home-based resources and the potential of the home market, these companies now became interested in exporting to, importing from, and investing in, neighbouring countries (Lim, 1994). As noted in a report prepared by the ASEAN Secretariat for the ASEAN Standing Committee,

> The private sectors in the individual countries have been pressing for an acceleration of the pace of ASEAN cooperation and are looking forward to taking advantage of the new opportunities that will accompany closer cooperation. As ASEAN becomes a more integrated area, foreign investors will also evaluate ASEAN as a more attractive place. Overall, the private sector has been a vocal and dedicated protagonist of a new, stronger ASEAN (Philippine Institute for Development Studies/ASEAN Secretariat, 1992, p. 8).

Indeed, the activities of the ASEAN Chambers of Commerce and Industry (ASEAN–CCI) suggest an activist private sector which in the past was responsible for many pro-integration initiatives – such as the ASEAN Industrial Joint Venture (AIJV) and the ASEAN Industrial Complementation (AIC) schemes – and has generally been more favourably disposed toward regional trade liberalization than government bureaucracies in the region (Lim, 1994; ASEAN–CCI, 1992). External pressures may be considered to have finally provided the push necessary to elicit government support for the private sector's long-held pro-integration, pro-trade position.

To be sure, the ASEAN private sector is by no means homogeneous in its views and interests, and some local industries – those most likely to be hurt by it – have continued to oppose regional trade liberalization, in some cases succeeding in winning over their governments. Few multinationals from advanced industrial countries are to be found in this group, since they have long favoured market integration that would enable them to rationalize their operations in the region according to the respective comparative advantages of individual host locations while serving a larger market, and are also well able to compete in the region without import protection as they do in other world markets.

NEW FORMS OF REGIONAL ECONOMIC COOPERATION

Regional Trade Liberalization: AFTA

AFTA involves implementation of a Common Effective Preferential Tariff (CEPT) scheme for manufactured products with at least 40 per cent ASEAN-wide content. Current tariffs on manufactures are to be reduced to no more than 20 per cent in five to eight years, and to no more than 5 per cent by 1 January 2003 (the original date was 2008). Fifteen product categories were selected for the first round of tariff reductions, and various ASEAN governments – notably Malaysia – announced that they would unilaterally accelerate this pace of tariff reductions.

Still, even if it proceeds on or ahead of schedule, the AFTA process may be less impressive than it might seem at first glance, and its impact is likely to be quite limited. Intra-ASEAN trade accounts for only 18 per cent of ASEAN's total trade, and 40 per cent of this is accounted for by Singapore's already tariff-free trade, including entrepot trade with its neighbours. Some unspecified proportion of the remaining intra-ASEAN trade consists of exchanges between enterprises located in Free Trade or Export Processing Zones in different countries, which also takes place under a free trade regime.

Unilateral tariff reductions have already led to relatively low average tariffs on processed goods, which by 1993 were close to zero in Brunei and Singapore, 10.36 per cent in Malaysia, 14.13 per cent in Indonesia, 8.25 per cent in the Philippines and 20.64 per cent in Thailand, for an ASEAN weighted average of 10.43 per cent (*Asiaweek*, 1994). Imada, Montes and Naya (1991) suggest that a 50 per cent preferential tariff reduction would enlarge the share of intra-ASEAN trade to total ASEAN trade by about 10 per cent or less, with correspondingly small gains in terms of total trade and income. Even these gains are limited by the fact that member countries are allowed to temporarily exclude specific products as required to protect 'sensitive' domestic industries, and many products have been successfully excluded, particularly in the automobile industry and in Thailand.

ASEAN's past history of regional trade liberalization does not inspire confidence. The extensive use of exclusions under the ASEAN Preferential Trading Arrangements (PTA) approved in 1977 resulted in barely 1 per cent of total intra-ASEAN trade being covered by the PTA by 1987, and the five-year plan announced at the 1987 ASEAN summit in Manila to extend PTA coverage to 90 per cent of total goods traded within the region never materialized. While both external and internal developments since 1987 may now be more favourable to regional trade liberalization, the fact remains that AFTA's modest goals, and the low level of intra-regional trade suggest that its impact, even if fully realized, is likely to be limited – and in some cases superseded by more rapid unilateral liberalization.

A major reason for this is that ASEAN trade flows continue to be determined mainly by comparative advantage based on relative resource endowments. While these resource endowments and the comparative advantages to which they give rise change over time – affected, among other things, by government policies and the actions of multinational investors – the trade flows generated still primarily link individual ASEAN member nations with a changing cast of more developed non-ASEAN trade partners. Thus, for example, the ASEAN countries mostly export food, raw materials, processed commodities, and labour-intensive manufactures – both final goods and components – to the US, Japan and other advanced industrial countries, while importing from them capital equipment, industrial materials, machinery, parts and more sophisticated consumer products. There is little reason for the ASEAN countries to trade with each other since they all have relatively similar resource endowments and comparative advantages and all export the same goods.

The one exception is Singapore, whose trade with its neighbours accounts for the largest single portion of intra-ASEAN trade. Besides entrepot functions, this reflects both Singapore's different resource endowment – it is land- and labour-scarce, for example, but capital-rich – and its higher level of technological development, such that its trade with its ASEAN neighbours reflects the pattern of their trade with other advanced and newly industrialized countries, i.e. Singapore exports intermediate and capital goods to its neighbours while importing from them raw materials and labour-intensive manufactures (Wu, 1991).

Outside of merchandise trade, the ASEAN countries tend also to be net importers of services from the advanced industrial countries and from Singapore. These invisible imports include transportation and communications services, investment income, and management and technology fees such as payments for the financial and engineering services exported by Singapore. Only relatively recently have intra-regional labour and tourism exports become significant; both Malaysia and Singapore are large net importers of labour from their ASEAN as well as some non-ASEAN neighbours, and the vast majority of tourists in the region come from elsewhere in Asia – among the ASEAN countries, especially from Malaysia and Singapore.

Thus it is arguably the persistence of an international division of labour based on comparative advantage which restricts the potential for and impact of regional trade liberalization within ASEAN – though this is counterbalanced somewhat by the emergence of a regional division of labour between Singapore (and, to a lesser extent, Malaysia) and its neighbours. It is in this context that Malaysia's proposals for, on the one hand, an expanded East Asian regional economic bloc including the more technologically advanced countries of Japan, Korea, Taiwan and Hong Kong and, on the other, the accelerated inclusion into ASEAN of the socialist Indochinese states, make intuitive sense for trade creation. Trade with EAEC countries (excluding Myanmar and Indochina) accounts for 54 per cent of total ASEAN trade, as compared with 18 per cent for intra-ASEAN trade alone (IMF, 1992).

Sub-Regional Cooperation Zones: The 'Growth Triangle' Concept

The pull of comparative advantage is revealed clearly in the recent emergence of 'growth triangles' in Eastern Asia in general, and in the ASEAN region in particular (Lee Tsao, 1991; Toh and Low, 1993; Lim, 1994). The concept was first articulated by Singapore's Prime Minister Goh Chok Tong in 1989, to promote the integrated development of Batam and other islands in the Indonesian province of Riau, the neighbouring Malaysian state of Johor, and Singapore. Under this form of cooperation, the governments of contiguous territories work together to attract investments into the 'triangle' – for example, through joint infrastructure development, joint investment promotion missions to third countries, and coordination of national investment policies – leaving it to the private sector to decide where the investments should go, according to the 'competitive advantage' of different areas. In the SIJORI (Singapore–Johor–Riau) triangle, Johor's and Riau's cheaper land and labour are combined with Singapore's human skills, managerial expertise, technology, transportation and communications infrastructure to attract ASEAN and non-ASEAN investment to all three locations.

The second sub-regional growth area within ASEAN is the Northern Triangle, based on the northern Malaysian port-city and industrial centre of Penang and its northwestern peninsular Malaysian hinterland, the city of Medan and north Sumatra across the Straits of Malacca in Indonesia, and five provinces of southern Thailand including the city of Phuket. A third triangle, the East ASEAN Growth Area, is emerging that will embrace the southern Philippines, Sabah in Malaysia, and northeastern Kalimantan, Sulawesi and Maluku in Indonesia. The organized ASEAN private sector enthusiastically endorsed the growth triangle concept (ASEAN–CCI, 1992) as a more realistic and viable, and speedier, localized alternative to region-wide free trade. But comparative advantage and private sector initiative alone would not have launched the triangle; a particular form of state intervention and public-private-sector cooperation also proved necessary. For example, the Batam Industrial Park was established as a commercial joint venture between Indonesian-owned PT Batamindo Investment Corporation (a subsidiary of the powerful Salim and Bimantara Groups closely connected with President Suharto) and Singapore-owned Batamindo Management (formed by two state-controlled companies in Singapore – Singapore Technologies Industrial Corporation and Jurong Environmental Engineering). These organizations were able to deliver the 'political will' necessary for this technically private sector venture to succeed, and to support it with public sector infrastructural projects in transportation, utilities and communications.

In the Malaysia–Singapore part of the triangle, private sector exploitation of comparative advantage – in the sense of labour-intensive Singapore-based companies (including multinationals) relocating to relatively land- and labour-abundant neighbouring Johor – did not need a push from or cooperation with the public sector, since Johor is a well-populated state with relatively well-developed infrastructure. Consequently a lower level of official cooperation is required and specifically triangle-linked projects are few. On the other hand, the existence of the growth triangle has not led to significant linkages between Johor and Riau, since their comparative advantages – at least vis-à-vis the main player, Singapore – are relatively similar. While necessary in order to realize Riau's comparative advantages for Singapore-based firms, the triangle is unnecessary for Johor–Singapore linkages, and insufficient to generate business linkages between Johor and Riau in the absence of complementary comparative advantages between them.

Most of the economic activity in the growth triangle is generated by the private sector, in manufacturing, processing, property development and tourism. While there is substantial representation by Singapore and Indonesian companies, including Singapore government-linked enterprises, in Batam, its industrial zone also hosts many non-ASEAN multinationals, including Hong Kong and Taiwan companies, and industrial-country multinationals, some with long-established operations in Singapore. In July 1992 the government of Taiwan announced that it would invest US$10 billion in Batam over the next decade 'to turn it into a global manufacturing, financial, shipping and re-export centre' populated by private and state-linked Taiwan companies.

Thus the growth triangle has so far been successful in its goal of attracting non-ASEAN investment into the zone – which is also the primary goal of AFTA. As a form of regional cooperation, a sub-regional zone like the Johor–Singapore–Riau triangle has several advantages over region-wide trade liberalization. It involves smaller-scale, decentralized negotiations among fewer parties, which are more committed to the partnership because of closer geographical proximity and associated historical ties. Commitments made are locally-based, looser and more informal, avoiding both complex national-level politics and the time-consuming and cumbersome bureaucratic machinery of the full ASEAN organization. Most of the activity is undertaken by private firms, thereby minimizing bureaucratic costs and coordination problems. Such zones may also facilitate eventual region-wide free trade, since 'for the different sub-regions to become complementary to one another, there has to be free movement of goods and services, including labour, across the boundaries of the zones' (ASEAN–CCI, 1992, pp. 18–19).

On the other hand, by providing an easy and convenient substitute for larger-scale regional integration, the proliferation of sub-regional cooperation zones could discourage more ambitious integration measures on a region-wide basis. It may merely concentrate non-ASEAN investment that would have come to the region anyway in a few privileged locations, diverting it from other, less-favoured, parts of each partner country or the region as a whole. There may also be conflicts between national/federal and state/provincial/local governments over aspects of growth triangle policy which could raise questions of sovereignty; for example, the state government of Johor might grant Singapore investors concessions that are at odds with federal government policy and with the interests of other states in Malaysia. Sub-regional cooperation might then widen regional disparities within ASEAN member nations and reduce national economic integration while causing national political friction – all of which might eventually hamper larger-scale region-wide integration.

The sub-regional cooperation zone is a new form of regional public–private sector economic cooperation within ASEAN which is unrelated to the ASEAN organization as such, but which nonetheless fosters regional economic integration at least on a bilateral basis. The Singapore–Johor–Riau triangle has so far been successful in achieving the

ASEAN-wide regional integration goal of attracting foreign and intra-regional investment, based on facilitating the exploitation of the different comparative advantages of triangle partners. Where comparative advantage does not favour it, however, the triangle itself cannot generate business linkages among contiguous partners. Thus on a sub-regional as well as region-wide basis, comparative advantage remains the basis of trade and investment linkages among the ASEAN countries, and a major determinant of success in regional cooperation efforts.

Regional Investment Linkages

Like intra-ASEAN trade, intra-ASEAN investment accounts for only a very small share of the ASEAN countries' total foreign investment inflows – typically less than 10 per cent, with over 90 per cent of this coming from Singapore alone (see Lee Tsao, 1994). Malaysia has the highest ratio of ASEAN-origin investments to total cumulative foreign investments – nearly a third in the manufacturing sector at the end of 1989 – but again most of this is from Singapore. ASEAN membership *per se* is incidental to the vast majority of intra-ASEAN investments. Rather, companies make their investment decisions based on their own competitive needs and strategies and the comparative advantages of different potential host countries.

Though they remain small relative to the large total foreign investment inflows that ASEAN countries have received over the past decade, intra-ASEAN investments have been increasing in absolute terms. This is the result both of shifting comparative advantages among ASEAN member countries – such as land and labour scarcities which have, for example, caused Malaysian agribusiness companies and small Singapore manufacturers to migrate to more land- and labour-abundant neighbours – and of corporate strategies based on the changing competitive advantages of ASEAN-owned firms. Home government policies towards capital outflows have also become more permissive – the Singapore government even provides financial and other assistance to local firms which wish to relocate in neighbouring countries. Motivations for outward investment vary by company and source country factors, as the following extracts demonstrate.

Many of [Singapore's] large, cash-rich, publicly-listed corporations – some of them partly government-owned – have fully exploited the mature, stagnant home market and are now venturing overseas in search of new sources of growth. Besides abundant capital ('deep pockets'), these companies often have firm-specific advantages in technology or management. (Lim, 1994, p. 148).

For ... Chinese-Indonesian businesses, intra-ASEAN investments reflect the influence of several factors: a commercially prudent diversification of their Indonesian home-based empires; record earnings made in the booming Indonesian home economy; a more liberal Indonesian government outlook toward outward investment; and security-motivated investments to hedge against the possibility that highly visible commercial success at home might lead to a revival of anti-Chinese ethnic tensions and discriminatory policies in Indonesia, especially after the rule of President Suharto ends. (Lim, 1994, p. 148)

The intra-regional flows of capital, technology, management, skills and goods which accompany intra-ASEAN investments certainly enhance regional economic integration. But the outward investment push of ASEAN companies is not restricted to ASEAN host locations alone, and may even favour non-ASEAN locations, particularly Vietnam and China (Lim, 1995). These less-developed socialist non-ASEAN locations offer several attractions: compared to the ASEAN countries, they have cheaper, more abundant land and labour, fewer binding regulations and restrictions on business (e.g. with respect to environmental standards and labour rights), and large untapped and relatively unsophisticated and uncompetitive markets likely to be hospitable to cheap ASEAN-made goods. In the case of Vietnam, the US-led economic boycott temporarily reduced competition from advanced industrial country multinationals, while Overseas Chinese have certain cultural and political advantages in investing and operating in China.

In the late 1980s and early 1990s, firms from the newly-industrialized economies (NIEs) – Taiwan, Hong Kong, Singapore and South Korea – relocated to the ASEAN–4 countries (Indonesia, Malaysia, Philippines, Thailand) many of their more labour-intensive manufacturing industries (garments, footwear, toys, consumer electronics) in response to changing comparative advantages at home. These NIE investments have contributed little to intra-ASEAN regional economic integration, since they mainly transferred standardized technologies and management from their home countries to multiple ASEAN host locations where they employ cheap labour in mostly low-skilled occupations, with the output being exported to third countries. There are few if any linkages between NIE subsidiaries located in different ASEAN countries.

On the other hand, investments in the region by multinationals from advanced industrial countries like the US, Japan, France and Germany are increasingly integrated on a regional basis, with the investing companies practising a regional division of labour which locates different activities in different neighbouring host countries according to their respective comparative advantages. Much of this has to do with Singapore's role as an industrial and services as well as goods entrepot for the entire ASEAN region. Because of its excellent infrastructure, services and skills, and free trade and capital flows, Singapore serves for many multinationals as a regional operational headquarters for their subsidiaries elsewhere in the region, as a warehousing and trans-shipment point, a purchasing and marketing centre, a financial and commercial services centre, and a research, design, training and technical centre supporting manufacturing facilities in neighbouring countries. In addition, Singapore is the site for capital-intensive high-tech manufacturing processes which provide parts to or use parts from more labour-intensive operations elsewhere (Lim and Pang, 1991; Lim, 1994). Thus many multinationals, particularly in the electronics industry, have built 'regionally-integrated production complexes' – regional operations which are vertically integrated through the ASEAN region. To the extent that many assembly facilities are located in free trade or export processing zones or bonded factories connecting with Singapore's free port, these multinationals may be considered to operate within a *de facto* regional free trade area. It is in this sense that ASEAN increasingly functions as a single investment location offering many different comparative advantages for potential multinational investors. In the 1990s, the emergence of the fast-growing ASEAN countries as increasingly important market destinations themselves has also begun to attract investment to serve the regional market by locating manufacturing facilities in one or more countries to sell in those host locations and to export to their neighbours.

With the exception of automobiles, multinationals' integrated regional investments in the region are a response not to ASEAN-related cooperation schemes, but rather to national investment promotion programmes which compete with each other to attract foreign investment. Bonded factory provisions and Free Trade Zones, for example, facilitate the location of different but related plants in neighbouring countries, all of them benefiting from relatively similar national investment incentive programmes. It is this convergence of individual ASEAN countries' investment policies – a product of national economic liberalization in the 1980s – which has enabled them to attract and retain foreign investors with regional requirements and interests. Together, the ASEAN countries as a group can offer investors cheap land, labour and raw materials combined with high skills and excellent infrastructure (in different locations) – a combination that no member individually possesses.

Thus, for example, when Singapore ran out of cheap labour, multinationals which invested there originally for that reason could and did relocate their labour-intensive activities to neighbouring countries – Bangkok, Johor or Batam – while retaining the skills and expertise of their Singapore-based skilled workforce and upgrading their Singapore activities to serve and complement the now relocated assembly plants. Thus Singapore was able to hold on to higher-value portions of these multinational investments. In this sense, the complementary advantages of neighbouring ASEAN countries provide them with some collective insurance against the kind of footloose behaviour once predicted for offshore sourcing multinationals but which has so far failed to materialize in this region. In the process, the multinationals' proliferating operations serve to regionally integrate the industries of neighbouring territories.

This process may not, of course, continue indefinitely. In particular, as other ASEAN countries build up their infrastructures and technological capabilities, Singapore may lose some of its industrial support activities to them as these activities move to realize the economies of being even closer to their production bases, and to respond to national host governments' desires for more advanced manufacturing technology. This may actually reduce the degree of intra-industry regional integration, consolidating national production bases instead. So far, however, only Malaysia among the other ASEAN countries is strategically moving up this road to compete more directly with Singapore for higher-value multinational investments.

CONCLUSION: A NEW MODE OF ASEAN REGIONAL ECONOMIC COOPERATION?

This chapter suggests that there has indeed been a sea-change as ASEAN moves toward regional economic integration in the 1990s. After fifteen years, the agonizingly slow and ineffective negotiations under the ASEAN PTAs appear to have been superseded by a more ambitious AFTA based on CEPTs. ASEAN state-to-state regional cooperation schemes based on regional import-substituting industrialization – the ASEAN Industrial Products (AIP), ASEAN Industrial Complementation (AIC) and ASEAN Industrial Joint Ventures (AIJV) schemes – appear to have been superseded by growing private sector intra-regional and regionally-linked investments both by ASEAN-domiciled firms and by multinationals from advanced industrial countries. And the sub-regional cooperation zone as manifest by the Johor–Singapore–Riau growth triangle has quickly gained popularity among governments and private investors alike.

Except for AFTA, the other two developments are not dependent on ASEAN as an organization *per se*. Perhaps the most distinctive feature of these new forms of regional integration is the shift from formal, state-led negotiated 'schemes' involving all members to informal, private sector-led and market-driven investment decisions involving only a subset of ASEAN members. Though both sub-regional cooperation zones and regional investment linkages could be enhanced by AFTA, they do not depend on it, and are likely to continue developing with or without AFTA, which at best will progress more slowly.

Singapore's prime minister Goh has characterized these developments as signifying a new phase of 'outward-looking, competitive (ASEAN) cooperation' – based on cooperation to develop each nation's own competitive advantage as decided by the market, rather than 'zero-sum cooperation' decided by bureaucrats insisting on 'an equal spread of benefits' among members. According to him, such cooperation should enhance the competitiveness of the regional grouping and of its members so that international investments will continue to flow into the region and ASEAN products can compete in the world market despite the emergence of other regional blocs in Europe and North America (*Straits Times Weekly Overseas Edition*, 9 March 1991; p. 1). These new forms of ASEAN regional economic integration are the result of both external and domestic, political and economic forces. Externally, pressures from the formation of regional economic blocs elsewhere have contributed to a recognition of the growing importance of the ASEAN market itself both for trade and investment, and a willingness to work harder to integrate it, largely via AFTA. Domestically, over two decades of rapid economic and industrial growth and one decade of domestic economic liberalization have led to shifts in national comparative advantage and the emergence of ASEAN-domiciled companies eager for the new business opportunities presented by closer regional integration, and possessing the firm competitive advantages necessary to take advantage of them. Multinationals from outside the region are also responding to these factors, and to their own global corporate strategic imperatives, by making regionally integrated investments in different ASEAN member countries.

Whether the push for integration from external pressures will last is uncertain. Already, NAFTA and the EU are both seen as lesser threats than they once were, and if this trend continues it could actually weaken the 'political will' in ASEAN to support accelerated regional integration for defensive reasons. On the other hand, if the two external blocs do strengthen and become more protectionist against non-members, then the external pressures will increase for ASEAN to integrate with its other East Asian trading partners, à la Prime Minister Mahathir's EAEG proposal, which could dilute ASEAN's own institutional significance. But acceleration of the currently slow-paced movement toward APEC free trade could either push ASEAN to step up its own regional free trade efforts or undermine AFTA by reducing the necessity for its very existence. Whatever the outcome of these and other external pressures, businesses from both ASEAN and non-ASEAN advanced and newly industrialized countries will continue to follow their own firm competitive strategies, which I have suggested will favour increased regional integration at the firm – and so eventually also at the national – level. Sub-regional cooperation zones will be one form of such integration which is not contingent on regional or even national-level policy agreements.

In sum, ASEAN's past and current experience with regional economic cooperation suggests that integration will proceed where it is supported by domestic or domestically-based business interests (e.g. long-established multinational investors), and that it will be supported by such interests when they can profit from it, which depends on the configuration of country and firm competitive advantages. This kind of partial, private sector-led, market-driven regional integration is likely to proceed where it makes economic and business sense, regardless of the progress of formal integration schemes (such as AFTA) at the region-wide, state-to-state level.

References

ASEAN–CCI (Chambers of Commerce and Industry) (1992) *ASEAN Economic Development and the Private Sector: Partners in Asian Economic Commentary Progress* various issues. Singapore: ASEAN–CCI.

Chng, Meng Kng (1990), 'ASEAN's Institutional Structure and Economic Cooperation', *ASEAN Economic Bulletin*, vol. 6, no. 3 (March), pp. 268–82.

Devan, Janamitra (1987) 'The ASEAN Preferential Trading Arrangement: Some Problems, ex Ante Results, and a Multipronged Approach to Future Intra-ASEAN Trade Development', *ASEAN Economic Bulletin*, vol. 4, no. 2 (November), pp. 197–209.

Holloway, Nigel (1991). 'Southeast Asia's golden triangles', *Far Eastern Economic Review*, 3 January), p. 34.

Imada, Pearl, Manual Montes and Seiji Naya (1991) *A Free Trade Area: Implications for ASEAN* (Singapore: Institute of Southeast Asian Studies).

International Monetary Fund (1992) *Direction of Trade Statistics Yearbook 1992*.

Kuntjoro-Jakti, Dorodjatun (1987) 'ASEAN's External Trade Relations in 1987: Entering a Growing Environmental Turbulence', *Contemporary Southeast Asia*, vol. 9, no. 2, pp. 113–19.

Lee Tsao Yuan (ed.) (1991) *Growth Triangle: The Johor–Singapore–Riau Experience* (Singapore: Institute of Southeast Asian Studies and Institute of Policy Studies).

Lee Tsao Yuan (1994) *Overseas Investment Experience of Singapore Manufacturing Companies* (Singapore: Institute of Policy Studies/McGraw-Hill).

Lim, Linda Y. C. (1994), 'The Role of the Private Sector in ASEAN Regional Economic Cooperation', in Lynn Mytelka, (ed.) *South–South Cooperation in a Global Perspective*, (Paris: OECD Development Centre).

Lim, Linda Y. C. (1995), 'Models and Partners: Malaysia and Singapore in Viet Nam's Economic Reforms', in Scott Christensen and Manuel Montes (eds) *Marketization in Southeast Asia* (Hawaii and Palo Alto: East-West Center/Stanford University Press).

Lim, Linda Y. C. and Pang Eng Fong (1991) *Foreign Investment and Industrialization in Malaysia, Thailand, Singapore and Taiwan* (Paris: OECD Development Centre).

Macintyre, Andrew J. and Kanishka Jayasuriya (eds) (1992) *The Dynamics of Economic Policy Reform in South–East Asia and the South-West Pacific* (Singapore: Oxford University Press).

Philippine Institute for Development Studies/ASEAN Secretariat (1992) *ASEAN Economic Cooperation for the 1990s: A Report Prepared for the ASEAN Standing Committee* (Manila).

Rieger, Hans Christoph (1991) *ASEAN Economic Cooperation Handbook* (Singapore: Institute of Southeast Asian Studies).

Stone, Eric (1992) 'Trading on ASEAN's Future', *Asian Business*, July pp. 20–27.

Timberman, David G. (ed.) (1992) *The Politics of Economic Reform in Southeast Asia* (Manila: Asian Institute of Management).

Toh, Mun Meng and Linda Low (eds) (1993) *Regional Cooperation and Growth Triangles in ASEAN* (Singapore: Times Academic Press).

Ungku A. Aziz (Moderator) (1990) *Strategies for Structural Adjustment: The Experience of Southeast Asia* (Washington, DC: International Monetary Fund/Bank Negara Malaysia).

Villegas, Bernardo M. (1987) 'The Challenge to ASEAN Economic Cooperation', *Contemporary Southeast Asia*, vol. 9, no. 2, pp. 120–28.

Wu, Frederich (1991) 'The ASEAN Economies in the 1990s and Singapore's Regional Role', *California Management Review* (Fall), pp. 103–14.

3 New Political Roles for ASEAN

Donald Crone

In the context of rapid changes in the external environment, the Association of South East Asian Nations (ASEAN) is searching for new political roles that adjust to relevant changes. From the ASEAN perspective, three interlocking sets of issues predominate in driving change: evolution in Pacific power structures; a new context of security concerns; and a rapidly proliferating set of diplomatically relevant institutions. Some aspects of these issues are 'fallout' from the wider international system: the Asian security system is undergoing change as a result of the collapse of the old Soviet threat, while the new Russian Republic is pressing to become an integral part of the emerging Pacific system; ASEAN economic and political cooperation has been reinvigorated by movement toward a more regionalized world order in other geographic arenas like Europe and the Americas. Other aspects are more of Pacific origin: Japan is searching for new political and economic roles; all Pacific states are adjusting to rapid change in US military and economic roles; Pacific economic and political institutions are developing rapidly.

These changes are significant, and they portend the need to adjust old approaches to a new set of realities. The situation is quite dynamic and complex, but the obvious conclusion is that the political roles of the ASEAN members in the Pacific require adjustment, and considerable agility will be required if ASEAN's own position in the Pacific international system is to be maintained or enhanced. For ASEAN, these are indeed 'interesting times'.

The ASEAN tradition has it that major changes and new directions can be launched only under the auspices of a meeting of the heads of government. The governments purposefully kept ASEAN subordinate, without the authority or ability to take initiative, for the first twenty-five years of its history. The first two summits, in 1976 and 1977, forged the Treaty of Amity and Cooperation and set out the beginnings of economic cooperation. The third summit, in 1987, was held to ratify significant changes in the programmes of economic cooperation; because of the timing, it also acquired the purpose of supporting the then new Aquino government (Crone, 1988). The 1987 summit also resulted in agreement that summits should be more frequent (every three years was the suggested interval). This, as it turned out, was not immediately followed.

Rather, a new summit was delayed until January 1992. A large part of the rationale for scheduling one then was to cope with the issues outlined above. While adjustment has been largely reactive to the external environment, domestic economic liberalizations of the 1980s have affected the content and urgency of ASEAN member foreign policy interests (Crone, 1992; Ng and Wagner, 1989). The remainder of this chapter elaborates the dynamics inducing change, the means of adaptation so far chosen, and the most likely directions that will result from these mechanisms. The ASEAN members are attempting to chart a new political role for themselves in the Pacific arena of a still-uncertain 'New World Order'.

THE CHANGING PATTERNS OF PACIFIC POWER

Patterns of power relevant to the Pacific have changed rapidly in the past several decades. There are two dimensions of those changes: the system of power relations among Pacific nations; and the place of the Pacific in the broader global arena. Within the Pacific, the predominant position of the US has eroded. Within the global arena, both the place of the Pacific and the broader structure of relations have changed, affecting the ASEAN members in important ways.

The stratification of power relations in the Pacific has changed quite dramatically over recent decades. For the first two decades after World War II, the United States was clearly hegemonic – the predominant economic power by any measure, and the only significant military power in the entire Pacific Basin. These two issue areas were firmly nested, with economic access and aid subordinated to security policy (Rostow, 1986). While questions about the erosion of US hegemony at the global level were raised by the early 1970s, within the Pacific that predominance was preserved by the Cold War competition with the Soviet Union, and by the constraints imposed on Japan's conversion of rising economic power into political power (Saito, 1990). The system of relations was an essentially bilateral one, between the US on one hand, and each of the countries the US chose to relate to on the other; the modal pattern was for the US to provide economic benefits in return for its

preferred pattern of security cooperation. The security and economic
access that the US did provide was part of a global strategy to contain
the Soviet Union and China, not a policy directly derived from the
region itself. US power was so predominant that regional concerns
were not important factors in policy.

By the 1990s, US predominance was no longer clearly the pattern.
This is largely a result of two parallel sets of changes. First, Japan has
risen to become a significant challenger in trade and direct foreign
investment, and the lead provider of aid. Both US and Japanese shares
of overall Pacific trade have fallen, but that of the US much more.
The surge of Japanese foreign investment is so dramatic, that it exceeded the total stock of US investment in the region, taking a leading
share in almost all countries. In foreign aid, Japan has clearly replaced
the US as the predominant provider, reflecting declining security concerns and fiscal austerity in the US, and certainly drawing on the Japanese view of aid as an important foreign policy tool in the absence of
military power (Japan, Ministry of Foreign Affairs, 1990). While trade,
stocks of direct foreign investment, and accumulated foreign aid indi-
cate a continuing, strong US presence, recent flows show an obviously different story. In 1988 for example, Japanese foreign investment
flows into East Asia amounted to $5.5 billion, while that of the US
was just over $2 billion. The US commitment for 1990 toward the
Philippine Assistance Plan, at $160 million, was just one-tenth that of
Japan. US economic pre-eminence has been replaced by that of Japan.

Second, the rapid economic development of a number of countries
in the region has substantially reduced the formerly vast gap in the
sizes of GNP, 'levelling the playing field' in some degree, and increasing the number of economically relevant players. The addition of
the Newly Industrializing Economies (NIEs) and the emergence of China
have been particularly significant. One sense of these changes is that
the sum of all other Pacific nations' GNPs together was only a bit
over one-quarter of US GNP in 1965; now they exceed it.

The results of these changes in patterns of relations are significant,
but not so simplistic as is usually portrayed. First, while Japan has
emerged as regional economic leader, it has only recently made progress
as a political leader (Haber, 1990; Saito, 1990). Japan's adoption of
'comprehensive national security' in the Ohira Report, more closely
linking economic and political objectives, characterized the policy as
a response to 'the termination of clear American supremacy in both
military and economic spheres' (Drifte, 1990, p. 29). While the US
relative economic position continues to decline, the political balance

is shifting more slowly. The US can no longer be said to be hegemonic in the region, but it clearly remains the major actor.

Second, the structure of linkages of the NIEs and near-NIEs (particularly Thailand and Malaysia) has changed significantly. The penetration of Japanese corporations in other Asian economies has linked Eastern Asia more closely together into a single structure (Pasuk, 1990). Rapid industrialization has transformed their economies, increasingly tying their futures into a Pacific economic structure that is set by the expansion of Japanese foreign investment and by continued US market access. The share of exports from one Pacific economy (defined as members of PECC, see below) to another increased from 56 per cent in 1970 to 69 per cent in 1991 (PECC, 1993: p. 56). For smaller Pacific countries, trade concentration in the region is even more significant. The newly industrializing economies have even become more important to each other as sources of investment. For example, in 1987 Taiwan and Hongkong ranked third and fifth as investors in Thailand, and in 1993 Taiwan had topped Japan in Malaysian investment approvals. The Asian NIEs, as a group, are anxious that the development of the Pacific economy should continue to their benefit in both economic and political terms, requiring maintenance of linkages to both Japan and the US. The weight of their opinion has increased to the point that it constrains the policies of the US and Japan.

The result is a new sense of assertiveness on the Asian side of the Pacific, tempered by uncertainty. The former subordination of regional relations to a global agenda is seen as a thing of the past, and all states, including the ASEAN members, are defining their interests in this new context and seeking to achieve them with a newfound confidence. At the same time, uncertainty as to how the regional balance of power will affect future opportunities is a central feature of the present Pacific system, in parallel to, but not entirely contingent upon, the same uncertainty at the global level. No one can be certain about the new boundaries created by power shifts, only that the old ones have been eroded. This leads to a necessity for probing, leaving retreat paths open, looking for new ideas, and experimenting.

The rapid evolution of the global system in the late 1980s and early 1990s is also a source of uncertainty and ambivalent signals. On one hand, the end of the Cold War shifts attention to economic, rather than security, structures. Shrouded by Cold War security concerns, the emergence of the Pacific as the dynamic centre of the global economy caught some by surprise: one estimate has East and Southeast Asia's share of global GNP in the year 2000 as 23 per cent, compared to the

US at 22 per cent and the EU at 21 per cent. The rapid growth of East Asia as an element of the global economy and the economic success of the ASEAN members have increased their weight and voice in global forums.

However, the same shift from security to economic issues, combined with increased concern for national development in the more industrialized countries has melded into heightened economic competition. The most obvious consequences were the near failure of the Uruguay Round of global trade talks and, partly as a result, the emergence of regional trade negotiations as a centrepiece of diplomatic effort in Europe, the Americas and the Asia Pacific. An emerging focus on economic security directs the use of political power into the more traditional array of economic policy issues.

For the ASEAN members the effects of the emerging economic focus are mixed. On the positive side, the grouping played an unprecedentedly large role in the Uruguay Round of trade talks, particularly as members of the Cairns Group focusing on agricultural trade liberalization. Prior trade rounds had left the ASEAN members to the mercies of larger powers' self-styled efforts to 'represent' ASEAN interests, with little positive outcome. But now ASEAN has achieved an enhanced diplomatic status more suitable to its place in the global scheme.

On the negative side, the impending formation of trade blocs has come close to a preoccupation for ASEAN. While both European and North American representations are that they have trade freeing rather than trade restricting in mind, economic blocs do not have to discriminate in a positive fashion to bring about diversion; they are intended to intensify trade among members, and that often comes at others' expense. In a climate of limited overall trade growth, the ASEAN members are worried that the smaller increments of growth will go elsewhere than to them, reversing their experience of the 1980s. Having hitched their futures more strongly than ever to an export orientation, the prospect of being all dressed up with no party to go to is, at least, dismaying, and perhaps even threatening to the stability of some ASEAN governments.

Questions about the viability of an open global trading system refocused ASEAN's attention on the regional trade system. The 'Singapore Declaration of 1992', the agreement among the heads of government at the 4th summit meeting of ASEAN, spoke of 'profound international political and economic changes that have occurred since the end of the Cold War' that press ASEAN to 'constantly seek to safeguard its collective interests in response to the formation of large and powerful economic groupings among the developed countries'. The image conjured up by Philippine President Aquino of a world in which the rich countries become richer and more secure by excluding the rest, where the middle countries join the poor, was typical of the linkage made between the trend toward economic blocs and consequences for ASEAN. The Singaporean foreign minister made the explicit linkage: 'ASEAN has no choice but to strengthen economic cooperation if we are to deal with the trend toward economic regionalism and remain an effective organization'.

The resulting 'Framework Agreement on Enhancing ASEAN Economic Cooperation' points to these changes as requiring 'more cohesive and effective performance of intra-ASEAN economic cooperation', lays out a significant enhancement of existing regional economic programmes including a timetable for an ASEAN Free Trade Area (AFTA), and, for the first time, tasks the ASEAN Secretariat with monitoring progress toward regional economic cooperation. While in some measure these changes were evolutionary from the 1977 start in economic cooperation, there is no question that the threat of economic regionalization accelerated both their timing and scope. What is on the surface an economic programme is more fundamentally a political response to a still uncertain New World Order.

CHANGES IN PACIFIC SECURITY PATTERNS

The US security presence has also undergone some, but less dramatic, change. Increasing Soviet interest and naval presence in the region up through the Reagan administration sustained the salience of an American role in the eyes of most states of the region. By the start of the 1990s sharp reductions in the perceptions of a Soviet threat reduced the value of an American presence, while increasingly sophisticated Japanese military capabilities sustained interest in an American presence in the eyes of some regional states for another reason. (Aligappa, 1990). However, the rise of trade tensions reduced political support for strategic ties with the US, as acceptance of the Pacific fabric was at least partially based on the US role in assisting growth as a route to domestic political stability (Gordon, 1988). An emerging world order posed new security issues for ASEAN.

One issue that, rather ironically, posed a question for ASEAN was the Cambodian peace process. ASEAN played a central role in keeping international attention focused on the situation in Cambodia for over a decade, and contributed significantly to the process of negotiations that resulted in a settlement of sorts. While the prospects for settlement were slim, partly as a result of lack of interest on the part of the United States in seeing any settlement emerge, ASEAN was delegated the 'lead' role, which the US publicly 'followed'; however, it should be noted that the 'end game' was clearly run by the five permanent members of the UN Security Council. A substantial portion of ASEAN's international identity became wrapped up in this role, as many members of the international system recognized ASEAN particularly in the context of the annual United Nations resolution to deny the Cambodia seat to the Vietnam-installed government. Many portrayed Cambodia as the 'glue' of ASEAN cooperation, the one issue on which the members could agree. This was mostly a myth: ASEAN members frequently disagreed on significant aspects of the issues involved, although mostly outside public forums. As Thai security was directly at stake, it was designated the 'lead state'. However, Singapore was often more hard line than the leader, while Indonesia and Malaysia were wary of any policy that confronted Vietnam. Thailand and Singapore rejected a major Indonesian diplomatic initiative, but the Thai government of Chatichai in 1989 completely shifted tactics unilaterally, turning from 'battlefield into a marketplace' (reflecting internal Thai divisions between military hardliners and civilians who thought the cost of that policy too great). That ASEAN unity could survive these differences is evidence of its resiliency.

Now, with that issue off the agenda in its old form, some in ASEAN feel that a new reason for its existence needs to be established. Regional security arrangements are thought to have increased relevance, especially for the prevention, containment and termination of conflict in a post-Cold War world (Aligappa, 1993). Philippine Foreign Minister Manglapus, for example, stated at the 1990 Annual Ministerial Meeting that, 'We can no longer excuse ourselves by saying "Let's fix Cambodia first".' Manglapus intended that regional military security should be discussed seriously. (The linkage to Philippine negotiations with the US over the bases treaty was rather transparent.) Debate over what direction ASEAN security cooperation should take has been quite prevalent. The extensive bilateral military exercises, close relations among top security staff, exchanges of intelligence, and several arrangements for training on each other's territory have formally been outside ASEAN auspices, and unconnected to wider security arrangements that several ASEAN members maintain with the US, the UK, Australia, and New Zealand. This fragmentation was intentional, but also problematic; defence procurement and manufacturing through six different systems, for example, is quite inefficient, and led to agreement in early 1990 to allow defence producers to coordinate in technology exchange, joint ventures and product acquisition and assembly.

The original pattern was set to avoid having ASEAN equated with the now defunct Southeast Asia Treaty Organization. Since the political disadvantages of an anti-communist pact faded away, calls for a more coherent arrangement have emerged, including hints that a regional security system is due. In late 1989 the Indonesian military commander responded by suggesting closer bilateral defence cooperation as an alternative to a military pact; this preference was affirmed in mid-1990 by President Suharto, who maintained that the present situation was sufficient to assure defence. But all ASEAN members do not share identical views on this (Buszynski, 1990). Singapore, having allowed the establishment of a US security depot over Malaysian and Indonesian objections, seemed convinced that it was important to keep an active US presence to deter the alternative possibility of Soviet, Chinese, and even Indian moves into the region. Malaysia and Indonesia prefer to reaffirm the ZOPFAN (Zone of Peace, Freedom and Neutrality) principle, continue to keep a Nuclear-Free Zone under discussion, and point to the 'bases are temporary' clause of ASEAN documents. The same line of thinking is evident in Indonesia's long-sought chairmanship of the Non-Aligned Movement. President Suharto, at the 1992 NAM Summit, emphasized that the 'New World Order' should not turn out, like the old, to feature the domination of the strong and rich over the weak and poor. Malaysian leader Datuk Seri Mahathir bin Mohammed also characterized the new order as every bit as threatening as the old.

However, the withdrawal of some US forces from the Asia–Pacific region, following from a general downsizing of the US military from budgetary pressures and the 'end' of the Cold War, keeps the issue alive. The US indicated that it will pursue a reorientation of its troop stationing policy, drawing some units back to US territory, but stationing small numbers more widely in the Pacific, including in the ASEAN countries. Any change in regional military arrangements naturally brings up the future role of Japan as an avowed (but undefined) political power in the region. A proposal by the then Thai Prime Minister Chatichai in mid-1990 for joint Japanese–ASEAN naval exercises presented bilateral defence cooperation as a tolerable alternative to a unilateral Japanese presence. The negative public Malaysian reaction prompted an immediate Japanese disavowal of the idea. No 'Pax Nipponica' seems desirable (Haber, 1990).

A number of countries' initiatives keep the possibility of a wider Pacific defence arrangement on the agenda. At the 1990 ASEAN Post-Ministerial Conference, Australia, with Canadian support, proposed a Conference on Security and Cooperation in Asia (to parallel the European model). This envisioned the ASEAN states as core members, then the dialogue partners, Vietnam and Cambodia, Papua New Guinea and the Indian subcontinent in concentric circles of lessening involvement. It was to bring the US and Japan more formally into Southeast Asian security arrangements on a long-term basis. In April 1991 the then President of the Soviet Union, Mikhail Gorbachev, voiced support for the CSCA proposal during his trip to Japan and Russian Republic spokesmen subsequently characterized a continued US military presence in the region as a factor for stability. Boris Yeltsin put stress on the need for a new security framework from the beginning of his term, especially talks among Russia, China, Japan and the US. However, the inclusion of Russia presented particular problems, especially for the US, which consistently sought to keep the Soviets out of Pacific arrangements (really preferring bilateral security relationships), and for Japan, which has still not negotiated a peace treaty with the Soviet inheritors to end World War II. A process modelled on the CSCE could also bring outside influence legitimately into both foreign (security), and domestic (human rights) arenas, an unwelcome intrusion for most ASEAN members.

Reacting to proposals from outside, the ASEAN members started exploring models that held more comfort for them. In 1990 and 1991, a series of seminars involving several dozen academics and government officials from around the region was held in Jakarta, Manila, Bangkok, and Kuala Lumpur to examine security issues, and to explore the outlines of an indigenous ASEAN initiative for a new regional order in Southeast Asia. The focus on regional order that emerged included bolstering internal consultative, confidence-building and conflict resolution mechanisms, extending them to the former Indochina states and the South China Sea, and considering non-governmental forums as supplements. In addition, the continuance of a US military role was seen as desirable, in part to help contain inevitable Japanese and Chinese expansion, and an extension of regional discussions to include China, India and Vietnam was suggested (ASEAN–ISIS, 1991).

That new regional order started to take shape in 1992. First, the January summit laid out a framework that included using the Treaty of Amity and Cooperation as a 'common framework' for regional cooperation, through opening it to accession to other Southeast Asian states (Vietnam and Laos acceded in June). The annual Post-Ministerial Conferences (PMC's) were identified as the vehicle for intensified political and security dialogues. In addition, the traditional group invited to this annual event was broadened in two ways: by bringing South Korea in as a regular dialogue partner, and India as a 'sectoral' partner; and by inviting as 'guests' China and Russia, with Vietnam and Laos as 'observers.' This new venture was tried out at the 1992 PMC, which highlighted a declaration aimed at reducing the tension between China and Vietnam in the South China Sea. Concerned with Chinese naval build-ups, with territorial disputes around the Spratly Islands that threaten armed conflict, and with control of oil deposits there, the ASEAN countries took the initiative to issue a formal statement calling on all states to settle sovereignty and jurisdictional disputes without resorting to force (see Chapter 13). The presence of China, Vietnam and Russia (along with the other dialogue partners) at the meeting added weight to the statement. With this dramatic gesture, ASEAN attempted to regain its diplomatic role, not just within Southeast Asia, but in the wider Pacific.

In early 1993 security cooperation was advanced by several developments. Japanese Prime Minister Miyazawa, on tour, gave critical assurances to the ASEAN states that Japan would support a regional security forum, and that it had no intent to rearm. The Clinton administration about the same time demonstrated the first American interest in a regional security forum since the 1950s. The earlier series of meetings to discuss the subject around the region intensified, to include forums in almost every one of the relevant countries. By May 1993 the issue had proceeded to the point that ASEAN held a formal meeting with the dialogue partners in Singapore on security cooperation. Confidence-building measures, non-proliferation, conflict prevention measures, and peacekeeping were identified as the most likely arenas for regional cooperation. In addition, Japanese and US reluctance to bring China and Russia into the dialogue was eroded, broadening the scope in ways formerly unimaginable. The ASEAN Regional Forum was agreed to in July 1993 among 18 actors (ASEAN, Australia, Canada, China, the EC, Japan, Laos, New Zealand, Papua New Guinea, Russia, South Korea, the US, and Vietnam) to serve as the central security body for the Asia Pacific.

The distinguishing feature of this forum is that it could be created at all. ASEAN's long-standing hesitation to engage security issues, Japan's questioned role, and American preferences for unilateralism had to be substantially settled first, in the Asian way. That ASEAN, an organization that has assiduously avoided any semblance of a security organization since its initiation, should emerge as the primary organ for a wide-ranging Pacific security dialogue is a real measure of how much change a 'New World Order' has induced.

Just as the declaration of ZOPFAN (Zone of Peace, Freedom and Neutrality) was intended in 1972 to fill an emerging power vacuum, ASEAN's new security role is a political response to one aspect of the New World Order. ASEAN is attempting to substitute a regional security order centered on itself for the old order based on a system of bilateral ties with the US. While all ASEAN members give at least some support for a continued US military presence in the region, their clear intent is to use it to contain Japan, China, and possibly India. The conception of a security arrangement run by the small states of the region is a bold one, worthy of a 'New World.'

THE INSTITUTIONAL BLOOM

If, as some suspect, the New World Order will be primarily concerned with issues of economic opportunity and security, organizations that focus on economic diplomacy will also rise in salience. ASEAN has long been the central economic institution in the Pacific Basin, both because of the lack of active competitors and because of the vitality of its members (Rieger, 1989). During the 1980s and extending into the 1990s a new, primarily economic institutional network that challenged ASEAN's primacy in this arena was created and solidified. The changing pattern of Pacific institutions poses several questions. Will ASEAN retain its central role? How will ASEAN relate to competitors? In which organization will issues be taken up and settled? ASEAN is increasingly crowded by institutional competitors in the new 'high politics' of economic diplomacy.

The Asia–Pacific Economic Cooperation (APEC) conference, is the primary competing intergovernmental organization. Formed in 1989 (by Canada, the US, Australia, New Zealand, Japan, South Korea and ASEAN), it rapidly overcame a series of political problems in order to bring in China, Hong Kong, and Taiwan (Crone, 1992). In part, its rapid progress was a result of its relationship, and growth out of, a prior, a more established organization. Formed in 1980, the Pacific Economic Cooperation Conference (PECC) had proved itself quite dynamic as a non-governmental organization devoted to the exchange of economic views and the construction of a wide-ranging network of economists, business leaders and government practitioners (Wanandi, 1989, Drysdale, 1988). At its 1991 meeting, PECC expanded its previously Asia–Pacific membership (Canada, Australia, New Zealand, the US, Japan, South Korea, China, Taiwan and ASEAN), to become more truly 'Pacific Basin': Chile, Peru and Mexico were admitted (as well as Hong Kong). The non-governmental nature of PECC limited the degree to which it directly challenged ASEAN, but the broader membership diluted any Southeast Asian perspective. PECC served as a foundation for APEC, and continues to provide policy services for the intergovernmental body. Both organizations are headquartered in Singapore, PECC led by a Singaporean and APEC by an American. In many regards, the APEC/PECC structure comprises a Pacific economic regime (Crone, 1993).

The existence and membership of APEC poses a formidable problem for ASEAN's identity and coherence. The problem has four primary dimensions. First, ASEAN has already to some degree been absorbed within the larger body of APEC, since the ASEAN members and their dialogue partners (except Europe) are all members of APEC. Preserving a distinct voice is difficult, and Malaysia's proposal for an East Asian Economic Caucus to accomplish that has been resisted. One of ASEAN's most distinctive values was its ability to focus the Post-Ministerial Conferences on its own agenda. In the economic arena, this may be displaced by APEC's yearly meetings. Second, the 'developing country' perspective of ASEAN is diluted by the membership in APEC of the US, Japan, Canada, Australia and New Zealand. To the degree that the ASEAN members have a common outlook on North–South economic issues, or on political values, these are moderated by APEC's membership. Third, given the similarity of agenda, APEC provides a forum that is an alternative to ASEAN's. This is particularly threatening where there is disagreement among ASEAN members, and the larger forum provides alternative lines of coalition formation. Cross-cutting interests could fragment and marginalize ASEAN. Finally, the inclusion of the US, Japan, and China in APEC introduces a layer of power politics that reduces the importance of the smaller, less powerful ASEAN members. The danger is a replication of global politics, where both the agenda and the outcomes are focused on the most important actors, leaving the second tier effectively out.

The ASEAN members reacted strongly to this institutional challenge. Its members were the most reluctant to form APEC. But, once it was formed, they also set in place a process of re-examination and reinvigoration of ASEAN itself, with the goal of countering that challenge. Several studies of the ASEAN organization were conducted, by a group of eminent persons and a United Nations team, with the explicit goal of strengthening it, which had been discussed frequently for a decade, but never seen as necessary by all members until the late 1980s. Several steps were taken: The Secretary General of ASEAN was raised to ministerial level to be used as an official representative in international meetings. Rather than a rotating ceremonial post, that office is now selected from nominees submitted by each member country, professionalizing the position substantially. All of the other senior ASEAN positions shifted to open recruitment as present occupants rotated out, professionalizing the staff as well. The structure of economic committees was completely changed, to make it capable of monitoring cooperative agreements and providing more suitable support for the enhanced role of the economics ministers. Summits of the ASEAN heads of government are to take place every three years, with informal meetings in between if necessary. More resources are to be provided for the Secretariat, both financial and political.

Strengthening ASEAN is primarily targeted toward its role in APEC. The ASEAN Secretariat organizes caucuses – Joint Consultative Meetings – prior to APEC ministerial and senior officials meetings among the ASEAN foreign ministers, economic ministers, and Directors General. Presently, the ASEAN foreign ministers are in charge at the APEC meetings as the primary concern is to buttress the importance of the Post Ministerial Conferences (where they also reign), but the economic ministers will eventually take a larger role as the APEC agenda shifts away from more political issues (such as membership and organization). The major question is whether collective positions can be preserved against the demands of national ones (this issue itself was the subject of a combined ASEAN Foreign and Economic Ministers meeting). Views are not identical, with Singapore feeling more confident about ASEAN's ability to take care of itself, and Indonesia watching more as a 'big brother', with concerns about losing its regional platform, one on which it has increasingly been the decisive member in recent years.

The goal of strengthening is to assure that ASEAN remains relevant in the changing global scene. Institutions matter in the international arena, and the commonplace is that old ones are replaced by new and become moribund (but are infrequently interred). While the ASEAN institution has not perfectly served the varied needs of its members, it is theirs, a point more acutely appreciated in the 1990s than before.

DEFINING A NEW POLITICAL ROLE

Overall, a New Pacific Order is presenting the necessity of ASEAN reinvigorating itself to address a regional system in flux that is nested within a broader international system also in flux. Change poses threats as well as opportunities. The current situation contains plenty of both for ASEAN: the threat of subsiding into irrelevance, and the opportunity of emerging as the strong core of a Pacific Basin organized to cope with the times.

As the broad power distribution changes, ASEAN members have attempted to insert their own influence more aggressively. Initiatives have been taken to counter outside tendencies toward economic blocs with their own enhanced trade area. ASEAN members have worked within GATT and other global organizations with a higher profile. Malaysia has even taken the lead in pushing for an East Asian Economic Caucus in the face of intense pressure from the United States to drop the idea; the debate has been quite acrimonious at times. Flux in the power system is being explored with care, but not reticence. ASEAN members are seeking a new political position.

Not the least impressive is the manner in which the ASEAN members are moving to provide the outlines of a new security system. The ASEAN Treaty of Amity and Cooperation is now established as a basis for security ties with neighbours, and the ASEAN Regional Forum is the basis of a new security dialogue for the Pacific. The fact that ASEAN has consistently downplayed the security aspects of its own nature in the past make this departure especially significant. ASEAN has stolen the march in security issues, and substituted a high profile political initiative for the lost Cambodia focus.

Faced with increased institutional competition, ASEAN is being pressured to boost its own organizational coherence, which has been, put politely, quite modest (Chng, 1990). One question is how to liaise with and to assert ASEAN views within the other Pacific organizations more effectively. With the previous structure of continuous ASEAN meetings, culminating yearly in a joint meeting with the more industrialized partners, the 'sides' were fairly clear – ASEAN had a structured centrality in the Pacific political and economic system. With a proliferation of venues and overlapping memberships, there is more room for fragmentation along lines that may cut across ASEAN, or more worrisome, cut ASEAN out. While the other organizations are not powerful or heavily institutionalized, neither is ASEAN. ASEAN may increasingly become structured as a 'pre-caucus' to other important meetings in an attempt to reduce internal fragmentation through prior formulation of a united position. The twenty-three years of waiting for ASEAN 'to mature' gave way to a proactive strengthening in the early 1990s. Chinese pressure could contribute to unity in the late 1990s.

To survive, the ASEAN organization will have to compete. The challenges facing ASEAN from global power fluctuations, from redefined security interests, and from institutional competition call for new political roles. The essence of political power in the international system is position. ASEAN manoeuvrings may improve that position with a combination of economic, political and institutional modifications to its prior programme. The future, impenetrable as always, could make much or little of their attempts. But ASEAN is not just waiting for a New World Order to become clear before adjusting. It is out in front.

References

Aligappa, Muthiah (1990) 'Soviet Policy in Southeast Asia: Towards Constructive Engagement', *Pacific Affairs*, vol. 63, no. 3 (Fall), pp. 321–50.

Aligappa, Muthiah (1993) 'Regionalism and the Quest for Security: ASEAN and the Cambodia Conflict', *Journal of International Affairs*, vol. 46, no. 2 (Winter), pp. 439–67.

ASEAN–ISIS (Institutes of Strategic and International Studies) (1991) ASEAN–ISIS Monitor, no. 1 (July) Kuala Lumpur: ISIS Malaysia).

Buszynski, Leszek (1990). 'Declining Superpowers: The Impact on ASEAN', *Pacific Review* vol. 3, no. 3, pp. 257–61.

Chng Meng Kng (1990) 'ASEAN's Institutional Structure and Economic Cooperation', *ASEAN Economic Bulletin*, vol. 6, no. 3 (March), pp. 268–82.

Crone, Donald (1988) 'The ASEAN Summit 1987: Searching for New Dynamism" in Mohammed Ayoob and Ng Chee Yuen (eds) *Southeast Asian Affairs 1988* (Singapore: Institute of Southeast Asian Studies).

Crone, Donald (1992) 'The Politics of Emerging Pacific Cooperation', *Pacific Affairs*, vol. 65, no. 1, (Spring), pp. 68–83.

Crone, Donald (1993) 'Does Hegemony Matter? The Reorganization of the Pacific Political Economy', *World Politics*, vol. 45, no. 4 (July), pp. 501–25.

Drifte, Reinhard (1990) *Japan's Foreign Policy* (London and New York: Royal Institute of International Affairs).

Drysdale, Peter (1988) *International Economic Pluralism* (New York: Columbia University Press).

Gordon, Bernard K. (1988) 'Politics and Protectionism in the Pacific', *Adelphi Papers 228* (London: International Institute for Strategic Studies).

Haber, Deborah (1990) 'The Death of Hegemony: Why 'Pax Nipponica' is Impossible', *Asian Survey*, vol. 30, no. 9 (September), pp. 892–907.

Habib, Hasnan (1990) 'Japan's Role in the Asia-Pacific Region: An ASEAN Perception', *Indonesian Quarterly*, vol. 18, no. 1, pp. 44–55.

Harrison, Selig, and Clyde Prestowitz, Jr (1990) 'Pacific Agenda: Defense or Economics?' *Foreign Policy*, vol. 79 (Summer), pp. 56–76.

Japan, Ministry of Foreign Affairs (1990) *Japan's Official Development Assistance, 1989* (Tokyo).

Ng Chee Yuen and Wong Poh Kam (1991) 'The Growth Triangle: A Market Driven Response?' Unpublished manuscript.

Ng Chee Yuen and Norman Wagner (eds) (1989) 'Privatization and Deregulation in ASEAN', *ASEAN Economic Bulletin*, vol. 5, no. 3 (March).

Pacific Economic Cooperation Council (PECC) (1993) *1993–1994 Pacific Economic Outlook* (Washington, DC: US National Committee for Pacific Economic Cooperation).

Pasuk, Phongpaichit (1990) *The New Wave of Japanese Investment in ASEAN* (Singapore: Institute of Southeast Asian Studies).

Rieger, Hans (1989) 'Regional Economic Cooperation in the Asia-Pacific Region', *Asian-Pacific Economic Literature*, vol. 3, no. 2 (September), pp. 5–33.

Rostow, Walt (1986) *The United States and the Regional Organization of Asia and the Pacific, 1965–1985* (Austin: University of Texas Press).

Rudner, Martin (1995) 'APEC: The Challenges of Asia Pacific Economic Cooperation', *Modern Asian Studies*, vol. 29, pt 2 (May), pp. 403–37.

Saito, Shiro (1990) *Japan at the Summit* (London: Routledge).

Simandjuntak, Djisman (1989) 'Southeast Asia in the Wider Pacific: Issues of Cooperation', *Indonesian Quarterly*, vol. 18, no. 1 (1990), pp. 22–33.

Wanandi, Jusuf (1989) 'The Role of PECC in the 1990s and Pacific Institutions', *Indonesian Quarterly*, vol. 18, no. 1 (1990), pp. 34–43.

4 The Emergence of Ecological Issues in Southeast Asia

James Clad and Aurora Medina Siy

INTRODUCTION

No other issue in Southeast Asia's contemporary history has so swiftly assumed prominence in the region's domestic, inter-regional and international affairs as the emergence of an increasingly politicized ecological awareness. A complex mix of external political pressure, multilateral diplomacy, aid conditionality, profligate resource extraction and local controversy has created an environmental awareness which has broadened the political agenda in Southeast Asia.

At first glance this may seem a somewhat sweeping assertion. Security issues also continue to preoccupy the region coincident with the disappearance of the Cold War. The Southeast Asian state system also faces enduring questions of trade access and economic development, even as a steadily more diversified export profile, greater intra-regional trade volumes, and rising middle-class prosperity give leverage to the ASEAN states. Still, the rapidly emerging impact of the environmental agenda – on multilateral, bilateral, regional, national and even parochial politics – has no precedent and few parallels in the region.

Much analysis of the environmental issues confronting Southeast Asia turns on the apparent intractability of political and economic elites reacting to the new environmental agenda. Yet environmental consciousness has not made an abrupt entry into the region, nor does it import a necessarily alien concept into local or even national-level politics. If one looks past ostensibly belligerent attitudes by governments to environmental pressure, one finds reforms quietly implemented in many Southeast Asian states since the 1970s. But what are the stimuli to which the often publicly obdurate leaderships have responded? To what extent is Southeast Asian environmental politics a creature of global trends, and to what extent is it anchored in local conditions and locally articulated? These questions lie at the core of this chapter.

Before venturing into specific accounts, our framework of analysis needs a cursory examination. Much contemporary theorizing about policy-making begins with an implicit assumption that narrowly defined and self-interested elites dominate and direct political discourse. The literature of political economy emphasizes the primacy of social class and interest groups via the 'public choice' approach, various 'pluralist' perspectives, or even neo-Marxist analysis. Most explanations of why governments make particular choices, and why they eschew others, depend heavily on notions of cohered class interest (Olson, 1965; Srinivasan, 1985, p. 43; dos Santos, 1970; Amin, 1977; Dahl, 1961, 1971; Shils, 1966, 1975). This perspective retains a tenacious hold on both the academic and popular imagination: whether in journals of political economy, or in journalistic surveys, the environment in Southeast Asia is invariably depicted as hostage to rapacious loggers, industrial polluters, or corrupted leaders, none of whom evince the slightest concern for the public welfare. There is considerable validity in this analysis.

A second paradigm for understanding of policy formation, also useful, emphasizes the monopoly position enjoyed by the state when defining the common good. Much of the theoretical writing by Joel Migdal or Theda Skocpol, for example, turns on how the state, any state, becomes a principal actor in the political process, with results that may, but as often may not, enmesh with elite concerns (Migdal, 1987; Skocpol, 1985). And various external imperatives, such as meddlesome aid donors, sometimes prompt reluctant action by bureaucratic leaderships, in full knowledge that these decisions will collide with elite interests. This takes us very far from the notion that the state necessarily sides with the economic elites. The explanation lies less in altruism or self-abnegation, and more in calculations of how to blunt and dissipate political pressure. Commitment to 'reform', and therefore to change, depends on what professors Grindle and Thomas describe as a choice between crisis and 'politics-as-usual' (Grindle and Thomas, 1991, pp. 14, 104–7). Crises prompt quick responses, lest an incumbent leader may be threatened. In the second category, parochial concerns or bureaucratic politics usually predetermine the outcome: environmental policy almost invariably falls into that category.

In the remaining sections of this chapter we examine (a) the extent of environmental distress in the region; (b) the various protagonists in this emerging politics; (c) the region's history of environmental activism, which predates the colonial period; (d) the role of contemporary international pressure on regional states for ameliorative action on the environment; and (e) the various Southeast Asian governmental responses.

THE EXTENT OF THE PROBLEM: A QUICK SURVEY

In Southeast Asia, the range of environmental issues now runs from the familiar excesses of affluent urban societies to incessant land degradation and water shortages adding inexorably to rural impoverishment. Plummeting air quality standards also afflict large metropolitan areas in Vietnam, Thailand, Indonesia and the Philippines. Lead additives in petrol continue to be used in some parts of the region, despite the risk of brain damage to children exposed (as shantytown children most often are) to motor vehicle exhaust. In Malaysia and Singapore, emission standards receive far better enforcement yet, as in Kuala Lumpur, heat inversions above the city still entrap pollutants in a low band of air.

In solid waste disposal, the picture is troubling. In Manila, nine million inhabitants generate 1,450 tonnes of solid waste each day; in Jakarta, this reaches 1,670 tonnes a day. In both cities, less than 70 per cent of solid waste reaches collection vans, incinerators or protected dumps. (US Agency for International Development, 1992). The percentage of treated waste drops even further in most secondary Southeast Asian cities. Most sanitary drinking water and sewage infrastructure built before the 1970s now suffers from acute over-usage and requires expansion and refurbishment.

Pressing as these are, no topic evokes more outrage nor prompts more resentment than the loss of Southeast Asia's tropical hardwood forests. Although forests once covered large tracts of the region, today only Burma, Malaysia and Indonesia count as major timber and timber product exporters; the latter two account for over 80 per cent of the world trade in tropical hardwood. The rapidity with which this forest cover has been disappearing troubles many: upland forest watersheds remained abundant until thirty years ago in Thailand, the Philippines and most of peninsular Malaysia. Within a generation's lifetime, a deepening cycle of lowered water tables, flooding, topsoil loss and ruination of irrigation and hydro-electric works has resulted from this deforestation. Comparisons of forested area in 1989 and 1993 (see Table 4.1) show the rate and extent of primary forest loss throughout the region. In 1990, a flash flood swooping down from the highlands of the Philippine island of Leyte killed more people in one evening than all the victims of a 22-year communist insurgency. (Table 4.2 summarizes the environmental problems of Southeast Asian countries and their causes.)

Outside Southeast Asia, analysts tend to see the region's environmental issues in an episodic way. Controversies such as well-publi-

Table 4.1 Extent of forest areas in Southeast Asian countries, 1980
vs 1990 (000 hectares)

	FOREST AREA		ANNUAL RATE OF DEFORESTATION (1981–1990)	
	1980	*1990*	*Hectares*	*Percentage*
Malaysia	21,546	17,583	396	1.8
Indonesia	121,669	109,549	1,212	1.0
Singapore	4	4	0	0.0
Thailand	17,888	12,735	515	2.9
Philippines	10,991	7,831	316	2.9
Vietnam	9,683	8,312	137	1.4
Cambodia	13,477	12,163	131	1.0
Laos	14,467	13,173	129	0.9
Myanmar	32,862	28,256	401	1.2

Source: *World Resources, 1994–1995* (World Resources Institute).

cized rejection by Southeast Asian politicians of Western inspired ecological agitation, or confrontations between governments and local communities (in which the latter assume the underdog's role) win attention. Hydro-electric dams, timber concessions and mono-culture plantation schemes have led to many protracted disputes since the 1970s. After 1984, plans to build a dam at Kedung Omo in central Java provoked villagers to resist relocation after the dam's lake drowned their farms. In another dam project, along the Chico river in northern Luzon, vehement opposition by tribal leaders to flooding of sacred tribal lands led to intense lobbying by foreign and domestic non-government organizations (NGOs) against World Bank funding in the 1970s. Another controversial project awaiting implementation is a stupendously expensive and ambitious scheme to send power from hydro-electric dams in Sarawak, in East Malaysia, across 1,200 kilometres of the South China Sea dividing it from peninsular (West) Malaysia.

Beside the high-profile controversies lie other issues: reliance on pesticides; habitual use by fishermen of dynamite or even cyanide to increase their yields; competing claims for water by agricultural, industrial and residential users; extravagant pollution of streams and rivers by industrial firms (textile factories are particularly notorious polluters); even esoteric forms of toxic waste – as in a 1980s controversy over a Japanese mining company, Rare Earth Ltd, whose byproducts irradiated Malaysian villages adjacent to its operations in Perak. All these examples reinforce a picture of accelerating despoliation throughout the region.

Table 4.2 Major environmental problems of Southeast Asia

Country	Problems	Causes
Cambodia	Deforestation	Logging, shrimp ponds; overpopulation; immigration.
	Habitat loss	
	Mangrove destruction	
Indonesia	Rainforest-degradation	Poor forest management practices; slash and burn agriculture.
Laos	Deforestation	Deforestation; shifting cultivation.
	Water management	Deforestation.
	Habitat loss	
Malaysia	Coastal degradation	Human overexploitation.
	Water pollution	Mining; silt and occasional oil spills; untreated sewage.
	Deforestation	Logging in primary forest.
Myanmar	Deforestation	Illegal logging.
(Burma)	Natural disasters	Geographical location in a climatic zone of heavy precipitation; river flooding, cyclones and earthquakes.
	Internal disorder and isolationism	
Philippines	Deforestation and land degradation	Illegal logging; increasing population and agriculture pressures.
	Coastal degradation	Excessive rainfall and tropical storms; deforested upland areas; destructive fishing methods; coral mining.
	Pollution	Air and soil pollution; industrial and other toxic waste disposal; urban overpopulation.
Singapore	Industrial pollution	Rapid industrialization; lack of land; inadequate water supply and growth of urban area near industries.
Thailand	Urbanization	Rapid growth; lack of land.
	Deforestation	Logging and encroachment by farmers.
	Wildlife destruction	Deforestation.
	Water scarcity	Destruction of forested watersheds; poor management of irrigation systems and inefficient water usage.

Vietnam	Urban environment quality	Rapid urbanization; industrial and air pollution; inadequate sewage system; traffic congestion.
	Deforestation	War damage (including defoliation by US forces); agricultural, legal and illegal cutting of wood for firewood and construction materials; accidental fires.
	Soil degradation	Overcultivation; intense precipitation.
	Water resources	Uneven distribution of water (dry season = water scarcity; wet season = flooding); industrial and domestic waste pollution; river sedimentation.
	Marine degradation	Oil spills; overfishing.

Source: 1994 Environmental Almanac (World Resources Institute).

THE ECOLOGICAL PROTAGONISTS

What has been the political response? On one side of the arguments around each project we find the most prominent concessionary lending institutions, the World Bank and the Asian Development Bank (ADB), figuring disproportionately in the major infrastructural projects which attract so much environmentalist criticism. Bilateral aid donors, notably the Japanese government's Overseas Economic Cooperation Fund (OECF), find themselves heavily criticized for helping to fund allegedly disruptive or damaging projects. But private financiers, especially major banks from the US, Western Europe and Japan, do not escape notice; a number of US institutions, notably the Bank of America, have even sought advice from NGOs as to how to build environmental sensitivity into their lending operations; their advisors include such NGOs as the Washington, DC-based World Resources Institute.

Meanwhile, the clients of these financiers – Southeast Asian governments and major domestic corporations – seek to meet steeply rising demand for electricity, irrigation water, roads and export revenue. Within the environmental debate, these concerns remain as 'constants', against which criticism often founders for a perceived lack of alternatives at the same short-term cost. Private ownership – as in the expansion of shrimp or prawn hatcheries – generates the same controversies. Local NGOs espouse ecological issues but may often lack a mass base. Behind these groups, foreign NGOs in such capitals as Bonn, Canberra, Copenhagen, London, Ottawa or Washington seek to influence aid budgeting in their respective countries, often with great acumen.

The environmentalists' Manichean world of 'good' (environmentally sensitive) and 'bad' (environmentally indifferent) leaders in Southeast Asia obscures the extent to which environmental politics in Southeast Asia already has become institutionalized within the respective national societies. The impression of governments in collusion with special interest groups, opposed only by earnest citified groups with no mass base, inadequately reflects reality. The maturation of environmental advocacy in Southeast Asia has a direct correlation to the growing impact of declining land, water, and resource quality on the lives of more and more people. For Southeast Asians, a deteriorating environment has an immediacy that traditional national security concerns lack.

The emergence of a distinct ecological politics in Southeast Asia results not primarily, as is sometimes alleged, from the agitation of forceful foreign lobbies (though these can bring influential voices to bear), nor from shadowy links between home-grown activists and international NGOs. Indeed, 'environmental politics' in large part emerged out of long-established community agitation. Village and local associations in Southeast Asia have a pedigree based on pre-colonial traditions. The maintenance of community consensus and cohesion occurred via self-help groups, as in Indonesia's *gotong-royong*, or mutual exchange, concepts or in the Philippine *bayanihan* spirit. Similar groupings in Thailand arose from community limits on land and water use in the commons as Garrett Hardin (1993, pp. 217–18) uses that word – meaning forests, watersheds, hunting or fishing grounds, and sacred areas. A myriad of associational forms emerged and developed in the region. Some remain distinctly indigenous, as in the communitarian organization of some native people; others, like trade unions and other non-government organizations based on livelihood, may have an evidently Western origin but operate in forms more familiar to consensus-seeking traditions.

Today's Southeast Asian environmental advocates are heirs to this indigenous legacy. Bit by bit, the intrusion of the formal state apparatus, and its protection of increasingly well-capitalized domestic and foreign resource-extraction companies, has led to a loss of local control of resources. With the expropriation of traditional practices, a process of disattachment began, with a tendency toward over-exploitation of local resources even by local people themselves who no longer have a stake, or a say, in their disposition. The monitizing of resources, and the intrusion and often very willing embrace of the modern consumer economy by local populations, also reinforces the disattachment, aided by monotheistic religious proselytizing which weakens animist belief in forest spirits. If this explanation holds, 'ecological politics', 'green advocacy' or dozens of other terms simply give new names to what are, or were, old habits of 'living within limits.' Hence the religious element – the reverence for trees, rivers, stones and animals – closer to an holistic, rather than anthropocentric view, of nature. For example, the Cordillera peoples in Luzon's northern highlands lived by an ancient but quite prudent practice of replacing every tree they cut with two seedlings. As Isagani Serrano (1994, p. 31) puts it:

> even swidden agriculture, or slash-and-burn farming, now thought to be destructive of the upland ecosystem, was once sustainable. Indigenous peoples and upland farmers, with their deeply ingrained understanding of ecospace, were guided by the regenerative cycle of a tree, leaving the first clearing untouched until second growth forests matured.

Western colonialism and then this century's far more comprehensive 'modernization' have displaced local 'sovereign' control over resources. The trend instead has been to vest this control in the state (Dove, 1994, p. 3). Commercial degradation of forests and upland ecosystems began in earnest when these abstracted rights became enmeshed with technological prowess. The opening of the Suez Canal, the expansion of railways, or the application of industrial rigour to agriculture – all these added to population pressures. By the time a full administrative imperialism was extracting natural resources for markets half the world away, the local ecosystem was in full retreat. Right up to national independence, only intermittent concern was heard about 'nature conservation' or 'wildlife protection', the words then favoured. Comparatively mild pollution and resource exploitation were seen as acceptable, demonstrating results of accelerated economic development.

Occasionally, colonial administrations set aside areas of pristine wilderness – as in the Dutch East Indies, where authorities created nature reserves on Java, or when the British imposed a degree of forestry control in possessions administered directly from London, as in Sarawak (for a brief time after World War II) and in Sabah. The US administration in the Philippine Islands created a few botanical reserves. But this was minuscule compared to the post-independence momentum toward galloping deforestation; for example, the Philippine archipelago's 24 million hectares of hardwood forests in 1940 had dwindled, by 1990, to less than 4 per cent of that area.

The accelerating rate of despoliation by the 1970s reflected an intensification of the development ethos, borrowed and 'indigenized' by local elites. In 1945, a zeal for environmental protection did not exist. No significant, politicized anxiety focused on pollution control, sustainable development, toxic land or water usage, abatement of forest-felling or hazardous waste disposal. Any protests were localized, devoid of any concept of environmental stress *per se*.

CONTEMPORARY ENVIRONMENTAL ACTIVISM

In the contemporary period, Southeast Asia's rapid transformation from agriculture to export-oriented economies has made both urban and rural dwellers aware of the intersection of deteriorating land and water quality, and of demographic growth. Marites Vitug, a prominent Southeast Asian writer on ecological issues, says that for most people in the region 'being green is neither easy nor comfortable; it is part of the struggle to survive' (Vitug, 1993, p. 44).

But this observation overlooks the fusion of environmentalism with the emerging middle class in the region. 'Environmentalism' in Southeast Asia has its origin as an echo effect from Western protest movements first arising during the 1960s. Inspired mainly by that activism, which included protests against chemical defoliation caused by US forces in Vietnam, a number of 'back-to-nature' movements sprouted in Asia with a mostly urban, middle-class orientation. They later widened their environmental focus to include rediscovery of traditional cultures and folk religions.

The first wave of environmental awareness in Southeast Asia crested in the 1970s, following the 1972 Stockholm UN Conference on the Environment. The most obvious manifestation was the addition of environmental planning methods which usually functioned in practice as a *pro forma*, 'add-on' procedure, tacked on at the end of the project planning process. Nearly all the current member of the Association of Southeast Asian Nations (ASEAN) created ministries of the environment at the central and, as within the Malaysian federation, at the state level as well.

The second wave of environmentalism, stronger than its antecedent, emerged during the 1980s and continues today. Its appeal rests on a deeper understanding than existed a decade earlier about the negative consequences of rapid economic growth, of urbanization, of steady population growth and of pressure on rural land. The new movement also reflected an increasing tension between the habits of political patronage and discontent within new middle-class constituencies about business-as-usual. Finally, the well documented and accelerating pace of biological resource exploitation and degradation in Southeast Asia, notably in fisheries and forests, could no longer be ignored by governments.

A few examples will suffice. The opposition in Sarawak to outside logging interests has resulted, since 1987, in the arrest of more than 400 members of the Penan ethnic group, a hunting-and-gathering culture. Protests by Indonesian villagers in 1985 against a dam likely to inundate prime farmland led to the deaths of four people in Madura. An ambitious plan to harvest West Irian forests for paper production collapsed after the foreign corporation involved, Scott Paper of the United States, opted to withdraw after opposition from both Indonesian and American NGOs. Residents of San Simon, in the Philippine province of Pampanga, after 1988 temporarily obstructed a newly constructed iron-smelting plant spewing toxic dust. In all these instances, a degree of community cohesion forced government regulators to close or curtail the activity, an action not seen in the past.

A shift in elite perceptions has followed. For Southeast Asia's growing class of professionals, entrepreneurs and technicians, environmental constraints have become a matter of routine. Industrial planners, logging operators, irrigation technicians, urban planners, transport operators, electricity suppliers, factory operators, plantation managers and other professionals routinely confront resource management and pollution problems. And an earlier inclination among governing and business elites to simply ignore environmental criticism is changing.

Dr Burton Oñate, an agricultural scientist and formerly the Asian Development Bank's Chief Statistician during the 1970s and 1980s, offers an example of this change. In a series of papers earning him, in one critique, the tag of 'enemy of the Green Revolution', Dr Oñate charged that the Philippines-based International Rice Research Institute (IRRI) had developed rice seed varieties which harmed small farmers and degraded the environment because they required large amounts of fertilizer and pesticide to produce profitable harvests. Farmers, he reasoned, become financially over-extended while intensive application of factory-produced nutrients add to soil acidity and contribute to river pollution. The net effect, he argued, was a reduction in productivity after initial, short-term gains.

The global issues thrown up by 1980s environmental debates – such as projected rises in median sea levels or changes in rainfall patterns – have not escaped attention from policy elites in Southeast Asia. Both regional economists and foreign groups, such as the US-based World Resources Institute, produce sophisticated analyses of lost opportunity costs in the destruction of Southeast Asia's coastal mangrove forests, or in the pollution of water supplies from pesticide and fertilizer run-offs. The effect of these analyses on what might be called the 'legitimization of environmental advocacy' should not be underestimated.

The budgets for remedial programmes also reveal the increasing importance of the issue. The Thai government by 1990 had announced multi-billion dollar programmes to prevent the eutrophication of streams and new maintenance spending to rehabilitate existing infrastructure, some of it built as recently as the 1970s. In Indonesia alone, broadly defined 'environmental project' outlays in the seventh Five Year Plan (ending in 1977) stood at $3.6 billion. An ADB report dating from 1988 estimated that nearly 40 per cent of Indonesia's infrastructural capital (roads, irrigation canals and dams) stands at risk of downstream silting. A 1994 estimate by the Asian Development Bank puts budgeted sums for 'environmental projects' (a definition which embraces everything from urban sanitation to tree-planting schemes) at $145 billion from 1990 to 1996 for all of Southeast Asia, plus Hong Kong and Taiwan.

Another dimension to the 'legitimation' of environmentalism results from the gathering clout of those ministries and departments set up in the 1970s, then seen merely as impotent add-ons to the bureaucratic process. No longer. The bureaucracies ostensibly responsible for supervising environmental issues have gradually achieved positions of real influence within their respective governments. As Indonesia's environment minister for fourteen years, Emil Salim had won grudging respect from President Suharto's closest advisers by the time he retired in 1992. Salim's successor continues to exercise a moderating influence over a range of projects, from petroleum refineries in Kalimantan to forest concessions in West Irian – an example of the autonomous momentum which some agencies develop in contrast to elite self-interest. Although still embryonic, at the regional level – within the largely passive ASEAN Secretariat, for example – a number of environmental programmes also attest to the issue's immediacy and maturation. Interest by outside donors in regional afforestation also enmeshes with ASEAN or bilateral projects.

In public atmospherics however, many national authorities still maintain a tough stance against outside advocacy of ecological issues. In this they employ arguments grounded in national sovereignty. Yet even they have made important moves since the mid-1980s to reduce heedless destruction, to abate grosser pollution and to redress environmental stress. Malaysia's Mahathir Mohammad, prime minister after 1981, has made 'those meddling foreign environmentalists' a regular target of his attacks – yet he has also presided over the continuing professionalization of his country's forest service, giving it real teeth in contests with the country's sultans (who rely on forest concessions as one of their few remaining sources of patronage). In 1987 Mahathir used Malaysia's Internal Security Act, which authorizes recurrent but court-sanctioned detention without trial, to arrest environmental critics – in the context of a wider crackdown on dissent. This action remains the most draconian measure employed to date against SE Asian green activism, although intimidation and death threats by and against protagonists in local environmental disputes continue to occur.

Maria Seda at the Singaporean Institute of Southeast Asian Studies puts the issue this way (Seda, 1993, pp. 2–3):

it would be disingenuous for Southeast Asian states to deny that they might benefit from efforts to improve resource use and environmental practices, and to promote broad, integrated and sustainable approaches to such international activities as trade and multilateral aid. Renewable stocks of natural resources are a key source of revenues and employment for most countries . . . Agriculture is still the largest employer [while] agribusiness and tourism are important sources of foreign earnings and employment . . . All these sectors are vulnerable to environmental degradation.

As ecological awareness grows, many home-grown NGOs have emerged, an important juncture in the pluralization of political life. The most prominent Indonesian NGO in this area, known by its Indonesian language acronym WALHI, took the novel step in 1987 of initiating civil litigation against both provincial and central governments, claiming that both had ignored legally-mandated environmental impact assessments for a hydro-electric and aluminum smelting project in Sumatra. Another organization, SKEPHI, has grown out of WALHI; it coordinated successful Indonesian NGO resistance to the Scott Paper Company's West Irian project.

The leading Malaysian environmental NGO, Sahabat Alam, has sought since the 1980s to restrain Malaysia's nine hereditary sultans from abusing residual prerogatives giving them control over forest resources. In Thailand, a coalition of NGOs capitalized after 1988 on popular revulsion against Thai–Chinese logging firms, whose clear-cutting of forests were seen as having contributed mightily to the unprecedented severity of upland flooding during 1988–9. Other points of activism include industrial pollution in areas adjacent to Bangkok. In the Philippines, the Haribon Foundation became the local partner of that country's first debt-for-nature swap. It has outgrown its initial conservation focus and now stands in the forefront of the Philippines' Green-Forum, an NGO coalition aiming at sustainable development.

Even smaller groups have gained a measure of success and standing. In the Philippines, combined efforts by the Malutok–Magarang tribal communities and several American Peace Corps volunteers enabled local residents to acquire legally acknowledged communal leases over their ancestral land. The lease has prevented migrants from encroaching on the communal perimeters; it has also slowed forest denudation (Lynch and Talbott, 1988, pp. 699–702). To take another example of local NGO activism, Indonesia's Prokasih programme has prompted community monitoring of blatant industrial pollution in Java (Brandon and Ramankutty, 1993, p. 80).

By the mid-1990s, therefore, an ecological dimension in Southeast Asian political life had won considerable acceptance. Some analysts professed to see in this hesitant politics of ecology a powerful engine for political liberalization. In countries like Malaysia, Indonesia or Vietnam, the analogy is with agitation during the 1970s about industrial pollution in central Europe: the argument is that authoritarian governments, wherever they exist, find it hard to label popular anger over pollution or deforestation as an overt challenge to governmental legitimacy *per se*. To take a public stance against *pembangunan*, the Indonesian and Malay word meaning 'development' (and possessing in Indonesia an almost sacral tone) still invites governmental hostility and suspicion, especially when a pervasive sense of limits to political action still exists. But throughout the region as a whole, including Indonesia, ecological activism by the mid-1990s had become a routine and usually admissible form of dissent. Environmental activists do not generally seek to displace the existing order but rather to tame its inherent rapacity – a characteristic some see arising from indigenous political culture (Kunio, 1988; Clad, 1991).

THE ROLE OF OUTSIDE PRESSURE

How has outside pressure promoted the development of ecological politics in Southeast Asia? In large part this has come through the unprecedented growth of regional NGOs after frustrations over failed, state-led development policies dating to the 1960s. In contrast to state-led, top-down development blueprints, NGOs have offered a bottom-up approach, promising efficient delivery of aid, innovative solutions, flexibility and empowerment of the poor. The United Nations Development Programme (UNDP) estimates that the worldwide amount of development aid channelled through NGOs rose from $1 billion in 1970 to over $7.2 billion by 1990 (UNDP, 1994). In its 1993 Human Development Report, the same agency reckons that about 100 million people in developing countries received some benefit or other from NGO activities during the 1980s, and more than 250 millions by 1993. More than half these organizations have emerged in Asia.

Given its position as a key primary commodities exporter, natural resource use debates have had special force in Southeast Asia. By the late 1970s environmental groups in western Europe and the United States had begun to press for radical changes in resource management; not content with the initially meager results, many foreign NGOs proceeded to argue over the heads of Southeast Asian governments, pitching appeals for specific 'green projects' to the international aid agencies and to the World Bank group while helping local protest groups organize. They began a sustained campaign to introduce quite specific 'green conditionality' in both bilateral and multilateral project funding. Much of this by the mid-1990s had become enmeshed with efforts to ensure that World Bank and ADB loans did not result in the displacement of indigenous people, of whom perhaps several million still dwell in Southeast Asia's forests and mountains, notably in Vietnam, Mindanao, Borneo and West Irian.

This pressure increasingly affected the processing of ADB and World Bank loans. In 1987 the World Bank allocated future loans to Indonesia's controversial transmigration programme only for rehabilitating and consolidating existing sites, and not for expansion. In the same year, the Bank's pipeline project for Nam Choan, in Thailand, was scrapped after agitation over its adverse impact on one of the country's few remaining tropical forests, and on six rare animal species (Seda, 1993, p. 19). Through the initiative of two American NGOs, and of an Asian NGO Coalition known as ANGOC, an ADB NGO lobby emerged in 1989 demanding reforms in that Bank's policies. At the ADB's 26th Annual Meeting in 1993, ANGOC's membership had exceeded 30 organizations. Partially in reaction, the Japanese-dominated ADB began to incorporate environmental and social impact criteria in its lending (Serrano, 1994, p. 81).

Similarly, the bilateral aid agencies have reacted to NGO advocacy by tying concessionary lending or grants to environmental objectives. Dismay over rapid felling of tropical forests, in Latin America as well as in Southeast Asia, also prompted groups in Europe and the US to organize consumer boycotts of tropical timber. Some campaigns tried to 'tag' timber product imports as coming from environmentally well managed areas; others called for outright bans on tropical timber imports. In 1992 the Netherlands minister for Overseas Development Cooperation sharply criticized Indonesia for its deforestation, an action representing perhaps the furthest extreme to which foreign governments would go to publicly challenge environmental management in Southeast Asia.

Much environmentalist intrusion into Southeast Asia's international relations can be traced to environmental activism in the US Congress in the mid-1980s. Legislation passed in 1985 required environmental assessment evaluations before US approval to any multilateral aid project. Subsequent legislation added more environmental impact criteria to project evaluation by the multilateral institutions. At American insistence, a comprehensive environmental agenda was gradually added to World Bank operations; the US also added environmental barriers to foreign product sales in the American market – as in the rejection of tuna caught by vessels using drift net fishing techniques. Advocacy for these moves came from Washington-based groups, such as the Rainforest Action Network, the National Resources Defense Council, the Sierra Club, the Environmental Defense Fund, the World Wildlife Fund and the Environmental Policy Institute. Southeast Asian governments watched this with misgiving.

International environmentalism also finds reflection in a large number of bilateral and multilateral conventions and agreements initialed since the 1980s. More than five hundred multilateral conventions have reached the signing ceremonies; these include such regional efforts as ASEAN-wide protocols for exchanging environmental information, or changes to the trilateral Indonesia–Malaysia–Singapore ship traffic management scheme operating in the Straits of Malacca. Common Southeast Asian bargaining positions on deforestation issues arising in the Osaka-based International Tropical Timber Organization also became routine; they also emerged during the intense talks on tropical timber guidelines preceding the UNCED conference.

There are sub-regional dimensions as well. After the Thai government's well-publicized tropical timber logging ban in 1989, Thai–Chinese business groups backed by the Thai military shifted operations to Burma, Laos and (with a cut of profits going to the Khmer Rouge guerrilla leadership) to western Cambodia. A Philippine ban on logging in 1990 also resulted both in intensified logging within existing concessions and in increased logging in adjacent forested areas of Malaysia and Indonesia. Ethnic Chinese Malaysian firms have shifted their logging operations to Papua New Guinea, Guyana and Belize; in Papua New Guinea the Minister of Forests had, by 1994, received numerous threats of intimidation or physical harm from loggers annoyed at government efforts to better monitor the amounts of cubic meterage being felled. Environmental depredation is indeed often the consequence of the pursuit of elite interests.

While studying implementation of 'integrated conservation development projects' or ICPDs, professors Wells and Brandon observed that 'international NGOs seldom become involved directly in project implementation . . . [their] principal role has been to contribute or raise funds and to provide expatriate technical assistance, sometimes in the form of the project manager or project leader' (Wells and Brandon, 1992, p. 52). This has contributed, however, to local NGOs becoming more truly 'national' in their composition, resources and acumen. Isagani Serrano (Serrano, 1994, p. 69) sees Southeast Asia's NGO movement as resting on two pillars – local development and self-governance, and he finds mixed results at best from intervention in local environmental issues by foreign NGOs. He says that increasingly sensitized advocacy by foreigners cannot change the fact that 'the concerns of citizens' movements in rich countries . . . differ from those in poor countries' (Serrano, 1994, p. 78).

Today, more and more environmental lobby groups within the region no longer rely on foreign inspiration, foreign funding or foreign advice.[1] Indeed, some regional NGO advocates dismiss certain Western NGO concerns as trivial; even the London-based Survival International claims that 'green marketing [in the West] will only make money for the marketers and may actually cause more damage by overexploiting products, destroying indigenous lifestyles, and distracting global attention from the real problems' (Dove, 1994, p. 2).

THE REGIONAL RESPONSE TO PRESSURE

Reaction from Southeast Asia's political and economic elites to the specific issues raised by the environmental NGOs has varied widely. At one end of the spectrum lies the ostensibly principled hostility to Western interference, typified by Malaysian prime minister Mahathir's stance prior to, and after, the 1992 UNCED conference in Rio de Janeiro. Mahathir has characterized Western campaigns to restrain logging in Southeast Asia's tropical forests as a transparent move to shift the timber trade back to temperate forest producers. More generally, he has become lead spokesman for the position taken by most Asian countries convening in Beijing, six months prior to the UNCED; in a resulting 'Beijing Declaration' they cast the entire global environment debate in the rhetoric of North–South division. Burma, the Indochinese states and Thailand also echo this view, with Indonesia and the Philippines taking a less antagonistic stance while doing little to abate the pace of deforestation.

At the other end of the spectrum, many government-backed development programmes are becoming slightly more receptive to innovations such as debt-for-nature swaps (as in the debt-burdened Philippines), new resource husbandry research (as in Thailand's new environmental centres) or new conservation strategies (as in a number of World Bank-sponsored forestry projects in Indonesia after 1990). It is worth acknowledging as well that Malaysia's domestic environmental protection policies have stiffened markedly since 1992, despite Mahathir's high-profile rhetoric against 'green imperialism'. (One factor in his domestic political calculations remains a perceived need to rein in the country's sultans, whose power base has narrowed to sources of patronage, such as forest concessions. Hence, for reasons not connected to a yearning for more restrictively managed forestry, the Malaysian political leadership by 1993 had moved to clamp down on logging concessionaires.)

The timber boycott threats from the West seemed, to the Malaysian and Indonesian delegations at the Rio UNCED conference, suspiciously similar to other boycott action motivated primarily by commercial advantages: in the early 1980s, controversial moves to label Southeast Asian palm oil, as having heart-stoppingly high levels of saturated fat, had harmed Malaysian export revenues. Was there a similar market-driven aim behind the purported altruism, anxious to protect tropical forests? Mahathir believed there was. In a series of statements up to the 1992 UNCED conference he accused American timber producers of coveting Japan's plywood market. He claimed they had financed environmental campaigns to shame Japanese trading companies into reducing their tropical hardwood purchases, but failed to document his claim, which has elicited firm denials from environmental groups. (Tropical hardwood is mainly used as ply in Japan's construction industry as a use-once-and-throw-away mould for casting concrete.)

From the standpoint of the region's governing elites, the focus on the global environment has resulted in important challenges to traditional concepts of sovereignty – a point debated with much vigour in the Non-Aligned Movement and in other forums in which the Southeast Asian states have representation. The various forms of foreign aid conditionality and the threatened environmental trade restrictions have created much unease in Southeast Asia; Indonesia's Foreign Minister Ali Alatas, speaking to the authors in April 1993, spoke of a 'new colonialism in a green guise'. An absolute right to conduct development within the national territory, and to accord (or not to accord) priority to environmental protection – that is still a favoured position in regional rhetoric.

Another view detects an undermining of sovereignty when foreign invested firms transfer unsustainable resource use practices, or grossly polluting industrial processes, to Southeast Asian locales. These instances rarely figure, however, in the often elegant elaborations by Singapore's diplomats of the Asian divergences from Western values

(Mabubhani, 1992, p. 45). Nevertheless, a domestic political commitment to environmental protection is increasing in the region, largely an aggregate of a myriad of incremental responses to local controversies and complaints. Yet the problem of effective implementation remains as intractable as ever: Brandon and Ramankutty, in proposing a comprehensive environmental strategy for Asia, admit that 'it is at the level of implementation – monitoring environmental impacts and enforcing regulations – that government institutions are weakest' (Brandon and Ramankutty, 1993, p. 4). Weak governments often face strong economic interests which profit from environmental destruction.

CONCLUSION

So is it, after all, just 'politics-as-usual' in Southeast Asia, with environmental consciousness playing a distinctly secondary role to elite-driven resource exploitation? In the absence of an emphatic, immediate perception of crisis – which still eludes the region – will bureaucratic process and customary patronage habits remain ascendent? In our view, they must adjust more as political power spreads. Environmental awareness in Southeast Asia rests on the increasingly indigenous politicized nature of the phenomenon. In a comparatively short period of time, environmentalism as an abiding expression of political choice has become consolidated in the region, coincident with (and perhaps hostage to) the burgeoning wealth and the accompanying embourgeoisment being created there.

Do the region's ecological policies depend, ultimately, on Western environmentalism? And has this pressure increased markedly since the end of the Cold War? The answers to both must be a qualified 'no'. If asked in the early 1980s, the answer would have been otherwise, but by the mid-1990s the gravity of the environmental agenda had prompted a broad spread of SE Asian constituencies to emerge, urban and rural, traditional and cosmopolitan. Insistent foreign advocacy had begun to lose much of its point and, for local NGOs, had sometimes become overly intrusive. At the same time, a readjustment in power and influence within international NGOs was also proceeding apace, with less of a correspondingly 'foreign' tag as and when these INGOs took an interest in local environmental issues. With the apparent, and possibly transitory, pause in great power manoeuvring in the region after the Cold War's demise, the available political 'space' in many Southeast Asian states unquestionably widened enabling, to a modest degree, some expansion of the political agenda if spoken in an environmental idiom.

Still, caution must dampen hopes that local green constituencies can, by themselves, quickly alter the region's deeply entrenched political culture of resource-extractive patronage. Theories of 'regime formation' rest on shared or complementary interests (Ruggie, 1975; Krasner, 1985; Young, 1985; Keohane, 1984), but for our purposes the utility of international regime analysis has some problems. One is the easy acceptance that signatories to international conventions incorporate the international norms into domestic law and, especially, practice. Standards of governance in Southeast Asia, while superior to many regions in the world, are still uneven; as elsewhere, 'environmentalism' has many converts reluctant to apply the credo's norms to their own activities. Governments strike a green pose, but no ostensibly or even predominantly 'green' political party remotely similar to the western European experience has emerged in Southeast Asia. Multinational corporations use it to market ecologically-friendly products, while some industrial organizations use it (as in Indonesia's forest concessionaires' public relations campaign in the US) to blunt criticism or remain well positioned in global markets.

Since the Cold War's end, compass bearings for the region's security concerns have shifted in other directions, but the dynamic remains the same – to blunt the intrusion of hegemonic powers. The April 1995 convening in Manila of ASEAN defence ministers to confer over China's intentions in the Spratly islands reinforced the sceptics who had seen the Cold War's end as but a momentary respite from longer, and more recurrent trends of rivalry and ambition. In this context, the imposition of environmentally 'correct' outside advice derives little extra momentum from the end of Soviet–American rivalry and the end of the diplomacy this spawned for four decades in Southeast Asia. It is rather the gradual expansion of international civil society, including within SE Asia, that has raised the salience of the environmental agenda without regard for great power alignments. Lastly, strong regionalism – in the form of regional institutions with autonomous freedom of action – lies many years away from political reality in Southeast Asia, foreclosing the possibility of truly multinational responses to urgent environmental problems.

The evolution of environmental awareness in Southeast Asia must continue, therefore, as a domestic, often intensely local phenomenon amplified, at best, by outside lobbies and advocacy.

72   *Ecological Issues*

Note

1. A case in point is the creation (in April 1993) of the Global Anti-Golf Movement (GAG'M) in Malaysia by three Asia-based citizens' networks. The movement was a response to the increasing outcry of local communities against the deleterious effects of golf courses on land resources and on farmers' income. Anti-golf campaigns have since elicited media interest and world-wide public attention. On 29 April 1993 citizen groups in Thailand, Hawaii, Indonesia, the Philippines, Japan, India, Nepal, Taiwan, the United Kingdom, Australia and Switzerland launched 'World No Golf Day.' (Reuter News Service, Far East, 1 June, 1993).

References

Amin, Samir (1977) *Imperialism and Unequal Development* (New York: Monthly Review Press).

Brandon, Carter and Ramesh Ramankutty (1993) *Toward an Environmental Strategy for Asia. World Bank Discussion Papers*, No. 224 (Washington, DC: World Bank).

Clad, James (1991) *Behind the Myth: Business, Money and Power in Southeast Asia* (London: Harper Collins).

Dahl, Robert (1961) *Who Governs? Democracy and Power in an American City* (New Haven: Yale University Press).

Dahl, Robert (1971) *Polyarchy, Participation, and Opposition* (New Haven: Yale University Press).

Dove, Michael R. (1994) *Marketing the Rainforest: Green Panacea or Red Herring?*, Analysis no. 13 (Honolulu: East-West Center).

ECO: The Magazine of Business & the Environment (1994) 'Refuse on the Pacific Rim.' vol. I, no. 2, (January).

Far Eastern Economic Review (1993) 'Turning Green in Manila', October 28.

Grindle, Merilee S. and John W. Thomas (1991) *Public Choices and Policy Change: The Political Economy of Reform in Developing Countries* (Baltimore: Johns Hopkins University Press).

Hardin, Garrett (1993) *Living within Limits* (New York: Oxford University Press).

Hill, Robert (1988) 'Maintaining Infrastructure', *Asian Development Review*, vol. 4, no. 2. (Manila: Asian Development Bank).

Keohane, Robert (1984) *After Hegemony: Cooperation and Discord in the World Economy* (Princeton, NJ: Princeton University Press).

Krasner, Stephen (1985) 'Structural Causes and Regime Consequences: Regimes as Intervening Variables' in Stephen Krasner (ed.) *International Regimes* (Ithaca and London: Cornell University Press).

Kunio, Yoshihara (1988) *The Rise of Ersatz Capitalism in Southeast Asia* (Singapore: Oxford University Press).

Lindblom, Charles E. (1977) *Politics and Markets: The World's Political Economic Systems* (New York: Basic Books).

Lynch, Owen L. Jr and Kirk Talbott (1988) 'Legal Responses to the Philippine Deforestation Crisis', *Journal of International Law and Politics*, vol. 20, no. 3.

Mabubhani, Kishori (1992) 'When Rights Go Wrong', *Foreign Policy*, vol. XI, no. 2.

Migdal, Joel (1987) 'A Model of State-Society Relations' in Howard J. Wiarda (ed.) *New Directions in Comparative Politics* (Boulder: Westview Press).

Olson, Mancur, Jr (1965) *The Logic of Collective Action: Public Goods and the Theory of Groups* (Cambridge: Harvard University Press).

Reuters Textline, *Business Times* (Singapore), 5 January 1994.

Ruggie, John Gerard (1975) 'International Responses to Technology: Concepts and Trends', *International Organization*, vol. 29, no. 3, (Summer).

Rush, James (1993) *The Last Tree: Reclaiming the Environment in Tropical Asia* (Boulder: Westview Press/Asia Society).

Santos, Theotonio dos (1970) 'The Structure of Dependence', *American Economic Review*, vol. 60, no. 2, pp. 231–6.

Saunders, Robert J. and Sunita Ghandhi (1993) *Energy Efficiency and Conservation in the Developing World: The World Bank's Role*, World Bank Policy Paper, (Washington, DC, 1993).

Seda, Maria (ed.) (1993) *Environmental Management in ASEAN: Perspectives on Critical Regional Issues* (Singapore: Institute of Southeast Asian Studies).

Serrano, Isagani R. (1994) *Civil Society in the Asia–Pacific Region.* (Philippines: CIVICUS–World Alliance for Citizen Participation).

Shils, Edward (1966) *Political Development in the New States* (Paris: Mouton).

Shils, Edward (1975) *Center and Periphery* (Chicago: University of Chicago Press).

Skocpol, Theda (1985) *State and Social Revolutions: A Comparative Analysis of France, Russia, and China* (New York: Cambridge University Press).

Srinivasan, T. N. (1985) 'Neoclassical Political Economy, the State and Economic Development', *Asian Development Review*, vol. 3, no. 2.

United States Agency for International Development, Bureau of External Affairs (1992) *USAID Facts* (Washington, DC).

Vitug, Marites (1993) in *Far Eastern Economic Review*, vol. 13, March.

Wells, Michael and Katrina Brandon (with Lee Hannah) (1992) *People and Parks: Linking Projected Area Management with Local Communities* (Washington, DC: International Bank for Reconstruction and Development/World Bank).

Young, Oran R. (1985) 'Regime Dynamics: The Rise and Fall of International Regimes' in Stephen Krasner (ed.) *International Regimes* (Ithaca and London: Cornell University Press).

5 Human Rights in Southeast Asia: Rhetoric and Reality

Geoffrey Robinson

INTRODUCTION

It was not so long ago that powerful western governments preferred to treat the appalling human rights records of their Southeast Asian allies and trading partners as unpleasant secrets among friends. The killing of more than 500,000 people in the aftermath of the 1965 Indonesian coup, the 1975 invasion of East Timor and the subsequent decimation of a third of its population, raised scarcely a murmur of protest, and still less in the way of concrete action. On the face of it, the situation has changed rather dramatically in the past few years. International reactions to the November 1991 massacre in East Timor, to the repression of the peaceful opposition in Myanmar (Burma) from 1988, and to a lesser extent the 1992 killing of scores of pro-democracy protesters in Bangkok, for example, were usually swift and strong.

It is no accident that this change coincided with the end of the Cold War. After 1989, the preoccupation with the fight against communism – which had so profoundly influenced western foreign policy in the region for four decades – grew increasingly difficult to sustain. Without the over-riding political imperative of anti-communism, there was no plausible reason for western governments *not* to extend their ostensible concern for the promotion of human rights and democracy to all states in the region, regardless of their political complexion. This political shift provided an unexpected opportunity for those genuinely committed to human rights, both in the West and in Southeast Asia, to push governments to match their rhetoric with action. Partly for this reason, and perhaps also as a guise for other, less noble, economic, and strategic objectives, the promotion of human rights has become an explicit foreign policy objective of an increasing number of OECD states within the past five years.

Yet, despite this apparent shift in attitude, serious human rights violations have continued to occur in virtually every country in South-

74

east Asia. A pattern of grave violations – including political killings, 'disappearance', torture, arbitrary detention, and a general climate of impunity – persists in Indonesia/East Timor and Myanmar, or Burma (Amnesty International, 1992d, 1993g, 1993i, 1994b, 1994d, 1994f, 1995b). Serious violations, such as political killings, torture and ill-treatment, continue to be reported with regularity from Cambodia, the Philippines and Thailand (Amnesty International, 1992b, 1993b, 1993h, 1994a, 1995c). And, while perhaps less dramatic, significant restrictions on civil and political rights – including sporadic detention without trial of real or alleged political opponents – have become institutionalized in Singapore, Malaysia and Vietnam (Amnesty International, 1991c, 1993k). The states of Southeast Asia also still lag behind those of some other regions in their record on ratifying key international human rights instruments, and the recent contributions of some to the human rights debate have been amongst the most retrogressive in the world. Not only have they worked to undermine the principles of international scrutiny and universality, they have attempted to suppress domestic human rights advocates. And when they have taken human rights initiatives, these have more often been aimed at improving the government's image than at addressing the root causes of abuse.

Why have such serious human rights violations continued in Southeast Asia in spite of open expressions of international concern, and the apparent readiness of foreign governments to intervene? Are the sceptics perhaps correct when they say that, in the Southeast Asian context, international intervention is ineffectual, perhaps even counterproductive, and that it ought to be abandoned? This paper attempts to address these questions. It does not chronicle developments in each country in the region, but instead looks comparatively at three somewhat more manageable questions.

First, what sort of international pressure has actually been exerted on Southeast Asian states to improve their human rights records in recent years, and what sort of intervention has proven most effective? Second, how and with what effect have the governments of the region responded to that pressure? And third, to what extent have domestic political developments been responsible for hastening or slowing improvements in the field of human rights? The paper concludes that, notwithstanding continuing violations in the region, international intervention has in some cases contributed to modest improvements. However, it finds that international pressure has proven effective only where the rhetoric of international concern over human rights has been matched by concrete action, and where it has complemented the actions and objectives of domestic human rights and political activists.

INTERNATIONAL PRESSURES

In a formal sense, human rights considerations have become an increasingly important factor governing the foreign policies of donor states in the past five years. Many have made respect for human rights an explicit foreign policy objective, and a condition for the maintenance of aid and trade relations. In March 1993, US Secretary of State Warren Christopher confirmed that human rights would be a cornerstone of the new administration's foreign policy; and that commitment has been reiterated on a number of occasions since. Some international bodies have done the same. The European Parliament resolved in 1991 that human rights issues should be automatically included in all future dialogues between the European Community (EC) and ASEAN ministers and parliamentarians (European Parliament, 1991); and in the same year, the EC announced that it would consider human rights performance in decisions about economic and development cooperation (Heinz, 1993).

This shift has unquestionably had some impact on foreign policy toward the region. Grave human rights violations in Myanmar (Burma) after the seizure of power by the State Law and Order Restoration Council (SLORC) in 1988, led eventually to strongly worded resolutions both in the UN General Assembly and the UN Commission on Human Rights (UNCHR), the appointment of a UN Special Rapporteur to examine the human rights situation there, the withdrawal of military attaches by EC governments, and cuts in overseas development assistance (ODA) from major western donors (Amnesty International, 1993i p. 4 and 1994b, pp. 13–15). The Paris Peace Agreements of October 1991, signed by four Cambodian parties and 18 states, included provisions specifically aimed at promoting and protecting human rights, and the United Nations Transitional Authority (UNTAC) was given explicit powers to oversee and implement those provisions (Amnesty International, 1993b). The 12 November 1991 massacre in Dili, East Timor, widely condemned by most western governments, resulted in a series of statements and resolutions by the UNCHR, and the European Parliament, and prompted some countries to reduce their ODA and military transfers (Amnesty International, 1994f, 1995b). Similarly, the May 1992 killings of peaceful pro-democracy protesters in Bangkok were widely condemned by the international community and led to the imposition of certain sanctions against the Thai military including, for example, the cancellation of joint exercises with US forces.

These moves are often cited as evidence of a new international commitment to human rights, and a new willingness to act in accordance with that commitment. Yet, the simple fact is that donor governments have been highly selective, indeed sometimes deeply hypocritical, in their expressions of concern for human rights in Southeast Asia; and their statements of principle have only rarely been translated into effective action (Amnesty International, 1994d, 1994f, 1994h). Most OECD governments – even those most vocal in their insistence on adherence to and respect for universal human rights standards – have found it expedient to modify their rhetoric and adjust their action to accommodate other foreign policy needs, such as the maintenance and improvement of trade relations, investment opportunities and security arrangements. Only where these other foreign policy goals have been positively served, or not unduly disrupted, or of no great importance have human rights considerations actually been accorded a significant priority, and the rhetoric matched by concrete action. Where, on the other hand, these objectives have collided in a significant way, concern over human rights has almost uniformly taken a back seat.

The problem has been exemplified by the posture of Japan. In April 1991, largely under pressure from western governments, the Japanese government indicated that it would take into account 'grave violations of human rights' in its decisions about foreign aid (Arase, 1993, p. 940), a commitment formalized in June 1992 with the promulgation of the 'ODA Charter' (*Newsletter on Aid*, 1993). The government reaffirmed its position on linking aid to human rights at the Regional Meeting for Asia of the UN World Conference on Human Rights, held in Bangkok in March–April 1993. Yet, with rare exceptions, Japan has not used its considerable economic leverage to make good on that promise. Even in the face of the most egregious human rights violations, the Japanese government has made only the most perfunctory gestures of disapproval.

While it did temporarily suspend aid to the military junta in Myanmar after the massive killings of 1988, in February 1989 Japan broke ranks with western governments by recognizing the SLORC and resuming some development and humanitarian aid; in February 1994, the amount of aid was significantly increased (*Guardian*, 26 February 1994). In 1991, and again in 1992, it attempted to prevent or soften UN resolutions criticizing the regime (Arase 1993, p. 946). Likewise, following the 1991 massacre in East Timor the Japanese government said that it saw 'no need' to adjust its aid policy toward Indonesia, despite evidence that some Japanese-supplied military equipment (principally vehicles and radios) had been used by Indonesian troops in East Timor (Arase, pp. 946–7). And, just five months after the massacre, it reportedly gave assurances to Indonesian officials that, despite its stated commitment to the contrary, 'Japanese economic aid will not be linked to the implementation of human rights' (cited in Arase, p. 947). The Japanese Government expressed 'regret' at the killing of some 50 peaceful demonstrators in Bangkok, but almost immediately announced that 'we are not considering changing ODA implementation' (cited in Arase, p. 948). These positions may, in part, reflect a sincere concern not to offend other Asian governments, particularly in view of sensitivities arising from Japan's historical role in the region, but it is at least as much dictated by Japan's substantial economic interests there. Whatever the motivation, Japanese actions have, in the view of one analyst, 'unavoidably contributed to the continuing repression of pro-democracy elements and shielded repressive regimes from the full brunt of Western economic sanctions' (Arase, p. 952).

Economic interests have, of course, shaped the foreign policies of many other governments as well, often at the expense of human rights. Economic considerations have been particularly important in relations between the dynamic ASEAN economies, and the considerably less dynamic economies of Europe. At an annual EC/ASEAN ministerial meeting in Manila in October 1992, for example, the EC agreed to delete all specific references to outstanding human rights concerns in the region – in particular those in East Timor – in order to secure ASEAN approval for a new trade agreement (*Reuter*, 30 October 1992). Economic interests have also become an increasingly important element in US foreign policy in the region. These economic interests have sometimes weakened the impact of the country's human rights initiatives. For example, while the US government has been among the most vocal critics of Myanmar's military regime, US businesses have been among the largest investors there. In 1992 they invested US$163.7 million, ahead of the Japanese (US$100.7 million) and the Netherlands (US$80 million) (*FEER* 1993, p. 94).

Yet nowhere have the contradictions between the concern for human rights and the pursuit of economic advantage been more acute than in government policies with respect to arms sales. Facing the prospect of declining defence-industry contracts with the end of the Cold War, western governments – in particular those of Britain, France, Germany and the United States – have been eager to find new markets for their new and used weapons. The thriving economies of Southeast Asia have offered a promising opportunity.

Successive British governments have tried to reconcile the quest for such opportunities with the rhetoric of concern for human rights – usually at the expense of the latter. While it joined in the chorus of international protest after the Santa Cruz massacre in East Timor, and even co-sponsored the 1993 UNCHR resolution concerning Indonesia's human rights record in East Timor, in June 1993 the government approved the sale, for about US$750 million, of twenty-four British Aerospace (BAe) Hawk Fighters to the Indonesian armed forces. Dismissing concern that BAe Hawks had been used in the past, and could be used in the future, for suppressing internal opposition, in December 1993 the government licensed the sale of a further sixteen jets. Similarly, claiming that the human rights situation had improved significantly since the Santa Cruz massacre, in October 1993 the German government sold Indonesia thirty-nine used navy vessels and three new submarines, along with a service contract for five years, and 5,000 tons of ammunition.

The Australian government has also sought to increase bilateral military cooperation with Indonesia, engaging in joint military exercises even with units notorious for committing flagrant human rights violations, such as Kopassus. Conscious of the apparent hypocrisy of this policy, the government has insisted that it continues to push for improvements in the field of human rights, but that it believes that this objective can be best achieved through a policy of 'quiet diplomacy' rather than overt criticism. Writing in late 1992, a former Secretary of the Australian Department of Foreign Affairs and Trade, summarized the government's priorities: 'With Australia's need to strengthen its economic and export performance, it would be foolish for the government not to seek actively to maintain a climate favorable to commercial interests.' (Woolcott, 1992, p. 76).

An additional problem has been the lack of clarity, on the part of some western governments, in distinguishing between the goals of 'democratization' and 'good governance' on the one hand, and protection of human rights on the other. The tendency to view the establishment of formal democratic institutions as a sufficient guarantee of human rights protection, has weakened their resolve in pressing for more fundamental or significant changes. The formal restoration of democratic rule under Corazon Aquino in 1986 appeared to promise a dramatic improvement in human rights policy and practice. Immediately after taking power, the new government ratified most of the major international human rights conventions, promulgated a new constitution which guaranteed most internationally-recognized human rights, and established a national human rights commission. Yet the reality was that these measures did not result in a substantial improvement in the human rights situation. In fact, the incidence of political killings and 'disappearances' may actually have increased under the Aquino regime (Amnesty International, 1992b, pp. 1–7). However, because the new government could claim the mantle of democratic legitimacy, there was a marked reluctance in international circles to be too critical. There were tactical political considerations as well. Within the human rights bodies of the United Nations, the Philippines began to play a relatively positive role after 1986, supporting many resolutions and proposals made for the improvement of international human rights standards that were openly opposed by other Asian governments. There was therefore a tendency within the UN not to criticize the government too heavily for its own human rights record, lest that might alienate the one Asian government that appeared to be voting the right way.

Broadly speaking, then, the new rhetoric of international concern for human rights has not been matched by effective action on the part of donor governments and international organizations. However, there have been important exceptions. Some states have jeopardized otherwise good relations with Southeast Asian governments by speaking out strongly, and by taking concrete action, in response to particular human rights abuses. The Netherlands suffered fairly serious repercussions for its reaction to the Santa Cruz massacre. When the government attempted to link future aid disbursements to an improvement in the human rights situation, the Indonesian government responded by rejecting Dutch aid on the grounds that the Netherlands was using 'development assistance as an instrument of intimidation' (Republic of Indonesia, 1992, p. 2). Canada's relations with Indonesia were also soured by its decision to suspend a portion of its new aid projects in 1992, despite criticism from human rights advocates that the measures did not go nearly far enough. Expressing a view widely held within the Indonesian government, the foreign minister, speaking to an Amnesty International representative in early 1992, described the Canadian reaction as 'irrational'.

Perhaps the most striking exception to the general rule of purely rhetorical flourish has been in the position taken toward Indonesia by the United States Congress and the Clinton administration. In 1992, and again in 1994, Congress voted to suspend international military education and training (IMET) to the Indonesian armed forces, worth about US$2.3 million annually, until there had been a significant improvement in the human rights situation; and in July 1994 Congress voted to restrict small arms sales to Indonesia on similar grounds. The administration barred the re-sale of four US-built F–5E fighters from Jordan to Indonesia, in June 1993, citing continuing human rights and other concerns. Earlier in the year it broke with past policy, and took the lead in pushing for a resolution on East Timor at the UN Commission on Human rights. In late 1993 the US administration threatened to suspend Indonesia's trading privileges under the Generalized System of Preferences (GSP) – which would allow the duty-free export of some US$600 million worth of Indonesian goods – if the government did not effect substantial improvements in the field of labour rights, and it continued to press openly for such improvements through 1994. At the Asia Pacific Economic Cooperation (APEC) summit held in Jakarta in November, President Clinton spoke in unusually critical terms about the human rights situation in Indonesia and East Timor (Amnesty International, 1994f, 1994i, 1994j).

It is true that there has been some resistance to this trend within the administration itself. The Departments of State and Defence worked hard in 1993 to prevent passage of an amendment (the Feingold Amendment) to the Foreign Aid Appropriations Bill which would have suspended all military assistance to Indonesia. The administration also undermined the intent of the suspension of IMET by allowing Indonesia to purchase military training in 1993 and 1994. And in early 1995, the vice-chairman of the US joint chiefs of staff reportedly gave assurances to the Indonesian armed forces that efforts were being made to resume IMET and sales of military equipment (*Reuter*, 16 March 1995). Still, given the long-standing friendship between the US and Indonesia, the moves taken by the administration and by Congress since 1992 have been genuinely surprising, and appear to have stimulated some minor improvements in Indonesia's human rights policy and practice, particularly in the field of labour rights.

Such exceptions have occurred, in part, because the gravity of the human rights situation in certain countries has simply grown impossible to ignore, but also because the rhetoric of concern for human rights that has emerged with the end of the Cold War has created its own political momentum at home. By making human rights an explicit foreign policy objective, western governments have provided an unprecedented political opportunity for those genuinely committed to human rights, both within governments and outside, to articulate and press their demands.

The new rhetoric has also served as a convenient guise for other, less altruistic, motives. The decision to bar the transfer of warplanes from Jordan, for example, was intended principally as a message to King Hussein for his support of Iraq during the Gulf War. And US concern over labour rights in Indonesia appears to have as much to do with the objective of strengthening the domestic economy by restricting cheap imports of textiles and other products, as with any principled desire to see a better deal for Indonesian workers. Similarly, though the amount of money involved is rather small, the decision to cut IMET spending is consistent with a more general desire in Congress to reduce the government spending.

Exceptions to the rule have also been the product of a new dynamic at the international level. Particularly since the end of the Cold War, it has become virtually unthinkable to express open opposition to human rights initiatives within the UN or the institutions of the EC and (after 1 November 1993) the European Union (EU). As a consequence, many western governments have found themselves formally supporting initiatives even where, in the interest of their bilateral relations with the target of condemnation, they would prefer not to. And, as European governments have sought increasingly to coordinate their foreign policies in recent years, the opportunity has arisen for the human rights concerns of one or a few states to gain the backing of the entire community. Thus, for example, Portugal's membership of the EC/EU has meant that its objectives *vis-à-vis* East Timor have been raised and pursued as a matter of European policy, both directly through European institutions, but also through the various United Nations bodies, including the General Assembly and the Commission on Human Rights.

The trend toward UN intervention in armed conflicts around the world in recent years has also resulted in some unprecedented human rights initiatives in the Southeast Asia region. By far the most significant was the inclusion of a human rights component in the Paris Peace Agreements on Cambodia of October 1991, and in the mandate of UNTAC which was empowered to oversee the implementation of the accord in the run-up to the May 1993 elections (Amnesty International, 1994c, pp. 7–8). As part of the peace agreements, Cambodia's Supreme National Council (SNC) acceded to seven major international human rights conventions, and agreed to incorporate basic human rights provisions in its future constitution (Amnesty International, 1993b, p. 4). According to the terms of the peace agreements, UNTAC's mandate included 'general human rights oversight' during the transitional period (1992–93), and the power to carry out 'the investigation of human rights complaints' and, where appropriate to take 'corrective action' (Amnesty International, 1994a, p. 3). Operating under this mandate, in 1992 UNTAC drafted a new penal code which contained substantial human rights provisions, and in January 1993 established a Special Prosecutor's Office with the authority to investigate human rights violations and bring to justice those found responsible. UNTAC also undertook to promote human rights education within the security forces, and to assist in the formation of local human rights organizations.

Needless to say, these measures did not bring an immediate end to human rights violations in Cambodia – which included political killings, 'disappearance', and torture – through 1992 and in the months preceding the 1993 elections (Amnesty International, 1993h, pp. 5–9 and 1994a, p. 7). Nor did they provide any absolute guarantee that abuses would not continue after the withdrawal of UNTAC in late 1993, as, sadly, they did.

Nevertheless, the Paris Peace Agreements and the work of UNTAC did contribute to an improvement of the human rights situation in the short term, and have arguably provided an important institutional basis for the future protection of basic human rights in Cambodia. It is fair to say that this success, however modest, was attributable in large measure to the fact that the peace agreements and UNTAC had the backing of an unusual coalition of eighteen western and Southeast Asian states, and entailed not simply the expression of concern about human rights violations but the establishment of institutions for their protection.

The Cambodian example, unquestionably unique in Southeast Asia, highlights many of the shortcomings in the nature of international intervention in other countries in the region. First, international criticism of other countries has not been sufficiently strong or sustained to bring about fundamental change. For the most part, interventions have been pro forma, designed to demonstrate a political commitment to human rights principles, without actually disrupting good trade or diplomatic relations. The targets of criticism in Southeast Asia know only too well that a few, carefully chosen, human rights initiatives, however superficial and ineffectual, will suffice to defuse international displeasure.

Second, the international community has, with rare exceptions, responded to individual human rights incidents in isolation, while effectively ignoring the less dramatic, long-term patterns of human rights abuse and their underlying causes. Not surprisingly, the recommendations offered have tended to be somewhat superficial, and often purely symbolic. Because the root causes of human rights violations are deeply embedded, genuine improvement in countries like Indonesia, East Timor and Myanmar (Burma), is likely to take many years, and will require fundamental changes in the structures of political power.

Third, the effectiveness of international pressure has been undermined by a lack of unity and coordination. As Canada and the Netherlands discovered after the Santa Cruz massacre, where foreign governments have acted bilaterally, rather than multilaterally, their criticism has been relatively easy to deflect. The threat of trade or aid sanctions, for example, can only be effective if it is backed by a broad coalition of significant trading partners. In the Southeast Asian context, the knowledge that some foreign governments, for example, Japan, Australia, Britain, Germany, not to mention China, will not take a firm stand – indeed, will gladly step in to fill the gap – has invariably weakened the resolve of others to do so.

Fourth, the effectiveness of international intervention in Southeast Asia has also been undermined by a lack of consistency, both in the choice of target and in the nature of the response. That inconsistency has often been viewed by the targets of criticism, quite rightly in many cases, as evidence of hypocrisy, and has given rise to accusations that human rights issues are being used to pursue other, less noble, objectives.

Finally, the rhetoric about human rights, good governance and democracy – and particularly the misleading conflation of democracy and human rights – has, in some cases, actually weakened the international response to grave human rights abuse, as in the Philippines.

SOUTHEAST ASIAN GOVERNMENT RESPONSES

Increasing international pressure on human rights issues, however selective and ineffectual, has triggered a variety of responses by Southeast Asian governments. These have ranged from the more purely defensive reactions, including denial and self-justification, to more sophisticated arguments and offensive strategies, characterized by an effort to re-cast the terms of the human rights debate in domestic, regional and international fora. Most governments in the region have also responded to criticism with high profile human rights initiatives, such as the repeal of a particularly odious decree, the promise of official investigations into a specific incident of abuse, or the establishment of a national human rights commission. Yet, all too often, these initiatives have been purely cosmetic, designed to deflect criticism, while doing little to improve the actual human rights situation.

Predictably, the most strident reactions have come from governments that have themselves been the object of international scrutiny and criticism. But the arguments advanced in recent years have demonstrated an increasing sophistication, as well as a greater consistency throughout the region. Through a variety of regional fora, including ASEAN and various UN-sponsored human rights conferences, Southeast Asia's governments have learned from each other how to deal with criticism from the international community.

At the forefront of the counterattack has been the government of Indonesia, but it has been eagerly, and skillfully, supported by the governments of Malaysia, Singapore and China (Amnesty International, 1994f, pp. 110–12). The military government in Myanmar (Burma), too, has echoed many of the more combative arguments developed by Indonesia. The governments of the Philippines, Thailand and Cambodia have taken somewhat more conciliatory and nuanced positions in recent years. The least sophisticated, but still common, response to allegations of human rights abuse has been simple denial. This strategy is still commonly employed by Myanmar and Indonesia. In February 1992, for example, a leading SLORC figure, Lieutenant-General Khin Nyunt, flatly contradicted conclusive evidence of widespread human rights violations since 1988, asserting that 'there are no restrictions on human rights, no torturing, and no religious discrimination at all in Myanmar' (Amnesty International, 1993i, p. 4). In a letter to Amnesty International, dated July 1991, the Indonesian government stated that: 'Accusations of human rights violations in Aceh . . . are pure inventions and are launched with the intention of discrediting the Republic of Indonesia in the eyes of the international community' (Amnesty International, 1993g, p. 16). In circumstances where the evidence of violations is difficult to obtain, or where powerful governments would prefer to turn a blind eye, this approach has proven to be remarkably effective.

Yet, as international scrutiny has intensified, the governments of the region have looked for more convincing arguments. One such argument is that fundamental cultural differences between the 'West' and 'Asia' make certain universal human rights standards – in particular, the rights of individuals enumerated in the International Covenant on Civil and Political Rights (ICCPR) and other covenants – inappropriate for Asian societies. In a speech reported by the official *Voice of Myanmar* in June 1992, the head of the SLORC, General Than Shwe said:

The western countries' human rights and standards of democracy cannot be the same as our Asian standards. We must choose the human rights standard and the democratic path compatible with the tradition of our country and people. (Amnesty International, 1993i, p. 4).

Indonesian authorities have presented this argument in a somewhat more refined form. Speaking at the Regional Meeting for Asia of the UN World Conference on Human Rights, in March 1993, the Indonesian delegate explained that Asians 'do not hold to an individualistic view of human rights for we cannot disregard the interest of society, State and nation' (Republic of Indonesia, 1993a, p. 4). The same point was made by Indonesia's foreign minister, Ali Alatas, at the World Conference itself, held in Vienna in June 1993 (Republic of Indonesia, 1993b, passim). In a variation on this theme, Southeast Asian governments have accused western governments of according a higher priority to civil and political rights, than to economic, social and cultural rights.

These arguments are based on two debatable premises. The first is that the human rights standards currently described as 'universal' are merely the product of western, liberal values, emphasizing the rights of individuals *vis-à-vis* states and societies. The second is that 'Asian' societies have a single, shared cultural understanding which places a higher value on duties than on rights or, as it is sometimes expressed by Southeast Asian governments, which seeks a 'symmetry' between the 'rights' of states and societies and those of individuals.

The reality, of course, is not so clear-cut. With the possible exception of the Universal Declaration of Human Rights (UDHR), promulgated in 1948, virtually all of the main international human rights covenants were framed, and later ratified, by a wide range of states, including many representing 'Asian' cultures. Most of those covenants, including the UDHR, actually seek to uphold the rights of communities and societies as well as individuals. Moreover, it is clear that there is a wide diversity of views, within both 'Asian' and 'Western' cultures, about the relative weight that should be accorded individual rights and duties. The diversity of 'Asian' thinking on this matter was eloquently expressed in the Declaration of Asian non-governmental organizations (NGOs) at the Regional Meeting for Asia of the World Conference on Human Rights, in Bangkok (NGO Declaration, 1993). What that declaration revealed was that, while Asian governments may agree on the primacy of the authority of states over the rights of the individual and the community, Asian peoples do not necessarily share their view.

It is significant that, in international fora, most Southeast Asian governments have found it expedient to water down their criticism of the principle of universality. Indonesia and other states in the region have been at pains to emphasize that they accept the universality of international human rights standards, bur argue that in their *implementation* consideration must be given to cultural and historical differences among states (Republic of Indonesia,. 1993b, p. 11). A related argument is that the implementation of human rights principles must make allowances for the different political priorities, and levels of economic development, of states. States must be free, so the argument runs, to pursue policies which guarantee stability, security and development. As expressed by the Malaysian delegation to the World Conference, there is a 'need to weigh human rights concerns against the pressing needs in some states [for] stability and economic development' (*Straits Times*, 8 June 1993). Some governments in the region have sought to buttress this argument by contrasting the high levels of violence and crime in western societies with the relative 'peace and order' of their own. Responding to US government criticism over its continued use of flogging to punish petty criminals, Singapore's Ministry of Home Affairs said: 'It is because of our tough laws against anti-social crimes that we are able to keep Singapore orderly and relatively crime free. We do not have a situation where acts of vandalism are commonplace as in cities like New York' (*Reuter*, 4 March 1994).

These sound like reasonable positions, but the problem is that in practice they have frequently been invoked to justify human rights violations, and to shield governments from international scrutiny (Amnesty International, 1994f, Ch. 8). In effect, they provide an excuse for states to run roughshod over individual, indeed even over collective, rights (Heinz, 1993, p. 17). For as important as declarations of principle may be it is, above all, in implementation that human rights standards find their real meaning. As noted in the NGO Declaration in Bangkok (1993, pp. 1–2):

Violations of civil, political, and economic rights frequently result from the emphasis on economic development at the expense of human rights. Violations of social and cultural rights are often the result of political systems which treat human rights as being of secondary importance.

Southeast Asian governments have also tried to meet international criticism by accusing their foreign critics in the 'West' of politicization, selectivity, and hypocrisy in their approach to human rights (Republic of Indonesia, 1993b, p. 15; *Star*, 12 October 1993). They have pointed out that many western governments are eager to criticize the violations committed by their enemies, while remaining silent when similar, or worse, violations are committed by their allies; and that many western governments have used human rights concerns to justify their pursuit of other, less noble goals. The Malaysian government, for example, has openly criticized western powers for their failure to intervene to prevent human rights violations against Bosnia's Muslims, while Indonesia has pointed to US reticence in condemning Israeli abuses in the Occupied Territories.

Southeast Asian states have taken a particularly strong line in rejecting any effort to link economic aid and trade to human rights performance. ASEAN ministers clashed openly with their EC counterparts at a meeting in Luxembourg in May 1991, when the latter proposed that human rights considerations should be included in a new EC/ASEAN trade agreement then being negotiated (Vatikiotis, 1992, p. 28). Following a visit to Indonesia later in the year, a member of the European Parliament reported that Indonesian authorities had left no doubt that 'the inclusion of human rights and environment clauses as *conditions* in cooperation agreements was unacceptable and counter-productive' (European Parliament, 1992). The same principle was enshrined in the Jakarta Message, issued at the Jakarta summit of the Non-Aligned Movement (NAM) in September 1992. Article 18 of the message, reads: 'No country . . . should use its power to dictate its concept of human rights and democracy or to impose conditionalities on others' (NAM, 1992a, p. 4).

Claiming that outside concern over human rights is not sincere, or is politically motivated, the governments of Southeast Asia have argued that international scrutiny and criticism constitutes unwarranted interference in a country's domestic affairs, and therefore a breach of its sovereignty. In the June 1992 speech cited earlier, for example, Myanmar's General Than Shwe claimed that: 'The external forces that bear malice towards us are inciting the people by using human rights and democracy as an excuse' (Amnesty International, 1993i, p. 4; also see, Republic of Indonesia, 1993b, p. 8). Indonesia's President Suharto struck a similar note in early 1992 when he claimed that any effort to impose 'foreign' values on another society constituted in itself a violation of human rights:

> There is not a single nation obliged to apply values of life which it cannot understand and are incompatible with its own fundamental values. If they are imposed, it would be equal to negating human rights itself and the fundamental rights of a sovereign state. (*AFP*, 1992)

Not surprisingly, most Southeast Asian governments have argued against any enhancement of the power of UN human rights institutions. During the UN World Conference on Human Rights in Vienna, for example, they explicitly rejected the proposal for the creation of a UN High Commissioner for Human Rights to coordinate, and give additional political weight to, the UN's various human rights bodies. For similar reasons, international human rights organizations, such as Amnesty International and Human Rights Watch-Asia (formerly Asiawatch), have also been the object of strident criticism by Southeast Asian states. The Indonesian government has consistently portrayed Amnesty International as an 'extreme leftist' organization, intent on overthrowing the New Order regime (Amnesty International, 1993a, pp. 5–8; 1994f, pp. 117–19). The governments of Malaysia and Singapore appear to harbour similar suspicious, and as of early 1995 refused to permit the organization to establish any official presence there. Even the Thai government, which like the Philippines has generally assumed a more benign attitude toward international rights organizations, has occasionally fallen into step with its neighbours on this issue. During the World Conference meeting in Bangkok, for example, a senior member of the Thai delegation publicly accused Amnesty International and Asiawatch of being fronts of the CIA (*Bangkok Post*, 31 March 1993).

Governments in the region have not developed these arguments in isolation. Partly moved by a common need to resist international pressure, but also driven by the agendas of the most powerful states among them, they have come increasingly to speak with a single voice. Following the 'Jakarta Message' of September 1992, a common Asian position was expressed, for example, at the Second UN Asia–Pacific Conference on Human Rights, held in Jakarta in January 1993; at the Asia Regional Meeting for the World Conference on Human Rights, held in Bangkok in March 1993; at the 26th ASEAN Ministerial Meeting in Singapore in July 1993; and most recently in the Kuala Lumpur Declaration on Human Rights promulgated by the ASEAN Inter-Parliamentary Organization (AIPO) in the same year; and in the run-up to the Jakarta APEC summit in November 1994.

The political impact of that unified voice has been enhanced by two key factors: the economic power of major Southeast Asian states *vis-à-vis* their critics, and their control of key positions within regional and international bodies. Southeast Asian states know that most western governments are anxious not to cut themselves off from economic opportunities, and they can therefore afford to assume a relatively aggressive posture. When conditions have been imposed by one trading partner, they have simply turned to others which are prepared to be more flexible. When threatened with cuts in military assistance and sales by the United States, for example, Indonesia announced that it would henceforth purchase its supplies from Germany, Britain, France and possibly Russia. As one ASEAN minister commented during a meeting with EC counterparts in October 1992: 'If they want to use it [aid] as a stick . . . you can well understand why some of the ASEAN countries may not lose a lot of sleep over it' *(Reuter,* 20 October 1992). Those with relatively weak economies, such as the Philippines, Vietnam, Cambodia and Myanmar are more vulnerable to cuts in aid and trade, and may perhaps be more responsive to pressures from outside. Still, even these countries have some room to manoeuvre. Economic sanctions imposed against Myanmar, for instance, have been rendered less effective as a means of influence because other Asian countries, such as Thailand, South Korea, Singapore, China and Japan have been more than happy to continue trading and investing.

Political cooperation among the countries of Southeast Asia, particularly within ASEAN, has also helped to strengthen their position *vis-à-vis* outside human rights critics (Vatikiotis, 1992, p. 28.). At a Ministerial Meeting in July 1992, ASEAN states expressed unanimous opposition to EC attempts to link trade and human rights (ASEAN). And, in October 1992, as noted earlier, ASEAN states took a unified stand against Portugal's attempts to make a new EC/ASEAN trade deal conditional upon an improvement of the human rights situation in East Timor – and won. At least since 1992, ASEAN states have also begun to discuss plans for establishing a regional human rights mechanism, with the explicit aim of deflecting *international* monitoring of the human rights situations in individual ASEAN states (Wanandi, 1992; ASEAN, 1993). The promulgation of the Kuala Lumpur Declaration of Human Rights in 1993 may be seen as a further move in the same direction (AIPO, 1993).

Regional solidarity has, at the same time, implied a good measure of hypocrisy in the ASEAN position on human rights, and has contributed to continuing human rights problems in the region. While Malaysia has complained bitterly about the failure of western governments to intervene on behalf of Bosnian Muslims, it has maintained an unseemly silence in the face of violations by Indonesian forces against Muslims in Aceh and elsewhere in Indonesia. It has also agreed not to grant refugee status to any of the hundreds of Acehnese who fled to Malaysia at the height of Indonesia's counter-insurgency campaign in 1989–90 (Amnesty International, 1993g, pp. 53–6).

While there has been some disagreement within ASEAN on how far to go in urging Myanmar's SLORC to improve its human rights practice, the overall ASEAN policy has been one of 'constructive engagement.' Most member countries have maintained friendly bilateral relations, both political and economic, with the military regime there. Thailand has shown no hesitation in expanding its trade relations with Myanmar, and invited Myanmar to attend the 1994 ASEAN summit. Malaysia has insisted that it will not 'judge over them' (*Jakarta Post*, 12 October 192). In 1992 President Ramos of the Philippines welcomed a high-level trade delegation from Myanmar (*Jakarta Post*, 8 October 1992). And in January 1994 Indonesia hosted a high-level SLORC delegation on an extended visit which included talks with President Suharto. Indonesia's foreign minister, Ali Alatas, paid a return visit in February, during which he praised the government's efforts at 'political restructuring and opening up of the economy' (*Guardian*, 26 February 1994).

The power of the ASEAN states has been further enhanced by regional and emerging international arrangements for increased economic cooperation, particularly APEC, which held its 1994 summit in Jakarta. Optimists may hope that such groupings will provide a forum for raising human rights issues, and they will have welcomed the statements of concern about human rights by various government leaders at the November 1994 summit. Yet, if ASEAN is any measure, the achievement of real human rights progress through APEC remains an unlikely prospect (Amnesty International, 1994h). Indeed, with the emergence of a new free-trade regime in the past few years, the opportunities for imposing such conditions appear, if anything, to be diminishing.

ASEAN states – in particular Indonesia and Malaysia – have also begun to play an increasingly assertive role in a range of international organizations; and to use their position in those bodies to pursue their own human rights agenda. As noted above, Indonesia has used its chairmanship of the Non-Aligned Movement (NAM), to advance its own interpretation of human rights, though opinion within the NAM is by no means undivided on this issue. The UN Commission on Human Rights has provided another useful forum for advancing the Indonesian agenda. In 1991, Indonesia became a member of the Commission, despite the fact that it has not ratified any of the UN's major human rights conventions. Through that position it has been able to influence the course of debate and voting in the UN.

In short, Southeast Asian governments have sought to defend

themselves against international scrutiny of their human rights records through a combination of defensive and offensive strategies, ranging from blanket denial to claims of cultural and political uniqueness, and aggressive political initiatives at the regional and international level. Taken together, the arguments they have put forward constitute a fundamental assault on basic human rights principles and standards. The considerable economic and political strength of the ASEAN states has given those arguments and strategies a unique force which does not bode well for the future of human rights policy and practice in the region.

However, the news has not been all bad. Despite their evident irritation, some Southeast Asian governments have responded to increasing international pressure with at least modest changes in human rights policy and practice. Faced with the prospect of international isolation, for example, between 1992 and early 1994 the military government in Myanmar (Burma) acceded to two important human rights covenants, announced the release of some 2,000 political detainees, disbanded the military tribunals that had been used to sentence political opponents, and commuted all death sentences to life imprisonment (Amnesty International, 1994b, p. 2). Similarly, following the Santa Cruz massacre, the government of Indonesia took the unprecedented move of conducting two official inquiries, and subsequently disciplined ten members of the security forces, albeit lightly, for their role in the incident. Still facing strong criticism, the government agreed to host a UN conference on human rights in January 1993, and in June announced the establishment of a National Commission on Human Rights. Since then it has given assurances that international human rights and humanitarian organizations would be allowed improved access to East Timor and has welcomed visits by a number of official UN delegations (Amnesty International, 1993a, pp. 7–9; 1994d, pp. 14–19; 1994f, Ch. 8; 1995b; United Nations, 1992 and 1995). These moves have not, by any means, solved the most fundamental human rights problems in each country, but they may be a step in the right direction.

DOMESTIC POLITICS AND HUMAN RIGHTS

Such human rights initiatives, in Myanmar, Indonesia and elsewhere in the region, have been stimulated in large measure by international pressure. Yet equally important has been the way in which external pressures have dovetailed with domestic political forces. In some Southeast Asian states – notably Indonesia, Cambodia and Myanmar – human rights issues have moved to the top of the domestic political agenda within the past five years. In others, such as the Philippines, Malaysia and Singapore, their importance appears to have remained roughly constant, or even to have declined in recent years. But in all cases the interaction of domestic and international forces has had some effect on the actual patterns of human rights policy and practice in different countries.

Dramatic human rights violations, like massacres, and mass arrests, have helped to provide a focus for political opposition both at home and abroad. The Santa Cruz massacre in East Timor provoked an unprecedented flurry of press commentary and critical discussion within Indonesia, not simply about the event itself but also about larger issues, such as the political role of the military, democratization and political openness. But just as important as the actual level and character of human rights violations in each country has been the strength and political importance of the social groups and classes predominantly concerned with such issues. Awareness of and concern for civil and political rights, and the rule of law, appears to have emerged most forcefully among Southeast Asia's professional middle classes; particularly lawyers, students and teachers. Members of these social groups founded the earliest human rights organizations, such as the LBH in Indonesia, FLAG in the Philippines, and the Penang Consumers' Association in Malaysia, and to a considerable extent, they continue to form the backbone of human rights activism in the region (Lev, 1990, passim; Lubis, 1992, pp. 33–4).

This is not to say that other social groups, such as farmers, workers and small traders have been uninvolved in the pursuit of these rights. But members of the professional middle classes have been critical in articulating those concerns and in mobilizing others in support of them. As a consequence, the political salience of human rights issues, broadly speaking, has increased as the size of this group has expanded. Countries with a relatively large professional middle class, such as the Philippines, Thailand and Malaysia, have had earlier and stronger human rights movements.

But size has not been the only factor. Equally important has been the political power of those classes, and the effectiveness of their strategies for articulating their objectives, and for mobilizing others behind them. Thus, for example, the strength of the human rights movement in the Philippines under martial law was a consequence not only of the considerable number of lawyers, students and teachers, but also of the fact that the human rights issue was taken up by a wide range of other groups and classes, including peasants, workers and women, and became a central preoccupation of powerful political organizations. There are indications that Indonesia might be moving in the same direction. With the help of professional middle-class groups, Indonesia's workers and farmers have increasingly begun to express their concerns in the language of human rights. And, in recent years, they have begun to voice those concerns directly, through wildcat strikes and demonstrations, sometimes without any assistance from their middle-class allies.

Though partly the result of increasing awareness of their rights and a concern to establish the rule of law, this process of politicization has depended, in part, on the changing *opportunities* that have been available within the political arena in different states. Rivalries and splits within the state elite have provided especially rich opportunities for advancing the cause of political openness generally; both the middle classes and others have taken advantage of that 'democratic space' in order to bring specific demands, including human rights issues, onto the political agenda. The final months and days before the 1986 EDSA revolution provided a critical breathing space for pro-democracy and human rights activists in the Philippines (Amnesty International, 1992b, pp. 87–92). In Thailand, inter-elite rivalry in the mid-1970s provided new opportunities for civilian participation in politics (Anderson, 1977, p. 24). The 'civilianization' of Thai politics eventually provided space for middle-class groups with liberal and human rights-related objectives. Indonesia may eventually follow a similar pattern.

Developments at the international level have helped to stimulate and to quicken these domestic political processes in a number of ways. The rhetoric of universal human rights has helped to shape the language and the work of domestic activists. Aware of the political advantages of international support, domestic political opponents have, both consciously and unconsciously, framed their concerns in that language, and have prepared information of a sort, and in a format, which directly addresses international as well as domestic audiences.

Of course, international linkage has not always produced positive results in the short term; sometimes it has proven highly problematic for local organizations. In the aftermath of the Santa Cruz massacre, for example, the Indonesian government accused domestic NGOs of treachery, and subjected human rights activists to intensive surveillance and, in some cases, imprisonment (Amnesty International, 1992c, 1995a). Following the government's decision to refuse Dutch aid, in April 1992 the Ministry of the Interior announced that NGOs too would be forbidden to receive any funding that originated with the Dutch government. The ministerial decree stated that 'social organizations and institutions, such as NGOs, which violate this determination will be penalized in accordance with existing legislative regulations' (Republic of Indonesia, 1992b). In subsequent months a number of Indonesian and East Timorese activists were jailed, or had their sentences increased, apparently because of their links with outside groups such as the International Committee of the Red Cross (ICRC) and Amnesty International (Amnesty International, 1993a, pp. 19–20).

In some countries in the region, the effect of international intervention has been more positive. As noted earlier, in Cambodia UNTAC placed human rights issues squarely on the domestic political agenda, and stimulated the growth of a large number of NGOs devoted to monitoring and promoting those rights. As a result Cambodia has developed a rudimentary human rights network in the space of just a few years, though it remains to be seen whether that network can prevent a future deterioration in the human rights situation.

International concern over human rights has also had an immediate impact on the domestic policy and practice of some Southeast Asian governments. Most states have, quite naturally, done the bare minimum necessary in order to satisfy their international critics. By establishing national human rights commissions, making statements of principle in support of human rights protection, hosting conferences and seminars on human rights issues and, in extreme circumstances, by promising to investigate alleged abuses and bring the perpetrators to justice, most governments have managed to deflect further international and domestic criticism. Still, even where governments have been able to satisfy international opinion with mere window-dressing, such moves have sometimes had unintended political and human rights consequences, by providing domestic groups with significant political and legal tools with which to press for more substantial changes.

CONCLUSIONS

There can be little doubt that human rights considerations are now of critical importance in the international relations of Southeast Asian states. Since the end of the Cold War, western governments have demonstrated an increasing willingness to speak out against the human rights practices of their erstwhile Southeast Asian allies. But how effective have international interventions been in changing the real human rights situation in Southeast Asian states? And what lessons can be drawn from recent experience about the role of foreign states, and institutions like the UN, in bringing about improvement in the coming years?

The answer to the first question is relatively simple. International intervention on human rights issues has, in the short term, produced only minor improvements in most countries in the region. The somewhat disappointing results would appear to lend support to those who would prefer to see an end to international scrutiny and intervention. But the evidence presented in this paper seems to support a different, and more optimistic, conclusion: that, in the medium and longer term, pressure from outside can and will bring significant improvements. Indeed, the evidence demonstrates clearly that the improvements to date, small and incremental though they may have been, have come principally where international intervention has been strong and coordinated and where, moreover, it has entailed the establishment of durable institutions and mechanisms for the protection of human rights, rather than bland and politically convenient expressions of concern. It also demonstrates that international pressure is likely to be most effective where it coincides with, and complements, the activities of the domestic advocates of human rights in each country and in the region as a whole.

References

AFP (*Agence France Presse*) (1992) 'Forcing Foreign Values on Other Countries Violates Human Rights: Soeharto', 13 February.

AIPO (ASEAN Inter-Parliamentary Organization) (1993) 'Kuala Lumpur Declaration on Human Rights'.

Amnesty International (1991a) *Philippines: 'Disappearances' in the Context of Counter-Insurgency* (February, ASA 35/05/91).

—— (1991b) *Philippines: Human Rights Violations and the Labour Movement* (June, ASA 35/16/91).

—— (1991c) *Malaysia: Administrative Detention of Sabahans* (October, ASA 28/09/91).

—— (1991d) *East Timor: The Santa Cruz Massacre* (November, ASA 21/23/91).

—— (1991e) *East Timor: After the Massacre* (November, ASA 21/24/91).

—— (1992a) *Indonesia/East Timor: Santa Cruz – The Government Response* (February, ASA 21/03/92).

—— (1992b) *Philippines: The Killing Goes On* (February, ASA 35/01/92).

—— (1992c) *East Timor: 'In Accordance with the Law' – Statement before the UN Special Committee on Decolonization* (July, ASA 21/11/92).

—— (1992d) *Myanmar: 'No Law at All' – Human Rights Violations Under Military Rule* (October, ASA 16/11/92).

—— (1992e) *Facing up to Failures: Proposals for Improving the Protection of Human Rights by the United Nations* (December, IOR 41/16/92).

—— (1993a) *Indonesia/East Timor: A New Order? Human Rights in 1992* (February, ASA 21/03/93).

—— (1993b) *Cambodia: Human Rights Concerns July to December 1992* (February, ASA 23/01/93).

—— (1993c) Oral intervention by Amnesty International, before the World Conference on Human Rights, Regional Meeting for Asia, 29 March 1993.

—— (1993d) Letter to H.E. Squadron Leader Prasong Soonsiri, Minister of Foreign Affairs, 31 March 1993.

—— (1993e) 'Asian Governments Defensive on Human Rights' (2 April, IOR 41/WU 04/93).

—— (1993f) Open letter to heads of state and government from Amnesty International's Secretary General (19 April, IOR 41/15/93).

—— (1993g) *Indonesia: 'Shock Therapy' – Restoring Order in Aceh, 1989–1993* (July, ASA 21/07/93).

—— (1993h) *Cambodia: Arbitrary Killings of Ethnic Vietnamese* (September, ASA 23/05/93).

—— (1993i) *Myanmar: The Climate of Fear Continues, Members of Ethnic Minorities and Political Prisoners Still Targeted* (October, ASA 16/06/93).

—— (1993j) *Papua New Guinea: Under the Barrel of a Gun* (November, ASA 34/05/93).

—— (1993k) *Socialist Republic of Vietnam: Continuing Concerns* (October, ASA 41/06/93).

—— (1994a) *Kingdom of Cambodia: Human Rights and the New Constitution* (January, ASA 23/01/94).

—— (1994b) *Myanmar: Human Rights Developments July to December 1993* (January, ASA 16/03/94).

—— (1994c) *Peace-keeping and Human Rights* (January, IOR 40/01/94).

—— (1994d) *Indonesia and East Timor: Fact and Fiction: Implementing the Recommendations of the UN Commission of Human Rights* (16 February, ASA 21/05/94).

—— (1994e) *East Timor: Who Is To Blame? Statement Before the UN Special Committee on Decolonization* (13 July, ASA 21/31/94).

—— (1994f) *Indonesia and East Timor: Power and Impunity – Human Rights Under the New Order* (28 September, ASA 21/17/94).

—— (1994g) *Myanmar: Human Rights Still Denied* (1 November, ASA 16/18/94).

—— (1994h) *Indonesia: 'Operation Cleansing' – Human Rights and APEC* (3 November, ASA 21/50/94).

—— (1994i) *Indonesia and East Timor: The 12 November Protests* (15 November, ASA 21/53/94).

—— (1994j) *Indonesia and East Timor: Update on the 12 November Protests* (23 November, ASA 21/56/94).

—— (1995a) *Indonesia and East Timor: Political Prisoners and the 'Rule of Law'* (January, ASA 21/01/95).

—— (1995b) *Indonesia and East Timor: Human Rights in 1994: A Summary* (January, ASA 21/03/95).

—— (1995c) *Kingdom of Cambodia: Human Rights and the New Government* (14 March, ASA 23/02/95).

Anderson, Benedict (1977) 'Withdrawal Symptoms: Social and Cultural Aspects of the October 6 Coup', *Bulletin of Concerned Asian Scholars*, vol. 9, no. 3, pp. 13–30.

Arase, David (1993) 'Japanese Policy Toward Democracy and Human Rights in Asia', *Asian Survey*, vol. XXXIII, no. 10 (October, pp. 935–52.

ASEAN (1993) *Joint Communiqué of the Twenty-sixth ASEAN Ministerial Meeting, Singapore, 23–24 July 1993.*

Asiawatch (1992) *Indonesia: Charges and Rebuttals Over Labor Rights Practices* (23 January).

Buszynski, Leszek (1992) 'Southeast Asia in the Post-Cold War Era: Regionalism and Security', *Asian Survey*, vol. XXXII, no. 9 (September), pp. 830–47.

Dagg, Christopher J. (1992) 'Human Rights and Aid: A Canadian Perspective', *Indonesian Quarterly*, vol. XXI, no. 1, pp. 38–48.

European Parliament (1991) 'Resolution on the Situation in South-East Asia' in *Minutes of Proceedings of the Sitting of Thursday, 12 September 1991.*

—— (1992a) Committee on External Economic Relations, 'Report by Mr Ben Visser, Rapporteur on Relations with the ASEAN Countries, on his Mission to Indonesia, 19–24 December 1991'.

—— (1992b) 'Resolution on East Timor' (17 December).

Heinz, Wolfgang S. (1993) 'Concepts of Democracy, Development and Human Rights in Asian Political Thinking. The Examples of China and ASEAN', paper prepared for the Conference on Nationalism and the Ethnicity in Southeast Asia, Humboldt-Universität zu Berlin, October.

Islam, Shada (1991) 'Values for Money: ASEAN, EC clash on human-rights criteria', *Far Eastern Economic Review*, June, pp. 9–10.

—— (1992) 'Stumbling Block: Indonesia–EC Agreement Ditched by Timor Issue', *Far Eastern Economic Review*, 30 July, pp. 9–10.

Lev, Daniel S. (1990) 'Human Rights NGOs in Indonesia and Malaysia', in Claude E. Welch Jr and Virginia E. Leavy (eds) *Asian Perspectives on Human Rights* (Boulder: Westview Press), pp. 142–61.

Lord, Winston (1993) Statement by US Assistant Secretary of State for East Asian and Pacific Affairs before the Senate on 31 March 1993, reprinted in the *Jakarta Post*, 13 and 14 April.

Lubis, T. Mulya (1992) 'Human Rights Standard Setting in Asia: Problems and Prospects', *Indonesian Quarterly*, vol. XXI, no. 1, pp. 25–37.

Mauzy, Diane and R. S. Milne (1995) 'Human Rights in ASEAN States: a Canadian Policy Perspective', in Amitav Acharya and Richard Stubbs (eds) *New Challenges for ASEAN* (Vancouver: UBC Press).

Muntarbhorn, Vitit (1993) 'Law and State: The Human Rights Challenge in Thailand', a study prepared for the Asian Studies Centre, St Antony's College, Oxford University.

NAM (Non-Aligned Movement) (1992a) 'Tenth Conference of Heads of State or Government of Non-Aligned Countries, Jakarta, 1–6 September 1992', *Indonesia News* (London), vol. 20, no. 37 (15 October).

—— (1992b) 'The Jakarta Message: A Call for Collective Action and the Democratization of International Relations', *Indonesia News* (London), vol. 20, no. 37 (15 October), Appendix.

Newsletter on Aid (Japan) (1993).

NGO Declaration on Human Rights. Bangkok, April 1993.

Republic of Indonesia (1992a) 'Indonesia Rejects Dutch Aid', press release, 25 March.

—— (1992b) Statement of the Minister of the Interior . . . Concerning the Ban on Receipt of Dutch Aid by Social Organizations and Institutions. (24 April). (Unofficial translation)

—— (1992c) Address by President Suharto of the Republic of Indonesia at the Inaugural Session of the Tenth Conference of Heads of State or Government of Non-Aligned Countries, Jakarta, 1 September 1992. *Indonesia News* (London), vol. 20, no. 37 (15 October), pp. 1–13.

—— (1993a) Statement by H. E. Mr S. Wiryono before the Regional Meeting for Asia of the World Conference on Human Rights, Bangkok (29 March).

—— (1993b) Statement by H. E. Mr Ali Alatas, Minister for Foreign Affairs, before the Second World Conference on Human Rights, Vienna (June).

Robinson, Geoffrey (1993) 'Some Thoughts on Political Violence in Indonesia and East Timor', paper prepared for the Annual Meeting of the Association of Asian Studies, Los Angeles (March).

Shawcross, William (1993) 'A New Cambodia', *New York Review of Books*, 12 August.

United Nations (1992) *Report of the Special Rapporteur on Torture on his Visit to Indonesia and East Timor in November 1991* (UN Doc. E/CN 4/1992/17/Add. 1).

—— (1995) *Report of the Special Rapporteur on Extrajudicial, Summary or Arbitrary Executions on his Mission to Indonesia and East Timor in July 1994* (UN Doc. E/CN 4/1995/61/Add. 1).

Vatikiotis, Michael (1992) 'Coping with the Critics', *Far Eastern Economic Review*, 29 October, p. 28.

Wanandi, Jusuf (1992) 'Asia, Too, Should Have a Human Rights Forum', *International Herald Tribune*, 20 October.

Woolcott, Richard (1992) 'Reality and an Asian Neighbour', *Time*, 7 September, p. 76.

Part III

Policies of External Powers towards Southeast Asia

6 US Policy Themes in Southeast Asia in the 1990s

Donald K. Emmerson

United States interests in the [East Asian-Pacific] region are mutually reinforcing: security is necessary for economic growth, security and growth make it more likely that human rights will be honoured and democracy will emerge, and democratization makes international conflict less likely because democracies are unlikely to fight one another. (US Department of Defense, *United States Security Strategy for the East Asia-Pacific Region*, February 1995, p. 3)

In the twentieth century three themes have predominated among the justifications of American foreign policy offered by its makers: *security*, *prosperity* and *democracy*. In 1993 the newly incumbent administration of President Bill Clinton intensified this tradition by repeatedly invoking all three of these Good Things. They were endorsed not only in their own right but also because each one of them was a means of furthering the other two – or so the administration argued. While their order and priority varied with the occasion, they epitomized what the Clinton administration said it wanted the world, including Asia and the United States, to be: secure, prosperous and democratic.

In July 1993 in Seoul, South Korea, for instance, Clinton proposed a new 'Pacific Community' based on 'shared strength, shared prosperity, and a shared commitment to democratic values' (Clinton, 1993, p. 509; Lord, 1993–4). It was natural that Clinton should have put security first, standing as he was on the divided and heavily armed Korean peninsula. In June, when Secretary of State Warren Christopher (1993, p. 1) addressed the World Conference on Human Rights in Vienna, Austria, it made sense that he should have begun with democracy. 'Democracy', he said, 'is the best way to advance lasting peace and prosperity in the world.' Given the American trade tensions with Japan, it was logical too that in Tokyo in May then Deputy Secretary of

Defence William Perry (1993, p. 1), when he cited the same trio of values, should have placed 'a top priority' on prosperity – calling on that occasion for greater American access to Asia's economic success.

'Security, democracy and prosperity' was not just a Democratic slogan. The administration of President George Bush (1989–93) had justified its Asian policies as ways of getting the same Three Good Things (Solomon, 1992a, pp. 410, 414.) Nor was the triad meant only for foreign consumption. At Senate hearings to confirm his nomination as Assistant Secretary for East Asian and Pacific Affairs, Winston Lord promised in dealing with the Association of Southeast Asian Nations (ASEAN) to promote 'American trade and investment', 'regional security', and 'the extension of freedom' (Lord, 1993b, p. 9).

This chapter is focused on security, prosperity and democracy because these are the terms that foreign policy decision-makers themselves used to justify what they were up to. I also want to use these themes to illustrate the ideological nature of American discourse on foreign affairs and the gap between foreign policy principles and practice. In the mid-1990s, I will argue, this gap showed just how limited was the actual capacity of US authorities compared with their rhetorical ambition; how misleading was their assertion that security, prosperity and democracy were mutually inducing, such that pursuing any one of them would help bring about the others; how contingent, divided, and unsteady was the American commitment to achieving any one of these goals, let alone all of them; and, finally, how difficult it was for the administration to fashion policies for Southeast Asia that could achieve these Three Good Things.

INTRODUCTION: FROM CONTAINMENT TO ENLARGEMENT

In America the Cold War coincided with a period of relative prosperity and economic confidence. Admittedly, in the Vietnam-wartime 1960s, under President Lyndon Johnson, the inflationary cost of funding guns and butter – trying simultaneously to win a war and build a 'Great Society' – undermined the economic optimism of the 1950s. Yet the counsellors of US foreign policy almost never couched their advice in terms of what it could do for their country's Gross National Product. The spheres of domestic and foreign policy – the experts, the constituencies, the budgets, the rationales – rarely overlapped or interacted.

In the early-to-mid-1990s, however, creating American 'jobs, jobs, jobs' became a litany first of the Bush and then the Clinton administration. Previously, the notion that domestic employment should have been a major goal of US foreign policy would have seemed, if not ludicrous, at least crass to Cold Warriors committed to what they considered a far nobler mission. That mission, at root, was to defend American, if not Western civilization, from what President Ronald Reagan (1981–9) called the 'evil empire' of Soviet oppression. The separation of economics from geostrategy and of domestic from overseas goals insulated foreign policy specialists from public opinion and sustained their passivity, even indifference toward the interests of American business or the demands of American labour. In the meantime undisputed politico-military leadership of the 'Free World' masked the incremental evidence of American economic slippage.

Beginning in the 1980s, however, the domestication of American foreign policy entailed a growing conjunction of home-focused domestic economic concerns with foreign affairs, as signs of US decline and the rise of Japan and Germany made the cost of the Cold War to Americans seem increasingly unfair. The breaching of the Berlin Wall in 1989 and the collapse of the Soviet Union two years later demolished altogether the Cold War as a grand rationale for American foreign policy. *Not right. US still supports dictators in the Middle East and Africa for their natural resources* This dénouement had diverse results. On the one hand, it opened an opportunity for US foreign policy to become more consistent ideologically. The case for tolerating dictatorships so long as they lined up with the 'Free World' against the USSR had vanished, along with the USSR itself. That the Clinton administration should have raised the priority on democratizing other countries and promoting respect for human rights was not inevitable, but it was opportune.

Without a plausible external threat to national security to preoccupy them, policy-makers could also focus on the domestic economy and make its health a priority goal of foreign policy. What was the new foreign policy about? 'The economy, stupid' – to cite the mantra of Clinton's campaign. This priority took dramatic shape at the White House in February 1994 when Clinton insisted that Japanese Prime Minister Hosokawa accept numerical targets for imports into Japan. Hosokawa refused, and both men allowed their summit to fail. During the Cold War, the US would not have pressed its case so hard; Japan would have conceded enough to ensure a compromise; or both.

At the same time, American voters who might find tawdry or at least uninspiring a call for US profits and paychecks to motivate relations with other countries could take heart from Clinton's reworking of the Cold War imperative in loftier terms. 'The successor to a doctrine of

containment must be a strategy of enlargement,' announced National
Security Adviser Anthony Lake in September 1993 – 'enlargement of
the world's free community of market democracies' (quoted by Friedman,
1993b). This peaceful, capitalist, democratic zone amounted to a plan-
etary counterpart of the 'new Pacific community' that Clinton had enun-
ciated two months earlier in Seoul.

For the United States this vision carried an activist agenda. By getting tough with countries that closed their markets to American goods
and services, the administration would help Americans to live better
and help create free markets abroad that would, in turn, enlarge the
global process of irenic democratization. By getting tough with countries that violated human rights, the administration would promote
democratization in tandem with freer markets, which would in turn
further world security and prosperity. By getting tough with rogue states
such as Iraq or North Korea, the administration would ensure the security and prosperity of the world's market democracies (c.f. Friedman,
1993b).

Yet Washington could not single-handedly change the world. The
Clinton administration knew this, despite having rebuked Under Secretary of State for Political Affairs Peter Tarnoff in May for suggesting that the US, with only limited means, must limit its objectives.
The 'Tarnoff Doctrine' was impolitic but realistic. What made Lake's
'strategy of enlargement' remarkable was the disparity between the
activist sweep of its principles and the modesty of its priorities and
practices.

Intervention on behalf of human rights was the fourth and last of
Lake's priorities for implementing the strategy. The other three con-
noted security more than enlargement: (1) strengthening 'the core of
major market democracies' in the West and Japan and their ability to
respond to crises such as the one in Bosnia; (2) helping 'market democracy' in Russia and Eastern Europe, 'where we have the strongest security concerns'; and (3) defending 'the circle of democracy and
markets' from the likes of Iraq and North Korea. 'Enlargement' by
these criteria seemed mostly to pass Southeast Asia by, given the inability of any of its states to threaten the countries inside Lake's charmed
circle. As for his fourth priority – intervening on behalf of human
rights – it was amply hedged by 'other considerations', including cost,
feasibility, and 'the willingness of regional and international bodies to
do their part' (Friedman, 1993b, quoting Lake).

This last proviso showed that, while rejecting the 'Tarnoff Doctrine'
as embarrassingly downbeat, the Clinton administration thought the US

ought to work multilaterally within the United Nations and the General Agreement on Tariffs and Trade (GATT) or, at a regional level, the North American Free Trade Agreement (NAFTA) and Asia Pacific Economic Cooperation (APEC). And for all the unilateralism implied by a 'strategy of enlargement' on behalf of American values, the major foreign policy successes of Clinton's first year were multilateral: in rapid succession in November and December 1993, the US Congress approved NAFTA, Clinton hosted the first summit of APEC, and the US together with more than a hundred other countries concluded the Uruguay Round of GATT. Clinton's Treasury Under Secretary for International Affairs promptly named 1993 'the most successful year for American international economic policy' since World War II (Nasar, 1994, quoting Lawrence Summers).

An administration committed to involving the US in such multilateral endeavours could hardly be called isolationist. Yet a crucial aspect of Clinton's outlook undercut that internationalism: his own lack of interest in foreign compared with domestic policy.

In 1992–3 much was made of Clinton's having avoided service in the Vietnam War. At least as important to an understanding of his relationship to foreign affairs, however, was the fact that he was the first president since World War II who had not personally absorbed the experience of that 'good war' – 'good' in the sense that it mobilized Americans against a clear and present danger to their national security and, more broadly, to Western democratic civilization. Despite having majored in international affairs at Georgetown University and spent two years at Oxford University as a Rhodes Scholar, Clinton centred his pre-White House career on a landlocked, poor and rural southern state. As governor of Arkansas he went on six trade missions abroad, including three to East Asia, but clearly foreign policy was his weakest suit.

In the 1992 presidential campaign, poverty, crime, drugs and spiraling health costs apparently persuaded Clinton to orient his candidacy inward and argue the need, above all, to get America's own socioeconomic house in order. But an inconsistency resulted that would bedevil Clinton's presidency in foreign affairs. Oriented outward by its allegiance to security, prosperity, and democracy as global goals, his administration was turned inward by its preoccupation with domestic policy, not to mention the limits on American power that Peter Tarnoff had acknowledged.

Nor were the policy implications of believing in the Three Good Things entirely clear. If the end of the Cold War had already made the world more secure, if the collapse of Leninism and a widespread trend toward privatization had already made prosperity possible, and if there was already a 'democratic tide running in the world' (Friedman, 1993a, quoting Anthony Lake), then championing those three values should have required that much *less* expenditure of American money and effort.

Further ambiguities were introduced by efforts to connect security, prosperity, and democracy to sustainability. In debating whether economic growth was necessary for environmental health (Bhagwati, 1993) or detrimental to it (Daly, 1993), experts agreed that prosperity and sustainability were related. For Southeast Asia, the American government-sponsored US–Asia Environmental Partnership offered preliminary evidence that sustainability was becoming a fourth Good Thing for Washington to pursue in interaction with the traditional three. But sustainability is omitted here for lack of space and because in 1994 it had not acquired the visibility of the other three themes. The rest of this chapter will review the Clinton presidency's ability to promote security, prosperity and democracy in Southeast Asia.

SECURITY: UNUSED LEVERAGE AND FAILED REFORM

During the Cold War American leaders defined 'security' negatively as protection from global communism and its protagonists – the USSR, China and their allies. In ruining that definition, the collapse of communism opened up several choices for the United States in Southeast Asia. American foreign policy-makers could have (1) reaffirmed the danger-based idea of security, declared victory, gone home and begun treating Southeast Asia as a place where American forces, absent any credible local threat, no longer belonged; (2) reaffirmed the old definition but argued that China or Vietnam, or both, still threatened Southeast Asia and thus warranted a major ongoing American military presence there; or (3) reconceived security as a process of lowering tensions and building trust, treating the absence of a present threat as an opportunity to help prevent future ones, reducing the American presence but not too quickly or too far, and shifting to a new defence posture based not on fear but on cooperation for the preventive maintenance of regional peace.

In the early 1990s the third, intermediate choice grew increasingly attractive. In the Philippines the eruption of a volcano in 1991 and a vote of the Senate in 1992, respectively, ousted American forces from Clark Field and Subic Bay – the last remaining US bases in Southeast

Asia. Disengagement made a virtue of necessity. Budgetary prudence in Washington further reinforced the logic of drawdown. But in 1990–91 the American–Iraqi war reminded Washington of the need for facilities to help the US Pacific fleet transit Southeast Asia toward possible assignments in the Middle East. And ASEAN governments themselves wanted at least some Americans to stay in the region to counterbalance China and Japan.

In 1990 the Department of Defense (DOD) under President Bush had announced an East Asia Security Initiative (EASI) to reduce, modestly and gradually, US forces in the region. If Clark and Subic had marked the American military presence in Southeast Asia as large, fixed and centred on bases located in a single country, under EASI all six ASEAN states would be to varying degrees involved in a very different US military profile – small, fluid and contingent upon access. Under EASI, low-profile bilateral arrangements were worked out in memoranda of understanding with various ASEAN member countries. Typically these accords afforded US military ships or planes rights of access to particular ports or airfields for repair, provisioning or training exercises. Singapore went the furthest by agreeing to host a small complement of American military personnel.

In July 1992 at its Foreign Ministers' Meeting in Manila, ASEAN for the first time went on record as favouring a continued American military presence in Southeast Asia. In May 1993, Winston Lord characterized a statement by the Singaporean chair of the ASEAN Post-Ministerial Conference (PMC) Senior Officials Meeting (SOM) as containing 'an expression of everyone wanting the US presence to remain out here' (Lord, 1993a, p. 5). Of all the ASEAN countries, Singapore had most outspokenly favoured a continuing American security presence in Southeast Asia. One can doubt that 'everyone' at the SOM had been equally enthusiastic. But certainly ASEAN did not want the US to cut and run. In Singapore in June, at a conference of Asian–Pacific opinion-makers, including many with official or semi-official status, Asian participants urged Washington to maintain an 'adequate military presence' in the region and become a 'co-architect' of Asia's new regional order (Koh, 1993, pp. 2–3).

EASI was meant to provide 'regional access, mutual training arrangements, periodic ship visits, intelligence exchanges, and professional military educational programs rather than permanently stationed forces' (DOD, 1992, p. 5). Alluding to the dispersion of these activities across multiple sites, in contrast to the previous concentration of US forces at Clark and Subic, one officer summarized EASI as 'places not bases'.[1]

The slogan matched the preference of ASEAN. Even 'places' for American access were locally sensitive subjects, however. Typically the agreements to implement EASI were kept confidential at the request of host governments.

Notwithstanding the sensitivity of such understandings, the removal of the Soviet pole from the bipolar Cold War had made them easier to reach, since doing so could no longer seriously antagonize any other big power. And although ASEAN diplomats were loathe to say so publicly, EASI also offered a reason, however small and symbolic, for any power, not just China or Japan but also Indonesia as the largest country in Southeast Asia, to hesitate to seek hegemony over the region. In the eyes of most ASEAN leaders EASI looked optimal: a dispersed and low-key network for sustaining a steam-and-fly-through American military presence in Southeast Asia that could help to alleviate local anxieties and serve local cooperation without compromising sovereignty and offending nationalists the way bases would have.

EASI also had advantages for the United States. Unlike the former, Philippine-focused strategy, EASI was not hostage to changing politics or opinion in any one ASEAN country. EASI also implied a much less substantial military presence in Southeast Asia – appropriate budgetarily. Finally, EASI could in theory be used to raise a question of leverage: What concessions or advantages would ASEAN governments be willing to cede to the US in return for American participation in the security of Southeast Asia? Strengthening the value of EASI to the US in this last regard was the lack of competition. For China and Japan were effectively prevented from playing a regional security stabilizing role either because they lacked the capacity or willingness to do so, or because Southeast Asians did not trust their intentions, or for both reasons.

The idea that security, prosperity, and democracy were causally linked could have been used to justify two radically opposed policies. One was a posture of *benign neglect* while awaiting the natural *evolution* of one value from another: democracy incubated by economic growth, regional peace emerging from democratization, and further prosperity made possible by regional peace. The other choice was *active intervention*, using prospective assistance on one score as *leverage* for reciprocal cooperation on another: offering to play a regional security role in return for better investment opportunities for American firms or better protection for American copyrights, for example, or making access to the US market dependent on local progress on human rights.

In the mid-1990s the US government was unable to implement either of these policies – either benign neglect anticipating evolution or active intervention employing leverage. This inability was especially striking in the realm of security. On the one hand, the executive branch could not prevent Congress from giving in to the temptation to punish Southeast Asian governments for human rights violations by withholding security assistance. The logic of such punishment – we will punish your lack of democracy by making you more insecure – contradicted the logic of evolution – your economic growth will gradually make you more democratic and therefore more secure – and made benign neglect impossible.

On the other hand, within the executive branch, the very idea of treating EASI as an asset for purposes of constructive leverage on ASEAN governments was simply not entertained. Clinton did not cancel EASI. But his foreign policy apparatus was in too much disarray and too distracted by crises elsewhere to evaluate let alone use whatever security leverage in Southeast Asia EASI might have represented. This ruled out active intervention based on linking security to economic or political goals. Absent any effort to make such linkage understood, EASI's Southeast Asian hosts could pretend that in permitting an American security role they were doing the US a favour, as if EASI were more important to the Americans than to themselves. By not trying to change such attitudes, the Americans in effect helped to minimize whatever leverage their security role might otherwise have given them.

For all the doctrinal clarity of Clinton's linking of security to prosperity and democracy, in Southeast Asia he could not put together mechanisms and policies to implement the connections. The region was, in any case, hardly prominent on Clinton's policy horizon. In 1994, to the extent that the US government had any clear outlook at all on Southeast Asian security, it seemed to be this: If it ain't broke, don't fix it. In the end, for all its talk of innovation and synoptic post-Cold War thinking, the administration fell back on the traditional, negative definition of security as protection from threat by a clear external enemy. There simply was no room in the crisis-driven mentality prevailing in Washington, either in Congress or the executive branch, for the idea that the absence of such a threat, far from warranting American neglect, could be an opportunity for the US, working proactively and preventively, to help keep the ASEAN region secure. Nor was Washington organizationally equipped to explore the use of American leverage on security to pursue other Good Things.

No damage was done in Southeast Asia. The ASEAN states went ahead on their own, more or less ignoring the United States. Indonesia hosted a series of 'seminars' among claimants to the Spratly Islands. ASEAN governments launched an ASEAN Regional Forum intended to bring together a range of Asian and Western powers to discuss mutual security concerns. ASEAN think tanks inaugurated a Council on Security Cooperation in the Asia Pacific. Americans participated in both initiatives. But from the standpoint of security policy, Southeast Asia for the US was largely a missed opportunity.

In February 1994 Clinton did lift the embargo on American economic relations with Vietnam. That long-awaited decision contributed more to the security of Southeast Asia than anything else his administration had done up to that point. Ending the embargo also seemed to have been driven by the logic of evolutionary linkage. Through expanded trade and investment ties, Vietnam could gain economic security and become a stronger buffer against prospective Chinese expansion in Southeast Asia. Economic intercourse with the US would open Vietnamese society to American ideas about democracy. Economic growth stimulated by the end of the embargo could strengthen a Vietnamese middle class whose members might in time demand greater respect for human rights, perhaps even an end to the Communist Party's monopoly of power. And if Vietnam together with the rest of Southeast Asia became more democratic, regional peace would ensue because democracies would not go to war against each other.

The decision to lift the embargo was ideally suited to justification by the president in terms of security, prosperity and democracy. Instead, when he explained his action, Clinton cited 'one factor and one factor only' (Clinton, 1994): the 2,238 Americans then still missing in action (MIA) from the Vietnam War. By ending the embargo he hoped to reward and encourage Vietnam's cooperation to determine their fate. The MIA lobby and its allies in Congress had preempted the debate. Already open to charges of callousness toward those who had fought and died in a war he had opposed and avoided, Clinton felt he could not appear to have been swayed by abstract considerations of security, prosperity or democracy for either the US or Vietnam – indeed by anything but a desire to lay to rest the ghosts of American MIAs for the sake of their surviving friends and families. Ironically, on the one occasion in Southeast Asia when he could have appeared to be turning his grand vision into a blueprint for action, the president felt obliged not to seem to be doing so.

PROSPERITY: PUTTING BUSINESS FIRST

President Bush had been inaugurated in January 1989. For eleven of the ensuing thirteen quarters American gross domestic product (GDP) grew at an annual rate of less than 2 per cent. Not since before World War II had the economy expanded under 2 per cent annually for so long. GDP actually shrank from July 1990 through March 1991 (Uchitelle, 1992).

Bush's vulnerability on domestic economic policy encouraged Clinton not only to focus on it but to subsume foreign policy under it. Of the 31 issue-specific chapters in his campaign volume, *Putting People First*, only two dealt with foreign affairs: one supported arms control, the other, Israel. He told an audience in Los Angeles that inattention to the economy had been the Bush administration's worst failure. A Clinton administration, he promised, would 'change the State Department's culture so that economics is no longer a poor cousin to old-school diplomacy' (Friedman, 1992, p. 16).

In keeping his promise, Clinton intensified trends already underway. Under President Bush the State Department had brought its ambassadors home from the ASEAN countries to travel around the US promoting American exports to Southeast Asia. The Clinton administration repeated the experiment in 1993 and again in 1994. By the early 1990s, on the organizational chart of State's Bureau of East Asian and Pacific Affairs (EAP), economic matters had already superseded military and human rights issues. The Clinton administration further enlarged the attention paid to economic affairs. But more important than an organizing chart was the general trend toward a more muscular trade policy. The sagging US economy as interpreted by the Democratic majority in Congress had already driven President Bush, against his ideological instincts, into a more activist stance on behalf of American companies angered by what they considered unfair foreign competition for American consumers or unfair efforts by foreigners to protect their markets overseas. In Asia Japan took the brunt of this new emphasis on trade fairness. But Southeast Asia too was implicated, beginning in the 1980s when 'voluntary export restraints' imposed by the US on Japan combined with the strong yen to pull investment capital from Northeast to Southeast Asia. Many of the resulting investments were aimed at exporting to the large and lucrative US market. In the eyes of economic nationalists in Congress these third-country or 'back-door' exports showed perfidious Japan evading its 'voluntary' agreements with the US.

In Southeast Asia during the Cold War the US had derived some policy leverage from the aid it provided to the ASEAN states. But by the early 1990s such assistance no longer amounted to much of an asset for Washington. In 1991 the fifteen top recipients of US assistance included only one Southeast Asian country, the Philippines, and that ranking would not survive the American departure from Subic and Clark. Over the next three years, the US Congress slashed aid to the Philippines by 85 per cent.[2] In 1991 American aid was obligated to only four other Southeast Asian countries: Indonesia ($98.9 million), Thailand ($11.5 million), Laos ($1.7 million), and Singapore ($20.0 thousand).[3] As proportions of either the donor's or the recipient's economy, these were small, even trivial sums. The Indonesian figure, at nearly $100 million, may seem high in isolation, but not compared with the $5 billion being channelled annually to that country by the World Bank and other donors, notably Japan.

In early 1994, as if to illustrate his priority on foreign affairs, Clinton sent to Congress a federal budget that cut funding for the State Department proportionally more than for any other cabinet agency (*New York Times*, 1994). Meanwhile, helping American business became, increasingly, the business of US foreign policy. Trade and investment were replacing aid as what America could offer other countries. In Southeast Asia the Department of Commerce and the office of the US Trade Representative (USTR) were encroaching further on the already diminished purview of the State Department, which Clinton had disparaged as the home of 'old-school diplomacy', while non-governmental bodies such as the US–ASEAN Council for Business and Technology, the American–Indonesian Chamber of Commerce, and the California–Southeast Asia Business Council played ancillary roles (see, for example, US–ASEAN, 1993). When a new public–private effort to promote investment and trade with the ASEAN countries – the US–ASEAN Alliance for Mutual Growth – was announced in 1994, for example, the lead agencies were Commerce and USTR, not State.

But business became State's business too. In 1993 I heard some specialists on security, politics or culture on the staffs of American embassies in the ASEAN countries lament, off the record, that their ambassadors had become mere salesmen for US firms. Typical of similar criticism heard occasionally in the US was the complaint that Clinton had demeaned his country by gearing its foreign policy so obsessively to commerce (Kauffman, 1994). In 1993 a public opinion survey found only modest support for 'aiding the interests of US business abroad' as a 'top priority' in foreign policy; among eleven such goals, it ranked seventh in popularity (*Harper's*, 1994).

But putting business first was popular with American corporations and rational for a region whose economic growth warranted a proportional shift in American priorities from aid toward trade and investment. Nor did the objects of all this commercial attention, the Southeast Asians themselves, find it crass. On the contrary, if my conversations with officials and academics from ASEAN countries were any indication, many in the region were pleased that Americans were involving themselves in Southeast Asia for reasons of economic self-interest – *realekonomik* – as if that were a more reliable, hence more reassuring motive for engagement than the fickle altruism of aid. That logic seemed especially persuasive in 1991–3 when Congress, reacting to the loss of Clark and Subic, slashed aid to the one ASEAN country that, apart from Indonesia, needed it the most – the Philippines.

America's pro-business policy in Southeast Asia was not, however, geared to maximizing the presumed beneficial interactions between prosperity on the one hand and security or democracy on the other. Within the bureaucracy in Washington officials specializing in different values worked independently and often in rivalry with each other.

Arguably, arms sales to Southeast Asia did serve both American prosperity and the security of the purchasing country. But one could counterargue that selling weapons to one Southeast Asian government gave its neighbours an incentive to add to their arsenals too, thereby triggering an arms race that could decrease the security of the original buyer – not to mention the difficulty of believing that arming an authoritarian state could enhance local prospects for democracy.

Nor was America's pro-democracy policy meshed with policies for prosperity or security. It is true that a modestly funded Democratic Pluralism Initiative (DPI) was administered by USAID, intended to help strengthen certain non-governmental organizations and media and to help legislatures and judiciaries become more effective checks and balances against executive power. But DPI officials interacted little with their counterparts responsible for trade, investment or military issues. By the mid-1990s the Clinton administration was discussing placing more emphasis on democracy in the curriculum of American military training and education courses for Southeast Asian officers. But that effort to wed pro-security with pro-democracy policies was made simply to render such aid less objectionable to Congress, which had already cancelled military education for Malaysia and Indonesia to punish these governments for violating human rights – respectively the right of Vietnamese refugees to asylum and that of the East Timorese to demonstrate against the forcible annexation of their homeland to Indonesia.

Compared with security and prosperity, democracy as a goal of American foreign policy was unique in that it entailed no leverage on the governments of other countries. It made no sense to think that the US could offer or withhold democracy the way it could, in principle, open or close access to the American market, or increase or reduce the frequency of US naval ship visits to Southeast Asian ports. Compared with security and prosperity, democracy was less a bargainable means to other values and more an end in and of itself. The absolute character of democracy as a value, in turn, tended to separate the pursuit of it from economic and security policy in Southeast Asia. While trade, investment, and military cooperation could, in theory, be used on behalf of the democratization of the region, the reverse was not true. The Clinton administration's specialists on democratization had no carrots or sticks, that is, no persuasive means to help achieve security or prosperity as outcomes of democratization, at least not in the short run.

Nor could American democratizers easily counter the arguments of some Asian governments that liberalizing politics too rapidly or too soon risked incurring insecurity by unleashing disorder and deadlock and promoting poverty by undercutting the social discipline needed for savings and productivity. Evident American social and political decay – violent crime, drug abuse, policy stalemate, proliferating litigation, and so on – added to these doubts about the contribution of democracy to security and prosperity in the US.

DEMOCRACY: THE LIMITS OF MORALPOLITIK

Compared with security and prosperity, the usefulness of democracy as a value in foreign policy was also undermined by its association with foreign intervention. Cooperation for security, typically government-to-government, did not threaten national sovereignty at all. Nor was sovereignty a serious issue for the governments that welcomed trade and investment with the US, despite occasionally expressed fears for the ability of their cultures to withstand American films and TV programmes. But the idea that Americans should tell Southeast Asians how to run their governments was interventionist to the core, especially to the governments themselves. One can imagine almost any ASEAN leader who read Morton Halperin's recommendation that the US 'guarantee' democracy around the world by 'military action when necessary' (1993, pp. 105–06) feeling nostalgia for the Tarnoff Doctrine and being relieved when Halperin was not allowed to put such ideas into practice in DOD.

Halperin (1993) did not advocate invading or overthrowing dictatorships. Only 'when a people attempt[ed] to hold free elections and establish a constitutional democracy' he wrote, should the US and the international community 'guarantee' the result (p. 105). But what if the attempt failed? Should the US then take over to ensure a democratic outcome? In the case of a newly democratic state, wrote Halperin, its government would first have to request American assistance to preserve democracy (p. 120). But he also wanted the US to 'commit to using force if necessary' against a dictatorship 'to restore or establish constitutional democracy' (p. 121). In the latter instance, he implied, if a people tried to restore democracy through free elections but were prevented from doing so by state repression, the US should intervene on the people's side against the state.

In Southeast Asia the test case for Halperin's views was Burma (Myanmar). There, following the violent repression of pro-democracy demonstrations, people did attempt to restore constitutional democracy. In 1990 the country's iron-handed rulers in the State Law and Order Restoration Council (SLORC) held an election. Aung San Suu Kyi's democratic movement won. But rather than accept the result, SLORC cancelled it and cracked down. Burma met Halperin's condition for intervention to guarantee the success of a failed attempt to restore democracy.

The Bush administration called for an arms embargo against Burma, suspended all non-humanitarian assistance, cancelled the additional access to the US market Burma had enjoyed under the Generalized System of Preferences (GSP), refused to renew the US–Burmese textile agreement, pressed international financial institutions such as the World Bank to stop lending to Burma, and campaigned for resolutions condemning Burma in the United Nations. Not to be outdone by the executive branch, the Senate, at the instigation of Senator Daniel Moynihan, who acted on the advice of a staffer married to a Burmese, refused to approve the administration's nominee for ambassador to Rangoon. Others in Congress argued for a ban on all US trade with Burma.

These efforts failed. SLORC stayed in power. Aung San Suu Kyi stayed under house arrest. The policy failed because the autocrats in Rangoon refused to give in and the US lacked leverage over the Burmese economy. Even if all US–Burmese commerce had been banned (in violation of GATT), trade between the two countries amounted only to some $50 million, or perhaps 2–4 per cent of Burma's total trade with the world (Solomon, 1992b, p. 8). (The US was, however, one of the top investors in Burma, even though amounts were small.) Burma's long-standing isolation from world politics and the world economy had sharply limited the ties outsiders might otherwise have used as leverage against the regime. American efforts failed too because other countries, including China, the ASEAN states and Japan were in varying degrees unwilling to join an American crusade for democracy in Burma.

One might have thought the Clinton administration and its Democratic majority in Congress would have reconsidered this approach to Burma. Instead they intensified it. They did so not, I think, because they believed it would guarantee a return to democracy in Burma, as Halperin would have wished, but because Burma did not matter compared with Clinton's domestic agenda or America's relations with more important countries. Responsibility for US policy toward Burma could, in effect, be delegated to the human rights lobbies and their patrons in Congress.

Compared with the intensity of conflict between the executive and legislative branches over US policy toward China, a country that mattered a great deal, condemning and isolating SLORC was easy to do. Ironically, the same disconnection of Burma from the US that facilitated Congress's hard line confounded the success of that line for lack of leverage. The leverage of one state over another, after all, presupposes some major and valued interaction between them.

Democratization is *moralpolitik*. The absolute character of democracy as an end in itself reflects its association with basic human rights considered inviolable and inalienable. It is this connection that tends to turn the campaign for world democracy into a crusade and to make punishment a tempting policy option. Violating rights is evil; the violators are therefore evil too; punishing them is therefore just. An interesting result of this syllogism is that policies meant to punish undemocratic regimes do not have to succeed abroad to be domestically successful. To denounce evil is to feel good; actually doing good as well need not occur.

Compared with Burma, Indonesia offers another frustrating case study in democratization as *moralpolitik*. Here too the human rights lobby was effective in getting Congress to punish an authoritarian regime. In 1992, thanks to the members of the Congressional human rights caucus, and because of intensive lobbying by human rights groups such as Asia Watch and Amnesty International, Congress cancelled $2.3 million worth of International Military Education and Training (IMET) for Indonesia, over the weak objections of the State Department and the stronger ones of DOD. Further lobbying by the same groups persuaded State to forbid Jordan from selling four US-built F–5 jet aircraft to Indonesia. (From 1993 Wisconsin's new Democratic Senator Russell Feingold made the Indonesian government his particular *bête noire*.)

Their proponents justified these moves as responses to the killing of unarmed demonstrators by Indonesian troops in Dili, East Timor, in November 1991. In 1993, from conversations with the person on Feingold's staff responsible for his Timor policy, it was clear that she did not seriously expect punishing Jakarta to cause it to lessen its repression, let alone relinquish East Timor or become a democracy. Standing up for human rights did make Feingold look good in the eyes of a small group of vocal, liberal Wisconsin voters outraged by the Dili killings. Similarly, the concentration of ethnic-Portuguese voters in Rhode Island helped to explain the eagerness of their senator, Foreign Relations Committee Chair Claiborne Pell, to punish Jakarta for violating the rights of the people of East Timor, which had been a Portuguese colony before its seizure by Indonesia in 1975. Earlier, the presence of Indochinese refugees in his state of Washington probably encouraged Senator Mark Hatfield to legislate the cancellation of IMET to Malaysia over reports that its government was refusing asylum to Vietnamese boat people. By mid-1994 IMET had been restored for Malaysia but not for Indonesia, though Indonesians could use the program if they paid for it.

I have argued that the effort to defend and achieve democracy or respect for human rights involved no leverage of the sort that flowed from American economic and security relations with Southeast Asia. But there was one way in which punishing a country for being undemocratic or violating human rights did create a resource: the prospect that if the offending regime changed its ways, the punishment would stop. That change was limited, however, to the same single theme – democracy and human rights. Had Indonesia allowed the duty-free importation of American automobiles, that would not have mollified Feingold or Pell, any more than the MIA lobby would have been ready to drop the embargo if Vietnam were willing to buy American. Nor would Feingold, Pell, or the human rights lobby have been swayed by the readiness of Jakarta to cooperate with Washington on regional security through EASI.

The lesson these lobbies wanted to teach Southeast Asia was clear: If you don't become more democratic, and if you don't stop violating human rights, your security and prosperity will suffer to the extent that we can punish you. But if you want us to stop, concessions you might offer on security and prosperity will not matter to us; all we care about is whether you become more democratic and respect human rights.

In 1994, for all its talk of enlarging market-democracies, the Clinton administration came to reconsider for Indonesia the value of punishment on behalf of democracy and human rights. In 1993 labour unions had joined the rights lobby to campaign for cutting more than $600 million in Indonesian earnings from its American trade by cancelling the country's access to GSP. Instead, in February 1994, the Clinton administration announced it was suspending its review of Indonesian GSP eligibility. The Indonesian government had in the meantime raised the minimum wage, but the chief demand of the Americans – that the government recognize an independent trade union – had not been met.

In June 1994 the Indonesian government banned three major news publications, making the State Department's new moderation that much harder to justify. Nevertheless, in July, to the dismay of human rights groups, State helped to beat back an attempt by Feingold and other senators to prohibit the use in East Timor of weapons that Washington might transfer to Indonesia in fiscal year 1995. Apparently to show why such a restriction was unnecessary, Secretary of State Warren Christopher reiterated the administration's policy of denying licences to sell Indonesia small arms and crowd-control weapons of the sort that could be used in domestic repression. The Senate promptly made this policy harder to change by writing it into the draft legislation.

Apparently, faced with the prospect of Clinton's visiting Jakarta later in the year to attend a second APEC summit with prosperity and (in bilateral meetings) security as its themes, State had decided to try to prevent relations with Indonesia from worsening. The administration had, in effect, acknowledged Jakarta's economic and strategic importance to the US. The Clinton administration would not easily sacrifice *realekonomik* for *moralpolitik* in deference to Congressional critics of Indonesia. The Democrats' loss of their Senate and House majorities in November 1994 elections was for Indonesia opportune. By 1995 Clinton officials were working with the new Republican Congress to restore US IMET funding for Indonesia while trying to reassure liberal Democratic legislators that IMET's human rights curriculum could help reduce abuses by the Indonesian military.

A more dramatic shift occurred on China. In May 1993 President Clinton had linked China's Most Favoured Nation (MFN) status with its performance on human rights. In May 1994 he reversed himself, explicitly delinking the two. ASEAN governments were pleased with the second decision. They failed to see how punishing China for its crackdown on dissidents could help make this vast, dynamic, and potentially dangerous state a cooperative partner for East Asian security and prosperity. For them the latter task was vital.

Similarly, despite the irritation of many ASEAN leaders with Tokyo for its failure to import high-value-added manufactures, Clinton's effort to open Japan's market did not earn him Southeast Asian support. Not even their common trade deficit with Japan could move ASEAN toward supporting the US position. US policy toward Japan was bilateral and acrimonious. No serious effort was made to adapt that policy to the interest of other Asians in fairer trade with Japan. Only with its discovery of APEC did the Clinton administration begin to consider the possible advantages of a more multilateral approach. Meanwhile, from watching the Americans pressure Japan, sometimes on behalf of specific US firms such as Chrysler or Motorola, ASEAN governments drew the conclusion that the Americans were looking out for their own, not Southeast Asian interests.

American criticism on human rights further disinclined its targets in Southeast Asia to want to join American efforts to increase foreign imports into Japan. Of all the Southeast Asian economies, Singapore's was the most committed to and dependent upon free trade. The city-state was the natural ally of an American campaign to remove barriers to freer trade with Japan. Instead, in June 1994, the caning of an American teenager for vandalism was allowed to obscure this common interest. The popularity of the verdict among graffiti-weary Americans removed any domestic political necessity for Clinton personally to intervene on the boy's behalf. Yet the president did so several times. Nor did the Singaporean government's unprecedented decision to reduce the number of strokes from six to four deter USTR Mickey Kantor from administering a retaliatory stroke of his own by thwarting the city-state's desire to host the first meeting of the new World Trade Organization (WTO) being created out of GATT. Unable to impose its values, the administration turned to vengeance, and men who denied the Tarnoff Doctrine wound up helping to illustrate it.

Against all these mixed signals, reversals, and failures, there was one instance of a pro-democracy policy that did have both economic and security benefits for Southeast Asians: American support for the May 1993 elections in Cambodia. Here at last the logics of positive intervention and beneficial evolution were complementary. A freely elected government in Phnom Penh would finally have the legitimacy to be able to deal with the notorious Khmer Rouge. The long hoped-for end to the Third Indochina War that had begun with Vietnam's invasion of Pol Pot's Cambodia in 1978 would, in turn, increase the security of mainland Southeast Asia. It would also help transform, in the Thais' phrase, Indochina's 'battlefield into a marketplace'. Commerce and peace would in turn permit the consolidation of Cambodian democracy.

In 1994 such optimism was still premature. Cambodia was deeply divided, the Khmer Rouge still active, peace still unachieved, corruption rampant, and stability let alone democracy still elusive. But pessimistic observers had already been wrong about the ability of Cambodians even to hold an election. What mattered more for future US policy in Southeast Asia was the thoroughly multilateral character of this one instance where security, prosperity, and democracy were beneficially interconnected and American intervention to help their evolution clearly warranted. It was the Security Council of the United Nations, not to mention preparatory Franco-Indonesian diplomacy, that had brokered and imposed the peace agreement signed in 1991 in Paris by all of the Khmer belligerents and eighteen other countries.

That fact suggested one lesson for American policy themes since the end of the Cold War. In keeping with the Tarnoff Doctrine of realistic limits, rather than Clinton's penchant for universal goals, security, prosperity and democracy were more likely to be served, especially in combination, if accompanied by a willingness to work multilaterally with other countries and not just bilaterally on behalf of American values, let alone unilaterally to punish Asians for presumptive failure to illustrate those values in their own behaviour.

CONCLUSION: PRINCIPLE AND PRACTICE

In the mid-1990s the ideological emblem of US foreign policy – the idea that security, prosperity, and democracy were Good Things that went together – looked better on paper than it did in practice.

The idea fell victim, first, to the gap between ambition and resources. In the wake of its costly victory in the Cold War, the United States lacked the resources to pursue such a grand and global design. Second, the design fell victim to the contradiction between the rhetorical ambition of 'enlargement' and the inward-looking retrenchment implied by Clinton's passion for domestic policy and his inattention to foreign affairs in the absence of a televised crisis – Somalia, Haiti, Bosnia – requiring Washington to act.

Third, as the story of EASI illustrates, Washington could not take advantage of something it had to offer that Southeast Asian governments clearly wanted – a security role in the region – to help bring about other goals. DOD was in too much flux, attention was focused elsewhere, and meanwhile Congress was sending a contrary signal to Indonesia, the most important country in the region: not that Americans could be relied on as partners for regional security, but that such cooperation could only occur once Indonesia complied with American demands. In 1993–4 those demands were for the right of self-determination for East Timor and an end to human rights abuses.

In 1994–5 the administration's effort to restore IMET funding for Indonesia notwithstanding a lack of progress on these issues reversed this democracy-first logic. But by emphasizing how much its security relationship with Indonesia mattered to the Clinton administration even in the face of Indonesian repression, the effort to revive US funding for IMET could only further shrink whatever policy leverage on other subjects American assistance for Indonesian security might imply.

Fourth, the notion that security, prosperity, and democracy were mutually inducing, such that pursuing any one of them would help realize the others, was too abstract to be useful as a guideline for foreign policy decisions. Nor was the contested and results-oriented character of the policy process congenial to patience as a policy option. To a harried, pressured official trying to decide what action to take now on a given country or issue, the thought that at some time in the indefinite future prosperity would induce democracy, or security prosperity, or democracy security, or vice versa, was unenlightening.

Officials also knew that these propositions could be wrong. While it was true, for example, that in the past democracies had not fought each other, in the post-Cold War era one could expect a proliferation of different kinds of democracies, some of which could prove to be less reliably irenic than their mostly Western antecedents had been. Freed of the constraints of a common struggle against communism, some of these post-Cold War democracies might turn nationalistic to the point of jingoism, hence potentially to the point of warring with other democracies.

Fifth, there was no public enthusiasm in America for conveying the Three Good Things to other countries. Consider the answers Americans gave to a 1993 poll asking them which of ten listed foreign policy activities should have a 'top priority'. The activities ranked *last* by respondents were 'promoting and defending human rights in other countries', 'promoting democracy in other nations', 'helping improve the living standard in developing nations', and 'protecting weaker nations against foreign aggression even if US vital interests are not at stake' (as presumably they were not in Southeast Asia). These same respondents ranked at the top of the list 'protecting the jobs of American' workers (prosperity for Americans), 'preventing the spread of weapons of mass destruction' (security for Americans and others), and 'insuring adequate energy supplies for the United States' (again, prosperity for Americans).[4]

Sixth, policy influentials inside the Beltway were divided. They ranked the three values differently. Some members of Congress sought to micromanage foreign policy and gear it to democratization and human rights. Many in DOD resisted these attempts in the name of security. The USTR and Commerce promoted trade, investment and market-opening moves. There were too many specialists. Few gave all three themes equal weight or scanned them for complementarity in the light of changing Southeast Asian conditions.

Seventh, those actual conditions were, compared with the smooth logic of the policy themes, recalcitrant. Far from persuading the ASEAN states that they really ought to adopt American-style democracy or American-style notions of the sanctity and precedence of the individual over the community, economic growth had emboldened some Southeast Asia leaders, notably in Singapore, Kuala Lumpur, and Jakarta, to defend an alternative, putatively 'Asian way' emphasizing order, social discipline, and the priority of the community over the individual. Far from pushing the region away from authoritarian temptations, American *moralpolitik* had in the end helped to trigger into being a counterimage of itself.

Not every pro-democracy policy followed by America in Southeast Asia failed. As noted above, the one pursued in Cambodia in 1993 worked well, at least in the short run. In 1994 one could at least argue that a pro-democracy policy had in fact improved the security of Cambodia and helped make possible its economic development. Similarly, although Clinton refused to justify his ending the embargo against Vietnam as a pro-prosperity move to improve either the security of Southeast Asia or the chance that democracy might evolve in Vietnam, that decision too illustrated and served his three themes.

But the eighth and final aspect of Washington's rhetorical eagerness to promote Good Things in theory was perhaps their most severe limitation on guidelines for the practice of foreign policy. Casting America's foreign affairs in such broad terms invited a conflict between two sets of domestic actors. One set, citing democracy and human rights as standards, wanted to punish countries that did not measure up, including withholding help on prosperity and security. Another set, for whom prosperity and security were more important values, opposed the first group, arguing that democracy and human rights were in the long run best served by trading with and investing in these countries and helping to assure their security. US policy zigged and zagged between these two positions.

In the end, policy themes that were meant to organize, focus and guide US foreign policy toward Southeast Asia, wound up mainly enabling Americans to have arguments with themselves about it. Security, prosperity, and democracy were too broad and innocuous to amount to a Clinton Doctrine. But by expanding American ambitions and phrasing them as universals, pursuit of these Good Things led Clinton farther and farther away from the modesty, the self-restraint, and the attraction to multilateral cooperation implied by the Tarnoff Doctrine that he had chosen to reject as an insult to the prowess of a superpower fresh from victory in the Cold War.

The rest of the 1990s will challenge the United States to fashion more consistent policies in Southeast Asia, policies that are less burdened by domestic inattention and conflict and more attuned to the region as it is, independent of what this or that group in Washington hopes it will be or wants to make it become.

Notes

1. Interview, Col. (USAF) Ralph A. Cossa, Chief, Policy Division, HQ, CINCPAC, Monterey, CA, 19 March 1993.
2. Holmes (1993). This figure was for all American assistance, economic or military. As late as 1993, among recipients of economic help from the USAID, the Philippines still ranked tenth (Barber, 1993).
3. Tarnoff (1992), 6. In contrast, nearly $6 billion – 41 per cent of all US aid that year – went to just two countries: Israel and Egypt.
4. Harper's 1994. The seven quoted activities were given 'top priority' by 22, 22, 18, 17, 85, 69, and 60 percent, respectively, of the 2,000 respondents polled. The Times Mirror Center for the People and the Press conducted the survey in September 1993.

References

Barber, Ben (1993) 'US Foreign Assistance Program Will Get New Focus in Overhaul.' *The Christian Science Monitor*, 7 October, p. 3.

Bhagwati, Jagdish (1993) 'The Case for Free Trade.' *Scientific American*. 269: 5 (November), pp. 42–4, 46, 48–9.

Clarke, Jonathan and James Clad (1995) *After the Crusade: American Foreign Policy for the Post-Superpower Age* (Lanham, Md.: Madison Books).

Christopher, Warren (1993) 'Democracy and Human Rights: Where America Stands.' Copy of remarks delivered to the World Conference on Human Rights, Vienna, Austria, 14 June. (Washington DC: Office of the Spokesman, US Department of State).

Clinton, Bill (1993) 'Fundamentals of Security for a New Pacific Community', *US Department of State Dispatch: Asia and the Pacific*, vol. 4 no. 29 (19 July), pp. 509–12.

Clinton, Bill (1994) 'In Clinton's Words: "Fullest Possible Accounting" of MIAs.' *The New York Times*. 4 February. p. A6.

Daly, Herman E. (1993) 'The Perils of Free Trade.' *Scientific American*, vol. 269: no. 5 (November). pp. 50–52, 54, 56–7.

Emmerson, Donald K. (1995) 'Region and Recalcitrance: Rethinking Democracy through Southeast Asia', *The Pacific Review*, vol. 8, no. 2.

Friedman, Thomas L. (1992) 'Clinton's Foreign-Policy Vision reaches across Broad Spectrum', *New York Times*, 4 October, pp. 1, 16.

Friedman, Thomas L. (1993a) 'Clinton's Securty aide Gives a Vision for Foreign Policy.' *The New York Times*, 22 September, p. A17.

Friedman, Thomas L. (1993b) 'Clinton's Foreign Policy: Top Adviser Speaks Up,' *New York Times*, 31 October, p. 4.

Gellman, Barton (1994) 'Perry Moves to Erase Aspin's Marks upon Pentagon Organization', *The Washington Post*. 17 February, p. A14.

Halperin, Morton H. (1993) 'Guaranteeing Democracy.' *Foreign Policy*, vol. 91 (Summer), pp. 105–122.

Harper's Magazine (1994) 'Foreign Policy: The Grass-Roots Approach', January, p. 64.

Holmes, Steven A. (1993) 'A Foreign Aid of Words, Not Cash.' *The New York Times*, 5 December, p. 5.

Kaplan, Robert D. (1994) 'The Coming Anarchy', *Atlantic Monthly*, vol. 273, no. 2 (February), pp. 44–46, 48–9, 52, 54, 58–60, 62–3, 66, 68–70, 72–6.

Kauffman, L. A. (1994) 'Trade Wins.' *SF Weekly* (San Francisco) 23 February, p. 9.

Koh, Tommy. (1993) 'America's Role in Asia: Asian Views.' *CAPA Report* (November) Center for Asian Pacific Affairs, Asia Foundation, San Francisco, CA.

Lord, Winston (1993a) Excerpts from Ambassador Winston Lord's Background Remarks for the US Press following the ASEAN-PMC SOM, Singapore, 21 May. Unclassified cable, US Information Service, Singapore-to-Washington, DC.

Lord, Winston (1993b) 'A New Pacific Community: Ten Goals for American Policy,' Opening Statement at Confirmation Hearings for Ambassador Winston Lord, Assistant Secretary of State-Designate, Bureau of East Asian and Pacific Affairs, US State Department, Washington, DC, 31 March.

Lord, Winston, (1993–4) 'The Horizons of US-Korea Relations', *The US-Koreas Review*, vol. 2, no. 6 (December-January), p. 5.

Nasar, Sylvia. 1994. 'Economists Trade Barbs over President's Policy.' *The New York Times*, 5 January, p. C2.

New York Times (1994) 'Who Wins, Who Loses', 8 February, p. A 12.

Perry, William (1993) Untitled, unpublished remarks, made at the Asia Society Conference, Tokyo, Japan, 13 May. (Tokyo: US Information Service Press Office).

Solomon, Richard H. (1992a) 'American and Asian Security in an Era of Geoeconomics.' US Department of State Dispatch: East Asia/Pacific, 25 May.

Solomon, Richard H. (1992b) 'US Policy and the Situation in Burma', testimony before the House Foreign Affairs Subcommittee on Asian and Pacific Affairs, 20 May.

Tarnoff, Curt (1992) *Foreign Aid: Answers to Basic Questions*, CRS Report for Congress, 25 March. (Washington DC: Congressional Research Service).

Uchitelle, Louis (1992) 'Even Words Fail in This Economy', *The New York Times*, 8 September, p. C2.

U.S.-ASEAN Council for Business and Technology, Inc. (1993) 'Position Paper: US Security and Competitive Interests Jeopardized in Indonesia', unpublished paper.

US Department of Defense, Office of the Assistant Secretary of Defense for International Security Affairs (East Asia and Pacific Region) (1992) *A Strategic Framework for the Asian Pacific Rim: Report to Congress 1992* (Washington DC: DOD).

7 Soviet and Russian Policy towards Southeast Asia (1986–93)

Vladimir Rakhmanin

Mikhail Gorbachev's coming into power started a new period in Soviet foreign policy – a rejection of the conservative scheme of opposing the US in the West and Japan and China in the East. This re-evaluation was a result of understanding the limited powers of the decaying Soviet empire, which could no longer afford confrontation on two fronts, sustain a powerful military machine and disregard developing consumer industries.

The new Soviet leaders also reviewed their policy towards Third World client states. In contrast to the earlier priorities given to military and economic assistance, Gorbachev offered Soviet clients a sort of declaratory 'profound sympathy'. He also called for restructuring of economic relations between socialist countries, trying to put them on a footing of mutual benefit.

It was also important for the USSR to create a favourable international environment for the beginning of radical reforms inside Soviet society. Asian policy became an important part of Gorbachev's foreign policy. By 1985 it became clear that in economic development, the USSR was lagging behind not only western countries but most of the eastern states as well. New Soviet leaders, more open to the world, saw the long-term political consequences of industrial growth of the four 'Asian dragons' and China. Besides, Chinese experience gave an example of successful reforming of Soviet-type economic structures from within.

The Soviet Union's military presence in the Pacific was very powerful. At the same time Moscow's political and economic positions in the region remained very weak. The huge Soviet military presence in Asia limited the possibilities of political manoeuvres and preserved the image of the USSR as a major threat to Asian countries. Unresolved territorial disputes and efforts to pursue dialogue with Tokyo from the position of force excluded the possibility of Soviet–Japanese rapprochement.

More than twenty years of hostility with China based on ideology and some unresolved practical matters (the famous 'three obstacles' – presence of Soviet troops at the Chinese border and in Mongolia, Soviet occupation of Afghanistan and Soviet support of Vietnam in Cambodia) slowed down the normalization of Soviet–Chinese relations, for which Moscow and Beijing seemed to be ready by that time.

Soviet great-power rhetoric, SE Asian countries' fears of communist subversion, as well as Cambodian and Afghan problems, prevented Soviet contacts with ASEAN from expanding. Undoubtedly, the Soviet–American confrontation and pro-American orientation of the majority of SE Asian countries also negatively influenced further development of contacts. The only allies of the USSR in the Asia-Pacific region were Vietnam, Laos, Cambodia, North Korea and Mongolia – the countries following the Soviet socialist model of development.

Taking into account negative and positive Soviet baggage in the region, Gorbachev and his close associates worked out a new doctrine for Soviet policy in Asia, later called the Vladivostok–Krasnoyarsk platform, after the names of the cities in the USSR where Gorbachev made important speeches on Asia in 1986 and 1988 (*Pravda,* 28 July 1986; 16 September 1988). The main ideas of this programme were as follows:

the Soviet Union is an Asian and Pacific state and should play an important role in the region;

the USSR stands for the early and fair resolution of regional conflicts (Afghanistan, Cambodia, Korea);

long-term security in the region can be provided only by collective efforts; radical reduction of armed forces and armaments, including nuclear, down to reasonable sufficiency is of great importance;

ecological security is an important part of regional security;

the USSR is interested in participating in regional economic integration.

Practically, the Vladivostok speech opened the door to Soviet–Chinese normalization. In Krasnoyarsk, Gorbachev hinted at the possibility of establishing diplomatic relations with South Korea. In 1986 the first Soviet–American political consultations on the Asia-Pacific took place. A new Soviet foreign minister, Eduard Shevardnadze, recognized the existence of the territorial issue in Soviet–Japanese relations. The Soviet Union started to speak seriously about reducing its military presence in the region and supported those statements with practical unilateral steps.

At Gorbachev's assumption of leadership, Soviet diplomacy had become both more active and more sophisticated in Asia and the Pacific, and that definitely influenced the USSR's position in SE Asia.

SOVIET POLICY IN SE ASIA (1986–91)[1]

By 1986 the USSR had long had relations with Vietnam based on mutual interests in containing China, and on ideological proximity. In the new Soviet policy in Asia the normalization of Soviet–Chinese relations, and gaining trust from ASEAN became of equal importance, leading to restructuring of relations with Vietnam: from Vietnamese dependency on the USSR to mutually beneficial cooperation. The key to achieving those priorities was the Cambodian problem. It was considered in the Soviet leadership that:

1. Settlement of or, minimally, achieving mutual trust with Beijing on, the issue of Cambodia would help to remove the main obstacle in Soviet–Chinese relations.
2. Vietnamese constructive cooperation on Cambodia would open the door in Hanoi to the international community, accelerate its cooperation with ASEAN, and provide the opportunities for building constructive Chinese–Vietnamese relations.
3. Constructive involvement of the USSR in the resolution of the Cambodian problem through Moscow's influence on Phnom Penh and Hanoi as well as Beijing's strengthened mutual trust with ASEAN, was a practical contribution of the new Soviet leadership to the security in SE Asia, and to realization of ASEAN's idea of turning SE Asia into a zone of peace, freedom and neutrality–a nuclear-free zone. Soviet Deputy Foreign Minister Igor Rogachev skillfully used shuttle diplomacy trying to persuade external powers involved in the conflict to be more flexible.
4. The consultations on Cambodia were becoming an important integral part of the Soviet-American dialogue in regional settlements.
5. In case of a Cambodian settlement, Soviet involvement in one more regional conflict would be stopped.

The Cambodian issue was at the centre of Shevardnadze's discussions with his Vietnamese and Cambodian partners during his visit to Indochina in March 1987. The same month he visited Indonesia, Thailand and Australia. In Bangkok and Jakarta one could hear criticism of Shevardnadze for being too reticent on Cambodia. The reason for this was that the Soviet minister did not consider it possible to have detailed discussions in Indonesia and Thailand without previously consulting Phnom Penh and Hanoi. In those capitals Shevardnadze suggested for the first time the use of a 'national reconciliation' formula to resolve the Cambodian conflict. The search for consensus among parties in the conflict and outside parties was not easy; bargaining was very tough. But the way to settlement was stimulated by serious changes in the world: US–USSR cooperation, normalization of Soviet–Chinese and Chinese–Japanese relations, beginning of the dialogue between the USSR and China and ASEAN, and the growing tendency for cooperation of Indochina countries and ASEAN.

At the same time searching for the Cambodian resolution was very emotional: under Pol Pot the ruling 'Khmer Rouge' killed (in accordance with different sources) somewhere between one and three million Cambodians. Vietnamese actions could be seen to have saved the country from further genocide but could also be defined as external aggression by the international community.

By the year 1987 Phnom Penh and Hanoi proclaimed the policy of national reconciliation and political settlement as the basis for the resolution of internal and external aspects of the Cambodian problem. Vietnam declared that it was going to withdraw all its remaining troops from Cambodia. The Soviet government strongly welcomed these intentions.

Moscow was sending a high-level diplomat to almost all bilateral meetings between Prince Sihanouk and Hun Sen; his mission was to observe and when possible to contribute to the success of the meetings. The Soviet representative was also an observer at two initial informal meetings of the four Khmer sides, ASEAN countries, Vietnam and Laos in Jakarta (July 1988 and February 1989). At those meetings a very important principle of a future Cambodian settlement was formulated – the linkage between withdrawal of all Vietnamese troops, a strict avoidance of genocide and cessation of all external interference and military assistance to any side in the conflict.

The first phase of the Paris conference on Cambodia (July 30 – August 1989) did not find a solution to the conflict, according to Soviet Foreign Ministry assessments, because of wide differences between the Khmer participants on four major problems:

who would rule the country during the transitional period (from Vietnamese withdrawal to national elections);
creation of an international control mechanism under UN auspices;
how to prevent resumption of genocide;
allegations about Vietnamese colonization of Cambodia.

In September 1989 Hanoi declared that all Vietnamese troops had been withdrawn from Cambodia. And although there was no international monitoring of the process, withdrawal of Vietnamese troops changed the framework of the conflict: its external aspect was significantly diminished and it became more a confrontation between Phnom Penh and Khmer opposition.

From January 1990 regular meetings of the UN Security Council Permanent Members' representatives started, and by August they worked out a Framework Agreement on Comprehensive Political Settlement in Cambodia. The Soviet Union actively participated in that process. In September 1990 during the Khmer sides' meeting in Jakarta the Supreme National Council of Cambodia was established. In November, again in Jakarta, France and Indonesia organized the meeting of the Friends of Paris Conference Co-Chairmen, in which the specific discussions of the Paris Conference final documents started. In December the whole package was presented to SNC for the Khmer sides' consideration.

Another round of behind-the-scene Soviet consultations with the Phnom Penh regime started. But the beginning of the dry season in Cambodia did not contribute much to further reconciliation: in spite of strong international pressure there was a continuation of fighting.

It was already clear, however, that the peace process on Cambodia could not be stopped. In June 1991 all Khmer sides agreed to an indefinite cease fire and decided not to accept any outside military assistance. By the end of August they reached final agreements on military issues and sharing power in SNC. All of this made it possible to sign an 'Agreement on Comprehensive Political Settlement in Cambodia' on 23 October 1991, in Paris, which created a fundamentally new situation in SE Asia.

Parallel to the Cambodian settlement the restructuring of Soviet–Vietnamese relations was taking place. Their strategic and ideological components were diminishing gradually. In 1987 a joint decision was taken to shift the emphasis in bilateral economic relations from loans and trade to production cooperation based on mutual benefit. Vietnam would have to pay market prices for Soviet goods. The question of bilateral relations was a subject for discussions during the talks in Moscow in May 1991 between M. Gorlbachev and General Secretary of the Communist Party of Vietnam, Nguyen Van Linh, and the Chairman of the Council of Ministers of Vietnam, Do Muoi. Both sides agreed that an increase in Vietnamese exports to the USSR would enable the countries to balance mutual trade and economic relations; in 1991 the turnover totalled US$500 million for each party. The accent was placed on direct relations between plants and organizations (Soviet Council of Minister's Report).

While discussing the debt of Vietnam (about 10 billion roubles) the Soviet party suggested an untraditional way of partial repayment – by reinvestments in joint ventures, created on the basis of Soviet–Vietnamese cooperation. But by that time bilateral Soviet–Vietnamese relations had in fact become hostage to political instability in the USSR, destruction of business relations among enterprises on the territory of the USSR, and the lack of clear perspective of further reforms in the country.

The last component of Gorbachev's policy in SE Asia was the development of relations with ASEAN countries. Shevardnadze's visit to Jakarta and Bangkok in March 1987 became an important event for Soviet diplomacy. During the previous twenty years no Soviet foreign minister had ever visited those countries. In the USSR they were viewed as strongholds of anti-communism and no place for Soviet leaders to be seen.

As the *Far Eastern Economic Review* (26 March 1987) wrote, Shevardnadze, avoiding direct criticism of the USA, showed a new image of the Soviet Union to the Indonesians and Thais, demonstrated openness, explained the essence of a peaceful approach, and called for the necessity of working out agreements on regional security taking into consideration the experience of Helsinki, the Bandung principles, the nonaligned movement and the New Delhi Declaration. In 1988 Shevardnadze even visited the Philippines. The Soviet Union was visited in return by the prime ministers of Malaysia (1987), Thailand (1988), and Singapore (1990), the President of Indonesia, Suharto (1989), and also by foreign ministers of Indonesia, the Philippines (1989) and Thailand (1987). In New York during the sessions of the UN General Assembly meetings between the Soviet foreign minister and his ASEAN colleagues took place again. In February 1990, visits were made, the first in the history of bilateral relations, by the Chairman of the Soviet Council of Ministers, Nikolay Ryzhkov, to Singapore and Thailand. During those visits many important new agreements were signed: for example, with

Thailand, a protocol of realization of agreements on scientific and technical cooperation and on establishing a Soviet–Thai commission on scientific and technical cooperation, and a programme of cultural and scientific exchange; and with Singapore, an agreement on establishing a joint economic commission for the development of trade, economic, scientific and technical cooperation (*Pravda*, 13–18 February 1990).

In 1989 Shevardnadze sent a message to the 22nd Annual Conference of the Foreign ministers of ASEAN in which he expressed readiness of the Soviet party to start consultations with the 'six' on the main components of the nuclear-free zone in SE Asia (*Izvestia*, 14 February 1989). In July 1990 the Soviet foreign minister suggested to the chairman of the permanent committee of ASEAN that there be a dialogue between the Soviet Union and ASEAN on peace, security and cooperation. For further mutual understanding and trust parliamentary contacts were being developed in 1990–91.

In July 1991 in Kuala Lumpur during the 24th Conference of the Foreign Ministers of ASEAN, official relations between the USSR and ASEAN as an organization were established. Trade and economic relations were developing too, but they were rather weak and lagged behind political contacts. In 1991 the total trade turnover with the six countries totaled 1.44 billion roubles (as compared with only 530.2 million roubles in 1990) with the deficit on the Soviet side of 206 million roubles.

On 1 October 1991 the USSR established diplomatic relations with Brunei, the last state with which the Soviet Union initiated diplomatic contact. A little bit more than two months later the Soviet Union ceased to exist.

THE GUIDELINES OF RUSSIA'S FOREIGN POLICY IN SE ASIA

A new independent and sovereign Russia emerged after the demise of the Soviet Union at the end of 1991. Russia is the successor state to the former Soviet Union and inherits Soviet international agreements and obligations, as well as the Soviet posture in the international arena, except for some Soviet actions, like, for example, invasion of Afghanistan, which were condemned by the Russian authorities. Although Russia is the successor to the USSR, its foreign policy, including toward the Asia–Pacific region, is different from that of the former Soviet Union.

The most important pecularity is that Russian foreign policy is strongly influenced by the domestic politics of radical economic and political reform, and reflects the process of Russia's re-emergence as an independent and sovereign state. To name just a few specific reform-related problems that are reflected in Russian foreign policy:

The state of Russia has not yet finished the process of 'self-identification'. That is why it is still difficult to define clearly genuine Russian national interests.

Economic difficulties and loss of great-power status produced the rise of national self-consciousness among politically active Russians. They become very sensitive to any action that could be perceived as humiliation of Russian dignity.

The high degree of corruption among state employees, bureaucrats and entrepreneurs. Sometimes Russian people see the market as a place where 'everybody lies to everybody'.

A fall in gas and oil production and in production of many heavy industry and reprocessing enterprises, including the high technology ones, seriously undermines Russian exports. For example, in 1991–2 Russian overall trade with Asia–Pacific countries fell by more than 20 per cent.

Reforms produced hardships for the military and military-industrial complex.

In comparison with the USSR, Russian geopolitical priorities have changed. Russia, at least for now, is going to pay more attention to its neighbouring countries, and will be less involved in global endeavours.

In the process of economic reforms the pragmatism and economic priorities of Russian foreign policy will be increasing: what is good for reforms will become good for Russian foreign policy.

The influence of local authorities in defining the Russian policy agenda abroad have increased.

Ethnic conflicts on the territory of the former USSR will influence policy.

Because of its geopolitical situation Russia is an Asian as well as a European state, and is going to play an active role in Asian affairs, especially those concerning its neighbours. Russia's attitude toward SE Asia lacks the global ambitions of the former Soviet Union. Russian interest in SE Asia is more pragmatic; it is founded on economic considerations. The priority interests of Russia in Indochina include the development of mutually beneficial cooperation with the Indochina countries, further interaction with these countries and other interested members of the international community in settling the Cambodian problem, and the implementation in SE Asia of the ZOPFAN concept put forward by the states of the region.

Russia considers Vietnam, Laos and Cambodia as independent sovereign states. However, in cooperating with the Indochina states Russia encounters some common problems: the need to reactivate, as far as possible, economic ties and to re-establish them on a new, essentially market-oriented and mutually beneficial basis; and to improve the efficiency of the use of the economic capacity generated with Russian assistance in Vietnam, Laos and Cambodia. (The Soviet Union spent nearly US$20 billion on the economic development of these countries.)

Relations between Russia and Vietnam have a rather special character. In previous years cooperation with this country was the most intensive in the region. Vietnam also has the greatest debt to the Russian Federation (nearly US$9.9 billion, which Vietnam started to repay in 1993). In Vietnam Russia has to deal with such problems as the completion of the national economic projects developed with Moscow's assistance and humanitarian issues.

Russian–Vietnamese relations suffered greatly from the loss of ideological closeness and of Soviet aid; Vietnam's GNP growth in 1991 with continued Soviet assistance could have been 8–10 per cent, but actually was 2.4 per cent. Yet it seems that the Vietnamese are gradually getting back on track: in 1992 Russian–Vietnamese trade was US$300 million and more or less balanced (Assessments of the Russian Ministry of Foreign Trade Relations). Of course, there will never be the same relations as in the late 1960s and early 70s, but traditional cooperation and broad industrial infrastructure created with Soviet assistance produced a strong foundation for further development of Russian–Vietnamese relations.

On 4 July 1992 Russia and Vietnam signed a trade agreement pledging to maintain the economic links forged during the Soviet era, and by 1994 Russian-Vietnamese trade was scheduled to be US$500 million. Vietnam will continue to pay off credits extended by Moscow by supplying food and goods and by providing services to Russian firms operating in Vietnam. Russia is to continue to help building factories and installations, particularly in the energy sector, in line with commitments made by the former Soviet Union, providing US$40 million in loans in 1993. The first meeting of the Russian–Vietnamese joint commission on economic, scientific and technological cooperation was held in Hanoi on 29–31 July 1992. As a result, some important documents were signed, among them an agreement between governments on scientific–technological cooperation (Interfax News Agency, 1 August 1992). During the first visit of the Vietnamese foreign minister to Russia (28–29 October 1993) both sides defined as the most beneficial areas of long-term bilateral cooperation: gas and oil exploration, construction of hydro-and thermo-power stations, coal development, production and processing in Vietnam of tropical agricultural products and their export to Russia, and shipbuilding and ship repair. The joint venture, VietSovPetro, continued to supply more than 80 per cent of all crude oil pumped in Vietnam.

Russia welcomed the fact that Vietnam and Laos became observers at ASEAN and saw a good prospect for them to become members. However, some frictions did develop in Russian-Vietnamese relations. In mid-1994 Russian security police seized cash and merchandise worth millions from Vietnamese traders in Moscow said to be operating illegally. Months before Vietnamese customs officials had impounded cargo of a Russian freighter for technical violations. And in June, when Premier Vo Van Kiet visited Moscow – the first time for a Vietnamese premier since the demise of the Soviet Union – President Yeltsin cancelled a scheduled meeting. There were apparently differences between the two countries over several matters, such as the terms for Russian forces remaining at Camranh Bay and the particulars of debt repayment by Vietnam. But on 11 April 1995 a new treaty of friendly relations was signed in Hanoi, without the provisions being announced (*Indochina Digest*, 17 June, 1 July 1994; 14 April 1995).

To become involved in the ASEAN economic potential, to enlarge the bilateral economic relations, as well as to promote the process of multilateral discussion of regional security problems, was an important part of the realization of Russia's national interests. The Russian foreign minister attended the ASEAN Foreign Ministers' Meeting in Manila in July 1992 and 1993 and continued the official dialogue with them. Russia expressed its desire to be a full member of ASEAN PMC dialogue and in the summer of 1994 participated in the ASEAN regional security forum. The Russian foreign minister in his address in July 1993 at the Consultative Meeting with ASEAN ministers of foreign affairs put forward the following proposals on 'Regional Security Community' in Asia Pacific:

Establishment of a Conflict Prevention Centre (capable in the future of effective peacemaking activities in accordance with the UN Charter);

Establishment of a Centre for Regional Strategic Studies;

Elaboration of an Arms Trade Code for the Asia Pacific
(Russia is ready to supply ASEAN countries with up-to-date defence weapons, provided a reasonable balance is maintained between regional stability requirement, the legitimate defence interests of states in the region and the interests of arms suppliers);

Political resolution of territorial disputes that still exist in Southeast Asia. (Russia supported the ASEAN proposal on the zone of freedom and neutrality in SE Asia and the idea of declaring this area nuclear-free. *Diplomaticheskii Vestnik,* July 1993)

Former Soviet Central Asian republics are very active in establishing working relations with ASEAN countries, especially with Muslims. The president of Uzbekistan, Islam Karimov, for example, very successfully visited Malaysia and Indonesia in June 1992.

Russia itself is interested in ASEAN experience in regional integration, because comprehensive strengthening of the Commonwealth of Independent States was declared as Russia's primary goal. Russia also wants to participate in APEC activities and is ready to consult with ASEAN countries on these issues. It is especially appropriate now because the APEC Secretariat is located in Singapore.

Trade and economic cooperation are important elements of Russia's relations with SE Asian countries. The volume of trade between Russia and ASEAN countries in 1992 was US$ 1.24 billion, with Russian exports of US$ 624 million, and imports of US$ 616 million. People from the Russian Far East would like to attract ASEAN investments, but mismanagement, confusion of power-sharing between central and local authorities and lack of legal regulations still prevent ASEAN business people from investing there.

Russia, as a new state in the process of radical reforms, is very much interested in the Asian experience of economic reforms; this is, so to say, another 'ideological sphere' of possible cooperation between ASEAN countries and Moscow. Development of bilateral relations with ASEAN countries is a very important part of Russia's contacts with this regional organization.

Russian–Indonesian relations have a long history, the most important bilateral ties with an ASEAN member. The first Russian vice-consulate in Jakarta was opened in 1865. In 1950 USSR established diplomatic relations with independent Indonesia. In the 1950s and early 60s Soviet-Indonesian relations developed rapidly, Moscow provided technical assistance to Jakarta. But after the attempted coup by the Maoist Communist Party of Indonesia and establishment of military rule, President Suharto sharply reduced contacts with all socialist countries, including the Soviet Union. The political dialogue resumed in the early 1980s, continuing with the leaders of the Russian Federation. Still trade between the two countries was fairly small: in 1992 US$ 46.5 million (Russian imports: $31.3 million, exports: $15.2 million). Indonesian business is interested in establishing joint ventures with Russian partners, first of all in Moscow and then in the Far East. There are good prospects for cooperation in palm oil processing and air transportation. Moscow and Jakarta are also exploring possibilities of developing military ties, and cooperation in military conversion.

The Malaysian minister of foreign affairs was the first high-level representative of ASEAN countries to visit the Russian Federation after the break-up of the Soviet Union in May 1992. He recognized that there were no limits for the development of Russian–Malaysian relations in all fields. Russia buys Malaysian palm oil, rubber and tin, and sells fertilizers and medicines. A number of joint ventures were established between the Russian and Malaysian firms in such spheres as palm oil processing, production of medicines from latex, export of technologies, etc.

On 7 June 1994, a deal was finally signed under which Kuala Lumpur would buy 18 Russian MIG-29 interceptors for about US$ 550 million. Malaysia will pay for the planes partially by supplies of palm oil. Attracted by bargain prices, Malaysia becomes the first non-communist state in Eastern Asia to operate Russian military equipment. Russia will set up a technical service centre in Malaysia to maintain the airplanes (Vatikiotis, 1994).

While Russia and Thailand established diplomatic relations in 1898, the contact remained cool due to several political differences between them. But it seems that nowadays Moscow and Bangkok are becoming closer. The Thai government authorized US$8 million for programmes of assistance to Russia for 1993, and already in 1992 had provided humanitarian assistance to Moscow. In 1992 bilateral trade was almost

US $400 million. A Russian trading company, Aviaexport, sold to the Thai army 33 MI–17V helicopters, spare parts, a simulator and one VIP model for US$130 million as a semi-barter deal (half of the money to be spent on imports of Thai products, including rice). Thai private companies are very active in Russia and vice versa. The perspectives for bilateral cooperation in science and technology are encouraging. Tourism between Russia and Thailand is flourishing.

Russian private entrepreneurs are very much attracted by Singapore and opportunities for doing business there. Trade between Russia and Singapore is increasing (in 1991: US$500 million.) By the end of 1992 over twenty joint ventures with investments from Singapore were registered in the Russian Federation (statistics from Russian Ministry of Foreign Trade Relations).

Russian relations were good with the Philippines under Marcos. Nowadays Moscow and Manila are in the process of deep reformation of their societies, which add new points of common interest to the political agendas of their leaders.

Russian foreign policy is going through a process of transition strongly affected by Russian domestic problems, but it is clear that 'the Greater ASEAN' (including Indochina) will be an important counterpart for Russia in the international arena and in political dialogue and economic cooperation; for instance, it now sits in the meetings of the ARF. Russia's role in the region is much smaller than was that of the Soviet Union. But the downsizing itself, removing any sense of threat, opens up new opportunities, especially economic, that were not available before 1990.

Note

1. The ASEAN academic point of view on this topic is well presented by Mathiah Aligappa (1990).

References

Aligappa, Muthiah (1990) 'Soviet Policy in Southeast Asia: Towards Engagement', East-West Center Reprint Series, International Relations Program.
Diplomaticheskii Vestnik (1993) July.
Far Eastern Economic Review (1987) 26 March.
Indochina Digest (Washington, DC) (1995) 14 April; (1994) 17 June, 1 July.

Interfax News Agency (1992) 1 August.

Izvestia (1989) 14 February.

Pravda (1990) 13–18 February.

Russia, Ministry of Foreign Trade Relations, *Statistical Series* (various).

Thakur, Ramesh and Carlyle Thayer (eds) (1993), *Reshaping Regional Relations: Asia-Pacific and the Former Soviet Union* (Boulder: Westview).

Vatikiotis, Michael (1994) 'Wings of Change', *Far Eastern Economic Review*, 16 June, p. 20.

8 China and Southeast Asia: The Challenge of Economic Competition

Robert S. Ross

The Soviet-Vietnamese alliance and the Vietnamese occupation of Cambodia polarized Southeast Asia throughout the 1980s. China opposed the Vietnamese occupation of Cambodia and founded the regional coalition resisting the Soviet-Vietnamese alliance. In that era of heightened threat perception, it was not difficult for Chinese diplomats to devise successful policy. An unyielding hard line against Moscow and Hanoi satisfied China's requirements *vis-à-vis* its adversaries while the strategic imperative encouraged Beijing's regional allies to develop cooperative relations with China. The diplomacy was relatively simple, but it was also successful. Thanks largely to the crumbling of the Soviet bloc, by 1989 China had accomplished its strategic objectives in Indochina.

But having won the contest over Indochina, Beijing must now adjust to the challenges of victory. Although it can take satisfaction from current trends in Indochina, Southeast Asia is no longer polarized by security concerns and China's contribution to regional security has diminished. Moreover, the Southeast Asian agenda has shifted from strategic to economic interests. This agenda affords Beijing reduced opportunities to contribute to regional objectives. Thus, despite having won the Cold War in Indochina, China faces an uncertain future in the region since the dawn of the 'New World Order'.

CHINA AND THE COALITION AGAINST SOVIET-VIETNAMESE COOPERATION

After failing to prevent Soviet-Vietnamese cooperation in Indochina in the late 1970s, in the 1980s China helped 'roll back' Vietnamese and Soviet influence on its southern periphery by inflicting high costs on their efforts to sustain the status quo. Simultaneously, Beijing focused attention on the members of the Association of South East Asian Nations (Thailand, Malaysia, Singapore, Brunei, Indonesia and the Philippines), seeking aid in punishing Vietnamese and Soviet expansionism. And while Beijing cooperated with ASEAN, it consolidated bilateral relations with the member countries. Because China was the crucial strategic component of the anti-Vietnamese coalition, the ASEAN states needed Chinese cooperation and they tailored their China policies accordingly.

Rolling Back Soviet-Vietnamese Expansion

On 23 October 1991 representatives of the warring Cambodian factions signed in Paris the Agreement on a Comprehensive Political Settlement for the Cambodian Conflict, formalizing a cease-fire between the parties and the basis for ending the thirteen-year war in Cambodia. The agreement established the domestic and international responsibilities of the Supreme National Council (SNC), a coalition body composed of representatives from all the contending groups and led by then Prince Norodom Sihanouk. It also called for the 1993 United Nations-sponsored election in Cambodia to choose the Cambodian leadership that would ultimately replace the SNC (*Agreement*, especially Section III). On this basis, representatives of all of the resistance factions returned to Phnom Penh supposedly to work with the former Vietnamese-supported government and participate in the elections. Although sporadic, low-level fighting continues to occur after the departure of UN peace-keeping forces, the UN process offered a realistic possibility to establish peace in Cambodia and signified the end of the military-based competition among the outside powers, including Vietnam and China, for influence in Cambodia. China was clearly pleased with the course of events and quickly welcomed the outcome of the elections.

But in the most important respects China achieved its strategic objectives in Indochina over two years prior to the signing of the 1991 agreement (Ross, 1991). Diminished Soviet influence in Vietnam was China's major objective and it held Sino-Soviet détente hostage to Soviet concessions on Indochina. By 1988 the combination of Chinese policy and Soviet domestic difficulties compelled Moscow to apply military and political pressure on Hanoi to withdraw from Cambodia. The most dramatic development was Moscow's failure to support Vietnam during its March 1988 naval clash with China in the disputed Spratly Islands. Moscow's security commitment to Hanoi further deteriorated as it drew down its naval presence at Cam Ranh Bay. It also significantly cut back its levels of new economic assistance to Vietnam, undermining Hanoi's ability to wage war in Cambodia, prepare for war against China and develop its economy.

China not only sought Soviet retrenchment from Vietnam to reduce Soviet encirclement but also to promote Vietnamese withdrawal from Cambodia and a corresponding increase in Chinese influence in a 'Balkanized' Indochina – China's second strategic objective for Indochina. Hanoi could tolerate civil war in Cambodia and Chinese military presence on the Sino-Vietnamese border as long as Moscow guaranteed Vietnamese security and paid the bills. But in the context of diminished Soviet military, political and economic support, Vietnam faced Chinese power in strategic isolation and was compelled to accommodate to China's demands. These developments culminated in Hanoi's withdrawal of its troops from Cambodia by September 1989.

But for the two years following the Vietnamese withdrawal from Cambodia, Beijing continued to support the Khmer Rouge, seeking the formal dissolution of the Vietnamese-installed 'puppet' Phnom Penh leadership and the transfer of formal sovereignty to the SNC. This demand reflected China's insistence that Vietnam gain nothing from its 1978 invasion of Cambodia, not even the possession of legal sovereignty by its Phnom Penh allies. China was inflexible and it was prepared to resist compromise and support the Khmer Rouge indefinitely. The Comprehensive Political Settlement reflected considerable Chinese success. The Phnom Penh government was legally dissolved and the SNC was recognized as the 'unique legitimate body and source of authority in which . . . the sovereignty, independence and unity of Cambodia are enshrined'. The SNC represented Cambodia in the United Nations and in other international organizations. The status of the former Phnom Penh government was reduced to mere 'administrative agencies, bodies, and offices'. Moreover, the role of the United Nations in Cambodia during the transition period also met Chinese demands. Not only did it supervise the elections, but also key government services, including foreign affairs, defence, finance, public security and information, thus attempting to deprive the Hun Sen leadership of many of the advantages of incumbency. Finally, the agreement did not criticize the odious policies of the Khmer Rouge during the 1975–8 period. On the contrary, it would have made possible full Khmer Rouge participation in the new post-election Cambodian government.

Developments in Cambodia since the UN-sponsored elections have clearly fallen short of international expectations. The continued unwillingness of the Khmer Rouge leadership to forsake war and to join the new government has led to continued violence and interferes with Phnom Penh's efforts to stabilize and develop the Cambodian economy. Chinese leaders have opposed Khmer Rouge recalcitrance and have publicly supported the position of Sihanouk and the other members of the Cambodian government regarding the role of the Khmer Rouge in post-war Cambodia. But their ability to influence the Khmer Rouge has declined. The Thai government has provided the Khmer Rouge army with a sanctuary in Thai territory and has tolerated the profitable trade between the Khmer Rouge and the Thai military. But despite the adverse circumstances within Cambodia, China can take considerable satisfaction from the outcome of the peace process and the resulting circumstances throughout Indochina.

China–ASEAN Cooperation

As with China's bilateral Soviet and Vietnam policies, Beijing formulated policy toward the ASEAN countries in the context of Soviet-Vietnamese military cooperation. The Soviet Union and Vietnam were China's adversaries, while China and the ASEAN states were strategic partners and Chinese interests benefited from the necessity for cooperation.

ASEAN's contribution to the anti-Vietnam coalition primarily consisted of its global diplomacy aimed at imposing on Hanoi and Phnom Penh diplomatic and economic isolation. Given the high standing of the ASEAN states among both developed and developing countries, they were able to make a vital contribution to the international economic isolation of Vietnam and, thus, to Vietnam's inability to sustain its war in Cambodia. China benefited immensely from ASEAN participation in the anti-Vietnamese coalition.

China's bilateral relationship with each ASEAN state also benefited from their opposition to the Vietnamese occupation of Cambodia. In the context of strategic cooperation, the ASEAN states sought consolidated bilateral relations with China. This trend was especially clear in Sino-Thai relations, central to which was a common interest in resisting the Vietnamese takeover. Although China's main focus was the Soviet presence on its southern border and Thailand's focus was the Vietnamese military presence on the Thai border, in practice they coordinated their policies to maximize the diplomatic and military pressure on Vietnam. After Hanoi occupied Cambodia in 1978, Bangkok permitted the Chinese-supported Khmer Rouge and the other anti-Phnom

Penh forces to use its territory and allowed China to transport military goods across Thailand to the resistance forces. In return, China stopped support for the Thai communists and even replaced the United States as Thailand's primary security partner, offsetting the threat of Vietnamese power which had arrived on the Thai border. The deployment of 300,000 Chinese troops on the Vietnamese border and the possibility that Beijing would teach Hanoi a second 'lesson' provided Thailand with sufficient security to resist Vietnam's occupation of Cambodia.

For China the relationship with Thailand was more than a convenient partnership against Vietnamese power, however. Beijing sought a long-term strategic relationship with Bangkok to assure China an ongoing voice in affairs on its southern periphery. Central to this effort was the development of Sino-Thai military relations. Since the early 1980s Chinese and Thai senior officers have frequently visited each other's countries to consult on mutual concerns. In recent years the Chinese Minister of Defence, Qin Jiwei, and the commander of the Chinese Air Force, General Wang Hai, visited Bangkok and the commander of the Thai Navy, Admiral Praphat Kritsanachan, visited Beijing. Lower-level exchanges have also occurred. In 1990 a Chinese naval training vessel visited Thailand (*FBIS/China*, 6 December 1990, p. 5; 13 December 1990, p. 19). Beijing and Bangkok also developed an arms-sales relationship. Although Chinese weaponry may be far from the latest in technological capability, it is often well-suited to Thai requirements of maintaining domestic stability in its outer regions and along the coastline. Moreover, Beijing has offered such weaponry at 'friendship' terms far below the international market price. Since 1987, when the two sides opened discussions on arms sales, China has sold Thailand tanks, artillery and armoured personnel carriers. It also completed construction on the first of six guided missile escort vessels it has agreed to build for Thailand (*FBIS/China*, 6 July 1990, p. 14; 13 December 1990, p. 19; 21 November 1988, p. 34; *FEER*, 8 December 1988).

China also moved to develop economic relations with Thailand. Sino-Thai trade has expanded and Thai investment in China has increased. Most important, China has become one of the largest purchasers of Thai rice, at times buying it despite a sufficient domestic supply.

Faced with what it perceived as an intolerable security threat, Bangkok developed a strategic relationship with Beijing as Hanoi's principal adversary. This same strategic complementarity helped consolidate relations between China and the other ASEAN states. China particularly benefited from Singapore's intense opposition to the Vietnamese occupation of Cambodia; Chinese and Singapore positions on a political settlement of the Cambodian civil war were nearly indistinguishable. Hence, despite the absence of formal Sino-Singaporean diplomatic ties prior to 1990, close political relations developed. Lee Kuan Yew visited Beijing numerous times and Chinese leaders frequently reciprocated. Singapore also developed the most extensive economic ties with China of any Southeast Asian country. Central to Singapore's calculation was the importance of China in the anti-Vietnamese coalition. Indeed, Singapore pursued good relations with Beijing despite its reluctance to offend Indonesia, which remained suspicious of Chinese ambitions.

Even China's relationship with Indonesia also benefited from the imperative of anti-Vietnamese cooperation. Although Jakarta consistently perceived China as a challenge to Indonesian regional leadership and was relatively sympathetic to Vietnamese objectives concerning China, it soft-pedalled its suspicions in the interest of ASEAN unity. To minimize intra-ASEAN friction, Jakarta had to acknowledge Thailand's strategic dilemma, the necessity for Vietnam to withdraw completely from Cambodia, and the corresponding importance of cooperation with Beijing. Moreover, Jakarta countenanced developing Sino-Singaporean relations and it also moved to develop its own limited economic ties with Beijing.

Thailand, Singapore and Indonesia were the ASEAN states most involved in the Cambodian conflict. Nonetheless, China's relationship with all of the ASEAN states reflected this general trend. In the strategic context of Chinese opposition to both Soviet and Vietnamese power in Southeast Asia as well as of US-China cooperation, there was a natural tendency for all of the ASEAN states to develop good relations with China. Simply put, the Soviet-Vietnamese military advance into Cambodia, while temporarily undermining Chinese security *vis-à-vis* the Soviet Union, enabled China to consolidate relations with the ASEAN states.

DEALING WITH SUCCESS: CHINA AND SOUTHEAST ASIA AFTER CAMBODIA

In the post-Cambodia era, Chinese leaders must make policy in the absence of a Soviet threat on China's southern border. This is surely a major improvement on the era of Soviet 'encirclement' and it creates opportunities for advancing Chinese interests. But in the absence of Soviet and Vietnamese expansionism, the ASEAN states no longer need such close cooperation with China. Moreover, although China has eliminated many of its traditional diplomatic liabilities in Southeast Asia, in the aftermath of the Cold War, regional diplomacy will increasingly focus on economic matters. China will have difficulty adjusting to these developments and, over the long term, may face insurmountable obstacles to maintaining even its present role in regional affairs.

Emerging Chinese Strategic Authority in Indochina

In the wake of the Soviet retreat from Indochina, no other state can offset China's considerable strategic power on its periphery. Having first helped to oust the United States and then the Soviet Union from Indochina, for the foreseeable future China will be the dominant military power in the region, which will significantly shape the developments to come. Not only has China sought improved relations with the Indochinese countries now that it is dealing from strength, but the Indochinese countries themselves will have little alternative other than to reconcile themselves to Chinese power.

Hanoi had long sought improved Sino-Vietnamese relations while it occupied Cambodia, but Chinese leaders resisted for fear of encouraging Vietnamese intransigence and undermining the anti-Vietnamese international coalition. Now, however, Sino-Vietnamese detente has been taking place on Chinese terms. With the emergence of Vietnam from strategic isolation and Vietnamese withdrawal from Cambodia, Beijing was prepared to be flexible. One of the first signs of this changing posture was the curtailment of the Chinese military incursions into Vietnamese territory that had required Hanoi to maintain a high state of military preparedness. China also agreed to open the border to trade between local residents. Then, shortly after Vietnam's January 1989 announcement that it would withdraw its troops from Cambodia by September 1989, the Chinese Foreign Ministry received a Vietnamese Foreign Ministry official for the first time since 1978 (*FBIS/China*, 12 January 1989, p. 9). In late 1990, when Hanoi appeared to have made significant concessions on a Cambodian political settlement, Chinese leaders hosted a Sino-Vietnamese summit in southwest China. Reflecting its recognition of China's developing regional authority, by early 1991 Hanoi had sent six delegations to Beijing while China had sent only one delegation to Hanoi.

This trend culminated in the visit to Beijing in November 1991 by Vietnamese Communist Party General Secretary Do Muoi and Premier Vo Van Kiet and the formal normalization of relations. Now that Vietnam had sent its senior leadership to Beijing to seek normal relations, in February 1992 Beijing sent Foreign Minister Qian Qichen to Hanoi. This was the highest-level Chinese delegation to Vietnam since the early 1970s.

Subsequently, the two sides reopened air and train service between the two countries and opened numerous ports to trade. In 1991 the value of two-way border trade between Guangxi Province and Vietnam alone was over US $150 million. The trend in 1992 suggested that the volume of trade for the year would be twice that of 1991. State-level trade should also begin to increase in the near future (*FBIS/China*, 10 August 1992, p. 11; 7 August 1992, p. 4).

China's relationship with Laos has also improved in recent years. Vietnam's preoccupation with domestic economic problems, its troop withdrawal from Laos in 1988, and its lack of Soviet strategic support meant that Vientiane had both the occasion and the need to improve ties with China. Likewise, Beijing, for the first time since the 1970s, saw the opportunity to establish a presence in Laos. In these circumstances, China and Laos began economic exchanges along the border and then improved political relations. In October 1989 Chinese leaders welcomed Lao Party Secretary Kaysone Phomvihane to Beijing for the first Sino-Lao summit since the 1970s and in December 1990 Li Peng paid a reciprocal visit to Vientiane. In 1990 the two sides also signed an interim border agreement calling for a joint aerial survey of the boundary. Furthermore, in an apparent contemporary strategic equivalent to Sino-Lao road-building in northern Laos in the 1970s, during the 1990s the two sides will cooperate in the development of an airfield in northern Laos (*FBIS/China*, 2 August 1990, pp.4–5; 27 August 1990, p. 8).

Sino-Cambodian relations suggest a similar trend. In the aftermath of retrenched Vietnamese power and Hanoi's diminished ability to contribute to Phnom Penh's economic or strategic security, Phnom Penh has the need and the opportunity to pursue Cambodia's traditional post-independence diplomatic practice of developing cooperative relations with both Beijing and Hanoi. In current strategic circumstances, only good relations with Beijing can bring peace to Cambodia and permit political stability, regardless of the composition of the Cambodian leadership. Hun Sen's willingness to hold SNC meetings in Beijing under *de facto* Chinese auspices indicates that this trend had already begun long before the culmination of the UN process. And, as Prince Sihanouk observed, that the SNC chose China as its first country to visit after the signing of the Comprehensive Political Settlement expressed

Cambodian 'respect for the Chinese government and people'(*FBIS/Chinc*, 9 April 1992, p. 15). Similarly, recent Chinese diplomacy reflects Beijing's confidence in its regional authority and a corresponding willingness to work even with the Vietnamese installed 'puppets' within a coalition leadership. China not only welcomed the SNC, including Hun Sen, to Beijing in July 1991, before the conclusion of the peace negotiations, but it has consistently treated the Hun Sen leadership with greater diplomatic respect than the other factional leaders, with the exception of Prince Sihanouk.

China's policy toward Cambodia since the deterioration of the coalition government and the resurgence of violence in Cambodia has not changed. Despite its limited influence over the Khmer Rouge, it has tried to persuade this faction to lay down its weapons and join the Phnom Penh government, thereby accepting the dominant powers in Phnom Penh and a limited governing role for the Khmer Rouge there. China continues to seek stability in Cambodia, regardless of the composition of the Cambodian leadership, confident that any Phnom Penh leadership will accommodate Cambodian foreign policy to Chinese power to both offset Vietnamese power and to promote Chinese support for domestic stability in Cambodia.

Toward Reduced Friction in China-ASEAN Relations

Thus, in the aftermath of its victory over Soviet-Vietnamese cooperation in Cambodia, Beijing looks forward to the benefits of being the dominant strategic power in a 'Balkanized' Indochina. Nevertheless, China's achievement of secure southern borders has undermined its ability to maintain cooperative relationships with the ASEAN states.

Chinese leaders recognize that as the Cold War continues to recede in Asia, economic diplomacy will gradually become the dominant form of competition in Southeast Asia. But they also argue that this is a transition era leading to a more uncertain and complex multipolar regional order in which more intense strategic competition between the great powers is likely and in which the economic and technological bases of power, developed during the contemporary period, will assume increased military significance. As one senior Chinese analyst explained, the 'race for overall national strength and high technology' will 'ultimately determine the balance of power in the world' (Wang Shu, in *FBIS/China*, 9 April 1992, pp. 3–4). Another Chinese analyst observed that the 1990s are a 'crucial period', during which the 'results of . . . competition in national strength will decide the places of various countries in the world in the next century, and their roles in the new world order' (Ren Zhengde, in *FBIS/China*, 25 August 1992, pp. 1–5).

Chinese leaders are concerned that as economic diplomacy assumes heightened salience in post-Cold War Southeast Asia, Japanese economic penetration of the region will increase, allowing Tokyo critical political influence. Because of China's deep suspicion of Japanese ambitions and its assumption that Japanese political and economic power will almost inevitably lead to military power, Beijing views this prospect with apprehension. One commentator argued that as an 'economic superpower', Japan is 'vigorously pursuing "superpower diplomacy"', increasing its political influence in the Asia–Pacific region'. Another analyst reflected that whereas the US military and economic position in the region is 'on the decline', Japan's 'economic strength is gaining dramatically', resulting in 'enormous political and economic influence on the ASEAN countries'(Wan Guang, in *FBIS/China*, 24 August 1990, pp. 2–3; Lin Xiao, in *JPRS/China*, 15 February 1989, pp. 4–5; Tao Bingwei, in *FBIS/China*, 14 May 1990, p. 16; Tian Zhongqing, in *JPRS/China*, 29 May 1990, pp. 6–9; Whiting, 1989). At minimum, Chinese leaders are asking if in the 1990s, Japan, as an 'economic superpower', will pursue 'economic hegemonism'? But concern for Japanese military power is also prevalent. When Japan sent minesweepers to the Persian Gulf, it signalled an initial step towards Tokyo's objective to becoming a 'political giant' and to 'seek military backing for its bid to become a political power'. Its decision to end its ban on sending troops abroad by agreeing to participate in UN peacekeeping activities revealed that, having achieved economic power, Tokyo was 'demanding a "major political actor's" position'. This ambitious objective also explains why Tokyo seeks a permanent seat on the UN Security Council (*FBIS/China*, 3 January 1992, pp. 18–19; Tang Tianri, in *FBIS/China*, 1 July 1992, pp. 7–8; *FEER*, 25 June 1992).

Thus, China's primary objective in post-Cold War maritime Southeast Asia is to contend with the potential prospect of Japanese regional dominance. Despite the ongoing tension in US–China relations, Beijing welcomes a continued US strategic presence in Southeast Asia. It is confident that so long as the United States remains an Asian power, Japan will restrain its military development programme. Nonetheless, as is the case with leaders of most of the Southeast Asian countries, Chinese leaders are not confident that in the post-Cold War era the United States will perform the role of regional balancer. Hence, Beijing is not prepared to rely on American foreign policy to achieve its regional objectives. It seeks to develop its own capability to contend with Japan's growing regional presence.

Thus, China currently seeks a 'peaceful international environment' in which to develop its economy and economic relations with the more advanced economies in preparation for a more contentious future: 'To China, a stable situation in the Asia–Pacific region undoubtedly offers a rare opportunity which is favourable to economic construction.' Ultimately, economic construction will provide the foundation for 'comprehensive national power' (Li Weiguo, in *FBIS/China*, 9 June 1992, pp. 1–2). Thus, as is the case with other regional powers, Beijing has been actively engaged in 'smiling diplomacy'. Chinese leaders make frequent visits to the region to hold friendly discussions on a wide range of issues. In 1992, for example, President Yang Shangkun, Vice Premier Yao Yilin and Foreign Minister Qian Qichen all visited Southeast Asia.

Moreover, in many respects China entered the post-Cold War era in a good position to pursue its objective of developing better relations with its neighbours. Primarily due to developments within the ASEAN states, the issues of Chinese ties to the illegal Communist parties and the ethnic Chinese in Southeast Asia no longer significantly obstruct relations with the ASEAN states. Since the 1970s China has distanced itself from the region's illegal communist movements so that its relations with these parties would not interfere with the development of official relations. But the major factor leading to the declining relevance of these Communist parties in China's regional diplomacy is the host government's enhanced stability and legitimacy. This trend is particularly clear in Malaysia. Beijing's relationship with the Malayan Communist Party (MCP) in the 1950s and 1960s continued to arouse concern in Kuala Lumpur through the 1980s. Then economic development and Thai-Malaysia border cooperation compelled the MCP leadership to concede defeat. In December 1989 the MCP agreed to destroy its weapons, 'respect' the laws of Malaysia, and 'participate' in economic development. Moreover, the Voice of Malayan Democracy, one of China's last ties to the MCP, ceased operation in January 1990 (*FBIS/Trends*, 18 January 1990, p. 36).

Malaysia may be the most dramatic example of the elimination of the diplomatic significance of the illegal Communist parties, but the same trend is evident in Sino-Indonesian relations. China's ties with the Communist Party of Indonesia (CPI) and the CPI's involvement in President Sukarno's anti-military plot in 1965 continued to create suspicion of Chinese intentions in Indonesia into the 1980s. Yet by the late 1980s Jakarta had gained sufficient confidence in its domestic security that it no longer feared CPI subversion, regardless of the Party's relationship with Beijing. To re-establish diplomatic relations with Beijing, Jakarta waited twenty-five years after the break and nearly fifteen years after both the emergence of a moderate Chinese leadership and the opening of relations with China by Malaysia, Thailand and the Philippines. Although this delay partially reflected the depth of the leadership's concern for domestic stability, Jakarta's decision to normalize relations also reflected Indonesia's changed domestic environment and its corresponding heightened confidence in its dealings with China.

This trend in the declining importance of the illegal Communist parties is mirrored by the diminished importance of the region's ethnic Chinese in China's relations with local governments.* For many years Southeast Asian governments feared that Beijing could manipulate their Chinese populations to undermine domestic security. Although actual Chinese leverage may have been minimal, Beijing worked assiduously to eliminate such suspicions (Ross, 1988). But similar to the trend concerning illegal Communist parties, the primary source of change was the domestic situation within the ASEAN states.

Beijing's perceived threat through ties to the ethnic Chinese had appeared strongest in Singapore, a predominantly Chinese state. In Indonesia and Malaysia the ethnic Chinese are in a minority but are a prosperous and economically influential sector of society. Therefore, they are politically suspect and the focus of potentially destabilizing racism. The economic success of the ASEAN states and historical circumstances, however, have done much to alleviate leadership concerns, despite the occasional and spontaneous outbreak of anti-Chinese violence in parts of the region. First, since the late 1980s the fruits of modernization have spread through the population, gradually reducing the economic basis for racial tension and the disproportionate economic influence of the Chinese minority in the host economy while also lessening the attractiveness of the Chinese mainland for Chinese abroad. Second, it has been nearly fifty years since Chinese emigration to Southeast Asia ended. The number of Chinese who were either born in China or whose parents were born there is rapidly diminishing. Only 5 per cent of the Chinese in Indonesia were born in China. This trend affects citizenship issues insofar as the majority of Chinese in Southeast Asia now have no claim to Chinese citizenship. This trend also points to the gradual assimilation of ethnic Chinese as their educational and economic outlook is becoming predominantly shaped by the indigenous culture. Local violence toward Chinese may not completely end, but the political and foreign policy significance of the local Chinese populations has diminished.

The first state to evidence reduced concern over Beijing's alleged manipulation of the overseas Chinese was Singapore, despite its Chinese majority. As the earliest ASEAN state to develop its economy and thus secure domestic legitimacy, Singapore has pursued improved relations with Beijing since the early 1980s, and now has the most extensive economic relationship with China of any ASEAN state. A similar trend is apparent with Indonesia and Malaysia. In 1990 Jakarta normalized relations, formalized trade and restored direct air service with China. This reflected confidence that expanded trade, political relations and contact between Indonesia's ethnic Chinese and China would neither enable Beijing to manipulate the Chinese minority to the regime's disadvantage nor significantly undermine the assimilation of ethnic Chinese (*FEER*, 14 February 1991, p. 55). Kuala Lumpur is further advanced in this direction. By 1991 there were thirteen Sino-Malaysian joint ventures in China, worth US$500 million, while Kuala Lumpur had approved seven such joint ventures for Malaysia. Moreover, in August 1990, it lifted restrictions on Malaysians wishing to visit China, an important step given traditional concerns (*FEER*, 14 February 1991, p. 55; *FBIS/China*, 11 December 1990, pp. 17–18).

These developments have reduced the diplomatic friction between China and the ASEAN states. They also permitted China to normalize relations with Indonesia and Singapore. Indonesia, as the largest and most influential of the non-communist Southeast Asia nations, was a target of Chinese diplomacy throughout the 1970s and 1980s. Beijing promoted cooperative relations and bilateral trade had already reached nearly $800 million in 1989 (*FBIS/China*, 5 July 1990, pp. 20–21). But Indonesia's reluctance to develop full relations with China inhibited its neighbours from doing so. Singapore was the most striking case of this: it insisted that it would not establish diplomatic relations with China until Indonesia did. Malaysia, Brunei, and, to a lesser extent, the Philippines also considered Indonesian suspicion of China when they decided on their China policy.

Normalization of relations between Jakarta and Beijing was a major contribution to China's regional objectives. President Suharto maintained that it was time to look toward the future rather than dwell on past conflicts and suspicions. He insisted that 'it would be unjust and unrealistic if we, who are living in the present . . . should constantly bear the burden inherited from history' and expressed his 'hope' that the two countries would 'see the re-establishment of the interrupted bonds of friendship and the restoration of positive cooperation' (*FBIS/China*, 8 August 1990, pp. 5–6). Shortly thereafter Singapore established diplomatic relations with Beijing. Then, during his December 1990 visit to Kuala Lumpur, Chinese Premier Li Peng heard Malaysian Prime Minister Mahathir affirm that the restoration of diplomatic relations with Indonesia and the establishment of diplomatic relations with Singapore prove that 'ASEAN recognizes the role that the PRC can play in affecting the prosperity and stability' of the region (*FBIS/China*, 11 December 1990, pp. 17–18). Thus, normalization of relations with Singapore and Indonesia not only contributed to China's immediate objective of offsetting the damage to its relations with the advanced industrial economies caused by the June 1989 Beijing massacre, but also contributed to Beijing's long-term regional objectives. With good reason, a symposium of Chinese international relations experts held by the State Council's Centre for International Studies concluded that the 'major progress' in China's Southeast Asia diplomacy is 'an important link' in its efforts 'to strive for a benign international environment' (*FBIS/China*, 7 January 1991, pp. 3–6).

China and the Economic Diplomacy of Southeast Asia

Thus, China enters the new era in an improved position. Two traditional obstacles to developing ties between China and the ASEAN states – ethnic Chinese minorities and illegal Communist parties – are becoming less salient. In addition, China has finally placed Sino-Indonesian relations on a new footing, promising enhanced bilateral cooperation and greater Chinese diplomatic access throughout the region.

But having cleared the agenda of Cold War issues, China must adjust to post-Cold War issues. Indeed, for the most part recent Chinese diplomatic advances have merely removed Cold War impediments to Chinese policy. Similarly, smiling diplomacy may produce headlines and eloquent speeches, but it cannot provide the foundation for a long-term regional role. Essentially, Beijing has yet to show that it has the ability to compete in the post-Cold War era as economic policy instruments assume greater prominence.

The major obstacle to effective Chinese participation in the economic diplomacy of Southeast Asia is the lack of close economic ties between China and its Southeast Asian neighbours. In the past there was little complementarity between China and the developing countries of Southeast Asia and thus little basis for Chinese economic involvement in the region. Indeed, for the most part, China and the ASEAN states have been competitors for market share in other countries, including the United States (Chia, 1988; Chia and Cheng, 1987). Moreover, China's combined trade with all six of the ASEAN countries was only $10.5 billion in 1993, approximately equal to total Sino-South Korean trade and considerably less than total trade between China and Taiwan. Singapore is China's most significant trade partner among the ASEAN states, yet in 1993 it ranked only seventh in total trade among Chinese trade partners, and had only 60 per cent of the combined trade between Russia and China and less than half of combined Sino-South Korean trade. Most revealing, China was only Singapore's tenth largest export market, absorbing a mere 2.6 per cent of total Singapore exports. This trend is even more pronounced among the other ASEAN countries. For example, China was Thailand's nineteenth largest export market, absorbing .01 per cent of Thai exports (*Direction of Trade Statistics Yearbook 1994*). Similarly, the ASEAN countries have not been major foreign investors in China or elsewhere outside their region. Singapore is the largest investor in China of the ASEAN countries, but actual investment in China during 1992 was only $120 million, less than one half that of Taiwan (*FBIS/China*, 7 May 1993, pp. 15–16; 1 April 1993, p. 64). Thus, despite China's rapidly developing and modernizing economy, economic exchange between China and most countries of Southeast Asia (Lardy, 1992; Ross, 1995) remains relatively small.

The consequence of limited ASEAN trade and investment relations with China is that the ASEAN countries have yet to develop significant economic incentives to consider Chinese interests in developing policy toward other bilateral issues or in relations with third parties. Moreover, in the context of an increased need for cooperation to minimize and resolve competition-based economic disputes, multilateral economic diplomacy will assume growing importance in regional affairs. But the impetus for regional cooperation will primarily arise from the problems associated with competition among the countries with close trade relations. As one senior Chinese analyst pointed out, 'In view of the bilateral and multilateral cooperation that is so obviously helpful to everyone's economic development, the prospects for economic trade cooperation in the region during the nineties are even broader' (Tao Bingwei, in *FBIS/China*, 14 August 1990, pp. 2–4).

China, however, may well be excluded from the major diplomatic trends in Southeast Asia. Indeed, Beijing recognizes that it cannot depend on economic capability to give it a voice and it is thus reduced to demanding participation in regional institutions. Wang Shu, former director of the Foreign Ministry's Institute of International Studies, reflected this attitude when he defensively asserted that 'all countries, large or small, strong or weak, poor or rich, should be equal in economic cooperation in the Pacific region'. He remarked that 'reaching a consensus is of great significance', that 'all countries should consult with one another patiently', and that it would be 'inadvisable to force hasty conclusions, still less bully others by dint of their strength'. Wang Shu concluded with the observation that China 'has always maintained a positive attitude toward economic cooperation in the Pacific' and the warning that 'cooperation of this kind will still be incomplete without the participation of China' (Wang Shu, in *FBIS/China*, 9 April 1992, pp. 3–4).

For political reasons the industrialized Asian countries may meet Beijing's demands that China be admitted to regional multilateral organizations, as was the case with Chinese admission to Asia–Pacific Economic Cooperation (APEC). But Chinese participation in such formal institutions as APEC or the ASEAN Post-Ministerial Conference will not yield Beijing the political benefits it seeks. At best, such gatherings will provide the setting for informal discussions among concerned and influential players on discreet issues. Thus, as economic issues replace Cold War security concerns, Chinese membership in such institutions will not guarantee that Chinese interests will be addressed. Indeed, Chinese analysts note that the economic disparities in Asia will undermine the effectiveness of region-wide cooperative institutions, and substantial diplomacy will take place in smaller forums comprised of states at similar levels of development (Shi Min, in *JPRS/China*, 18 April 1990, pp. 1–4; *FEER*, 8 August 1990, pp. 9–10).

Moreover, Chinese economic weakness will likely lead to a reduction of Beijing's influence on its southern periphery. With the war in Cambodia drawing to a close, Thailand can look forward to an influential economic role in Indochina and feel less dependent on Chinese goodwill. At the same time, Tokyo's influence in Bangkok will continue to grow as Japanese investment plays an increasingly crucial role in Thai development. In this context, Bangkok's offhand suggestion that Japan and Thailand conduct joint naval exercises must have been disconcerting to Chinese leaders, despite the short-term improbability that Japan would consider naval operations more than 1000 miles beyond the home islands (*FEER*, 13 September and 24 May 1990). More recently, Japan has been active in developing economic relations with Vietnam and in 1993 became Vietnam's largest trading partner. As Hanoi emerges from the isolation of the Cold War, Japanese direct investment in Vietnam will undoubtedly grow, creating a significant Japanese economic presence in Vietnam, thus offsetting China's strategic advantages and affording Vietnam greater foreign policy flexibility. Similarly, as Hanoi gains access to capital from international financial institutions, it will purchase technology and industrial equipment from the advanced industrial countries, such as Japan, and not from China. One Chinese analyst warned of Japan's 'pronounced interest' in Indochina. Given Vietnam's historical animosity toward China and its current resentment of China's role in Indochina, Beijing must expect Vietnam to use economic diplomacy to free itself from the constraints of Chinese power (Tian, in *FBIS/China*, 1 August 1992, pp. 18–19; *FEER*, 16 July 1992).

Territorial Disputes and China's Expanding Military

Thus, China's role in Southeast Asia will be significantly determined by the trends in China's economic relations with the ASEAN countries. Perhaps the limited economic ties between China and the Southeast Asian countries merely reflects the relatively later start of the ASEAN countries toward economic development compared to the more advanced NIEs in East Asia. As their economies mature, they may well trade more with and invest more in China. Should this occur, China's economic presence in Southeast Asia will expand, thus minimizing Beijing's need to rely on its military to project power into the region. The entire region would benefit from such a development.

But should economic relations between China and the Southeast Asian countries fail to expand significantly, as suggested by their similar level of economic development and their ongoing competition for international markets, China will lack the ability to contend with other regional powers, including Japan, for political influence through economic competition. Moreover, China's economic handicap may well converge with regional apprehensions over China's expansive claim to the Spratly Islands and China's increased defense activities, thereby alienating China from the ASEAN states and further undermining China's effort to develop a positive regional presence.

In addition to China, the Philippines, Malaysia, Brunei, Vietnam and Taiwan claim some or all of the Spratly Islands. During the 1970s and 1980s, China and the ASEAN countries finessed this conflict in the interest of their larger common objective of cooperation against the Soviet-Vietnamese alliance. In the post-Cold War era, however, the necessity for strategic cooperation has diminished and the salience of the territorial dispute has increased. China's claim to islands just off the Malaysian coast, for example, has raised understandable security concerns throughout the region over Chinese intentions. Moreover, now that the ASEAN economies are more developed and their technological abilities have advanced, their interest in mining the ocean floor in the vicinity of these islands has increased. Thus, in recent years the territorial conflict has assumed increased importance in relations between China and the region.

But China's interest in the southernmost islands is only partially related to the surrounding natural resources. Insofar as China lacks the technology to mine the ocean floor, it would have to depend on Western corporations to mine the resource on China's behalf – provoking opposition from the closer claimants. Indeed, it would be far less expensive and more reliable for China to import oil, for example, than try to undertake the expensive and long-term project of off-shore drilling in the vicinity of the disputed southern islands. China's claim, however, may deter other interested parties, including Japan, from mining this area. This is no small achievement. But China also has military interests in the region. One reason for its extensive sovereignty claim is that it enables its navy to manoeuvre in the South China Sea without the difficulties of operating in 'international waters' and with the logistical facilities that the islands can support. Similarly, secure possession of larger islands – essentially unsinkable aircraft carriers – would give China a position astride the primary sea lanes between Northeast Asia and the Middle East. Given Beijing's concern for Japan's ultimate intentions and its interest in preventing Tokyo from developing enhanced regional authority, this must be considered a major strategic asset.

China is unlikely to relinquish its sovereignty claim, but has tried to finesse the issue through diplomacy. While remaining inflexible on the principle of sovereignty, it has promoted the idea of joint economic ventures in the disputed waters with the other claimants. In August 1990 Li Peng reaffirmed Beijing's interest in joint exploitation and indicated that 'after Sino-Vietnamese relations are normalized' in the aftermath of a settlement in Cambodia, China would welcome Vietnamese participation. China has also welcomed Indonesia's effort to organize a regional forum of all claimants, including Vietnam, on the condition that the agenda exclude political issues and focus on economic concerns (*FEER*, 30 August 1990, p. 11; 10 January 1991, p. 11). During his attendance as a guest at the July 1992 ASEAN foreign ministers' meeting, Chinese Foreign Minister Qian Qichen maintained that China sought a 'peaceful settlement' to the dispute. Failing that, China was prepared to 'shelve' the differences over the Spratly Islands and develop cooperative economic ventures in the South China Sea (*FBIS/PRC*, 22 July 1992, p. 1; Ji, 1992; and Chapter 13 in this volume).

But Beijing's diplomatic and economic overtures can only go so far toward ameliorating regional suspicions over Chinese territorial claims. In addition to apparent Chinese impatience to begin exploration for oil in territorial waters also claimed by Vietnam, recent Chinese military activities have aroused regional apprehension. In March 1988 Chinese forces easily overwhelmed Vietnamese units to take possession of several Spratly Islands and in early 1995 it was discovered that China had erected buildings on certain of the islands also claimed by the Philippines. Moreover, Beijing's growing interest in developing its naval capability in the South China Sea has aroused significant concern throughout the region. It has constructed a helicopter landing facility and a small port capable of receiving patrol vessels in the Paracel Islands. Small army detachments, some equipped with artillery, have conducted landing exercises on the islands. China has also improved its navigational guidance systems for naval operations in the South China Sea (*Jane's Defence Weekly*, 9 June 1990, p. 1156; *FBIS/China*, 9 March 1989, p. 35; 4 October 1989, pp. 27–8; 9 March 1990, p. 6; 14 March 1990, pp. 6–7; 19 February 1992, pp. 30–31). In 1991 Beijing announced that after three years of training it was formally incorporating the 'first ship-based aircraft unit' into its navy, apparently outfitting flat-top vessels to serve as aircraft carriers for helicopters (*FBIS/China*, 16 January 1991, p. 46; 10 January 1991, pp. 36–7; *FEER*, 9 July and 24 September 1992). Then, in 1992, Chinese acquisition from the Soviet Union of SU-27 military aircraft and of primitive air-refueling capability, and Chinese interest in late-model sophisticated Ukrainian aircraft carriers further aroused apprehension over Chinese military aspirations on the part of many Southeast Asian countries (*New York Times*, 7 June and 23 August 1992; Tai Ming Cheung, 1990; *FEER*, 6 August 1992).

Chinese naval equipment is technologically primitive. SU-27s do not enhance China's ability to defend its claims in the southern reaches of the South China Sea, even with refueling capability, and even a late-model Ukrainian aircraft carrier would not significantly expand Chinese blue-water capabilities. Similarly, purported access to military facilities in Burma will do little to improve China's limited power-projection capability. Thus, although Chinese military modernization may grant Beijing a high-profile military presence in Southeast Asia, only Vietnam need fear China's actual military capabilities amid disputed waters (Ross,1994; *FEER*, 22 December 1994). But capabilities often matter less than the perception of intentions on the part of other countries. This is exactly China's dilemma. Already handicapped by its minimal economic presence in the region, its military activities have converged with its considerable territorial claims so that many in the region have begun to see China as a potential threat rather than as a potentially constructive force for regional stability. Similarly, Beijing's increasing defence budget has aroused considerable concern throughout the region, despite the fact China's high inflation rate has offset announced budget increases so that there has been minimal real growth in this spending. The result is the undermining of China's ability to achieve its primary objective in Southeast Asia – developing a regional presence enabling it to resist the potential for increased Japanese economic and political presence in Southeast Asia.

CONCLUSION

Geography dictates that military capabilities will still matter in Indochina and that Beijing will develop a major role in shaping political relations on its southern border. A division of labour may well emerge whereby China remains the dominant strategic power in Indochina and other countries establish a significant economic presence in this subregion. China is likely to accept this arrangement quite readily. But in the rest of Southeast Asia the agenda will focus on economic development and on the corresponding importance of economic diplomacy. As in Indochina, China will not be able to compete on the economic chessboard. Furthermore, Beijing's defence programme may actually weaken China's regional presence, insofar as it will not significantly improve Chinese capabilities but may create a significant anti-China blacklash throughout the region. This is Beijing's post-Cold War dilemma and it remains unclear whether Chinese leaders recognize this dilemma and whether they have the policy-making sophistication and diplomatic ingenuity to adjust Chinese policy to maximize both Chinese interests and regional stability.

Editorial Note

The unrelenting pace of change continues in the mid-1990s to transform economic and strategic relationships between China and Southeast

Asia. Strong economic growth in China, Vietnam, Laos, Thailand and Burma has boosted trade between them. Alongside China's growing, post-1990 military, aid and trade ties with Laos there is increasing pressure for the implementation of several highway-building projects that would result in Laos becoming the main road link between China and Southeast Asia. The geopolitical as well as the economic consequences would be considerable.

China's 'special relationship' with another neighbouring Southeast Asian state predated the end of the Cold War but has increased in significance since the late 1980s. The Burmese military regime faced a widespread international arms and aid embargo in the wake of its brutal suppression of the Burmese pro-democracy movement in 1988, but in late 1989 discovered a generous and sympathetic ally in Beijing. The Chinese government offered substantial amounts of economic assistance and military hardware to the State Law and Order Resoration Council (SLORC) in Rangoon. However, SLORC's consequent economic and military dependence on China, with an accompanying flood of imported Chinese consumer goods and the considerable inflow of mostly illegal Chinese immigrants from Yunnan into urban areas in Upper Burma, has provoked a backlash against all ethnic Chinese. Burma is likely to prove to be the exception to the general downward trend in the significance of resident ethnic Chinese as an influence on China's relations with Southeast Asian countries. If highway links to Laos expand traffic rapidly, a similar phenomenon could occur there.

In the relationship with Vietnam, still to be resolved are major land and maritime boundary and territorial disputes and the future of the ethnic Chinese who fled to China from Vietnam in the late 1970s. Hanoi remains wary of Chinese intentions and of its growing power. While official Sino-Vietnamese trade expanded in the 1990s, it still ranked below China's trade with any ASEAN country except the Philippines (Womack, 1994, p. 501). Even so, Hanoi has sought to curb that expansion in order to prevent cheap Chinese imports from forcing too many Vietnamese companies out of business. Nor is it eager to encourage capital investment from China, which in February 1995 ranked only twenty-eighth in the list of sources of foreign investment in Vietnam. (The four Asian 'tigers' – Taiwan, Hong Kong, Singapore and South Korea – headed the list, followed by Japan.)

Hanoi's success in achieving full ASEAN membership in 1995 may pose a fresh challenge to Beijing's Southeast Asian policy. Vietnamese participation in ASEAN is likely to increase regional concerns about China's territorial claims and naval expansion (for information about recent Chinese activities in the South China Sea see Chapter 13), and thus make it harder for Beijing to realize its objective of promoting cooperation with ASEAN. From the Chinese point of view, however, there is one possible reassuring factor. The organization's enlarged membership will make it harder for it to reach consensus on key policy issues and if Chinese diplomacy is skilful enough it should be able to exploit differences among the member states. In any case, a multi-polar 'New World Order', while the US is distracted elsewhere and Japan is under major constitutional and political constraints, gives China more leeway than it has had for a very long time.

Note

* I am grateful to Evelyn Colbert for this insight.

References

Agreement on a Comprehensive Political Settlement of the Cambodian Conflict (1991).
Chia Siow-yue (1988) 'China's Economic Relations with the ASEAN Countries,' in Joyce K. Kallgren, Noordin Sopiee and Soedjati Djiwandono (eds), *ASEAN and China: An Evolving Relationship* (Berkeley: Institute for East Asian Studies, University of California).
Chia Siow-Yue and Cheng Bifau (eds) (1987) *ASEAN-China Economic Relations: Trends and Patterns* (Singapore: Institute of Southeast Asian Studies).
Direction of Trade Statistics Yearbook, 1994 (Washington, DC: International Monetary Fund).
Far Eastern Economic Review (FEER).
Foreign Broadcast Information Service (FBIS), *Daily Report: China.*
Ji Guoxing (1992) *The Spratly Disputes and Prospects for Settlement* (Kuala Lumpur: Institute for International Studies).
Joint Publications Research Service (JPRS), *China.*
Lardy, Nicholas (1992) 'China's Growing Economic Role in Asia,' in *The Future of China, NBR Analysis*, vol. 3, no. 3.
Li Weiguo (1992) 'How to Approach the Current Favorable International Situation', *Shijie Zhishi,* 16 April.
Lin Xiao (1989) 'Shake Off the Influence of the Cold War – ASEAN Members Adjust their Foreign Polices', *Shijie Zhishi,* 1 November.
Ren Zhengde (1990) 'Turbulent International Situation – Multipolar, Changeable, Eventful', *Liaowang,* 3 August.
Ross, Robert S. (1988) 'China and the Ethnic Chinese: Political Liability/ Economic Asset', in Joyce K. Kallgren, Noordin Sopiee and Soedjati

Djiwandono (eds) *ASEAN and China: An Evolving Relationship* (Berkeley: Institute for East Asian Studies, University of California).

—— (1991) 'China and the Cambodian Peace Process: The Value of Coercive Diplomacy', *Asian Survey*, vol. XXXI, no. 12 (December).

—— (1994) 'China Threat Not What it is Made Out to Be', *Straits Times* (Singapore), 30 November.

—— (1995) 'China and the Stability of East Asia' in Robert S. Ross (ed.) *East Asia in Transition: Toward New Regional Order* (Armonk, NY: M. E. Sharpe).

Shi Min (1990) 'Looking Ahead to the Political and Economic Situation for the Asia-Pacific Region during the 1990s', *Liaowang*, no. 5 (overseas edn, 29 January).

Tai Ming Cheung (1990) *Growth of Chinese Naval Power, Pacific Strategic Papers* (Singapore: Institute of Southeast Asian Studies).

Tao Bingwei (1990) 'On the Asia-Pacific Situation in the 1990s', *Guoji Wenti Yanjiu*, no. 1 (January).

Tang Tianri (1992) 'Why Did Japan Pass Bill on Dispatching Troops Abroad?' *Fazhi Ribao* (11 June).

Tian Zhongqing (1990) 'The Pattern of International Relationships in the Asia Pacific Region in the 1990s', *Guoji Zhanwang*, no. 3 (8 February).

Wan Guang (1990) 'Evolution of the Postwar Asia-Pacific Pattern and its Prospects in the 1990s', *Liaowang*, overseas edn, no. 33 (13 August).

Wang Shu (1992) 'Study thoroughly the Global Competition for Economic Power – Grasp the Foundation of Changes in the International Situation', *Liaowang*, (16 March).

Whiting, Allen S. (1989) *China Eyes Japan* (Berkeley: University of California Press).

Womack, Brantly (1994) 'Sino-Vietnamese Border Trade: The Edge of Normalization', *Asian Survey*, vol. XXXIV, no. 6, pp. 495–512.

9 Japan and Southeast Asia: Facing an Uncertain Future

Michael W. Donnelly and
Richard Stubbs

Nations within the Asia Pacific have been among the most economically dynamic in the world during the past two decades. Divergent in terms of economic resources, at different levels of economic development, politically following various paths, few regions of the world offer such a wide variety of political and economic experience. Nevertheless, except the Philippines, Burma (Myanmar), Cambodia and North Korea, the countries of the region are achieving high, in some cases, quite remarkable gains in economic growth. A global economy of relatively open trade and investment has been indispensable to the growing prosperity in the region (World Bank, 1993).

While developing world-scale commercial ties, economic links among the countries of the region have also deepened. What gives this some special distinction is that it has taken place without significant discrimination against economies outside the region, has been achieved without elaborate regional institutional infrastructure, has escaped the need for a common security framework, and has not produced a regional communal 'consciousness' or obvious claims to political leadership that prevail in Europe and North America (Bergsten and Noland, 1993). These distinctive features may not last much longer.

Rapid growth of economic links has produced new requirements for governments in the region to give more attention to how market-driven commerce must be linked to regional 'institutionalization', diplomacy and military security. How these issues are addressed will depend significantly on Japan. Already the country's economic interests in Southeast Asia have expanded dramatically, especially since the Plaza Accord of the Group of Five finance ministers in 1985 which realigned currencies among major industrialized nations. Since then, Japanese firms have substantially increased their investment in the region. Some analysts have suggested that Japan is increasingly viewing the Asia Pacific generally as its own backyard, as an extension of the Japanese economy itself. Based on substantial evidence, including flows of trade, investment, foreign aid, government-provided credit and transfers of technology, Richard P. Cronin and others suggest that Japan has emerged as the 'nerve centre' of the Asia–Pacific region, the 'core economy' of the future (Cronin, 1992).

Economic data certainly do suggest shifts in patterns of international commercial activity. But of course the question about Japan and the region is more than economic. It is also political. Yet it is not at all clear that Japan will be able to convert its position as 'core economy' into a more influential political role or enable the country to become more directly involved in military security arrangements.

Our view is that Japan will surely continue to have a very large place in Southeast Asia's commercial and industrial activity. The area is entering a new era of growing multilateralism and governments in the region want Japan to be part of it. The Asia Pacific more generally will also require creative government policies and the capacity to muster support for them – creation of new collective security arrangements, controls on arms proliferation, coordinated management of economic disputes, decisive action in crisis situations. New initiatives will be required to sustain regional, and not just domestic economic growth, while avoiding the drift towards either narrow nationalism or protectionist blocs. The outside world more than ever expects a clear expression of objectives from Tokyo that can be understood and judged.

In response, a younger generation of Japanese politicians, bureaucrats and managers who want their country to play a larger regional and world role are gaining power in the country. Early in 1994 an ambitious agenda for policy change proclaimed by the reform-minded coalition of seven political parties headed by Prime Minister Morihiro Hosokawa included a promise that Japan would contribute to the global community in a way commensurate with its abilities and responsive to 'international expectations'. Later in the year Tomiichi Murayama, a lifelong socialist, was selected as head of a new coalition government dominated by the right-leaning Liberal Democratic Party. Murayama's first overseas trip, besides a previously scheduled Group of Seven summit meeting, was to Asia. He declared that no region of the world was more important to his administration.

Nonetheless, the habits of low-key strategic coping, with its emphasis on national self-interest are proving difficult to break. External expectations and pressures will only partially determine the timing and scope of Japan's political and security policy choices in the next few years. More decisive will be unpredictable domestic conditions reflected most recently in Lower House elections held in the summer of 1993 which ended almost forty consecutive years of one-party Liberal Democratic Party (LDP) government. In this new period of multiparty governing, there are fewer certainties in Japanese politics regarding how national interests will be perceived, overseas strategies adopted, and policies implemented. In Southeast Asia there is uncertainty as well: about Japan's economic presence and, even more, about a potential military place in the region for Asia's most economically powerful state.

JAPAN'S HABIT OF STRATEGIC COPING

The geopolitical struggle between the Soviet Union and the United States no longer exists to give foreign policy-makers in Tokyo predictable political parameters of debate, self-evident reasons to go along with Washington, or an excuse not to explore a wider range of geostrategic choices. The Gulf crisis severely jolted Japan even further. Japanese foreign policy has been chiefly determined by American behaviour and in this first post-Cold War challenge Tokyo found it extremely hard to go along. A call for greater emphasis on the United Nations has been defined by the government as the most effective way to ease Japan into the international world of geo-political and military security. Yet for all its economic power and rhetoric about a UN-oriented foreign policy, in the Gulf Tokyo was unable to share the 'defence-burden' with the United States except by cheque-book diplomacy.

Since the end of World War II, the country has been able to concentrate rather narrowly on national economic development, avoid geostrategic conflicts by maintaining a low international political profile, open up its markets to foreign competitors only very gradually, and rely on the United States to guarantee the nation's external security (Pyle, 1992). Caution overseas helped avoid rancorous debate at home while liberating the energies of the Japanese people for the challenge of economic recovery. The Cold War kept America committed to Japan while modest military expenditures and close diplomatic ties with the United States assured both Japan's regional security and its acceptance in Asia.

Michael Blaker has described this minimalist diplomatic policy as 'strategic coping' (Blaker, 1993). Politically passive, ideologically reserved, and cautiously reactive, the architects of Japan's foreign policy understood international affairs for the most part through the prism of ties with the United States. It was extremely difficult to discern any kind of world view that went beyond the vague ideas of 'comprehensive security' and the political requirements of junior alliance partner. Military ties served as the linchpin. The US–Japan Security Treaty aimed at permitting Japan to maintain a comparatively limited, purely self-defensive military capability.

In retrospect, it is clear that Japan was able to use the Cold War and American power – economic, political, military, ideological and even cultural – to national advantage. With the country's emergence as a major economic power in the 1970s, however, Washington and other Western allies increasingly began to criticize this approach to foreign affairs (Inoguchi and Okimoto, 1988). Still, in the eyes of most American policy-makers until the very end of the Bush administration, Japan remained a bulwark against communism, a helpful security ally in Northeast Asia, a foothold in the Asia Pacific region, a showcase for the dynamics of a market economy and a display of the virtues of democratic politics.

JAPAN INVESTS AND REGIONAL EXPECTATIONS GROW

For years memories of Japanese occupation aroused bitterness in Southeast Asia (Tilman, 1987). During the late 1970s and early 1980s, however, a number of trends emerged which allowed Japan a higher profile. Indeed, by the late 1980s and early 1990s these trends had crystallized to such an extent that Japan was widely viewed as the one state that had the resources, and the commitment to Southeast Asia's stability, to enable it to address the key economic and even on occasion specific security concerns of the ASEAN governments. Japan was being sought out as a leader on a number of significant issues.

Three broad, inter-related developments had become apparent in the late 1970s, gradually encouraging the governments of the ASEAN states to reassess their attitudes toward Japan. The first development concerned the changing role of the United States, which had come to dominate the region by the 1960s. President Nixon's announcement in 1969 of the Guam Doctrine signalled that apart from any nuclear threat to the region the US would expect the Asian states to be responsible for their own security. The departure of US troops from Vietnam and the subsequent victory of the communist forces also underscored the altered commitment of the US to the region. This was followed in 1979 by the obvious unwillingness of the US to take the lead in dealing with the Vietnamese invasion of Cambodia. The failure of the US to live up to the expectations of the ASEAN governments, led to a general appreciation in the region that the US could no longer be relied upon to help solve their problems (Chanda, 1990), and was reinforced by reductions in the levels of American aid to the region.

The second development concerned a gradual change in Japan's approach to the ASEAN region represented best by the so-called Fukuda Doctrine of 1977. Japan's more active approach to ASEAN was generally welcomed as were the more formal arrangements for cooperation which were prompted by new Japanese initiatives. Japan agreed in the 1980s to boost its aid to the ASEAN region in general and to Thailand – as the country most threatened by the continuing guerrilla war in Cambodia – in particular. The Japan–ASEAN Investment Corporation was established in 1981 to boost ASEAN economic development. Japan's gradual, but nonetheless perceptible, emergence as a regional player was juxtaposed with America's apparently increasing reluctance to maintain its old position of paramount regional leader.

The third trend which reinforced the first two was the changing emphasis that the governments of the ASEAN region gave to security issues as opposed to economic development issues. During the period of the Cold War, at least up until the early 1980s these governments were preoccupied with the external threat posed by the Communist powers, the Soviet Union, China and Vietnam, as well as with the continuing threat posed by communist subversion. The problem was seen in essentially military terms and it was to the US, as the premier military power, that the ASEAN governments turned to help them devise a military solution. However, during the early 1980s, as the ASEAN region moved into a period of relatively rapid economic development, government leaders began to put more value on the stability that accompanied prosperity. It came to be appreciated that communist insurgencies were undermined by increased employment and higher wages and that Communist states were interested in sharing the growing economic prosperity of the region by developing better trade links with the ASEAN states. As a consequence of these changing perceptions, it was the growing economic power of Japan rather than the military might of the United States on which more and more emphasis was placed by the governments of the ASEAN states.

While changes in ASEAN–Japan relations gathered momentum during the 1970s and early 1980s, the major changes in ASEAN attitudes to Japan have taken place since 1987 and have been prompted by the extraordinary increases in Japanese economic penetration of the region. The most startling increase came in Japanese foreign direct investment (FDI) as a result of the Plaza Accord of September 1985. The rapid increase in the price of the yen, which went from an average of 238 to the dollar in 1985 to 128 to the dollar in 1988, when combined with other structural imperatives which were overtaking Japanese industry, forced a number of companies to consider moving beyond Japan's borders. South Korea and Taiwan were initially targeted as the most attractive places to relocate. However, their currencies also began to appreciate and they faced a growing labour shortage and rising wages as well as the threat of the removal of the US Generalized System of Preferences (GSP). In a parallel development the ASEAN governments in the wake of the 1985–86 recession eased their FDI regulations so as to allow most foreign owned firms producing mainly for export to invest in their country. (Phongpaichit, 1990). This coincidence of economic imperatives paved the way for Japanese FDI looking for a new home in suitable lower cost economies.

Initially Thailand and Singapore were the preferred destinations for Japanese manufacturing companies seeking to relocate in the ASEAN region (see Table 9.1). However, in Thailand the infrastructure became stretched to the limit and investment dropped in the early 1990s. In Singapore the removal of the GSP by the US, the relatively high wages and the steady appreciation of the Singapore dollar meant that Japanese investment declined after the peak year of 1989. As a result, Malaysia and particularly Indonesia have also become major destinations for Japanese FDI. Overall, then, the ASEAN region saw direct Japanese investment grow from US$3.7 billion in the four years 1983–6 to US$16.3 billion in the four years 1989–92.

Alongside this massive private sector investment in the region there has been a marked increase in the Japanese government's investment through its aid programmes. Starting in 1977 with the Japanese decision to double official development assistance (ODA), over the following three years aid became an increasingly significant factor in Japan–ASEAN relations. Between 1976 and 1986, Japan's ODA increased fivefold with the ASEAN members annually receiving roughly one third of all Japanese bilateral disbursements (Japanese Government, Ministry of Foreign Affairs, 1992; Rudner 1989). Over the period from 1982 to 1986 the four largest ASEAN states – Indonesia, Malaysia, the Philippines and Thailand – received nearly US$1 billion per year in aid. In 1987 ODA to the four ASEAN states rose sharply to nearly US$1.7 billion and reached US$2.3 billion in 1990 and US$3.25 billion in 1992 (*JEI Report*, various dates; Japanese Government, Ministry of Foreign affairs, 1993). A high percentage of this aid was in the

Table 9.1 Japan FDI in ASEAN (US$ million)

	1985	1986	1987	1988	1989	1990	1991	1992	1993
Indonesia	408	250	545	580	631	1,105	1,193	1,676	813
Malaysia	79	158	163	387	673	725	880	704	800
Philippines	61	21	72	134	202	258	203	160	207
Singapore	339	302	494	747	1,902	840	613	670	644
Thailand	48	124	250	859	1,276	1,154	807	657	578
ASEAN* Total	935	855	1,524	2,713	4,684	4,082	3,696	3,867	3,042

* ASEAN members excluding Brunei

Source: ASEAN–Japan Statistical Pocketbook (1993) (Tokyo: ASEAN Promotion Centre on Trade, Investment and Tourism, 1993).

form of loans and was, for the most part, geared to helping the ASEAN states expand their export manufacturing base. Emphasis was placed on developing the economic infrastructure – roads, railways, ports and airports – and on providing bilateral structural adjustment loans so as to ease policy reforms. In combination the increased Japanese ODA and the massive influx of investment have changed the face of the ASEAN economies.

As a result of the enormous influx of Japanese FDI, ASEAN's imports from Japan have risen sharply. Much of this is accounted for by the machinery and equipment that has been required to set up the export-manufacturing industries and the Japanese components needed to manufacture or assemble the final products. At the same time the ASEAN countries have increased their exports to Japan, most especially their exports of manufactured goods (see Table 9.2). This has meant that whereas in 1986 the ASEAN economies exported US$15.2 billion worth of goods to Japan, of which US$2.09 billion or 13.75 per cent were manufactured goods, by 1993 the ASEAN economies were exporting US$34.01 billion worth of goods to Japan, of which US$13.84 billion or 40.7 per cent were manufactured goods (*ASEAN–Japan Statistical Pocketbook*, 1994). Yet it must be emphasized that overall the shift in the balance of trade has been in Japan's favour. Hence, whereas in 1985 the ASEAN members had a US$8.95 billion trade surplus with Japan, by 1993 this had become a US$15.46 billion trade *deficit*. Interestingly, this was offset in part by an increase from US$5.8 billion to US$8.8 billion over the period from 1986 to 1989 in ASEAN's trade surplus with the US (US Government, 1989). However, this surplus has been reduced in the last few years as the US economy has gone into a slump.

Overall, then, while the ASEAN economies – even at times the Philippines – have experienced remarkable growth rates in their GDPs of from 6 to 13 per cent and enjoyed considerable prosperity in the process, they have also become more and more tied to the Japanese economy. The almost overwhelming economic presence of Japan, therefore, has persuaded the ASEAN governments to press it into playing a regional role commensurate with its increasing capacity and involvement. In contrast with the nation's aggressive business firms, the Japanese government has still been extremely cautious in seeking greater engagement on political and especially military issues.

Table 9.2 Japan–ASEAN trade (US$ million)

Japan's trade with:		1985	1986	1987	1988	1989	1990	1991	1992	1993
Brunei	Exports	90	58	41	67	83	86	129	158	127
	Imports	1,892	1,285	1,184	1,117	1,086	1,262	1,500	1,357	1,408
	Mfd goods*	0.1%	0.1%	0.1%	0.1%	0.1%	0.1%	0.1%	0.1%	0.1%
Indonesia	Exports	2,172	2,662	2,990	3,054	3,301	5,040	5,612	5,576	6,022
	Imports	10,119	7,311	8,427	9,497	11,021	12,721	12,770	12,244	12,478
	Mfd goods*	4.3%	6.7%	11.6%	14.3%	19.7%	15.6%	16.8%	19.6%	26.4%
Malaysia	Exports	2,168	1,708	2,168	3,060	4,124	5,511	7,635	8,116	9,649
	Imports	4,330	3,846	4,772	4,710	5,107	5,402	6,471	6,573	7,642
	Mfd goods*	9.2%	9.8%	9.0%	12.8%	15.0%	20.2%	28.2%	31.0%	35.5%
Philippines	Exports	937	1,088	1,415	1,740	2,381	2,504	2,659	3,517	4,814
	Imports	1,243	1,221	1,353	2,044	2,059	2,157	2,351	2,333	2,380
	Mfd goods*	22.3%	20.1%	20.7%	26.7%	27.2%	35.5%	39.5%	42.5%	43.5%
Singapore	Exports	3,860	4,577	6,008	8,311	9,239	10,708	12,213	12,974	16,601
	Imports	1,594	1,463	2,048	2,339	2,952	3,571	3,415	3,097	3,602
	Mfd goods*	28.5%	41.2%	42.1%	50.8%	55.8%	50.9%	58.0%	64.0%	71.9%
Thailand	Exports	2,030	2,030	2,953	5,162	6,838	9,126	9,431	10,366	12,261
	Imports	1,027	1,391	1,796	2,751	3,583	4,147	5,252	5,947	6,502
	Mfd goods*	27.7%	26.5%	29.4%	32.6%	42.0%	48.1%	51.8%	53.7%	56.0%
ASEAN	Exports	11,257	12,123	15,575	21,394,	25,966	32,975	37,679	40,707	49,474
	Imports	20,205	16,517	19,580	22,458	25,808	29,260	31,759	31,551	34,012
	Mfd goods*	10.1%	13.7%	16.8%	21.5%	26.9%	27.3%	31.7%	35.1%	40.7%

* Manufactured goods as a percentage of total imports.

Source: ASEAN–Japan Statistical Pocketbook (1993) (Tokyo: ASEAN Promotion Centre, Investment and Tourism, 1993); United Nations, Statistical Yearbook for Asia and the Pacific (Bangkok: Economic and Social Commission for Asia and the Pacific, various years).

THE REGIONAL NEED TO TRY SOMETHING ELSE

Nevertheless since 1989 Asia has become a dramatically different place. The collapse of the Soviet empire has eliminated Russia as a major player in regional power politics, and thus undermined many of the basic premises underlying the Japan–US alliance. In partial reflection of these new circumstances, diplomatic and economic ties with America are more fragile than ever.

The Soviet collapse has come at a time when China is emerging more significantly as a regional military power, adopting open-door policies, and pursuing new economic and diplomatic initiatives. The reconciliation of communist and noncommunist regimes made possible the development of regional ties linking the ASEAN countries with Indo-China. While President Clinton has reaffirmed his nation's political and military commitment to the region, there is still a potential for reduction of the American presence. ASEAN countries are uncertain about how to build an effective security framework given the changed structure of power in the region, a rapidly growing arms trade, and the rising potential of regional or subregional military conflicts.

No doubt some further economic integration of the region is inevitable, driven largely by market forces but facilitated by government policies. If the nations in the region believe themselves seriously disadvantaged by regional arrangements in North America and Europe, then they will probably pursue even greater regional integration as a kind of second-best option. What, then, of Japan?

JAPAN'S CAPACITY TO CHANGE

The task of reorienting and explaining Japan's approach to Asia has been underway for well over a decade. Prime ministers Fukuda, Ohira, Takeshita, Kaifu, Miyazawa, Hosokawa and Murayama have all sought opportunities for proposing a broader Japanese role in Southeast Asia. High ranking officials have been firmly on record that openness and a respect for plurality is indispensable for the continuing economic development of the Asia–Pacific region. A wide consensus among bureaucratic policy elites is also firm that in an extremely fluid situation Japan requires a 'long-term vision', perhaps even a prime minister's personal 'doctrine', that will enable the country to play a considerably greater political and even military security role in the area.

Many politicians go along with officialdom. For example, a special study group set up by the LDP unveiled a draft report in early 1992 which pronounced that one of the four major new roles for the country is to 'strive to preserve peace and maintain stability in the Asian region, always seeking the understanding and support of other Asian countries' (LDP Special Study Group, 1992). Late in the same year a blue-ribbon advisory group to then Prime Minister Miyazawa offered an extensive set of views and recommendations regarding Japan's future ties to the Asia–Pacific region (Round Table, 1992). In his visit to Southeast Asia in early 1993, Prime Minister Miyazawa referred to the need to engage in quiet dialogue with nations of the region, a part of the world which he also referred to as 'Japan's constituency'.

Within a few days after being appointed, Prime Minister Morihiro Hosokawa openly recognized that Japan had fought 'a war of aggression in Asia'. In subsequent days, he expressed his 'profound remorse and apologies' to Asian countries for Japan's behaviour during World War II which 'caused unbearable suffering and sorrow for so many people'. (*Asahi Shimbun*, 23 August 1993) This was the first time that a Japanese prime minister had so explicitly apologized for Japan's actions during wartime. The statement was seen as another move towards opening the door to a more activist policy in Asia. The Murayama Administration has continued this movement towards settling issues left over from Japan's record as an imperialist power in the region.

What all these pronouncements add up to is not altogether apparent. Challenged to try something else, does Japan in a new era of coalition politics have the capacity and will to consider a wider range of political and military choices? In order to consider 'whither Japan in Southeast Asia' the following considerations are most important.

The American Alliance and Military-Rooted Independence

Japanese military forces constitute the most modern, technologically sophisticated non-nuclear power in Asia. Japanese industry is now a formidable competitor in global markets for dual-use technologies. While security forces are defensive in overall concept, Japanese minesweepers were dispatched to the Gulf, following the end of hostilities, to join the operations of eight other nations at the request of the Saudi Arabian government. More recently, Japanese soldiers returned to the soil of Southeast Asia for the first time since World War II, as part of a United Nations peace-keeping force in Cambodia. The UN Peace-Keeping Operations Law, enacted in June 1992, authorizes the overseas dispatch of Self-Defense Forces personnel to provide *un*armed support to UN sponsored peacekeeping missions. Most observers have hailed this action as a critical turning-point in Tokyo's post-war diplomacy. However, passage of the law was bitterly fought by opposition political parties, who viewed deployment of Japanese military personnel outside the vicinity of the home islands to engage in collective security efforts as a violation of Article 9 of the Constitution. Nevertheless as Japanese troops prepared to leave Cambodia in August 1993 the head of the Defence Agency stated that Japan should assume a more positive stance on UN peace-keeping activities, including sending *armed* units overseas.

The Japanese government has also proposed that ASEAN post-ministerial meetings with 'dialogue partners' include a new forum for discussion of regional security questions. This led to the formation of the ASEAN Regional Forum. The ARF will meet regularly to discuss military stability in the region. In light of this a good deal of discussion, re-thinking and debate is going on in Tokyo right now regarding the country's defence organization, crisis decision-making processes, overseas military activities and military-spending priorities. This in itself is hardly new; defence-related political differences have produced contentious issues in Japan throughout the post-war period.

During the past decade or so the American side has been pressuring the Japanese government to assume a larger role in its national defence, nevertheless, in striking contrast to economic relations, the security ties linking the two countries have been relatively free of acrimony. Still, conflicts will probably emerge on matters related to high-technology, proprietary rights and technology transfer, involving economic as well as security issues. But most government officials and private analysts on both sides of the Pacific, still see the US-Japan Mutual Security Treaty as the best guarantor of regional stability, especially since it keeps the United States in the region.

There have been no concrete signs that Japan's measurable military strength might be used in direct or even indirect support of political goals in Southeast Asia. The evidence suggests that no major security threat is yet seen by Tokyo to exist in that region, no important domestic constituencies are active in Japan advocating an increased military role there, no important viewpoint suggests that the present balance of power requires Japan to be there except with UN peace-keeping forces, and no one is suggesting that a larger military role would help provide greater economic gains.

Indeed, there is some evidence of moves in a different direction. The Japanese government under the LDP pushed up by one year a review of the nation's 1991–5 defense build-up plan and Prime Minister Miyazawa in a statement in the Diet in early 1992 also suggested that the 1976 defence outline, which constituted the overall framework for self-defence, may also be re-examined in an effort to scale back overall military programmes. Defence spending is being reduced. The government has also recently declared that economic assistance to developing nations should be linked to limits on military spending and arms exports. There is no reason to expect governments in the near future to repudiate these initiatives.

Constitutional Ideals, Divided Public Opinion, and Cautious Diplomacy

The Japanese public has enjoyed forty-five years of stability and growing affluence, without being asked directly to consider the possibility of conscription, nuclear weapons, or war and death on the battle field. An important reason why economic power is not easily transformed into more ambitious geo-strategic diplomacy has been the way in which the values of post-War democracy are linked by many members of the public to Article Nine of the Constitution.

While the wording of the Constitution has remained unchanged, the precise interpretation of a number of provisions, especially Article Nine, has long been in contention. Over the years, the government has been able to expand and upgrade its military strength and redefine the geographical scope of its defensive mission even under the limitations set out by Article Nine. The range of military-related activities openly discussed in political debate has widened. The constitutionality of the Self-Defence Forces and the Security Treaty with the United States no longer inspires much dissent. Instead, issues considered are now much more specific: the meaning of 'self-defence' especially in the light of the adequacy of evolving post-Cold War security arrangements both globally and in Eastern Asia; the concrete missions of the Self-Defence forces and the capabilities necessary to fulfil these missions; types of permissible weapons; the relationship between military defence and other forms of national security, and military ties with the United States, when linked to economic disputes.

The Defence Agency continues to state in various publications that the war-renouncing clause 'does not deny the inherent right of self-defence that Japan is entitled to maintain as a sovereign nation.' Its White Papers also assert that effective exercise of the right of self-defence may require activity outside Japan's immediate sea and air space. Government constitutional experts, however, remain firm that Article Nine does not permit the dispatch of Self-Defence equipment and personnel abroad to engage in combat. It was partially for this reason that the carefully worded United Nations Peace-keeping Operations Law was required to give the government authority to send contingents of no more than 2,000 to Cambodia and other areas supervised by UN forces. Still, the fact that enactment of this legislation was possible is more evidence that Japan's present 'peace constitution' is not a complete obstacle to a more activist foreign policy.

But constitutional constraints cannot be dismissed even as talk in Japanese politics about revision persists. As Masaru Tamamoto suggests, 'Four political values the Japanese hold dear – the democratic condition, minimum involvement in international politics, a limited military establishment, and American protection – are thought to form an organic whole. Thus to tamper with one is to tamper with the others. The Japanese attachment to these four values is expressed in the high public support for the constitution in which they are enshrined' (Tamamoto, 1990, p. 503). Japan's response to the Persian Gulf War and the difficulties encountered in enacting the new peace-keeping legislation are simply the most recent examples to demonstrate that, similar to uncertainties outside Japan, there is no consensus regarding how the country should play a political and military role in the post Cold War period.

The norms of international politics which may require the use and threat of force tap a deep-rooted aversion and fear among many Japanese towards extensive overseas political and military involvement. A substantial portion of the Japanese public remains reluctant to acknowledge that changing global conditions have profound implications for what 'self-defence' means. In an opinion poll conducted in the summer of 1993 only 32 per cent of those polled felt that 'Japan should participate in UN peacekeeping efforts'. In contrast, 66 per cent said Japan should not do so. As many as 74 per cent of respondents felt that their country had no responsibility to assist militarily in world trouble spots (*New York Times*, 6 July 1993). All signs suggest that a large portion of Japanese people are unlikely to support any dramatic changes in their nation's defence posture no matter what academics in universities, officials in Kasumigaseki or some politicians in Nagatacho might advocate.

Stalemated Reciprocal Consent

The extreme difficulty that Japan experienced in dealing with the Gulf crisis and the Cambodian peace-keeping effort underscores problems of political direction at home. On many routine matters, Japan's approach to foreign affairs is formulated in a highly bureaucratized policy-making process which favours consensual decisions. But if proposed actions become controversial, policy is also shaped by politicians who are severely divided, without loyalty to a majority party, lacking firm leadership at the top, and ever-shadowed by scandals and constant charges of political corruption. Forging a consensus among members of an ideologically diverse coalition will be especially difficult.

Politics becomes the vaunted Japanese art of compromise, consensus, balance and immobilism. Some outside observers see power in Japan as 'enigmatic', the state as 'illusive', and the process excessively laborious. As John Haley writes about public policy, government remains in a chronic dependence upon what might be called 'consensual governance' (Haley, 1991). The political parties are a tangle of factions, the bureaucracy a maze of competing agencies, the process of decision often quite opaque, and with no one at the top helping to make clear what the country's official views might be. The growing intervention of Japanese politicians in what heretofore have been considered purely diplomatic matters has also weakened somewhat the continuity and predictability of the nation's foreign activities. While some members of Japan's foreign policy establishment might recognize the need to redefine the country's diplomacy on such occasions as the G–7 Summit held in Tokyo in 1993, the nation nonetheless often reaches almost a state of paralysis, distracted as it is by internal squabbles or domestic problems of one kind or another. Any attempt to dramatically change the nation's geo-political orientation towards the external world in general and Southeast Asia in particular would surely be accompanied by political difficulties.

Decentralized Foreign Economic Policy

A decade ago there was a tendency in the literature on Japan to contrast 'chronic immobilism' in Japan's military-political policies with considerable 'strategic rationality' in industrial and trade policies. Recent research suggests, however, that the notion that Japan has some kind of coherent economic strategy does not withstand close scrutiny. A broad range of foreign *economic* policy areas are also marked by division and political disagreement. In an extremely pluralistic political setting, the Japanese government often lacks an effective coordinating or integrative institution capable of implementing innovative policies in the face of vested interests or divided opinion. Thus a recent study of trade policies has argued that the country's position on trade issues is largely the result of policies adopted by various autonomous sectoral power centres, each of which consists of a key ministry, the industry under its jurisdiction, and in some cases relevant members of the LDP (Wolff and Howell, 1992). Pempel has written about 'The Unbundling of "Japan, Inc."', Fukui has commented on 'too many captains' in the Ministry of Foreign Affairs; Kernell has remarked upon 'the primacy of politics in economic policy' that parallels the particularism of the United States; and a number of studies have shown how uncertain the government has been in using foreign aid as an instrument of foreign policy (Pempel, 1987; Fukui, 1987; Kernell, 1991).

The argument here is not that the government has no role in the private sector's overseas investments and other commercial activities. It is not to suggest that the firms and public agencies in Japan do not have close ties. Japanese firms can sometimes influence foreign aid projects, for example. However, public and private goals cannot be achieved without competition and conflict with one another. The difficulties of a constrained Japanese state are thus reflected not only in historically defining moments such as the PKO debate but also on many ongoing economic issues as well.

A growing number of Japanese academics, government officials and political leaders are enthusiastically expressing ideas regarding regionalization in Asia along the lines of new divisions of labour and patterns of trade. The idea of somehow coordinating production in the region in a way to minimize wasteful competition and duplication of production while making use of each country's special advantages certainly would have a special appeal given Japan's own domestic experience. But it is not clear that the Japanese government has a deliberate strategic approach to the organization of production in the region that puts official programmes at the service of Japanese industry. It is extremely difficult to discern deliberate and coordinated purposes on matters of investment, trade, foreign aid, the role of the yen, technology transfer, or even matters of formal, government-to-government political cooperation.

THE VIEWS FROM SOUTHEAST ASIA

While there is clearly a consensus in Southeast Asia that Japan should play a greater role in solving the region's problems, there is no clear consensus as to what that role should be. Confounding this uncertainty over Japan's role in Southeast Asia is the debate over the nature and degree of integration of the wider Asia–Pacific region and the way in which the region should respond to changes that are taking place in the global political economy.

Symptomatic of this lack of consensus has been the response to the Malaysian proposal for an East Asia Economic Grouping, now called the East Asian Economic Caucus – EAEC. The idea, first put forward by the Malaysian prime minister, Mahathir bin Mohamed, in December 1990 was originally to bring together the ASEAN states, Hong Kong, South Korea, Taiwan, Japan and possibly the countries of Indo-China in a group which could give a focus for discussions prior to negotiations at the GATT or with the EC or the US (Low, 1991, p. 374). This proposal, however, caused a good deal of debate.

For Mahathir and, indeed, others in the region, such as Singapore's prime minister Goh Chok Tong, the EAEG/EAEC proposal was in many ways a logical response to events. The post-Plaza Accord patterns of private sector investment, production and assembly have created a network of economic activity which is bringing about greater regional integration and, therefore, a need to discuss common interests. At the same time, the increased regional integration represented by recent developments in Europe and North America means that there is a clear necessity for the Asia–Pacific region, including Southeast Asia, to coordinate its actions so as not to be out manoeuvred in global economic negotiations. For Malaysia, therefore, Japan is a major factor in the success of a possible EAEC or similar grouping. As the Malaysian minister of international trade and industry has argued: 'Japan has a definite role to play as leader of the region. You can come up with a club but you don't have to be chairman yourself' (*Straits Times*, overseas edition, 26 January 1991). Moreover, as a Singapore-based economist has pointed out, Malaysia would also like 'to anchor Japan to East Asia, arguing that East Asia should be Japan's natural constituency rather than have it uproot industries and move them away to Europe and the United States' (Low, 1991, p. 375). In other words there are those within Southeast Asia who would like to see Japan make a clearer commitment to the Eastern Asian or Asia–Pacific economy.

The Malaysians, however, ran into opposition to their proposal. For the Thai and Indonesian governments the major concern was that the ASEAN states, which are primarily export-oriented economies and heavily dependent on the large markets in the US and to a lesser extent the EU, should not be seen even considering the possibility of reinforcing the disintegration of the global economy into protectionist regional blocs. Critics of the EAEC appeared much happier with the inclusive philosophy of the Asia–Pacific Economic Cooperation (APEC) meetings than with any institutional arrangement which might exclude the US. Generally, those who have been wary of the EAEC would rather have Japan as a link to the US than as a champion of Asian interests in competition with the US. While at the July 1993 ASEAN foreign ministers meeting a compromise was brokered by the Singaporeans which makes the EAEC a caucus within APEC, there is still considerable ambiguity as to how the arrangement will work in practice and what role Japan will play.

A further compounding factor is the lack of a clear understanding of how Japan's foreign economic policy towards the region will unfold. The ASEAN governments would like to see Japan open up its economy to an even greater extent than it has in the last few years and absorb an even higher percentage of the region's exports. This would be one way of combating the rapidly expanding trade deficit. They would also like to see Japan develop its regional economic leadership role within the wider context of one of the emerging institutional frameworks, be it as Indonesia and Thailand would prefer within APEC or as Malaysia would prefer within an EAEC. There are also certain fears that what some, perhaps exaggerating official Japan's coordinating capacity, have detected as Japanese plans for their firms in Southeast Asia – for example, those developed by MITI – may serve as a blueprint for regional development over which the region itself would have little or no control (Arase, 1991, pp. 270–78; *Asian Wall Street Journal*, 21 Aug. 1990). While the ASEAN governments appear to value the prosperity that Japanese involvement in the economy has brought, there are emerging concerns in some quarters about the extent to which the ASEAN economies are becoming beholden to decisions being made in Tokyo without their input.

In contrast to the lack of any clear consensus on Japan's economic policy in the region there would appear to be more of a consensus on Japan's role in the security of the region. Past concerns about the revival of Japanese militarism have been on the wane in recent years. Certainly, it appears that the governments of Southeast Asia are now less apprehensive about Japan's military tradition than are their Northeast Asian neighbours. The extent to which the ASEAN governments are so far relatively comfortable with the changing Japanese security role can be seen from the fact that they supported Japan's decision taken in April 1991 to send six minesweepers of the Self-Defence Forces to the Gulf to take part in United Nations clearing operations. Equally, the Japanese action in sending engineers from the Self-Defence Forces to Cambodia has not caused the unease that might have been expected a few years ago. Indeed, Japanese increased involvement in attempts to find a solution to the Cambodian crisis has generally been encouraged by the ASEAN states. It is widely recognized that only Japan has the resources to underwrite the peace-keeping campaigns and reconstruction programmes that are needed to once again bring peace and stability to the Indo-China region. The cautious leadership that Japan has displayed in this respect has been generally welcomed.

However, there are signs that the consensus could dissolve in the future. The key issue is the question of how to come to grips with the possible changes in the region's security relations in the wake of the US withdrawal from the Philippines. Some indication of the differences of opinion that might arise followed the then Thai prime minister Chatichai Choonhaven's suggestion to the director of Japan's Self Defence Agency in May 1990 that Thailand and Japan should conduct joint naval exercises in the event that the US withdrew from the Philippines. He was roundly criticized in Thailand as well as in Malaysia and Indonesia (Cronin, 1991, p. 64). But for Southeast Asian governments and more broadly for the people of the region there is an important question here. With the increasing evidence of China's interest in expanding its influence in the South China Sea through its claims to the Spratly Islands and its issuing of a drilling permit in waters within Vietnam's continental shelf and the continuing uncertainty in the region as to Washington's ability and willingness to ensure regional stability, what role can and should Japan play? All the ASEAN governments agree that Japan must, in the prime minister of Singapore's words, remain 'firmly anchored to the US alliance system' (*Straits Times*, May 1991). However, if the US-Japan security relationship should falter, then the uncertainty and instability that might follow would create many problems for all of Southeast Asia and there can be no guarantee that all would agree on a common course of action.

CONCLUSIONS

The portrait provided in this analysis of Japan's present and future place in Southeast Asia is a mixed one. There can be little doubt but that in economic terms Japan has the national capacity to play an ever larger role in Southeast Asia and is doing so. In a very cautious manner, Tokyo will also continue to search for some kind of larger political and security purpose. The countries of the region seem willing to go along with an increased Japanese presence as long as there are substantial benefits, as it does not close off other options or become in any way threatening, and as the United States remains engaged in the region. The last condition is important. In *Japan and Southeast Asia* there is agreement that Japanese security and political links with the United States must be maintained.

But beyond general agreement on these conditions, uncertainty and doubt cloud the future of Japan's place in the Southeast Asian region. This is the case both in the domestic debate in Japan and in discussions amongst Southeast Asian governments and attentive publics. The Asia Pacific economic miracle has been cast into a new strategic environment. What will drive future geo-political relationships in Southeast Asia will be a new inter-weaving of economics, politics and military security choices, but the texture of the mix cannot yet be determined.

References

Arase, David (1991) 'US and ASEAN Perceptions of Japan's Role in the Asian–Pacific Region' in Harry H. Kendall and Clara Joewono (eds) *Japan, ASEAN and the United States* (Berkeley: Institute of East Asian Studies).

ASEAN–Japan Statistical Pocketbook (1994) (Tokyo: ASEAN Promotion Centre on Trade Investment and Tourism).

Bergsten, C. Fred and Marcus Noland (eds) (1993) *Pacific Dynamism and the International Economic System* (Washington, DC: Institute for International Economics).

Blaker, Michael (1993) 'Evaluating Japan's Diplomatic Performance' in Gerald L. Curtis (ed.) *Japan's Foreign Policy After the Cold War: Coping with Change,* (Armonk: M. E. Sharpe).

Chanda, Nyan (1990) 'The External Environment for Southeast Asian Foreign Policy' in David Wurfel and Bruce Burton (eds) *The Political Economy of Foreign Policy in Southeast Asia* (London: Macmillan).

Cronin, Richard P. (1991) 'Changing Dynamics of Japan's Interaction with Southeast Asia' in *Southeast Asian Affairs 1991* (Singapore: Institute of Southeast Asian Studies).

Cronin, Richard P. (1992) *Japan, the United States and Prospects for the Asia–Pacific Century* (Singapore: Institute of Southeast Asian Studies).

Cumings, Bruce (1991) 'Asia and the Pacific since 1945: A US Perspective' in Robert H. Taylor (ed.) *Asia and the Pacific* vol. 2 (New York: Facts on File)

Far Eastern Economic Review Yearbook, 1990.

Fukui, Haruhiro (1987) 'Too Many Captains in Japan's Internationalization: Travails at the Foreign Ministry', *Journal of Japanese Studies*, vol. 13, no. 4 (Summer), pp. 359–81.

Haley, John O. (1991) *Authority Without Power* (Oxford: Oxford University Press).

Inoguchi, Takashi and Daniel I. Okimoto (eds) (1988) *The Political Economy of Japan: The Changing International Context* (Stanford: Stanford University Press).

Japanese Government, Ministry of Foreign Affairs (1992) *Annual Report of Japan's ODA*.

Japanese Government, Ministry of International Trade and Industry (various years) *Tsusho Hakusho* (Annual White Paper).

Kernell, Samuel (ed.) (1991) *Parallel Politics* (Washington, DC: Brookings Institution).

LDP Special Study Group (1992), 'Japan's Role in the International Community' in *Japan Echo* (summer), pp. 49–58.

Low, Linda (1991) 'The East Asian Economic Grouping', *Pacific Review*. vol. 4, no. 4, pp. 375–82.

Pempel, T. J. (1987). 'The Unbundling of "Japan, Inc": The Changing Dynamics of Japanese Policy Formation', *Journal of Japanese Studies*, vol. 13, no. 4 (Summer), pp. 271–306.

Phongpaichit, Pasuk (1990) 'Japanese Investment in ASEAN after the Yen Appreciation' in Soon Yee Ling (ed.) *Foreign Direct Investment in ASEAN*. (Kuala Lumpur: Malaysian Economic Association).

Pyle, Kenneth (1992) 'Japan, the World and the Twenty-first Century' in Takashi Inoguchi and Daniel K. Okimoto (eds) *The Political Economy of Japan, Volume 2: The Changing International Context* (Stanford: Stanford University Press).

Roundtable on Japan and the Asia–Pacific Region (1992) *Japan and the Asia-Pacific Region in the 21st Century* (photocopy).

Rudner, Martin (1989) 'Japanese Official Development Assistance to Southeast Asia', *Modern Asian Studies* vol. 23 (February); pp. 73–116.

Tamamoto, Masaru (1990) 'Japan's Search for a World View,' *World Policy Journal*, vol. 7 no. 3, pp. 493–520.

Tilman, Robert O. (1987) *Southeast Asia and the Enemy Beyond: ASEAN Perceptions of External Threats* (Boulder: Westview Press).

US Government, Department of Commerce (1989) *US Foreign Trade Highlights* (Washington, D.C.: Department of Commerce).

Wolff, Alan Wm. and Thomas R. Howell (1992) 'Japan' in Thomas R. Howell, Alan Wm. Wolff, Brent L. Bartlett and R. Michael Gadbaw (eds) *Conflict Among Nations* (Boulder: Westview Press).

World Bank (1993) *The East Asian Miracle* (New York: Oxford University Press).

10 Australian and Canadian Policy towards Southeast Asia

Kim Richard Nossal

INTRODUCTION

In the two and a half decades after the formation of the Association of Southeast Asian Nations in 1967, Australian and Canadian attitudes and policies towards the Southeast Asian region underwent a considerable transformation. From a policy of relative detachment from the region, both of these middle powers moved to dramatically increase their engagement in Southeast Asia, both politically and economically, matching in particular the evolving political economy of the region. Trade, investment, and development assistance all increased from the early 1970s to the mid-1990s, often at an accelerating rate. Diplomatic interest and involvement likewise showed a rapid rise over this period, with both the governments in Canberra and Ottawa moving to formalize their ties with the ASEAN community. In short, the portrait of Australian and Canadian links with Southeast Asia over the 1970s and 1980s is one of rapid, and indeed at times frenetic, growth.

It is common to attribute the often spectacular increase in these links to the evolving importance of the political economy of the Southeast Asian region on the one hand, and the changing position of Australia and Canada in the evolving international division of labour on the other (for example, Stubbs 1990; Evans and Grant, 1991). There can be little doubt that both the governments in Canberra and Ottawa sought over the course of the 1970s and 1980s to relocate themselves in the international system (Cooper, Higgott and Nossal, 1993), in large measure in response to shifts in the global political economy. Likewise, it is clear that the increasing dynamism of the ASEAN economies attracted both Australian and Canadian attention. The interconnection of these two developments, it is argued, prompted the governments in Canberra and Ottawa into a more active engagement in the Southeast Asian region.

One would not want to deny the obvious impact of the shifts in the international economy on the evolution of Australian and Canadian policy: clearly, the increasing dynamism of the Southeast Asian economies in the 1970s and 1980s proved attractive to both business and government in numerous OECD countries, Australia and Canada included. By the same token, however, one would not want to minimize the importance of global politics as a powerful determinant of state behaviour. In this chapter I will suggest that the approach to the region of both Australia and Canada was strongly affected not so much by the evolving economic conditions *within* the region but rather by the foreign policies of states *outside* the region.

In particular, I will argue that the bipolar politics of the Cold War were critical in explaining the approach of these two countries towards the region. As in other geographic areas of the world, the regional politics of Southeast Asia were heavily influenced by the impact of the super-powers during the Cold War era, an impact that was as keenly felt on the evolving international political economy of the region. The imperatives of the bipolar conflict between the Soviet Union, on the one hand, and a loose anti-Soviet coalition consisting of the United States, China, Japan, the Western European states, and the states of ASEAN, on the other hand, shaped much of the politics both within the region and towards the region. With the collapse of the Soviet Union, and the transformation of the bipolar rivalry, most of the imperatives associated with that rivalry essentially disappeared.

The transformations of the post-Cold War era also had an impact on the policies towards Southeast Asia of smaller states outside the region, such as Australia and Canada. I will argue that these two middle powers, members of the formal Western alliance system led by the United States and generally committed to the anti-Soviet coalition operating in the Asia–Pacific region, had shaped their general approach to Southeast Asia within the parameters set by the Cold War. Specific policies towards the region – on human rights, economics and trade, and defence – were fashioned by the needs of a fundamentally extraregional dynamic that was geostrategic rather than economic.

With the changes in the international system brought about by the collapse of the Soviet Union and the end of the Cold War, we can see the approach of Australia and Canada towards Southeast Asia shifting considerably. This chapter argues that the end of the Cold War in essence liberated Australian and Canadian policy-makers to pursue more autonomous policies towards the states of Southeast Asia and the evolving political economy of the region.

THE CONSTRAINTS AND IMPERATIVES OF COLD WAR

The regional manifestations of the Cold War had a clear impact on the evolution of Australian and Canadian policies towards the region in the post-Second World War era. During much of this period, both countries were clearly small-power 'outsiders' – former appendages of a Western imperial power, but states which had struck out to play middle-power roles in the post-1945 world order. To be sure, both states had links to the Southeast Asian region through the Commonwealth. Both states had economic ties of investment, trade and development assistance. And both were actively involved in the region during the Cold War era, although they were active in different ways and for different reasons, reflecting Andrew F. Cooper's contention that Australia and Canada may be like-minded states in the contemporary international system but they tend to have very different diplomatic styles (Cooper, 1992). However, I will argue that the general approach of both Canberra and Ottawa towards Southeast Asia during this period was driven by the imperatives and constraints of great-power politics.

For Australians, perched on the edge of the region, the politics of Southeast Asia during the early years of the Cold War represented a direct threat to the security of Australia. In part, this threat was perceived in the light of Japanese expansionism of the late 1930s and early 1940s. Japan's military successes of the early 1940s created a lingering fear among many Australians that invasion and occupation by Japan had been narrowly averted only because of the intervention of a great power protector, the United States, seen by many Australians as assuming the role of Australia's 'great and powerful friend', displacing Britain (Harper, 1987; Cheeseman, 1993).

After the war, the fear of physical attack from an Asian power was no less potent, though the source of concern had shifted to the threat posed by the rise of communism. This fear found expression on numerous occasions and in different contexts, and was very much part of the discourse on security in Australia in the 1950s. A statement to Parliament by the Australian Minister for External Affairs, Richard G. Casey, in October 1954 (quoted in Millar, 1991, p. 218) is illustrative of how many Australians tended to see their security dilemma during this period:

> If the whole of Indo-China fell to the Communists, Thailand would be gravely exposed. If Thailand were to fall, the road would be open to Malaya and Singapore. From the Malay Peninsula the Com-

munists could dominate the northern approaches to Australia and even cut our life-lines with Europe.

The concern with the Communist threat to Southeast Asia was, not surprisingly, reflected in Canberra's general policy approach to the region during the Cold War era. While Australia opened diplomatic links and development assistance programmes with the states of Southeast Asia in the period of decolonization after World War II, there was a distinct defence orientation to Australian policy towards the region (Angel, 1992). This was reflected in direct and active military involvement, ranging from the participation of Australian forces in the Malayan Emergency of the 1950s and in opposing Indonesia's 'crush Malaysia' campaign of 1963-6, to the sending of troops to fight alongside the United States in Vietnam. It was reflected in the military aid extended to Singapore and Malaysia, such as the squadron of Sabre fighter aircraft given to Malaysia in 1969 (Richardson, 1974, p. 248).

The preoccupation in Australia with security concerns continued to be evident even after the strategic environment in Southeast Asia changed dramatically in the late 1960s and early 1970s with the withdrawal of Britain east of Suez and the military withdrawal of the United States from Indochina. It could be seen in the eagerness with which Canberra embraced the Five Power Defence Arrangements, a collective security agreement among five Commonwealth members (Australia, Britain, Malaysia, New Zealand and Singapore) which was intended to compensate for Britain's withdrawal east of Suez. It can also be seen in Australia's reaction to the Indonesian invasion and occupation of East Timor, where the blunt outrage of Australian public opinion contrasted sharply with the more muted and understanding reactions of the Australian government (Viviani, 1978; Albinski, 1977, pp. 106–10). Likewise, the Australian concern with security and stability can be seen in Canberra's reactions to the eventual military victories in 1975 of the Communist forces of the Khmer Rouge in Cambodia, of the Pathet Lao in Laos, and of the North Vietnamese and Viet Cong in South Vietnam; Malcolm Fraser, whose conservative coalition between the Liberal Party and the Country Party (later the National Party) came to power in December 1975, embarked on a strongly anti-Vietnamese policy designed to blunt both Soviet and Vietnamese threats to regional stability (Renouf, 1986, p. 166). And when the Vietnamese invaded Cambodia in 1978, and the Indochinese peninsula again became the focus of intense political rivalry among the great powers, Australia strongly supported Western and ASEAN efforts to limit Soviet involvement and Vietnamese power in the region. Canberra backed ASEAN's anti-Vietnamese diplomacy, even though there was considerable distaste at the involvement of the Khmer Rouge in the ASEAN-supported Coalition Government of Democratic Kampuchea.

By the late-1980s the security environment in Southeast Asia had shifted again, mainly as a result of shifts in the foreign policy orientations of the great powers. By this time it was evident that the Soviet Union under Mikhail S. Gorbachev was no longer so eager to expand its presence in the region; the government in Beijing was pursuing a more feisty foreign policy, one that mixed strenuous attempts to take advantage of the economic dynamism of the region and efforts to be more assertive in regional issues, such as a settlement in Cambodia and the dispute over the Spratly Islands; and the United States was experiencing what some were maintaining was 'imperial overstretch' in the Asia Pacific, leading to a diminished desire to maintain a strong presence in the region.

For Australia the shifting policies of the great powers were cause for concern. Although the strategy of trying to keep the great powers of the West engaged in the region as the 'cornerstone for Australia's Southeast Asian policies' had by this time 'come into question' (Angel, 1992, pp. 156–7), the government of Robert Hawke nonetheless continued to try to link Australian security to regional security: as late as 1989, the Minister for Foreign Affairs, Gareth Evans, and the Minister for Defence, Kim Beazley, were defining Australia's security concerns in terms of the dangers of regional instability (Cheeseman, 1993, pp. 20–22, 143–56). Moreover, Australia's defence posture still included military aid to the countries of ASEAN under the Defence Cooperation Program throughout this period (Cheeseman, 1993, pp. 161–2).

During this same period, by contrast, Canadians had no security involvement in Southeast Asia comparable to those of Australia. Rather, Canadian concerns tended to focus on the impact that regional conflicts in Southeast Asia might have on politics at the global level. Thus, for example, though Canada had no direct security interests in the war in Indochina in the early 1950s, the government in Ottawa had become involved in that conflict by allowing Canada's name to be put forward as a member of the International Commission of Supervision and Control that was established by the 1954 Geneva Conference to oversee the ceasefires in the three new Indochinese states.

It is true that the Canadian government did not originally view its service on the truce supervisory commissions with much enthusiasm, but its willingness to become involved in conflict resolution in an area where it had few concrete interests was largely predicated on the tenets of what has come to be known as middle power diplomacy, or, more ironically, 'middlepowermanship.' (Gordon, 1966; Painchaud, 1966; Holmes, 1966; Holbraad, 1984; Hawes, 1984; Wood, 1990; Cooper, Higgott, and Nossal, 1993). Middlepowermanship involves a style of diplomacy premised on the notion that it was in Canada's broad security interests to involve itself in the settlement of local conflicts that involved the great powers, on the assumption that an increase in great power tensions over local 'brushfire' conflicts might lead to a great power conflagration, which was persistently defined by Canadian governments to be antithetical to core Canadian interests.

To the extent that Canadian participation in the work of the truce supervisory commissions prevented a larger conflict involving Canada's allies and friends, Canadian security interests were served (Ross, 1984). And later, with the escalation of the Vietnam War in the mid-1960s, the Canadian government was to use Canada's membership in the International Commissions to try to play the honest broker in the conflict. To be sure, as American involvement in that war increased, membership in the ICSC brought a related benefit, affording Ottawa some protection from requests to send military forces to assist the United States in the conflict. However, while the government in Ottawa might have expressed publicly its doubts about the wisdom of escalation in Vietnam (English, 1992), or privately its relief at being able to use its membership on the ICSC as a means of deflecting suggestions of a Canadian military contribution to the conflict, there was never any doubt about where Canada stood on the broader issue of Communist influence in Southeast Asia during the Cold War era.

That Canada was generally sympathetic to the efforts to limit Communist expansion in the region can be seen in virtually all other facets of Canadian policy towards Southeast Asia during this period. For example, Canadian policy during the *konfrontasi* between Malaysia and Indonesia, which saw Ottawa provide military aid to Malaysia and withhold food aid to Indonesia, was in part predicated on the value that Ottawa placed on the Commonwealth as an international institution (Cohn, 1980; Keenleyside, 1988; Stubbs, 1990, p. 354) and the fear that unless concrete support were given to Malaysia, the confrontation would end up fracturing the Commonwealth, and in part on a concern about the regional impact of the Chinese-backed Sukarno regime in Jakarta.

Likewise, Canada's development assistance policies towards the states of Southeast Asia were in large measure designed to complement other efforts to stem Communist expansion. The Colombo Plan had begun as a development assistance scheme for the newly independent states of the Indian subcontinent. One of the catalysts for this programme was a Western concern that if the economies of the subcontinent, particularly India, were not given external assistance, these states might end up as China had in the late 1940s, with a popular revolution and a Communist government allied to the Chinese or Soviets. Over the 1960s, Canada's development assistance program was slowly extended to the states of Southeast Asia. In 1970, with the emergence of a pro-Western regime in Jakarta, the government of Pierre Elliott Trudeau selected Indonesia as a 'country of concentration' for Canadian development assistance (Hainsworth, 1986, p. 16). It can be argued that the choice of Indonesia as a target 'country of concentration' was determined by a concern in Ottawa for the implications of strategic shifts in great power politics in the region, and a desire to bolster the region's largest power against the putative expansionary designs of the Communist states of Indochina (Nossal, 1980). On the other side of the coin, the halting evolution of Canadian development assistance policies towards the states of Indochina after the end of the war in 1975 was clearly driven by Cold War considerations. After 1975 Ottawa was slow to fulfill its promise, made in 1970, to extend a full reconstruction package to the states of Indochina once hostilities had ceased: I have argued (Nossal, 1978) that this hesitation was primarily driven by Canadian concerns about Vietnamese intentions towards the Southeast Asian region. The Vietnamese invasion of Cambodia in December 1978 and the overthrow of the Pol Pot regime in January 1979 was seen as vindication of these concerns, and the aid sanctions imposed on Vietnam and Cambodia in February 1979 were held to be the most appropriate response to the intrusion of the Soviet Union into the region (Nossal, 1994).

Finally, it can be argued that Cold War considerations helped shape Canada's human rights policies towards the region. The main impact of the Cold War, it can be argued, was to dampen or mute concern for violations of human or civil rights in those states sympathetic to the West (for example, the Philippines and Indonesia), and sharpen concern for human rights violations in those states allied or friendly to the dominant rival, the Soviet Union, such as Vietnam (Keenleyside, 1988, pp. 197–8). It is equally revealing that in those cases where human rights violations were occurring in a state that was not playing an important part in the rivalry of the great powers – such as Burma – the government in Ottawa remained largely indifferent.

REGIONAL ECONOMIC ENGAGEMENT

To argue that the policies of Australia and Canada towards Southeast Asia tended to be shaped by the broader concerns of great power rivalry is not to suggest that this was the sole factor that determined the Australian and Canadia approach to the region. For it is undeniable that as Southeast Asia's importance in the Asia–Pacific political economy grew over the waning years of the Cold War, transnational links of all sorts – trade, development assistance, investment, education, tourism and immigration – grew up between the countries of Southeast Asia and both Australia and Canada.

This is most clearly seen in the development of two-way trade between these middle powers and the region. As Table 10.1 shows, Canada's trade with the nations of ASEAN grew at an accelerated rate in the early years, from 6 per cent between 1970 and 1975, to 19 per cent between 1975 and 1980. By the late 1980s there was over $3 billion in two-way trade between Canada and the countries of ASEAN, representing over 1 per cent of Canada's imports and exports. Australia's trade with the countries of ASEAN demonstrated even stronger growth. As Table 10.1 demonstrates, exports to ASEAN countries grew from 6 per cent of total exports in 1970 to 11.5 per cent in 1990, when Australia was sending $5.61 billion to Southeast Asia, and importing $2.98 billion, or 6.1 per cent, from the region. This two-way trade represented an increase of 50 per cent over the the percentage of trade with Southeast Asia in 1985.

Likewise, both countries put in place active development assistance policies in the region over the course of the Cold War era. By the end of the 1980s Australia's development assistance programme to the countries of ASEAN stood at $40.2 million, or 18 per cent of total ODA (Official Development Assistance) disbursements, and representing an increase of 33 per cent from 1985. In Canada's case, the development assistance programme to Southeast Asia grew as dramatically: bilateral disbursements to ASEAN countries doubled between 1971–2 and 1972–3, increasing from 6 per cent of bilateral aid to all Asia to a high of 15 per cent by 1975–6. By 1984 a total of $74 million was being disbursed by the Canadian International Development Agency in the ASEAN countries, a figure that rose to $134 million a mere four years later.

Moreover, one could not deny that the evolving importance of Southeast Asia to the international political economy was being mirrored by sharp changes in both the Australian and Canadian economies, prompting both

Table 10.1 Australian and Candadian trade with ASEAN, 1970–90 (millions of Australian/Canadian dollars and percentage of total imports/exports)

		1970	1975	1980	1985	1990
Australia	Imports from ASEAN	119 2.6%	317 3.3%	1,268 6.7%	1,659 4.9%	2,980 6.1%
	Exports to ASEAN	296 6.0%	659 6.8%	1,615 8.4%	2,218 6.4%	5,580 11.5%
Canada	Imports from ASEAN	60 0.4%	146 0.4%	388 0.6%	760 0.7%	1,742 1.3%
	Exports to ASEAN	79 0.4%	210 0.6%	741 1.0%	767 0.6%	1,689 1.1%

Source: Australian Bureau of Statistics; Statistics Canada.

the governments in Canberra and Ottawa to reassess their broad economic and trade policies. In the 1980s both the Australian and Canadian governments sought, actively and consciously, to expand their economic relations with Southeast Asia, particularly the countries of ASEAN.

In Australia's case this took the form of a policy of 'comprehensive engagement' (Evans and Grant, 1991, p. 182). Seeking to expand relations with Southeast Asia was part of a wider projection of Australia into the Asian region during the 1980s, a process by which politicians, diplomats, and many in the private sector have pushed the notion that Australia has to 'catch up with its geography' (Evans, 1990, p. 421). In other words, Australia could no longer afford its previous role of a largely white European outpost on the periphery of Asia, dependent on Britain for trade and the United States for defence. Rather, Australian elites in the 1980s began pushing the notion that Australia was an Asian country. To be sure, they recognized that Australia was different from other Asian countries, but it nonetheless should seek to be (as Australian policy-makers are fond of putting it) 'odd man in' rather than 'odd man out' in Asia.

The policy framework of 'engagement' propelled increased economic and cultural links between Australia and the countries of ASEAN in particular. A special 'dialogue' relationship between Australia and ASEAN had been concluded as early as 1974, but economic links between Australia and the countries of the region had been slow to grow, in part because of complementarities between their economies (Evans and Grant, 1991, p. 189). But by the late 1980s, as we saw above, Australia's trade with the countries of ASEAN began to rise spectacularly.

In Canada's case there was also the push for more active engagement. While Canada's 'dialogue' relationship with ASEAN had been inaugurated in 1977, three years after Australia's, it was not until the 1980s that there was a sustained effort to expand the relationship. As Stubbs (1990, pp. 351–2) has noted, the government of Brian Mulroney actively sought to expand official relations with Southeast Asia over the course of the 1980s. One concrete manifestation of this interest was the establishment of the Canada–ASEAN Centre, opened in Singapore in July 1989. After the official opening of the centre, Joe Clark, the Secretary of State for External Affairs, described it as Canada's 'anchor' in the region, an institution which would provide a base for the Canadian government's local activities. The centre's mission was to provide a focal point for training, education and research, and to provide a home for CIDA's development cooperation programme for the ASEAN region (*Canadian International Relations Chronicle*, July–Sept. 1989, p. 25).

Mirroring this increased governmental interest, there was a comparable rise in Canadian trade with Southeast Asia during this period, as we saw above. However, it should be stressed that as a percentage of total Canadian trade, the trade with Southeast Asia was still minute. Although the efforts to increase the total volume of trade between Canada and the countries of ASEAN bore considerable fruit, there can be little doubt that trade with the industrialized north (the United States, Japan, and the countries of the European Community) still dominated Canadian trading patterns.

THE POST-COLD WAR ERA

One of the key indications of the degree to which the policies of these middle powers towards Southeast Asia were affected by the constraints and imperatives of the Cold War is to examine what occurred when the constraints evaporated with the effective withdrawal of the Soviet Union from the region at the turn of the decade, and then the collapse of the Soviet state in 1991. Four illustrative cases suggest themselves: the approach of these middle powers towards Vietnam; the case of Cambodia; the attitude of Australia and Canada towards human rights observance in the region; and the Australian–Malaysian spat of November/December 1993.

In the wake of the weakening of great power tensions in the region in the late 1980s, both the Australian and Canadian governments involved themselves in trying to mitigate the antagonism between Vietnam and virtually all of its neighbours ranged in a broad anti-Soviet coalition led by China and the United States. As the 1980s wore on, both Canberra and Ottawa became distinctly uncomfortable with the continuing efforts of the coalition to punish the key Soviet ally in the region, Vietnam. Indeed, the Australian Labour Party government of Bob Hawke, when it was first elected in 1983, tried to take the initiative to bring Vietnam's isolation to an end, but was firmly rebuffed by both the United States and China, and roundly criticized by ASEAN (O'Brien, 1987; Harris, 1988). The Canadian government, mindful of the treatment meted out to Australia when Canberra stepped out of line, maintained its own sanctions against Vietnam throughout the 1980s, despite growing discomfort with the policy in official Ottawa (Nossal, 1994).

But by 1989, with Vietnam's withdrawal from Cambodia, both governments decided that the time had come to bring the ostracism to an end. In November 1989 Australia publicly recommended that the Asian Development Bank lift its ban on loans; in January 1990 the Canadian government moved to restore Vietnam's eligibility for official development assistance; by March 1992, Australia had approved a A$100 million aid package for Vietnam. In each case, these initiatives met with opposition from others in the region, particularly from the ASEAN countries; but each was taken in the hope that it would catalyze others into rethinking the wisdom of the ostracism of Vietnam. Moreover, both middle powers took these initiatives despite the annoyance that officials in Canberra and Ottawa knew they would cause in ASEAN capitals.

A related example of the transformative opportunities that came with the waning of the Cold War was the opening available for conflict-reduction initiatives in one of the most intractable conflicts in the region – that of Cambodia. As early as 1983, the newly elected Labour government of Bob Hawke actively involved itself in attempting to broker a solution to the Indochina problem, eagerly embracing the role of mediator in the conflict. However, as in the case of his Vietnam initiatives, Hawke was to discover that Australia's other friends and allies in the region were not overly interested in Australia playing that role.

As a result, the government in Canberra abandoned its attempts to act as an mediator, which had meant essentially trying to find common ground between the contending sides from a 'middle' position. Rather, Canberra quickly recognized that the costs of moving outside the position of a committed member of the anti-Vietnamese coalition were too high. Instead the Hawke government embraced the role of trying to facilitate a process of conflict resolution within the Western coalition. Using the opportunity afforded by the virtual collapse of the anti-Soviet/anti-Vietnam coalition after the Tiananmen massacre in 1989, the Australian government devoted considerable effort to breaking the diplomatic impasse that had stalemated the Paris International Conference on Cambodia. Adopting what has been termed a middle-power technical and entrepreneurial leadership role (Cooper, Higgott and Nossal, 1993), the Australian government produced a series of studies that comprised essentially a step-by-step peace plan – the 'Red Book' on Cambodia, entitled *Cambodia: An Australian Peace Proposal*. This technical document stressed an enhanced role for the United Nations as the means of breaking the power-sharing impasse, outlining in detail the role that the UN could play in civil administration, in organizing and conducting fair elections and in monitoring cease-fires and military withdrawals. It is no coincidence that the UN Security Council Framework Document on Cambodia bears such a striking resemblance to the Red Book's executive summary. Nor is it any coincidence that Australian peacekeeping troops were called on to play a leading role in the UN Advance Mission in Cambodia (UNAMIC) or that an Australian was appointed to head the military component of the UN Transitional Authority in Cambodia (UNTAC) (Evans and Grant, 1991, pp. 206–18). In this case, then, we can see how Australia managed to take advantage of the loosening of the tight anti-Soviet coalition that had marked regional politics in the 1980s to push its own policy preferences.

A third telling example of the impact of the end of the Cold War on Australia's and Canada's approach to Southeast Asia has been on the issue of human rights. As we saw above, the geostrategic constraints imposed on Australian and Canadian policy during the Cold War era had had the impact of dampening the expression of concerns among officials in Canberra and Ottawa over human rights violations.

This was particularly evident in policy towards Indonesia. On 12 November 1991, Indonesian troops in Dili, the capital of Timor, attacked a group of approximately 2500 mourners at a funeral service for a young Timorese pro-independence activist who had been killed two weeks earlier by Indonesian soldiers. By all accounts, the only provocation that the mourners were offering was to carry the flag of Fretilin, the outlawed Timorese independence movement, and pictures of its guerrilla leader, Xanana Gusmao. At the cemetery, Indonesian soldiers opened fire on the group, and subsequently moved in on the mourners, allegedly bayonetting many of them. In the immediate aftermath of the massacre, it was claimed that numerous Timorese were 'disappeared' by Indonesian authorities. Numerous foreign journalists witnessed the massacre itself; and it was recorded on video by Yorkshire Television.

Canada's Secretary of State for External Affairs, Barbara McDougall, who was at the third Asia–Pacific Economic Cooperation (APEC) conference in Seoul when the massacre occurred, immediately held a meeting with the Indonesian Foreign Minister, Ali Alatas, during which she expressed Canadian 'outrage' over the behaviour of the Indonesian troops. The same day, the Indonesian ambassador to Ottawa was called in to External Affairs to hear further criticism and Canada's ambassador to Indonesia called on the government to convey Canada's anger. At the United Nations, Canada's permanent representative condemned Indonesian actions in Dili before the Third Committee (see the account in Canada, 1991).

This was followed by the imposition of development assistance sanctions. On 9 December 1991 the Canadian government announced that it was suspending approval of all new development assistance projects that might 'directly benefit' the Indonesian government. The value of the projects affected was approximately $30 million (*Globe and Mail*, 10 Dec. 1991; *Canadian International Relations Chronicle*, Oct.–Dec. 1991. p. 23).

The immediate reaction from the Hawke government was to call for an international investigation into the massacre. However, public opinion in Australia pushed the government to do more, particularly when the Yorkshire film was smuggled out of Indonesia some days after the massacre and widely shown on TV. Pressure on the government in Canberra for harsher action came from the Timorese community in Australia, church groups, aid and university groups, unions, and indeed from the Left faction of the Australian Labour Party (Feith, 1992, pp. 3–4). While the Australian government did not, like Canada, respond to this pressure by invoking sanctions against Jakarta – instead it pronounced itself satisfied with the internal investigation of the massacre conducted by the Indonesian government – there was little doubt that the massacre prompted Canberra to back away somewhat from its previous pro-Indonesian position.

However, the more active pursuit of human rights concerns by Australia and Canada, which tended to accelerate in the post-Cold War era (Schmitz, 1992), introduced an element of disharmony in the relations between these middle powers and the ASEAN states. In particular, there has been a tendency in some Southeast Asian states to rebuff human rights representations as merely manifestations of European culture and not necessarily reflective of Asian standards (Evans and Grant, 1991, p. 148). As Paul M. Evans (1992, p. 75) has argued, 'The tensions produced by these differences will not only be manifested in more difficult bilateral relationships, but unless very carefully managed will have an effect on inter-regional interactions.'

One final case indicating the impact of the end of the Cold War can be found in the dispute between Australia and Malaysia over Asia–Pacific Economic Cooperation (APEC). The APEC idea, closely associated with Hawke and the Australian government (Higgott, Cooper and Bonnor, 1990), was designed to construct an inclusive forum for economic cooperation that would not only keep Japan and the United States within the same multilateral economic cooperation forum, but, as importantly, would also provide a legitimate place for Australia. Canberra was therefore concerned when the Malaysian government of Prime Minister Mahathir decided to push for another conception of regional cooperation, one that focused exclusively on the East Asian economies, pointedly excluding not only the North American members – the United States and Canada – but also Australia (Nossal and Stubbs, forthcoming). The dispute intensified when Mahathir decided to boycott the Seattle meeting of APEC hosted by President Bill Clinton in November 1993. In Seattle, the Australian prime minister, Paul Keating, said that he couldn't care less whether Mahathir attended APEC forums, calling him a 'recalcitrant.' While the word 'recalcitrant' made little sense in the circumstances, there could be no mistaking Keating's pejorative intent, and the statement stirred a brief spat between the two countries. In Malaysia, some senior members of the governing party called for the adoption of a 'Buy Australia Last' campaign, and there were threats to terminate a lucrative $3 billion contract for patrol vessels that Malaysia was planning to buy from Australian shipyards. The dispute turned out to be relatively short-lived: the two prime ministers moved quickly to dampen the rhetoric. However, it did reveal some of the tensions that have become more apparent since the end of the Cold War. And while Keating may merely have been giving vent to a concern about Mahathir's Asia-first proclivities that was more widely held in the Asia Pacific, the fact that he would express such concerns in public revealed the degree to which the cohesive bonds of the Cold War coalition had weakened, lowering the costs of squabbling for smaller states.

These four case studies suggest that when the constraints imposed by the Cold War rivalries of the great powers were lifted after in 1989, the governments in Canberra and Ottawa felt much freer to pursue more autonomous policies towards the countries of Southeast Asia. No longer did the Australian or Canadian governments have to worry about the effects of breaking coalition unity on issues of importance to other states, particularly the great powers, such as the isolation of Vietnam or the issue of human rights in Indonesia. No longer did prime ministers in Canberra or Ottawa have to be concerned that their policy preferences would not fit with the larger geostrategic objectives of their friends and allies in the region. To be sure, bilateral economic interests did serve to dampen what otherwise might have been greater pressure on such aspects as human rights – as, for example, was the case in Australia's reaction to the Dili massacre – but on the whole it can be argued that both these middle powers were able to give much freer expression to their foreign policy concerns once the constraints imposed by the Cold War had been lifted. Their actions more than ever were affected by the political role of NGOs.

CONCLUSION

Given the rapid rise in Australian and Canadian economic, diplomatic and cultural relations with the countries of Southeast Asia in the 1980s and early 1990s, it is tempting to conclude that what has propelled these relationships is primarily a concern for economic gain as middle powers like Australia and Canada seek to relocate themselves in a evolving international political economy. There can be little doubt that the increasing dynamism of the Southeast Asian economies in the 1980s drew increasing attention from business and government in Canada and especially Australia.

However, I have suggested in this chapter that when one examines the Australian and Canadian approach to Southeast Asia over the course of several decades, it can be argued that the policies of these middle powers towards the region were heavily influenced not so much by the search for economic advantage as by the imperatives and constraints of great power rivalry. I have suggested that geostrategic concerns played an important part in shaping Australian and Canadian policies towards the countries of Southeast Asia throughout the Cold War, and that we can see the degree to which the policies of these states were influenced by strategic concerns by looking at what has occurred in the

"New World Order". With the effective end of the Cold War in 1989, the great power rivalry in the region dissipated, with the result that Australian and Canadian policy-makers have been liberated from the constraints imposed by the coalition politics of the Cold War. There has been evidence of an increasing fracturing in the relationships, as both the Southeast Asian countries and Australia and Canada are no longer so tightly bound to one another as they were before 1989.

Editorial Note

In 1995 the Australian desire to become part of EAEC and otherwise benefit economically from its physical proximity to Asia has appeared to cause modifications of Australian policy on human rights and other issues that might upset Indonesia or other ASEAN members.

Canada under Prime Minister Jean Chretien has explicitly abandoned the earlier attempt to link human rights to Canadian economic relations with Asia.

References

Angel, J. R. (1992) 'Australia and Southeast Asia', in P. J. Boyce and J. R. Angel (eds) pp. 146–66.

Albinski, Henry S. (1977) *Australian External Policy under Labor* (St Lucia: Queensland University Press/Vancouver: University of British Columbia Press).

Boyce, P. J. and J. R. Angel (eds) (1992) *Diplomacy in the Marketplace: Australia in World Affairs, 1981–90* (Melbourne: Longman Cheshire).

Canada (1991) Parliament, House of Commons, Standing Committee on External Affairs and International Trade, Sub-Committee on Development and Human Rights. *Minutes of Proceedings and Evidence*, Issue 9, 9 December.

Cheeseman, Graeme (1993) *The Search for Self-Reliance: Australian Defence since Vietnam* (Melbourne: Longman Cheshire).

Cohn, Theodore (1980) 'Politics of Canadian Food Aid: The Case of South and Southeast Asia', in Theodore Cohn, Geoffrey Hainsworth and Lorne Kavic (eds). *Canada and Southeast Asia: Perspectives and Evolution of Public Policies* (Coquitlam, BC: Kaen Publishers).

Cooper, Andrew Fenton (1992) 'Like-minded Nations and Contrasting Diplomatic Styles: Australian and Canadian Approaches to Agricultural Trade', *Canadian Journal of Political Science*, vol. 25 (June), pp. 349–79.

Cooper, Andrew F., Richard A. Higgott and Kim Richard Nossal (1993) *Relocating Middle Powers: Australia and Canada in a Changing World Order* (Vancouver: University of British Columbia Press).

English, John (1992) 'Speaking Out on Vietnam, 1965', in Don Munton and

John Kirton (eds) *Canadian Foreign Policy: Selected Cases* (Scarborough: Prentice-Hall Canada), pp. 135–52.

Evans, Gareth (1990) 'Australia is Catching Up with its Geography', *Australian Foreign Affairs and Trade: The Monthly Record*, vol. 61 (July), pp. 420–28.

Evans, Gareth and Bruce Grant (1991) *Australia's Foreign Relations in the World of the 1990s* (Melbourne: Melbourne University Press).

Evans, Paul M. (1992) 'A North American Perspective on the Pacific in the 1990s: On the Pacific or of the Pacific?' *Australian-Canadian Studies*, vol. 10, no. 1, pp. 61–80.

Feith, Herb (1992) 'East Timor after the Dili Massacre', *Pacific Research*, vol. 5 (February); pp. 3–5.

Gordon, J. King (ed.) (1966) *Canada's Role as a Middle Power* (Toronto: Canadian Institute of International Affairs).

Greenwood, Gordon and Norman Harper (eds) (1974) *Australia in World Affairs* (Vancouver: University of British Columbia Press).

Hainsworth, Geoffrey B. (1986) *Innocents Abroad or Partners in Development? An Evaluation of Canada–Indonesia Aid, Trade, and Investment Relations*, Field Report Series 15 (Singapore: Institute of Southeast Asian Studies).

Harper, Norman (1987) *A Great and Powerful Friend: A Study of Australian American Relations between 1900 and 1975* (St Lucia: University of Queensland Press).

Harris, Stuart (1988) 'Australian Government Perspectives and Policies', in Colin Mackerras, Robert Cribb and Allan Healy (eds) *Contemporary Vietnam: Perspectives from Australia*. (Wollongong, NSW: University of Wollongong Press) pp. 31–44.

Hawes, Michael K. (1984) *Principal Power, Middle Power, or Satellite?* (Toronto: York Programme in Strategic Studies).

Higgott, Richard A., Andrew Fenton Cooper and Jenelle Bonnor (1990) 'Asia Pacific Economic Cooperation: An Evolving Case Study in Leadership and Cooperation Building', *International Journal*, vol. 45 (Autumn), pp. 822–66.

Holbraad, Carsten (1984) *Middle Powers in International Politics* (London: Macmillan).

Holmes, John W. (1966) 'Is There a Future for Middlepowermanship?' in J. King Gordon (ed.), pp. 13–28

Keenleyside, T. A. (1988). 'Development Assistance', in Robert O. Matthews and Cranford Pratt (eds) *Human Rights in Canadian Foreign Policy* (Montreal and Kingston: McGill-Queen's University Press), pp. 187–208

Millar, T. B. (1991) *Australia in Peace and War*, 2nd ed. (Canberra: Australian National University Press).

Nossal, Kim Richard (1978) 'Retreat, Retraction and Reconstruction: Canada and Indochina in the Post-Hostilities Period', in Gordon P. Means (ed.) *The Past in Southeast Asia's Present* (Ottawa: Canadian Council for Southeast Asian Studies), pp. 171–81

Nossal, Kim Richard (1980) 'Les Droits de la Personne et la Politique étrangère canadienne: le Cas de l'Indonésie', *Etudes internationales*, vol. 11, pp. 223–38.

Nossal, Kim Richard (1994) *Rain Dancing: Sanctions in Canadian and Aus-*

tralian Foreign Policy (Toronto: University of Toronto Press).

Nossal, Kim Richard and Richard Stubbs (forthcoming) 'Mahathir's Malaysia: an emergent middle power?' in Andrew F. Cooper (ed.) *Niche Diplomacy: Middle Powers in the Post-Cold War Era* (Boulder: Westview Press).

O'Brien, Philip G. (1987) *The Making of Australia's Indochina Policies under the Labor Government (1983–1986): the Politics of Circumspection?* Research Paper 39 (Nathan, Qld: Centre for the Study of Australian–Asian Relations, Griffith University).

Painchaud, Paul (1966) 'Middlepowermanship as an Ideology', in J. King Gordon (ed.), pp. 29–36.

Renouf, Alan (1986) *Malcolm Fraser and Australian Foreign Policy* (Sydney: Australian Professional Publications).

Richardson, J. L. (1974) 'Australian Strategic and Defence Policies', in G. Greenwood and N. Harper (eds), pp. 233–69.

Ross, Douglas A. (1984) *In the Interests of Peace: Canada and Vietnam, 1954–1973* (Toronto: University of Toronto Press).

Schmitz, Gerald J. (1992) 'Human rights, democratization, and international conflict', in Fen Osler Hampson and Christopher J. Maule (eds), *Canada Among Nations, 1992–93: A New World Order?* (Ottawa: Carleton University Press), pp. 235–55.

Stubbs, Richard (1990) 'Canada's Relations with Malaysia: Picking Partners in ASEAN', *Pacific Affairs*, vol. 63 (Fall), pp. 352–66.

Praagh, David van (1976) 'Canada and Southeast Asia', in Peyton V. Lyon and Tareq Y. Ismael (eds). *Canada and the Third World* (Toronto: Macmillan), pp. 307–42.

Viviani, Nancy (1978) 'Australians and the Timor Issue: II', *Australian Outlook*, vol. 32 (December), pp. 241–61

Wood, Bernard (1990) *The Middle Powers and the General Interest*, Middle Powers in the International System, no. 1 (Ottawa: North–South Institute).

11 Western Europe and Southeast Asia

Brian Bridges

The end of the Cold War brought significant changes to international patterns of interaction and the relationship between Western Europe and Southeast Asia was not immune to these broader shifts. European attention was diverted by the primacy of coping with the disintegration of communism, first in Eastern Europe, and then in the Soviet Union itself, coupled with the dynamics – and hiccups – of the European Union[1] attempts to create a single integrated market. Southeast Asia quietly slipped down the list of European priorities until 1992–3, when primarily Cambodia and human rights issues, but also re-evaluated economic prospects, heralded another surge of interest.

In writing about European policies towards Southeast Asia, two difficulties present themselves. Firstly, 'Europe' is an entity lacking clear definition or agreed boundaries. For the purposes of this chapter, the emphasis is on the European Union and its current fifteen member countries. However, on occasions, the terms 'Western Europe' and 'Europe' will be used to denote wider geopolitical concerns. Secondly, the EU-level relationship with ASEAN and individual Southeast Asian countries has become increasingly entangled with the relationships between individual EU member states and those same Southeast Asian countries. The difficulty is compounded by the EU's strong influence over economic matters but its restricted, though slowly expanding, competence over foreign policy issues. The EU is not a fully-fledged state-like actor in the international arena and on certain issues individual EU countries can play a key promotional or blocking role. The idea of a coherent and comprehensive EU strategy towards Southeast Asia is, therefore, an unrealistic one.

LEGACIES AND PATTERNS

In the first three decades after the World War II, the European withdrawal from Southeast Asia, involving the removal of colonial administrations and the reduction of military commitments, was accompanied by a loosening or severing of economic and commercial ties. Although after the Vietnamese invasion of Kampuchea European governments were keen to support and boost ASEAN, European commercial activity in the region remained low-key into the 1980s (Harris and Bridges, 1983, pp. 23–55).

In practice, by the early 1980s the EC's policies towards the developing world had become structured into a 'pyramid of privilege' (Stevens, 1981, pp. 60–82). Despite the EC belief that regional organizations such as ASEAN could contribute not only to economic development but also to stability and security against communist influence, the ASEAN countries fell into the category of developing countries with no 'association agreement', even though a cooperation agreement was concluded with the EC in 1980.[2] The Indochinese states and Burma ranked below. This structure remained basically unchanged through the 1980s, until the dramatic changes in Eastern Europe led to the insertion higher up in the pyramid of the newly emerging democracies, or at least some of them, by means of association agreements.

The EC–ASEAN Cooperation Agreement provided the framework for consultative discussions on commercial, technological and developmental issues. But, although a variety of government and private sector formats were tried out, particularly during the mid-1980s when the sustained economic growth of the region began to attract greater European corporate interest, the record was mixed. Moreover, it was undoubtedly an unequal economic relationship, in which the ASEAN countries inevitably found themselves in the weaker bargaining position.

The growth in EC–ASEAN political cooperation, by contrast, was a markedly more successful feature of the 1980s, when the Afghanistan and Cambodian problems, clearly of particular importance to the EC and ASEAN respectively, brought about a coincidence of interest (Mols, 1990, pp. 71–3). Cambodia remained a focus of EC–ASEAN meetings throughout the decade, but the dialogues gradually broadened to cover a much wider range of regional and international issues. By contrast with the economic dialogue, ASEAN felt able to meet the EC on a more equal basis on political questions.

Post-colonial relationships tend to be an amalgam of contradictory emotions and unrealistic expectations. The relations of Britain, France, the Netherlands and, in the specific East Timorese case, Portugal, with their former colonies in Southeast Asia have been no exception to this rule. Although the United States and Japan maintain greater leverage in Southeast Asia, the Europeans feel that they are less hampered by emotional baggage and could therefore be better able to contribute to the resolution of conflict and the development of more open political systems in the region. Also, Southeast Asians do tend to see the Europeans as a much less dominant or potentially threatening alternative to the Japanese and the Americans. Nonetheless, the Europeans have not always found it easy to exorcise the ghosts of the past and, as the Dutch found out in 1992 when Indonesia cut them out of its aid partner programme (shades of the 1981 Malaysian 'buy British last' campaign), a rethinking of attitudes has had to continue. The result has been that, whatever the French might claim about their links with Indochina (recalled evocatively in the award-winning film, *Indochine*), it is some time since there were any 'special relationships' which worked substantially in the favour of European interests.

EU–ASEAN: REORDERING PRIORITIES

The main axis of recent European involvement in Southeast Asia has been and continues to be the relationship with the ASEAN countries. There has been no fundamental change over the past few years in the Europeans' basic perception of ASEAN as a relatively stable, accessible and politically compatible grouping. However, there have been some fluctuations in the economic relationship and some new tensions brought into what had been a relatively trouble-free politico-strategic dialogue.

Following on the resurgence of European commercial interest in the ASEAN countries in the mid-1980s, EC exports to the ASEAN countries grew from US$7.7 billion in 1985 to $21 billion in 1991, while EC imports from ASEAN rose from US$8.9 billion to $25.8 billion over the same period. ASEAN as a group, therefore, remained in surplus with the EC throughout the period. However, while the absolute value grew, the relative importance to each side remained basically unchanged. For the EC, trade with ASEAN still represented less than 2 per cent of its total trade, while for ASEAN, the EC still accounted for around 15 per cent of its total trade. In 1988–9 for Brunei, Burma, Indonesia and Thailand trade with EC was greater than that with the US and Canada together.

From 1985 onwards, manufactured goods represented more than half of the total value of EC imports from ASEAN and that proportion has continued to grow. The key change was the massive increase first in clothing, textile and footwear imports, and then in electrical machinery and components and consumer electronics. The EC became increasingly concerned that Singapore, and, to a lesser extent, Malaysia and Thailand, were following too closely in the footsteps of Japan, South Korea and Taiwan by creating difficulties for certain European industries. With unemployment high inside the EC, the pressure from affected sectors for some degree of control on imports was strong. Anti-dumping actions became more common and the EC began moves in late 1991 to 'graduate' Singapore from the class of 'developing countries'.

To the ASEAN countries, these kinds of actions seemed part of a new and worrying phase in the evolution of the international economic order, in which the GATT regime appeared threatened by regionalist tendencies. In particular, ASEAN became concerned in the late 1980s about the implications of what appeared to be a 'Fortress Europe' emerging out of the EC's ambitious programme for creating economic, monetary and even political union, known by the shorthand form of the '1992 process'. ASEAN countries feared that their access to their traditional European markets would be substantially reduced and that the EC would seek reciprocity in ASEAN markets for access to the newly-integrated EC markets in services and investment.

Symbolic of ASEAN concerns was the unexpected appearance of ASEAN trade ministers accompanying the foreign ministers to the 1990 Kuching EC–ASEAN Ministerial Meeting. EC representatives took considerable pains, in their various meetings with ASEAN, to try to dispel the myth of 'Fortress Europe', with a certain amount of success, but if the ASEAN countries became less vocal with these fears, it did not mean that they had forgotten them. The actual impact of the '1992 process' will vary depending on the ASEAN country; studies have suggested that the net effect for Singapore and Malaysia would be negative, while the other three main ASEAN economies would gain, though only Indonesia to a significant degree (Davenport and Page, 1990, pp. 96–100; Kwarteng, 1992, pp. 223–39).

Direct investment – and associated technology transfer – has come increasingly to the fore in EC–ASEAN discussions since the mid-1980s. Following the first ever EC–ASEAN Economic Ministers' Meeting in October 1985, which highlighted European investment in ASEAN as 'a key element in a long-term strategy to strengthen economic links between the two countries' (Luhulima, 1992, p. 313; Maurier and Regnier, 1990), steps were taken to encourage European participation in ASEAN Industrial Joint Ventures and other projects in the region and joint investment committees were gradually established in all the ASEAN countries. As a result, although the EC still lags well behind Japan and the United States in historic cumulative totals of foreign direct investment (FDI) in the region, over the 1985–90 period the EC invested US$4.7 billion in ASEAN (excluding Brunei) by comparison with $4 billion by the United States and $6.5 billion by the Japanese.

The simple statistics which show an apparently steady growth in trade and FDI flows between the EC and ASEAN do, however, mask the fact that, particularly during the 1989–91 period, the integrating EC market and the emerging Eastern European markets distracted EC companies from capitalizing on the fast growth in ASEAN; the surge of commercial interest in the mid-1980s was not consolidated. Anecdotal evidence suggests, however, that by 1992 EC companies, disillusioned by the immense problems facing the Eastern European countries and by the EC's own currency and economic problems, had begun to look anew at the Southeast Asian markets. British exports to Southeast Asia grew by more than double the rate of overall British exports in 1992.

EC interest was also stimulated by the agreement on the ASEAN Free Trade Area (AFTA), which, like the EC's single market, in theory came into effect in January 1993. The progressive cutting of tariffs over the next fifteen years was expected not only to boost trade but to encourage outside investors, including the Europeans. This was a mirror image of the argument for outside manufacturers to be inside the EC single market. However, given the opt-out clauses on 'sensitive' products and ASEAN's poor past record in trade cooperation, some Europeans remained sceptical about how effective the new agreement would really be.

As the Cold War order began to crumble, the basic convergence in EC and ASEAN views in the politico-strategic sphere began to waver slightly. With Germany, so often the lead EC country in the political dialogue with ASEAN, overwhelmed by its reunification problems, intra-European policy differences became more visible; so too did differences with ASEAN. France made more of the Cambodian issue, as discussed in the next section, and the Netherlands and Portugal became prominent in the politicization of aid and economic cooperation policy.

By the late 1980s, total development assistance to ASEAN from the EC and its twelve members had reached an annual level of around $500 million, not as large as Japanese aid, but comparable with US efforts. It may have been 'politically invisible' before (*Far Eastern Economic Review*, 7 Feb. 1991), but it became controversial when, encouraged by the democratization of post-communist Eastern Europe and aware of growing popular environmental concerns, EC countries, led by the Netherlands, began to look at ways of introducing human rights and environmental criteria into their aid programmes (Godemont, 1993, p. 97). This heightened tensions with ASEAN nations, none of whom feel comfortable in discussing these issues, and, in the case of Indonesia, Malaysia, and Singapore brought forth quite strident criticism. This, indeed, led the Indonesian government, which became increasingly upset with Dutch 'lecturing' on human rights in the aftermath of the East Timor killings of November 1991, to disband its Dutch-coordinated international aid support group, the Inter-Governmental Group on Indonesia, and to refuse any further Dutch bilateral aid in March 1992. Indonesia then reformed the group, with World Bank assistance, but without the Netherlands. This move was popular within Indonesia and had little deleterious economic impact, since Dutch aid to Indonesia in 1991 had only been $91 million. The new World Bank-chaired Consultative Group on Indonesia, in July 1992, actually pledged Indonesia its largest ever aid package of $4.9 billion.

Most EC governments condemned the East Timor actions and a few suspended aid programmes, at least until an Indonesian inquiry censured the army. Portugal, which happened to hold the rotating presidency of the EC in the first half of 1992, however, was determined to utilize the Dili killings to crank up its long-standing campaign for UN involvement in mediating the future of its former colony, which had been annexed by Indonesia in 1976. Portugal unsuccessfully urged an EC trade embargo on Indonesia but was able to gain EC support for a resolution to the UN Human Rights Commission protesting the situation in East Timor. Due to intensive Indonesian lobbying, no formal vote was taken at the UNCHR, however (MacIntyre, 1993, p. 206).

Portugal then blocked EC–ASEAN negotiations for a new cooperation agreement. The 1980 agreement had been extended several times after its initial five years, but by the early 1990s officials on both sides felt a new agreement with a much broadened scope would be advantageous. Both at the July 1992 ASEAN PMC dialogue with EC representatives and the October 1992 EC–ASEAN ministerial meeting in Manila, Portugal refused to allow a decision on new negotiations to be taken. While the declarations which came out of the Manila EC–ASEAN meeting did refer in greater detail than ever before to respect for UN charters on human rights and to endeavours for social justice, Portugal's proposed specific reference to East Timor was omitted (*Agence Europe*, 26 Sept., 29 and 31 Oct. 1992). Most EC representatives were encouraged by the ASEAN willingness to make some reference to human rights, but despite efforts by Britain, then holding the EC presidency, Portugal could not be persuaded to relent in its opposition to new

negotiations. The old agreement was left in force. Yet, while fellow
EC governments (even the Dutch) were certainly embarassed by Portuguese vehemence, the EC had decided as a matter of general policy
that all future economic cooperation agreements with developing countries
should include a human rights clause.

Environmental issues, in particular the destruction of the tropical
rain forests of Malaysia and Indonesia, have also pitched these governments against European pressure groups and, as was seen in the run-
up to the Rio Earth Summit of 1992, certain European governments as
well. Malaysian prime minister Dr Mahathir Mohammed has taken the
lead in criticizing Europeans for double standards over development
and the environment. The EC Commission, in reviewing its aid policies towards the developing world in mid-1992, did agree to the need
to provide more focused aid for projects such as protecting the ASEAN
rain forests. Specific aid for environmentally-related projects is, therefore, likely to be taken up in the negotiations for a new EU–ASEAN
cooperation agreement.

THE INDOCHINA CONNECTION

The key element in the political dialogue between EC and ASEAN
throughout the 1980s was the Vietnamese occupation of Cambodia and
the ways in which a resolution might be achieved. The winding down
of US–Soviet and Sino–Soviet rivalries in the late 1980s altered the
stakes for the major powers in the Cambodia embroglio and facilitated
moves towards a settlement. This, in turn, allowed a more nuanced
European approach. Until the late 1980s, the position of the EC and
most of its member countries was closely allied with that of ASEAN,
the United States and China. This meant essentially a low profile for
the Europeans while both the fighting on the ground in Cambodia and
the international diplomatic stalemate continued. Most European governments, even the British, felt that there was little that they could do.

The key exception, however, was France, which, supported by Ireland, refused to ban all humanitarian aid to Vietnam and Kampuchea
and consistently abstained on the UN credentials vote for the ASEAN-
backed Coalition Government of Democratic Kampuchea (CGDK) because of the presence of the Khmer Rouge in this coalition. Successive
French governments, given their strong feeling of 'responsibility' for
bringing peace and stability to the region, continued to discuss possibilities with Indonesia, which was trying to break the deadlock. Finally,

in December 1987 and January 1988 France hosted the first substantive negotiations between the opposing Cambodian factions, when Hun Sen, Prime Minister of the People's Republic of Kampuchea (PRK) and Prince Norodom Sihanouk, President of the CGDK, at last met. The French undoubtedly felt a sense of pride in setting up these meetings, but no real breakthrough was achieved.

However, the pace of diplomatic activity increased, culminating in the month-long international conference on Cambodia held in Paris during August 1989 and co-chaired by France and Indonesia; Britain as a permanent member of the UN Security Council (P–5) was the only other West European state to attend. But after a promising start, the conference ended in stalemate. (Wright, 1989, pp. 57–60; Turley, 1990, pp. 437–53).

After the Paris conference, France (together with Australia) became deeply involved in the negotiation process on Cambodia. So too did the UN P–5 group as a whole, particularly after the US government changed policy in July 1990 and came out specifically against Khmer Rouge participation in the CGDK. The withdrawal of Vietnamese troops from Cambodia in September 1989 caused European governments and public opinion to become increasingly concerned about the Khmer Rouge seizing power again. In February 1990 the EC issued a statement clearly setting out the 'non-return to power' of the Khmer Rouge as 'a central element' of EC policy on Cambodia (Than, 1991).

The European governments also increasingly favoured raising their diplomatic profile with Vietnam, as well as relaxing international economic sanctions on it, as part of a step-by-step approach to encourage Vietnam to move along the path of reform. This pushed them ahead of ASEAN and American policy. At the February 1990 EC–ASEAN ministerial meeting the ASEAN side had asked the Europeans to be extremely cautious in approaching Vietnam diplomatically. However, the UN P–5's agreement in August 1990 on a Cambodian peace plan framework and its broad acceptance by the four Cambodian factions made it possible for a number of West European governments to begin to upgrade their diplomatic representation in Vietnam and in November 1990 the EC itself established diplomatic relations with Vietnam for the first time. Long an advocate of restoring Vietnam's eligibility for International Monetary Fund (IMF) loans, France in April 1991 tried to organize a 'friends of Vietnam' gathering at the end of an IMF/World Bank meeting in Washington, primarily to try to make a bridging loan to Vietnam to enable it to clear its $120 million in arrears with the IMF, but it failed to get US (or Japanese) support.

Meanwhile, agreement on the finer details of the P–5 peace plan for Cambodia was painstakingly hammered out and in October 1991 Paris was once again the site of an international conference to sign the comprehensive political settlement. By the end of 1991 a small advance UN guard, principally consisting of French and Australian troops and headed by a French general, had arrived in Cambodia (Roberts, 1993, pp. 71–6).

The degree of European participation in the UNTAC (UN Transitional Authority in Cambodia) operations marked a new phase in European involvement in Asia. By the eve of the May 1993 elections, ten West European countries had either military forces or police stationed in Cambodia. Of these, the French had by far the largest contingent, with 1362 soldiers and 139 police, followed by the Netherlands with a total of 831. Even Germany, which had balked at sending troops to the multinational forces fighting in the 1990–91 Gulf War because of constitutional constraints, found it possible to send 149 military and 76 policemen to Cambodia. The EC and its constituent members also, collectively, were the largest provider of funds – $230 million pledged in 1992 – to the UNTAC operation, although, in practice, like other donors, they were dilatory in actually supplying the funds. With the elections over and the new government installed, several EC governments – the French in particular – committed themselves to infrastructural reconstruction funding.

This did not, however, mean that all the Europeans were in complete agreement with how UNTAC carried out its operations, particularly when the Khmer Rouge proved intransigent about meeting pre-election cease-fire and disarming provisions. In July 1992, French General Michel Loridon, the second in command of the UNTAC forces – who was angry with repeated Khmer Rouge violations – was reassigned after his arguments in favour of the forcible disarming of the Cambodian factions set him against his UNTAC superiors. (Other senior UN officials complained that the French were not acting as 'team players' and disliked the requirement for all UNTAC activities to be conducted in French as well as English. *Economist Foreign Report*, 3 Dec. 1992.) Towards the end of 1992, the French also began to promote the idea of presidential elections before the planned May 1993 parliamentary elections, thereby reversing the timetable provided for in the October 1991 Paris peace accord, despite strong British and American reservations. Despite a personal plea from President François Mitterrand, when he visited Cambodia in February 1993, Prince Sihanouk remained adamant against becoming a presidential candidate.

Mitterrand's visit to Vietnam in the same week, the first by a Western head of state, was intended to open a new chapter in France's relationship with its former Indochinese colonies. It was a visit strong on symbolism, but also replete with commercial overtones, for French business had consistently been pushing the government to move quicker on aid and economic/technological assistance for Vietnam. Total EC trade with Vietnam had grown from only US$77 million in 1985 to $443 million in 1991, with France the leading EC trader and, having $490 million invested in Vietnam by April 1993, also the leading EC investor.

Mitterrand's visit also acted as a catalyst for spurring negotiations already quietly under way between the EC and Vietnam for a cooperation agreement. The EC Commission, in laying down the negotiating guidelines in July 1993, made it clear that, as proposed in the ASEAN case, the cooperation agreement should have some clause referring to human rights and democracy (*Agence Europe*, 16 July 1993). Nonetheless, economic and technical assistance provisions eventually formed the bulk of the agreement. The EC governments believed that by assisting in Vietnam's transition to a market economy, new commercial opportunities would emerge. Visions of Vietnam as the next dynamic Asian economy certainly began to loom large amongst European businesses in 1992–93. Paradoxically, while European governments urged the Americans to ease their restrictions on IMF loans to Vietnam (which they gradually did during 1993), European businessmen saw advantage in having US commercial rivals still excluded from doing business there. So the lifting of the American embargo in 1994 was viewed with mixed emotions.

One element of European aid to Vietnam which began in 1991 and grew in importance was aid for the re-integration of returning 'boat people', which was set to reach $32 million in 1993. In fact, Vietnamese efforts to stem the exodus of boat people had acted as an important subsidiary reason, after the withdrawal of Vietnamese troops from Cambodia, for the EC's 1990 decision to establish diplomatic relations.

A sudden influx of Vietnamese 'boat people' into Hong Kong had begun in 1988–9 (on levels paralleling the earlier 1979–80 inflow) and, under new regulations introduced in June 1988, the Hong Kong government tried to distinguish genuine refugees from 'economic migrants'(Casella, 1991, pp. 160–4). Despite appalling living conditions in the crowded, closed camps, only a miniscule number volunteered to be repatriated. In December 1989, therefore, the first group of Vietnamese was 'forcibly' repatriated to Vietnam. The British found themselves hindered by US government opposition and by critical media coverage, but could see no alternative.

Eventually, the British, Hong Kong and Vietnamese governments reached an agreement in October 1991 for an orderly repatriation programme for all Vietnamese non-refugees from Hong Kong. By April 1993 only 495 Vietnamese had returned under the mandatory programme, but the number of new arrivals had dropped drastically (from 20,206 in 1991 to 12 in 1992) and voluntary repatriations had risen to an average of over 1,000 per month. Over 30,000 Vietnamese migrants still remained in Hong Kong camps.

BURMA

By contrast with Vietnam, Burma (Myanmar) had rarely figured in European deliberations on Southeast Asia until its military government's violent suppression of pro-democracy demonstrators in 1988 brought it into the international spotlight. Burma, about which policy debates revolve around human rights, has tended to be a divisive issue in EC–ASEAN relations since 1988. After the bloody events of 1988 the EC condemned the killing of pro-democracy demonstrators and suspended aid programmes (though these had already been fairly small scale). It has called on the ruling junta to recognize the results of the 1990 general elections, has sought an official arms embargo, and, on a number of occasions, urged trade sanctions against Burma. In July 1991 the European Parliament awarded the confined opposition leader Aung San Suu Kyi its Sakharov human rights prize.

Whilst the EC has taken a vocal line on Burmese repression, the ASEAN governments have argued that 'constructive engagement' (a phrase which can cover a multitude of sins) is the best way of coaxing Burma into a more normal socio-political system (Bray, 1992, pp. 291–6). Despite the more robust statements which for a short period emanated from Malaysia, as the problem of Burmese Muslim refugees being forced into Bangladesh came to a head in early 1992, the disagreements at the July 1993 ASEAN–PMC meeting between the EC and ASEAN representatives showed that the differences in approach to Burmese democracy were as marked as ever.

It is, of course, true that the West European countries have little security interest and very limited economic interests in Burma. This has enabled them to take a principled stance over Burmese repression. But, events in Burma did also coincide with the general shift in emphasis to human rights issues in EC foreign policies.

THE MULTILATERAL CONTEXT

The EU–ASEAN or EU–Southeast Asian relationships cannot be considered in isolation; there are further complex triangular and multilateral interactions, particularly with Japan and the United States, but also with the emerging forms of Asian–Pacific regionalism.

Although the European governments have welcomed Japanese participation in the UNTAC operations in Cambodia as a helpful (though too limited) first step towards a more responsible international political role, they have continued to be concerned about Japanese commercial activities in Southeast Asia. Japanese companies are not just fierce competitors within the region, but, indirectly, have contributed to the EU's trade problems with regional states.

The United States too is a commercial rival in the region, but, also, ultimately, the protector of European strategic interests. The Europeans had paid close attention to Soviet, Chinese and Vietnamese actions in the region during the 1980s, but had generally let the Americans make the running in politico-military responses. The British were involved with Malaysia, Singapore, Australia and New Zealand in the consultative Five-Power Defence Arrangement (FPDA), but, despite a first-ever defence ministers' meeting in 1991, it remained practically dormant and not a crucial factor in regional security (Chin, 1991, pp. 193–203). Europeans shared with most Asian states the appreciation that the US should act as an engaged balancer in the region. For Southeast Asians, on the other hand, Western Europe has continued to act as a useful means of diversifying away from US and Japanese influence and domination.

The EC's own moves towards the integrated single market and further enlargement, coupled with the emergence of the North American Free Trade Agreement and its potential enlargement, have raised concerns amongst Southeast Asians about the negative effects of the growth of regionalism – possible 'economic blocs'. The Europeans, in turn, have been concerned about the direction of the Malaysian East Asian Economic Caucus concept and, as a more serious contender, the Asia–Pacific Economic Cooperation (APEC) process. British Foreign Secretary Douglas Hurd spoke for many in Europe when he urged that APEC should not turn itself into 'an Asian economic fortress' (*South China Morning Post*, 16 Sept. 1993). At the July 1993 ASEAN–PMC meeting, the EC made it clear that it wanted to have some kind of working relationship with APEC, either through observer or dialogue partner status. The announcement of an 'East Asia–EU' summit meeting to be held in Thailand in 1996 went a long way to fulfilling that aspiration.

Discussions on regional security structures in the Asia–Pacific region have been even more embryonic. Even though several of the proposals on the table drew on the European experience of the Conference for Security and Cooperation in Europe, the Europeans – like many Asians – saw limitations as to how far the European model could be adapted to the more complex Asian environment. These doubts were increased by the evident failure of the existing European multilateral mechanisms to solve the crisis in the former Yugoslavia. Nonetheless, the revamping of the ASEAN–PMC format into an ASEAN Regional Forum, which brings the EU representatives directly into the joint political and even security discussions with other ASEAN dialogue partners, is a useful step forward.

CONCLUSIONS

The end of the Cold War did not bring about a sudden change to Europe–Southeast Asian relations, but a number of subtle shifts can now be discerned. Western Europe turned in on itself, swamped by the need to cope with the socio-political transformation of Eastern Europe and tempted by the, albeit transient, commercial opportunities there. Together with this came the traumas of the EC's own economic and political integration. However, by 1992–3 Europe was beginning to turn back again to Southeast Asia.

In inter-regional economic relations, the gap between expectations and accomplishments widened. While trade, aid and investment flows did increase, the Europeans missed out on significant commercial opportunities in fast-growing Southeast Asia. The Southeast Asians, in turn, felt that Europe's preoccupations elsewhere worked to their disadvantage. It needed a certain degree of European disillusionment with markets closer at hand to come together with ASEAN's renewed attempts to promote economic cooperation and the emergence of new, potentially dynamic markets in Indochina before European eyes seriously turned again to the region. The mid-1980s push to heighten economic interchanges had proved short-lived; old patterns and mind-sets prevailed. The test for both the EU and ASEAN, as they move towards further enlargement through the drawing in of regional neighbours, is whether regional economic groupings can promote, rather than hinder, new, closer inter-regional economic relationships.

The winding down of the Cold War also produced a subtle change in European political and strategic perceptions of Southeast Asia. By

1992, because of a greater interest in extra-European UN-sanctioned actions, for which the Gulf War had acted as a catalyst, several European countries were prepared to break with past practice and contribute forces to the United Nations peace-keeping operations in Cambodia. However, the political and budgetary limitations on the European capability to play a military role in the region are unlikely to change in the near future. The Europeans are likely to remain outside the Southeast Asian regional strategic equation (Lau, 1990, p. 73), even though common political interests will continue to grow. The 'new agenda' of international relations, including democratic and environmental issues, also had a crucial impact on the political relationships. In any case, whatever the obstacles, political, economic and civic interactions between Western Europe and Southeast Asia are likely to grow more rapidly in the late 1990s than they did in the late 1980s. The 1996 EU–ASEAN summit meeting is symbolic of the increasing intensity, as well as complexity, of those interactions.

Notes

1. When the Maastricht Treaty entered into effect on 1 November 1993, the European Community (EC) became the European Union (EU). Thus the latter term will generally be used except when referring to certain pre-1994 agreements or relationships.
2. Association agreements are 'characterized by reciprocal rights and obligations, common actions and particular procedures', whereas cooperation agreements give no special preferences, but are designed to stimulate cooperation in areas of common interest such as industrial development, energy and environmental protection. Unlike the association agreements, cooperation agreements contain no financial element to support such commitments (Flaesch-Mougin, 1990; pp. 35–6).

References

Bray, John (1992) 'Burma: Resisting the International Community', *Pacific Review*, vol. 5, no. 3.
Casella, Alexander (1991) 'The Refugees from Vietnam: Rethinking the Issue', *The World Today* (Aug./Sept.).
Chin Kin Wah (1991) 'The Five Power Defence Arrangements: Twenty Years After', *Pacific Review*, vol. 4, no. 3.
Davenport, Michael and Sheila Page (1990) *Europe: 1992 and the Developing World* (London: Overseas Development Institute).

Flaesch-Mougin, Catherine (1991) 'Competing frameworks: the dialogue and its legal basis', in Edwards, Geoffrey and Elfriede Regelsberger (eds), *Europe's Global Links: The European Community and Inter-Regional Cooperation* (London: Pinter).

Godemont, François (1993) 'Europe and Asia: The Missing Link', in *Asia's International Role in the Post-Cold War Era: Part II*, Adelphi Paper no. 276 (London: International Institute for Strategic Studies).

Harris, Stuart and Brian Bridges (1983) *European Interests in ASEAN* (London: Routledge & Kegan Paul for RIIA).

Kwarteng, Charles (1992) 'Confronting the European Single Market of 1992: Challenges for the ACP and ASEAN Countries', *Journal of Developing Societies* (July–Oct.).

Lau, Tek Soon (1989) 'Regional Security: Problems and Prospects in South-East Asia', in Giuseppe Schiavone (ed.), *Western Europe and Southeast Asia* (London: Macmillan).

Luhulima, C. P. F. (1992) 'ASEAN–European Community Relations: Some Dimensions of Inter-Regional Cooperation', *Indonesian Quarterly*, third quarter.

MacIntyre, Andrew (1993) 'Indonesia in 1992', *Asian Survey* vol. 33, no. 2 (February).

Maurier, Jean-Luc and Phillippe Regnier (1990) *Investment Flows between Asia and Europe: What Strategies for the Future?* (Geneva: Modern Asia Research Centre).

Mols, Manfred (1990) 'Cooperation with ASEAN: A success story', in Geoffrey Edwards and Elfriede Regelsberger (eds) *Europe's Global Links: The European Community and Inter-Regional Cooperation* (London: Pinter).

Roberts, David (1993) 'Cambodia's Uncertain Future', *Pacific Review*, vol. 6, no. 1.

Stevens, Christopher (ed) (1981) *EEC and the Third World: A Survey* (London: Hodder & Stoughton).

Than, Sina (1991) 'Cambodia 1990: Towards a Peaceful Solution?', in *Southeast Asian Affairs 1991* (Singapore: ISEAS).

Turley, William (1990) 'The Khmer War: Cambodia after Paris', *Survival*, Sept/Oct.

Wright, Martin (ed) (1989) *Cambodia: A Matter of Survival* (London: Longman).

Part IV

Regional Policy Conflicts in a 'New World Order'

12 The Evolution of Great Power Involvement in Cambodia

Pierre Lizée*

In many regards, the Cambodian peace process symbolized the beginning and the 'end' of the 'New World Order'. The signing of the Paris peace agreement, in October 1991, followed a flurry of diplomatic activities which represented one of the first instances of the type of great power cooperation made possible by the end of the Cold War. The Paris agreement itself embodied an unprecedented commitment to build upon that atmosphere of cooperation in order to assist a country which had been engulfed by violent conflicts for more than twenty years: the United Nations Transitional Authority in Cambodia (UNTAC) set up by the agreement constituted the largest peace-keeping operation ever mounted and its exceptionally broad objectives aimed at radically altering Cambodian society in order to make it more amenable to a durable peace.

Precisely because the Cambodian peace process had been seen as one of the key components of a 'New World Order', however, the difficulties it encountered led to a certain pessimism about the actual possibilities afforded by the emerging international situation. Were the combined efforts of all the great powers unable to resolve conflicts which, it seemed, had lost their original *raison d'être*? Each attack by the Khmer Rouge on UNTAC personnel, each act of political violence during the electoral period in Cambodia, and each postponement in the implementation of the peace plan, appeared to provide an affirmative answer to that question.

The fact that the elections on which the whole peace plan was based did go ahead brought only mild comfort to those championing the idea

* I received scholarships from the Social Sciences and Humanities Research Council of Canada and from the Department of National Defence Military and Strategic Studies Program. A research grant from the Cooperative Security Competition Programme of External Affairs Canada allowed me to observe the May 1993 elections in Cambodia.

that an incipient global order was taking shape in Cambodia. The high level of participation at the polls owed much more to the courage of numerous Cambodians when confronted by repeated threats on their lives than it did to the ability of UNTAC to bring peace to Cambodia. Furthermore, the elections ushered in a new era of instability in Cambodian politics. The *Front Uni National pour un Cambodge Indépendant, Neutre, Pacifique et Coopératif* (FUNCINPEC), the winner of the elections, was in effect forced to share power with the leaders of the State of Cambodia (SOC) who did not want to forego the hold they maintained over most of Cambodia. Enormous tensions thus still remained. Members of the FUNCINPEC argued that the letter of the Paris agreement had to be followed and that, therefore, power should be held by their party since it had won the elections. Others claimed that the coalition with the SOC had to be maintained in order to placate its leaders and prevent a renewed civil war. The option of having Prince Sihanouk form a coalition government to fend off the possibility of renewed hostilities had been broached by the backers of the Paris plan and the coalition could therefore be given some measure of legitimacy by being placed under the tutelage of the Prince.

In this sense, UNTAC had failed to achieve its principal objectives: the distribution of power in Cambodia was still determined to a large extent by factional infighting rather than by democratic processes. The installation and strengthening of liberal democratic institutions which had been seen in the Paris agreement as the only basis for a durable settlement of the Cambodian conflict had therefore still not been realized. The great powers and the United Nations were thus compelled to ask themselves if the cause of peace was better served by continued attempts to implement the letter of the Paris agreement or by a decision to come to terms with the reluctance of the SOC to surrender power in order to provide Cambodia, at least for a time, with some political stability. In that sense, they were forced into dealing with a new set of problems and dilemmas.

What does all this say about the policies pursued by the great powers and the United Nations in Cambodia? Why were they unable to bring the Paris plan to a successful conclusion? Conversely, what do the obstacles they encountered in Cambodia and, additionally, the stark alternatives thrust upon them by these problems, reveal about the way in which they will be able to exercise influence over future events in that country? Understanding the policy shifts which marked the implementation of the Paris plan can indeed reveal, it would seem, the constraints shaping the future strategies of the great powers and those of the United Nations *vis-à-vis* Cambodia, and thus bring into relief the real repercussions of the 'New World Order' on that country.

This chapter will argue that UNTAC could not complete its mandate because the conflict resolution mechanism it employed did not take into account some basic characteristics of the Cambodian war. The dynamics of factional infighting which constituted the basis of this war could not lend themselves to the type of institutionalization of conflict which the United Nations endeavored to create through the promotion of liberal democratic institutions. Delays in the implementation of the plan were thus to be expected. Furthermore, the leaders of the different Cambodian factions were bound to resist the installation of democratic institutions since it entailed profound modifications in the traditional structures of authority on which their power rested.

Confronted with these difficulties, it will be shown, some of the great powers advocated a fundamental change in the purpose of the Paris plan. Power, they said, should ultimately be handed to the only Cambodian leader whose legitimacy could not be questioned, Prince Sihanouk, who would then try to form a coalition government with the heads of the different factions. Relying in such a way on an established structure of power in Cambodia involved a deferral of the democratization process since it posited that power would be a function of customs and time-honoured traditions, but, according to those who held such a view, it would at least bring peace to the country. The uncertainty which preceded the elections led to a *de facto* acceptance of that scenario.

The fact that the May 1993 elections attracted a very considerable number of voters caused many in the international community to contend that handing power to Prince Sihanouk would mean betraying the confidence countless Cambodians had put in the ideal of democratic rule. The great powers thus found themselves in front of what represented basically two divergent ways of attaining peace in Cambodia. On the one hand, they could argue that the democratization of Cambodian society had been advanced through the popular success of the elections and that the process should be encouraged further in order to develop the democratic institutions which would ultimately bring peace to Cambodia. On the other hand, it could be said that peace would be possible only if traditional power structures were maintained: allowing Prince Sihanouk to create a coalition government identified with his own legitimacy rather than with the actual results of the election would safeguard the alliance concluded by the FUNCINPEC and the SOC and would thus prevent the latter from launching a new civil war to protect its position of power.

The chapter will suggest that the post-election situation in Cambodia will lead the great powers to add a new form of power to the sort of pressures on which they have relied in the past to influence Cambodian politics, one more subtle and long-term than its predecessor. Frictions between great power policies, it will be proposed, will be articulated on the different courses of action possible within these parameters. Before proceeding with this argumentation, however, it is important to begin by explaining in greater detail the logic of the Paris peace plan and that of the diplomatic process which led to its conclusion.

THE CAMBODIAN CONFLICT: 1979–89

William S. Turley notes that the first years of the Cambodian conflict have 'aptly [been] described as a "stable war" because the non-Indochinese actors could tolerate, or saw advantage in, its prolongation' (Turley, 1990, p. 438, citing Emmerson, 1985). What led to this 'stable war'? The Vietnamese invasion of Cambodia in late December 1978 and the subsequent Chinese campaign against Vietnam, in February and March of the following year, first created an 'interlocking structure of relationships' (Leifer, 1985–6, p. 627). Indeed, by early 1979, the hostility expressed by opposing Cambodian factions, the rancor which had always marked the relations between Cambodia, Thailand and Vietnam, the regional conflict between ASEAN and the Indochinese states, and, finally, the global contest between the United States, China and the Soviet Union, were all part of the same 'conflict nebula' (Regaud, 1992, p. 13).

In this sense, each actor knew that forceful actions on the ground could have unforeseen implications within the rest of the 'interlocking structure' of the conflict. A sudden escalation of the fighting, for instance, would have many regional repercussions. Low-intensity, long-term strategies were thus designed. The coalition including the ASEAN states, China, the United States and the Coalition Government of Democratic Kampuchea [CGDK], recognized by the United Nations and composed of the Khmer Rouge, Prince Sihanouk's party and the Khmer People's National Liberation Front (KPNLF) tried to 'bleed Vietnam white', as the Chinese put it. This strategy was based on the international embargo which had been imposed on Hanoi after it seized control of its neighbour: the longer the conflict lasted, the weaker Vietnam would become, and the stronger the pressure on it to withdraw from Cambodia would grow. Furthermore, the strain imposed on its economy by the embargo and the cost of maintaining a large number of troops in Cambodia would weaken Vietnam to the point where it would not be a regional threat. The opposing coalition, composed of Vietnam, the government installed by the Vietnamese in Phnom Penh (which later become the SOC), and the USSR, hoped to create a *fait accompli* in Cambodia. The longer the conflict lasted, according to that logic, the likelier a *de facto*, if not *de jure*, international recognition of the government installed in Phnom Penh by Hanoi would become.

The negotiation strategies of both coalitions also reflected this long-term approach to the conflict. Vietnam and its *protégés* in the Cambodian capital insisted that the military action of December 1978 was justified by the behaviour of the Khmer Rouge during their stay in power. Therefore, the government in place in Phnom Penh was legitimate. Seen in this perspective, the Cambodian conflict was essentially a civil war between the Phnom Penh government and the different groups trying to undermine its power. It would, therefore, have to be included in any negotiation on the Cambodian situation, a fact which served the strategy of *de facto* recognition which it was pursuing in concert with Hanoi. The coalition headed by China and the CGDK contended, for its part, that the Cambodian conflict resulted from Hanoi's occupation of Cambodia: it was not a civil war, but an international conflict caused by the 1978 Vietnamese attack against the Khmer Rouge government, a government which was at the time, and still remained in the eyes of the international community, the legitimate authority in Cambodia. Negotiations held according to these terms would encourage condemnations of Vietnam and thus justify even more the pariah status of that country on which the coalition had based its strategy.

Such a divergence in the definition of the Cambodian conflict led to a complete stalemate at the negotiation table: the parties could not discuss how to resolve the conflict since they could not get past the question of the very nature of that conflict. As Michael Leifer put it (1989, p. 12): 'The diplomatic stalemate over Cambodia appeared to have become entrenched, with neither Vietnam nor ASEAN apparently prepared to compromise over how the conflict should be represented and, therefore, on the terms on which negotiations might begin to resolve it. At that juncture, compromise seemed impossible because of the stark alternative representations of the Cambodian conflict.'

That stalemate itself, however, was part of the strategy of the two coalitions. Both sides, in fact, wanted to block the negotiations in order to give to the long-term strategies they were pursuing the time necessary to their success. All these factors thus conspired to bring about the 'stable war' described by Turley, though it must be noted, to add to his remarks, that it benefitted not only the 'non-Indochinese actors' involved in the conflict but all the other ones as well.

Nicolas Regaud was therefore correct when he described this period as one of complete stalemate at the 'global, regional and local levels of the conflict' (Regaud, 1992, pp. 12–14). A 'transition period' began, however, in 1986. It was marked by substantial transformations at the global and regional levels of the conflict (Regaud, 1992, p. 14). The most important of these transformations was the new Soviet outlook on the Asia–Pacific region. The speech given by Gorbachev in Vladivostok in July 1986 gave the first indications of that change. Beyond general comments aimed at 'marking a rupture with past policies . . . of confrontation and militarization of the region', the speech included 'concessions . . . which were all meant to reassure and seduce China' (Regaud, 1992, p. 290). The following October, Moscow also indicated that it would be willing to discuss the Cambodian conflict with Beijing. This opened the possibility of movement on the issue which had always been seen by the Chinese as the most important problem standing in the way of a normalization of their relations with the Soviets.

These developments put Vietnam in an untenable situation. Moscow, which had been Hanoi's principal supporter since the beginning of the Cambodian conflict was now in effect signalling its intention to seek a settlement of the conflict and to improve its relations with the leader of the coalition opposed to the Vietnamese presence in Cambodia. The embargo which by then had been in place for a number of years was also taking a heavy toll on the development of the Vietnamese economy, a fact brought into relief by the promotion, at the Sixth Congress of the Vietnamese Communist Party held in late 1986, of reformist leaders intent on improving Vietnam's economic performance. The other side of that coin was that by then the government installed in Phnom Penh by the Vietnamese had grown quite strong. Hanoi could thus withdraw its forces from Cambodia and yet maintain a certain measure of control over that country.

These factors led many in the international community to believe that Hanoi might be willing to come to a compromise on the Cambodian conflict. The diplomatic activity which ensued brought about the Jakarta Informal Meeting, in July 1988, where occurred, in the words of Michael Leifer, a '[revision of] the long-standing representation of the conflict' (Leifer, 1989, p. 16). Since Vietnam had promised repeatedly that it would withdraw its troops from Cambodia, the conflict was now seen as the consequence of the opposite claims to legitimacy of the CGDK and the Phnom Penh government. In this context, the negotiations focused on the mechanisms able to bring about 'national reconciliation' among these two groups. The CGDK argued that a quadripartite authority including its three components and the Phnom Penh authorities should be established immediately. This authority would then be responsible for the organization of elections in Cambodia. The Phnom Penh government argued on the contrary that 'national reconciliation' was possible if elections were held while it was still in power. A quadripartite authority, it maintained, would be created only after these elections. Those who would control the organization of the election, both sides evidently thought, would also control its results and use them to their advantage. Behind the willingness to discuss reconciliation thus remained a fierce opposition between the two camps.

The development of the Sino–Soviet dialogue and the acceleration of the negotiation process after the Jakarta Informal Meeting led France to believe that an international conference could apply enough pressure on the Cambodian factions to compel them to find an agreement on some form of power-sharing. The Paris International Conference on Cambodia, which eventually took place from 30 July to 30 August 1989, was the largest international gathering yet devoted to the search for peace in Cambodia. The greater part of the discussions occurred within different committees set up after the ministerial declarations which opened the Conference.[1] The so-called Ad Hoc Committee, in charge of 'examin[ing] questions regarding the implementation of national reconciliation' (Document CPC/89/4; Acharya, Lizée and Peou, 1991, p. 129) clearly represented the focal point of the talks. 'Failure on its part to arrive at an agreement on the internal aspects of the Cambodian conflict', as Tommy Koh has noted (Koh, 1990, p. 84), 'would doom the conference itself to failure.' And indeed, the Cambodian factions, with the acquiescence of their respective backers, did not arrive at a compromise on the issue of national reconciliation, a situation which prevented any meaningful agreement from being reached in Paris at that time. (For two conflicting analyses of the Conference, see Haas, 1991, and Koh, 1990.)[2]

THE CAMBODIAN CONFLICT: 1989–91

After the Paris Conference began a period which Regaud described as one of 'relocalization' of the conflict (Regaud, 1992, p. 14). First, the Vietnamese withdrawal from Cambodia, in September 1989, 'pushed the Cambodian civil war to the forefront of the conflict' (Regaud, 1992, p. 14). In the wake of Hanoi's withdrawal, the CGDK, with the full support of the Chinese, launched new offensives against the Phnom Penh regime in the hope of toppling it. Phnom Penh proved itself strong enough to resist those offensives. The realization that a stalemate on the ground could continue for years then persuaded many regional and extra-regional actors to renew their efforts to find a political settlement to the Cambodian conflict, the second aspect of the 'relocalization' of the conflict (Regaud, 1992, p. 14). The dynamics underlying these efforts determined the very nature of the peace agreement which was signed at the second Paris Conference, in October 1991.

Essentially, four dynamics were at play:

(1) The profound foreign policy reorientation inaugurated with the Vladivostok speech and the upheavals brought about by *perestroika* and *glasnost* progressively caused the Soviet Union to disengage itself from the peace process. When it became apparent that the Khmer Rouge would be prevented from coming back to power in Phnom Penh, Moscow basically withdrew from the great powers negotiations on Cambodia.

(2) Moscow's changing attitude, followed by the collapse of communism elsewhere in the world, forced Vietnam and China into a closer relationship. China slowly modified its demands on the role which should be played by the Khmer Rouge in a national reconciliation government. Once it sanctioned the idea that the group should be confined to a limited role in future Cambodian governments, an understanding was worked out with Hanoi: pressures would be applied by China and Vietnam on the Khmer Rouge and the Phnom Penh government to compel them to come to terms with one another.

(3) The American and Chinese positions on Cambodia grew apart. The United States feared that Sino–Vietnamese collusion could shift the center of gravity of the peace negotiations towards a compromise between the two communist Cambodian factions (the Khmer Rouge and the Phnom Penh government) which would in effect exclude the two non-communist groups (Sihanouk's group and the KPNLF). In order to prevent this, the Americans concentrated their efforts on a peace proposal, put forward by Australia, which claimed that the question of

power in Cambodia should ultimately be settled by democratic elections.

(4) The pressures exercised by the United States, China and Vietnam brought about many agreements among the Cambodian factions. These added up to a recognition of the need for elections in Cambodia but left the different factions in control of their respective political and military structures in the period preceding these elections. By playing the positions of the great powers against each other, the leaders of the Khmer Rouge and the Phnom Penh government, the two strongest of the four Cambodian factions, thus each managed to secure the means of influencing the electoral process in their favour. This ensured in their eyes that the distribution of power in Cambodia would remain a function of inter-factional agreements and that, therefore, their own position of power would be preserved.

The reorientation of Soviet foreign policy undertaken at Vladivostok had prompted Moscow to broaden its contacts with the countries of Southeast Asia in the hope of participating in the economic dynamism of the region. As the focus of Soviet interest in the region shifted from politico-military to economic concerns, relations with Hanoi were readjusted accordingly: military aid was discontinued while economic assistance was reorganized in order to eventually permit more autonomy on Vietnam's part. This compelled Hanoi to continue to improve its relations with China. The main corollary of the Soviet foreign policy reorientation, the amelioration of relations with Beijing symbolized by the May 1989 summit and continued thereafter though numerous bilateral meetings, also required Hanoi to move somewhat towards China.

The collapse of Eastern Europe, the unfolding of massive economic and political reforms, and, finally, the disintegration of the Communist Party of the Soviet Union after the aborted coup of August 1991, then greatly reduced the influence Moscow could exercise in the Cambodian peace process. But these events helped bring Vietnam and China together since both countries feared the type of political liberalization which had engulfed the Communist governments of Europe. As Carlyle Thayer has noted, 'an element of *realpolitik* . . . influenced the normalization process [between Vietnam and China]', but this normalization was also the consequence of a 'nascent Asian socialist community [linked by] a commonality of interests based on ideology which [made] their relations with each other qualitatively different from relations with non-socialist states' (Thayer, 1992, p. 402).

The Cambodian 'end-game' (Rowley, 1991) was thus played within the context of an increased Sino–Vietnamese collaboration which took the form of high-level meetings in 1990. It became apparent, at talks held in September of that year that 'against the backdrop of the collapse of communism, the war in Cambodia [had] lost its usefulness and the Khmer Rouge lost its value to China as a knife in Vietnam's side' (Thayer, 1992, p. 404). From that point on, both Hanoi and Beijing exercised pressures on their respective Cambodian *protégés* to bring them to a settlement on the Cambodian question.

This created some Western fear that a 'Red solution', whereby China and Vietnam 'would encourage or induce an agreement between the Khmer Rouge and the Phnom Penh regime, excluding the non-communist resistance and obviating the feasibility of an open election' (Frost, 1991, p. 138), might somehow emerge. This fear produced a new approach based on a complex and detailed peace initiative which had been put forward by Australia in February 1990 (the text can be found in Acharya, Lizée and Peou, 1991). The Australian plan argued that the way out of the stalemate created by the incompatibility of the positions of the CGDK and Phnom Penh government on the issue of national reconciliation – who had the right to organize elections and would these elections be fair? – could be solved by being, in a sense, pushed aside. It was the United Nations, the document suggested, which should organize and supervise the electoral process. Under such circumstances, neither side could contest the legitimacy of the government which would be brought to power by these elections. The conflict would thus end at that point. The Australian Minister for Foreign Affairs, Senator Gareth Evans explained:

> The central concept of the Australian proposal to reinvigorate the peace process was very simple. So as to sidestep the power-sharing issue which had bedevilled the Paris conference, and constrain the role of the Khmer Rouge in the transitional arrangements, we proposed that the United Nations be directly involved in the civil administration of Cambodia during the transitional period. Along with a UN military presence to monitor the cease-fire and cessation of external military assistance, and a UN role in organising and conducting elections, UN involvement in the transitional administration arrangements would ensure a neutral political environment conducive to free and fair elections. (Senate Daily Hansard [Australian], 6 Dec. 1990, quoted in Frost, 1991; pp. 141–2)

In a series of meetings on Cambodia, the Permanent Five Members of the United Nations Security Council (P–5) discussed the Australian proposal and, in August 1990, agreed upon a 'Framework Document' for peace which followed its principles quite closely. It is in the context of these discussions and of the subsequent P–5 talks that Washington defended its position. The United States believed that democratic elections in Cambodia could achieve two objectives. First, elections could guarantee a certain measure of power to the two non-communist Cambodian factions, the KPNLF and Prince Sihanouk's group, which were militarily much weaker than their Communist counterparts. Elections, secondly, would also undermine the two Communist factions. The Phnom Penh government, an *interlocuteur obligé* since it controlled most of the Cambodian territory, would nonetheless see its power greatly reduced once the electoral process got under way. The Khmer Rouge, from which Washington had withdrawn its support in July 1990, would be forced out of the jungle and into the political arena, where it would wither away.

Washington's attempts to curtail the power of the Khmer Rouge and its insistence on the establishment of democratic institutions in Cambodia put it at odds with Beijing's goals in the region. In effect, the Cambodian conflict became one of the focal points of the Sino–American rivalry which had emerged in the wake of the Soviet Union's demise. As Kelvin Rowley (1991) put it:

> as viewed from Beijing, Soviet influence was on the wane on China's southern flank. The emerging danger was that this would now be replaced by US and/or Japanese influence, rather than China's. As the Cambodian end-game was played out, the context was increasingly one of Sino–American competition rather than Sino–American co-operation.

The Cambodian factions, subjected to numerous pressures to resolve their conflict following the adoption by the P–5 of the 'Framework Document', used the Sino–American rivalry to conserve a certain leeway in these negotiations. They knew that the United States would rather accept a compromise formula derived from the 'Framework Document' than see them abandon that approach and eventually move towards a settlement akin to the 'Red Solution'. Therefore, they worked out a series of agreements which in fact did depart from the fundamental principles of the 'Framework Document' in ways that favoured each of them and they convinced the P–5 to accept these modifications. During fours sets of talks held in June, July and August 1991, the factions agreed for instance that a 'partial demobilization', rather that the 'total demobilization' which had been recommended by the

P–5, would take place. This made it more difficult for the United Nations to verify if a demobilization had in fact occurred since any troops encountered in the field could pretend that were not part of the contingents required to disband. Such an accord also left the two strongest factions with enough weaponry to influence the implementation of the peace plan according to their own priorities. These agreements, combined with previous understandings leaving the main structures of the Phnom Penh government and those of the coalition government intact and simply putting them under the supervision of the United Nations, meant that even if a peace agreement based on the P–5 plan was signed the leaders of the opposing factions could maintain a certain degree of autonomy *vis-à-vis* each other and the United Nations peace-keeping forces. Power, then, would not primarily come out of the democratic process put in place by the United Nations, but would remain largely in their hands.

By the end of August 1991, these four dynamics converged. Beijing and Hanoi recognized that the framework of Cambodian politics for the foreseeable future had been set by then in a way that was acceptable to both of them: their talks and the agreements reached by the Cambodian factions themselves guaranteed to their respective clients a position of power in Cambodian affairs. Moscow, unable by then to influence events anyhow, was nonetheless pleased with such a situation. Washington, for its part, could see the P–5 framework, even if emptied of some of its substance, serve as the basis of an emerging settlement of the Cambodian conflict. The leaders of the different Cambodian factions, finally, knew that they had manoeuvred themselves in a position which would let them, if pressed to sign a peace agreement based on the P–5 framework, retain most of their influence. The control they maintained over certain political structures and the troops they still had on the ground would let them be the power brokers in Cambodia, whatever the outcome of the electoral process.

THE PARIS AGREEMENT

The Paris Conference was reconvened in late October 1991. It set up an operation of enormous proportions which would eventually involve more than 22,000 people under the direction of the United Nations and cost close to US$2 billion. The goal of the operation was to organize 'free and fair elections' which would put in place a constituent assembly. The task of this assembly would be to adopt a new constitution and then turn itself into a legislative assembly which would in turn establish a new government. The organization and the success of the elections would rest on the creation of a social environment conducive to the establishment of democratic institutions.

UNTAC's 'Electoral Component' was thus to be complemented by a Police Component, responsible for 'ensur[ing] that law and order are maintained effectively and impartially', a Military Component charged with, among other assignments, the 'supervision of the ceasefire and related measures, including regroupment, cantonment, disarming and demobilization of forces of the Cambodian parties', a Civil Administration Component, which had 'direct control over existing administrative structures acting in the field of foreign affairs, national defence, finance, public security and information', and three components focused on deeper socio-political concerns:

(1) a Human Rights Component, making UNTAC responsible 'during the transitional period for fostering an environment in which respect for human rights and fundamental freedoms is ensured';
(2) a Rehabilitation Component, dealing with 'food security, health, housing, training, education, the transport network and the restoration of Cambodia's basic infrastructure and public utilities';
(3) a Repatriation Component, in charge of the 'movement of returnees, the provision of immediate assistance and food, and a reintegration programme' (Boutros-Ghali, 1992, pp. 34–5).

The magnitude of the operation was undoubtedly a function of the international context at the time. The idea of a 'New World Order' under which the international community would attempt to resolve regional conflicts, an idea articulated to a large extent by the reinvigoration of the United Nations, made possible by the end of the East–West standoff, served as a catalyst in the effort to gather the resources needed to take the P–5 framework to the level of international commitment envisaged by the second Paris Conference.

UNTAC aimed at being a 'peace-building', rather than a 'peacekeeping', operation. For all intents and purposes, its goal was to 'identify and support structures which [would] tend to strengthen and solidify peace in order to avoid a relapse into conflict', to use the language of the UN Secretary-General's report on the broadening of peace-keeping operations permitted by 'the improvement in relations between States east and west' (Boutros-Ghali, 1992, pp. 11, 5). It was meant, in other words, to exploit the potential for international cooperation of the New

World Order in order to not only contain the Cambodian conflict, an objective which would have paralleled the goal of most peace-keeping missions organized elsewhere, but also to permit its resolution by establishing a democratic culture in Cambodia. By protecting human rights, by developing a 'free and fair' political environment for the elections, and by assisting in the reconstruction of Cambodia's economic infrastructure, UNTAC would set in motion social transformations allowing the implantation of democratic institutions on which peace would then be based. Its objectives and its size in fact made UNTAC one of the first symbols of the New World Order.

As such, it acquired an autonomy of its own in the sense that the potential for its manipulation by the great powers was curtailed, on the one hand, by the worldwide attention it received and, on the other hand, by the great number of states and international actors involved in its action in Cambodia. The setting in motion of this enormous international effort solely oriented towards the resolution of the Cambodian conflict did not mean, however, that peace would be forthcoming in Cambodia. The four Cambodian factions, now feeling threatened by the extent of the mandate given to UNTAC, were bound to resist the implementation of the Paris peace plan.

CONFLICT AND CONFLICT MANAGEMENT IN CAMBODIA

As he describes the 'success of constitutionalism in delimiting the role of violence in political life', Sheldon Wolin (1936, p. 20) notes that

> the theory and practice of constitutional democracy have signified a concerted effort to restrict the application of violence by setting defined limits to power, by insisting on the observance of regularized procedures and by establishing strict methods for rendering those in power accountable for their actions. The paraphernalia of constitutionalism – the rule of law, due process, the separation of powers, checks and balances, and the system of individual rights, with its significant emphasis on privileges and 'immunities' – have not eliminated power, but they have contributed to its regularization, to eradicating that unpredictable, sheerly destructive quality that epitomizes all violence.

The logic of the Paris Agreement was rooted in this approach to conflict management. The 'peace-building' efforts of UNTAC were supposed to create in Cambodia the 'paraphernalia of constitutionalism'. The establishment of the 'rule of law' and a 'system of individual rights' would then allow the articulation of conflict in Cambodia on non-violent, political structures. Political struggles would not be 'eliminated', but, as Wolin puts it, they would be 'regularized' in order to 'eradicate their unpredictable, sheerly destructive qualities'.

The peace agreement, though, did not take into account the fact that the ability of political structures to contain violence is predicated on a particular series of socio-historical developments. It is the 'intersection', as Anthony Giddens puts it, of very particular dynamics, such as the growth of state institutions, the increasing importance of interstate relations, or the development of the political demands of the bourgeoisie, itself a function of the societal transformations caused by the extension of industrialization and capitalism, that produced, in certain societies and at specific times, it must be noted, the twin processes on which the 'success of constitutionalism in delimiting the role of violence' is based: centralization of the means of organized violence in the hands of the state and pacification through the elaboration of a framework of rules and laws regulating the use of these means of violence (see Giddens, 1987, Shaw, 1989; Wolin, 1963).

Cambodia's development, however, has not encompassed all the same social processes nor has it produced similar 'intersections' between them. The 'paraphernalia of constitutionalism', therefore, could not have a great resonance in Cambodian society. Much less could they be expected to 'regularize' political infighting and bring about a form of non-violent politics in Cambodia.

What are the factors which explain this situation? The state, as an institutional framework, has always been extremely weak in Cambodia. This results mainly from the constant pressures exercised on it by Cambodia's two powerful neighbours, Thailand and Vietnam, and by the French colonizers. Nor have economic developments caused in Cambodia transformations similar to the ones which took place in many other societies. Business activities have been concentrated in the hands of the royal entourage and in those of the Chinese community. There has never been, therefore, a Cambodian bourgeoisie powerful enough to challenge traditional patterns of authority through demands for an extension of the political franchise.

These factors were compounded by the influence of Brahmanism and Buddhism in Cambodia. Both religions posit that the social order is a reflection of a much broader cosmic order which stands outside human intervention and human comprehension. These religions have propounded in Cambodia the values of a 'pyramidal social order', to use Abdulgaffar Peang-Meth's expression (Peang-Meth, 1991, p. 445), whereby the king, situated at the top of this pyramidal structure, draws his power from the position he occupies in the cosmic order and not, in any measure, from a concern for popular representation within the political hierarchy. In this context also, the notion of the individual does not receive the preeminence it enjoys in some other societies. Finally, the ceaseless wars of the post-colonial era, and, most notably, the desolation that befell Cambodia during the Khmer Rouge period, have also provided innumerable social dislocations which have weakened Cambodian political institutions (see Chandler, 1992; Forest, 1980; Peang-Meth, 1991; Martin, 1989).

These processes and their amalgamation have prevented the emergence of a strong central authority able to control the means of organized violence and that of a framework of rights and institutions which would have contained and supervised their use. Cambodia has not developed, therefore, the institutional framework on which the movement from a violent to a non-violent form of politics could have been articulated. For these reasons, political struggles in Cambodia have tended to be expressed through violence. To quote Douglas Pike's brilliant phrase, 'the opposite of war in Cambodia is not peace; it is government. To reverse this, if there is government there can be peace; without government continued warfare is inevitable' (Pike, 1989, p. 847).

In these conditions, the only model of peace possible is one where the different factions refuse to surrender any power to political institutions and establish, for all intents and purposes, a system of balance of power between them. Such a model is bound to be stable only for a short period of time – witness the countless upheavals which have defined Cambodia's history – but it is the sole representation of an alternative to war conceivable within the present Cambodian context.

The Paris Agreement, however, was another story. The emphasis put in this case on democratization efforts meant that peace was supposed to be based on 'constitutional paraphernalia' which could not hold the conflict in check since they were not anchored in Cambodia's socio-political traditions. Furthermore, the creation of this 'paraphernalia' would endanger the configuration of beliefs and practices on which the power of the faction leaders is predicated. It could be assumed, therefore, that they would try to prevent it.

As could be expected, then, the actions of the four factions cast doubt on their support of the UN operation as soon as it got under way. For example, the separate political alliances which were concluded early on between certain factions, such as the one established between the Sihanoukists and prominent figures in the Phnom Penh government, rendered the Cambodian Supreme National Council (SNC) set up to embody Cambodian national sovereignty totally meaningless. It was thus prevented from becoming the guarantor of a 'neutral political environment' in Cambodia, as was envisaged in the UN plans. The refusal of the Khmer Rouge to participate in the disarmament phase of the peace plan and the unwillingness of the Phnom Penh government to cede control of many of its components to the UN personnel then kept UNTAC from creating the conditions necessary to a 'neutral political environment' during the electoral process.

The last few months before the elections were spent trying to achieve some agreement among the factions and the backers of the Paris plan on the role of Prince Sihanouk before and after the elections. Much time was spent discussing eventual presidential elections where only the Prince would have been the candidate. As president, Sihanouk would then have tried to form a government of national reconciliation including the four principal factions. Such an option had the merit of permitting the inclusion, and thus the neutralization, of the Khmer Rouge even though the group had refused to participate in the electoral process. This meant, however, that the UN accepted that the elections had lost their *raison d'être*. Though the idea of a presidential election was dropped, it was clear that the UN was in fact looking for options that would bring stability to Cambodia, no matter what the result of the vote was going to be.

By doing so, the UN put Cambodian political models back at the centre of the peace process in Cambodia. What UNTAC was encouraging from that point on was a return to the traditional pattern of Cambodian political life where the god-king, drawing his legitimacy from long-established customs and institutions, tries to create some balance of power between deeply divided factions. Democratization and political representation, the basis of the peace-building approach of the Paris framework, were obviously missing from that new approach to the search for peace in Cambodia. Peace through democracy, the formula at the centre of the Paris framework, had given way to the notion that peace involved stability only. This squared with the way the Cambodians themselves considered conflict resolution.

And indeed, it was possible to think at the time that some form of accommodation between the factions would be possible after the elections. But the overwhelming enthusiasm of the Cambodian people for the elections, to say nothing of their courage, changed the equation.

With a level of participation approaching 90 per cent, it was impossible to ignore public opinion. A debate on the nature of the political rules of the game in Cambodia thus emerged. Should power be vested in Sihanouk after the election? This would bring into play traditional modes of authority which would be less threatening to the Cambodian leaders and would guarantee a certain measure of stability in the post-election period. Should the Paris agreement, on the contrary, be followed to the letter since any departure from that framework would take Cambodia away from the democratization process on which all hopes for a durable peace had been pinned?

This debate was presented in a stark fashion when Prince Norodom Ranariddh, Prince Sihanouk's son and the leader of FUNCINPEC, called his father's attempt at creating a government of national reconciliation a 'constitutional coup' (*The Nation*, 5 June 1993, p. 1). The secession attempt led by another of Sihanouk's sons, Prince Norodom Chakrapong, and the difficulty of taking power away from the SOC then led the international community to accept a new power-sharing agreement between its leaders and the FUNCINPEC after guarantees were given that this would only be an interim arrangement. Matters were complicated by the wrangling over the new Constitution. The same tensions remained, however, between those advocating a close adherence to the letter of the Paris agreement, and those promoting a return to a more traditional model of politics, for instance by a return to the 1947 Monarchical Constitution (*Phnom Penh Post*, 17 Aug. 1993, pp. 1, 8). And the last segment of this episode of Cambodia's history, the promulgation of a new Constitution in September 1993, confirmed that these tensions were most likely to endure. For example, the Constitution restored the monarchy and established that 'the King shall hold the supreme role as referee to guarantee the normal functioning of public authorities', but claimed simultaneously that the 'King shall comply with . . . a multi-party, liberal democratic system' (*Constitution of the Kingdom of Cambodia*, Chapter 2, article 9, and Chapter 1, article 1). In any case, a modicum of peace was established, permitting the UNTAC to withdraw, proclaiming success.

TOWARDS A REDEFINITION OF POWER?

In the near future, the involvement of the great powers in Cambodia will probably revolve around two interdependent sets of factors related to these tensions. First, great-power policy will likely be shaped by the political configuration which will emerge in Cambodia as the factional infighting in that country lets the proponents of a given model of peace gain the upper hand over their adversaries. Second, policy may also be a function of the desire of the great powers to influence this political struggle. This will be done either by establishing alliances with certain groups within Cambodia or by supporting the model of peace which will give preeminence to these groups.

The implications of that second mode of influence should be understood. If they choose to support a search for peace based on the letter of the Paris agreement, the great powers will have to deal with the weaknesses of that agreement. This would involve putting forward an implementation framework which would target the social structures underlying the type of factional politics prevailing in Cambodia and then attempt to modify them in order to permit the development of democratic institutions; a long-term programme of international economic and political aid would have to be aimed more directly at these structures, while a peace-keeping force would have to remain in place to prevent the groups threatened by this programme from disrupting it. If, on the contrary, peace is seen as a corollary of balance of power politics in Cambodia rather than a consequence of democratization, international action will tend to revolve around pressures on the faction leaders aimed at shoring up their coalition. Economic aid patterns, for their part, will remain similar to what they were during UNTAC's mandate. The definition of a precise position on those issues will rest on the particular capacities of each great power, for instance the role played within the aid consortia operating in Cambodia.

If the United States chooses to support the democratic model of peace, for instance, a 'self-reinforcing constellation' of socio-political developments (Chan, 1992, p. 19) would include a capitalist market economy and a decentralization of political processes. In this context, Cambodia would be integrated, via the development of economic flows and shared values, within the regional order centred around ASEAN. This integration would in turn reduce Cambodia's margin of manoeuvre and make the country more responsive to the pressures of the United States and to those of ASEAN. Conversely, if a peace based on a balance of power between the different Cambodian factions is sought in Cambodia, the attendant political tussle might frighten international investors and thus slow the type of economic development on which a greater integration with ASEAN is predicated. The persistence of a centralized political system would also bring Cambodia closer to the two regional actors whose goal is now to contain demands for greater democratization: Vietnam and China. This would in turn curtail the institutionalized arrangements between ASEAN and Cambodia.

Previous understandings of power will thus have to be supplemented with the type of broad, long-term pressures generated by the sustained integration within a particular regional grouping fostered by the promotion of a given model of peace. This form of power will represent, furthermore, a fundamental component of the creation of a regional order, or indeed of regional orders, in Southeast Asia. These considerations will most probably shape great power involvement in Cambodia. They explain, also, why it is possible to see the Cambodian peace process as the end of the early conception of the New World Order.

Editorial Note

In 1995 it appears that the coalition between First Prime Minister Ranaridh and Second Prime Minister Hun Sen has worked surprisingly well, surviving longer than would have been expected. This is, at least in part, a result of Ranaridh's willingness to give up more control over day-to-day functioning of government to Hun Sen's Cambodia People's Party – especially in the provinces – than he had originally intended.

Internationally, Cambodia's ceasing to pose a threat to a great power or one of its allies may actually prove to be a disadvantage; this unlucky country may suffer as much from great power neglect as from manipulation. In fact, greater than any 'great power' is the influence of Thailand, even more influential than many Khmer regard as desirable. Thus Cambodia is being integrated into Southeast Asian regional politics at the same time its salience for great powers is declining. Among Western states in Cambodia, Australia has become a 'great power', rivaling the role of the US.

With the positions of China and Russia in Phnom Penh having become quite insignificant, there is a 'new' line of cleavage among outside powers, harking back to the nineteenth century: the Francophone–Anglophone (or 'all the rest') divide. It is apparent in NGO circles and international agencies as well as in aid programmes.

Notes

1. The documents which were circulated at the first Paris Conference (August 1989) and some of the statements issued by the Five Permanent Members of the Security Council are presented in Acharya, Lizée and Peou (1991).

The peace agreement signed at the second Paris Conference (October 1991) will be included in Acharya, Lizée, and Peou (forthcoming), *Cambodia: The Elusive Search for Peace*. The United Nations published many documents relating to UNTAC. One can consult, for example, UN (1992), *United Nations Peace-Keeping Operations: Information Notes* (New York: UN). The debate on the future direction of peace-keeping operations which is under way at the UN stems from the arguments presented in Boutros Boutros-Ghali (1992).

2. A wealth of information on the Cambodian peace process was presented in Cambodia's two English newspapers, the *Phnom Penh Post* and the *Cambodia Times*. Thailand's two English newpapers, the *Bangkok Nation* and the *Bangkok Post* also reported regularly on the situation in Cambodia. Finally, commentaries on UNTAC were found in the publications produced by Cambodian human rights organizations. *Le salut khmer*, which was published in France by the well-known human rights activist Douc Rasy, is very interesting in that regard.

References

Acharya, Amitav, Pierre Lizée and Sorpong Peou (1991) *Cambodia: The 1989 Paris Peace Conference, Background Analysis and Documents* (Millwood, New York: Kraus International Publications).

Alagappa, Muthiah (1990) 'The Cambodian Conflict: Changing Interests', *Pacific Review*, vol. 3, no. 3, pp. 266–71.

Boutros-Ghali, Boutros (1992) *An Agenda for Peace. Preventive Diplomacy, Peacemaking and Peacekeeping* (New York, UN).

Brown, Frederick Z. (1992) 'Cambodia in 1991: An Uncertain Peace', *Asian Survey*, vol. XXXII, no. 1 (January), pp. 89–96.

Brown, Frederick Z. (1993) 'Cambodia in 1992: Peace at Peril', *Asian Survey*, vol. XXXIII, no. 1 (January), pp. 83–90.

Chan, Steve (1992) 'National Security in the Asia-Pacific: Linkages among Growth, Democracy, and Peace', *Contemporary Southeast Asia*, vol. 14, no. 1 (June), pp. 13–32.

Chandler, David P. (1991) *The Tragedy of Cambodian History. Politics, War, and Revolution since 1945* (New Haven and London: Yale University Press).

Chandler, David P. (1992) *A History of Cambodia* (2nd edn) (Boulder and Oxford: Westview Press).

Emmerson, Donald K. (1985) 'The Stable War: Cambodia and the Great Powers', *Indochina Issue*, no. 62 (December).

Forest, Alain (1980), *Le Cambodge et la colonisation française. Histoire d'une colonisation sans heurts (1897–1920)* (Paris: L'Harmattan).

Frost, Frank (1991) 'The Cambodia Conflict: The Path towards Peace', *Contemporary Southeast Asia*, vol. 13, no. 2 (September), pp. 119–63.

Giddens, Anthony (1987) *The Nation-State and Violence*, Vol. 2 of *A Contemporary Critique of Historical Materialism* (Berkeley and Los Angeles: University of California Press).

Haas, Michael (1991) 'The Paris Conference on Cambodia, 1989', *Bulletin of Concerned Asian Scholars*, vol. 23, no. 2, pp. 42–53.

In, Thaddée (1991/2) 'Cambodge, an I', *Politique internationale*, vol. 54 (Winter), pp. 273–89.

Koh, Tommy T. B. (1990) 'The Paris Conference on Cambodia: A Multilateral Negotiation that "Failed"', *Negotiation Journal*, vol. 6, no. 1 (January), pp. 81–7.

Lechervy, Christian (1992/3) 'Le Khmer rouge: Homo bellicus versus homo economicus', *Culture et Conflits* (Hiver).

Leifer, Michael (1985–6) 'Obstacles to a Political Settlement in Indochina,' *Pacific Affairs*, vol. 58, no. 4 (Winter), pp. 626–36.

Leifer, Michael (1989) *Cambodian Conflict. The Final Phase?* (London: Institute for the Study of Conflict).

Leifer, Michael (1990) 'The Stakes of Conflict in Cambodia', *Asian Affairs*, vol. XXI, no II (June), pp. 155–61.

Lizée, Pierre (1993) 'Peace-keeping, Peace-building, and the Challenge of Conflict Resolution in Cambodia', in *Peacekeeping and the Challenge of Civil Conflict Resolution* (Fredericton: Centre for Conflict Resolution).

Martin, Marie Alexandrine (1993) 'La paysannerie khmère et le processus démocratique', in Christian Lechervy and Richard Petris (eds) *Les Cambodgiens face à eux-mêmes? Contributions à la construction de la paix au Cambodge* (Paris: Fondation pour le progrès de l'homme), pp. 127–42.

Martin, Marie Alexandrine (1989) *Le mal cambodgien. Histoire d'une société traditionnelle face à ses leaders politiques 1946–1987* (Paris: Hachette).

Peang-Meth, Abdulgaffar (1992) 'The United Nations Peace Plan, the Cambodian Conflict, and the Future of Cambodia', *Contemporary Southeast Asia*, vol. 14, no. 1 (June), pp. 33–46.

Peang-Meth, Abdulgaffar (1991) 'Understanding the Khmer: Sociological-Cultural Observations', *Asian Survey*, vol. XXXI, no. 5 (May), pp. 442–55.

Peschoux, Christophe (1992), *Les 'nouveaux' Khmers rouges 1979–1990* (Paris: L'Harmattan).

Pike, Douglas (1989) 'The Cambodian Peace Process: Summer of 1989', *Asian Survey*, vol. XXIX, no. 9 (September), pp. 842–52.

Regaud, Nicolas (1992) *Le Cambodge dans la tourmente. Le troisième conflit indochinois 1979–1991* (Paris: Fondation pour les études de défense nationale L'Harmattan).

Roberts, David (1992) 'Cambodia: Problems of a UN-brokered Peace', *The World Today*, vol. 48, no. 7 (July), pp. 129–32.

Rowley, Kelvin (1991) 'The Cambodian Conflict after the Vietnamese Withdrawal', unpublished paper.

Sopiee, Noordin (1993) 'The New World Order: Implications for the Asia–Pacific', in Rohana Mahmood and Rustam A Sani (eds) *Confidence Building and Conflict Reduction in the Pacific*, 3–29, (Proceedings of the Sixth Asia-Pacific Roundtable, Kuala Lumpur, June 1992), (Kuala Lumpur: Institute of Strategic and International Studies).

Shaw, Martin (1989) 'War and the Nation-State in Social Theory', in David Held and John B. Thompson, (eds) *Social Theory of Modern Societies. Anthony Giddens and his Critics* (Cambridge and New York: Cambridge University Press), pp. 129–46.

Thayer, Carlyle A. (1992) 'Comrade Plus Brother: The New Sino-Vietnamese Relations', *Pacific Review*, vol. 5, no. 4, pp. 402–06.

Thion, Serge (1986) 'The Pattern of Cambodian Politics', *International Journal of Politics*, vol. XVI, no. 3 (Fall), pp. 110–30 (Special issue devoted to *Cambodia: Politics and International Relations*, Guest Editors: David A. Ablin and Marlowe Hood).

Turley, William S. (1990) 'The Khmer War: Cambodia After Paris', *Survival*, vol. XXXII, (Sept./Oct.), pp. 437–53.

Wanandi, Jusuf (1990) *The Cambodian Conflict* (Tokyo: International Institute for Global Peace).

Wolin, Sheldon S. (1963) 'Violence and the Western Political Tradition', *American Journal of Orthopsychiatry*, vol. XXXIII, pp. 15–28.

Yeong, Mike (1992) 'Cambodia 1991. Lasting Peace or Decent Interval?', in *Southeast Asian Affairs*, pp. 103–19, (Singapore: Institute of Southeast Asian Studies).

13 The Spratly Imbroglio in the Post-Cold War Era

Mark J. Valencia[1]

For the first time in a generation, Southeast Asia seemed to have an opportunity for lasting peace. The end of the Cold War, the ebbing of the Cambodian conflict and *rapprochement* between Vietnam and the Association of Southeast Asian Nations (ASEAN), and even between Vietnam and China, have set the stage for a positive regional security relationship. But the dispute over the Spratly Islands in the South China Sea has become an obstacle to realizing this goal.

THE SPRATLYS: RECENT BACKGROUND TO AND STATUS OF THE DISPUTES

Introduction

Five countries and six governments – Brunei, Malaysia, the Philippines and Vietnam and the governments of both China and Taiwan – claim all or a part of the Spratly Islands and/or their attendant maritime area. This group of islands and reefs, some of which are submerged in storms or high tides, is thought to harbor oil and gas,[2] and is of strategic significance for sealane defence, interdiction and surveillance. Military forces of the claimants occupy the islands in a crazy-quilt pattern (Figure 13.1), and the territorial and jurisdictional disputes could result in further conflict (Valencia 1988), and even encourage new regional divisions. In addition to their strategic significance, what makes these disputes particularly sensitive and dangerous is that they are perceived as challenges to the integrity of the nation states and to the strength and effectiveness of their governments by both internal and external polities. Recently, all but Brunei have strengthened their claims by reinforcing their troop presence, making it more difficult to disengage and demilitarize, and, on the contrary, leading to an incipient arms race in the region. In addition to the claimants, the disputes

244

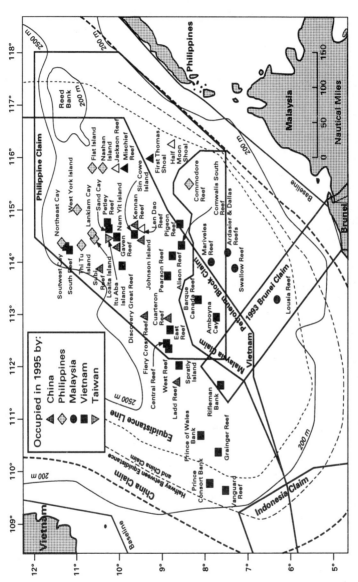

Figure 13.1 The Spratly Islands: occupants and claims (open triangles denote features on which China has placed markers but has not occupied)

involve the interests of the United States and Japan, and thus have become the main security problem affecting the entire region.

All of the claimants have been meeting annually since 1990 in a series of nongovernmental talks brokered by Indonesia. These 'Track Two' (unofficial) talks involve government officials and a few academics – both participating in their private capacities – from China, Vietnam, Taiwan, Laos, Cambodia, and the six ASEAN states (Thailand, Indonesia, Malaysia, Singapore, Brunei and the Philippines). In order to avoid an exclusive focus on the contentious claims, the agenda covers a broad range of topics. These talks are the only regional security dialogue in which both China and Taiwan have agreed to participate.

This novel process – a cross between formal government-style negotiations and an academic think-tank atmosphere – allows frank discussion of issues and solutions, although governments can ultimately disgregard the results. The idea is to build confidence that multilateral cooperation is possible. The approach has borne some fruit in the establishment of technical working groups on resource assessment and development, marine scientific research, environmental protection, biodiversity research, and – more significantly – legal matters. On the resolution of conflicting claims, however, there has been no progress, with participants unwilling to even specify or explain their positions. Even the working group on legal matters that convenes in Thailand in late 1995 is explicitly forbidden to discuss maritime claims or sovereignty issues.

Confidence-building measures agreed upon at the second workshop in 1991 have not dampened the disputes. Participants were to recommend that their respective governments (1) agree to avoid the use of force to settle territorial and jurisdictional disputes; (2) consider resolving conflicting claims by cooperating for mutual benefit, including joint development; and (3) exercise self-restraint in order not to complicate the situation. Although the use of armed force in combat has been avoided to date, there has been little progress on the other points. Malaysia is unenthusiastic about multilateral joint development and Vietnam is firmly opposed to it on its claimed continental shelf. China and Taiwan profess to support joint development but want the scene to encompass almost the whole South China Sea and thus the continental shelves claimed by other countries – and China wishes to negotiate individually with its smaller neighbours so as to dominate the arrangements.

Though the parties have voiced the desire to avoid destabilizing the situation, many claimants have done precisely the opposite. Military forces of the claimants occupy the islands in a crazy-quilt pattern and all are upgrading their military capabilities, some by building airstrips, harbours and defences. The claimants are also increasing economic activity in the islands; the Vietnamese by setting up fishing enterprises, Taiwan by building a lighthouse and harbour, and the Malaysians by building a tourist resort, something the Philippines may do as well. China, Vietnam, and the Philippines have granted concessions allowing foreign oil companies to explore in the disputed areas they claim.

Background

The Spratly issue was high on the agenda at the July 1992 ASEAN Foreign Ministers meeting as well as its Post-Ministerial Conference which included China, Japan, Russia, and the United States (Greenburger 1992). The movement of this once marginal issue to centre stage followed the lack of significant progress in the Indonesian-brokered Jogjakarta talks in June 1992, which were aimed at finding a solution to these disputes, and China's unilateral actions in the area (*Oil and Gas Journal*, 13 July 1992, pp. 20–21; Walsh, 1992; Jacob, 1992; *Asiaweek*, 17 July 1992, pp. 21–2; *Indonesian Times*, 3 July 1992, p. 2). The Jogjakarta discussions were wide ranging, but in the end the participants were unable to agree on fundamental matters such as the area in dispute or even to discuss its exact dimensions (Third Workshop on Managing Potential Conflicts, 1992; McDorman, 1993). Although the participants reaffirmed their desire to resolve the disputes in a peaceful, cooperative manner, they could not agree to discuss a cooperative solution and where, how and by whom it would be implemented. The participants also rejected an attempt to elevate the future dialogue to a more formal, official level. Thus the only concrete result was the setting up of milquetoast 'working groups' on resource assessment and scientific research, as well as the perfunctory commitment to meet again. Even the latter was in some doubt since China began implementing a new policy by which it would not allow its present or former officials or even academics to participate in discussions on security if participants from Taiwan were to be present. Nevertheless participants from all parties including China and Taiwan did attend the follow-up technical meeting on scientific research in Manila in early June 1993.

China was clearly the main obstacle to satisfactory progress in Jogjakarta, backing away from earlier commitments to resolve the issue (Valencia, 1992). Ironically, it was Li Peng's 13 August 1990 announcement in Singapore that China was prepared to put aside the question of sovereignty and jointly develop the Spratly area (Chanda and Cheung, 1990) that had seemed to simultaneously remove the major obstacle and set the stage for resolution of the problems there. Indeed it appeared to be a significant *volte-face* from the showdown following the violent clash between China and Vietnam on Johnston Reef in March 1988 in which three Vietnamese ships were sunk and 77 Vietnamese sailors were killed or missing (*Honolulu Advertiser*, 15 March 1988, p. D1, *FEER*, 26 April, 1990, p. 8).

Although all claimants agreed at the 1991 Indonesian-sponsored meeting in Bandung to resolve their differences peacefully and avoid unilateral actions that would jeopardize the process (Hadipranowo, Townsend-Gault and Djalal, 1991), subsequent Chinese actions eroded the crucial atmosphere of goodwill. China strengthened its naval and air capacity in the South China Sea area, acquired aerial refueling technology, and considered buying an aircraft carrier from the Ukraine.[3] It passed a Law on Territorial Waters and Their Contiguous Areas that formalized and made rigid its claim to territorial sovereignty over the Paracel and Spratly islands (Law on the Territorial Seas, 1992; *FEER*, 12 March 1992, pp. 8–9). Sometime in this period, it apparently drilled a stratigraphic test on Fiery Cross Reef called Nanyang #1 (Crestone Energy Corporation, 1992). Then it gave an oil concession – Wan'an Bei – in the Vanguard Bank area on Vietnam's claimed continental shelf to Crestone Energy Corporation, a US company, and pledged to protect the company with force (*Ta-Kung Pao*, 9 May 1992, p. 2 *FEER*, 18 June 1992, p. 8; *Straits Times*, 27 June and 3 July 1992). And even while the Jogjakarta participants were supposed to be seeking solutions to the problems, China was in the process of sending fresh troops to six islands it occupies and landing troops to erect a sovereignty marker on the Vietnamese-claimed Da Lac, the nearest feature to the Crestone concession area (MacDonald 1992; *Asiaweek*, 17 July 1992, pp. 21–2; *Time*, 27 July 1992, p. 40; Christ, 1992). Naturally, Vietnam argues that the concession area is on its continental shelf and in its 200-nautical-mile Exclusive Economic Zone (EEZ), and demanded of both China and Crestone that the deal be scrapped (UPI, 1992, Statement of the Ministry of Foreign Affairs, 1992).

In the face of alarm and mounting criticism from other claimants, China abruptly reoffered to negotiate the Spratly disputes and reiterated a pledge not to use force to defend its claims. But this was too little too late. In response to China's actions, the 1992 ASEAN Foreign Ministers' meeting promulgated its first ever formal declaration touching on regional security, called the ASEAN Declaration on the South China Sea (MacDonald, 1992; Pura, 1992a, and 1992b; Shenon, 1992; *FEER*, 6 Aug. 1992, pp. 8–9 and 13 Aug. 1992, pp. 14–6; *Asiaweek*, 7 Aug. 1992, pp. 20–3). It urged all claimants to settle the disputes peacefully and called for regional cooperation in furthering safety of navigation and communication, pollution prevention, search and rescue, and in combatting piracy and drug smuggling. Vietnam immediately supported the declaration while China's response was more equivocal. In September 1992, ASEAN's position was endorsed by a paragraph in the final document of the Non-Aligned Movement's political committee, although China opposed its inclusion (Smith and Aznam, 1992). And then China redeployed three Romeo-class conventional submarines from its North Sea Fleet to the South China Sea with a mission to patrol the contested areas (*FEER*, 8 April 1993, p. 9). This raised the possibility that China was simply using the Indonesian-sponsored process to stall for time while it consolidated and strengthened its position. Indeed, its small step-by-small-step approach has ameliorated foreign reaction because each step is so small and the costs of calling China's bluff are so large. But China was close to 'crossing the line' in other countries' strategic analysis of the situation, particularly that of Vietnam which, probably because of its relative diplomatic isolation, bore the brunt of China's advance. In the fourth Indonesian-sponsored talks in Surabaya in August 1993, China rejected the Indonesian proposal to formalize the talks (*FEER*, 2 September 1993).

The resolution of the South China Sea issues had been high on the agenda for the December 1992 talks between Premiers Li Peng and Vo Van Kiet in Vietnam (Hiebert, 1992b; Shirley, 1993; *South China Morning Post*, 3 Dec. 1992, p. 13; Kanwerayotin, 1992; Gao, 1992). Although little progress was made, China and Vietnam did agree to settle their disputes peacefully and upgrade the level and pace of the settlement process. Regarding the Crestone concession, China did propose to Vietnam that Vietnam take the continental shelf area between China's traditional claim line and the western edge of the Crestone concession while China retained the Crestone area. In China's version of 'joint development', each side would have full responsibility for developing its area. Vietnam rejected China's proposal arguing that the entire area was on its continental shelf as defined by the Law of the Sea Treaty and thus belonged to Vietnam. Regarding the Spratlys, China preferred bilateral talks while Vietnam insisted on multilateral negotiations by all countries concerned. The third round of Vietnam/

China technical talks was held on 3 January 1993, but these only explored the principles by which the dispute would be settled.

RECENT DEVELOPMENTS

China/Vietnam

Tension flared again in May 1993 when China's Ministry of Geology sent a seismic survey vessel into a concession let by Vietnam to British Petroleum Norway's Statoil and India's ONGC (*Petroleum Argus*, 24 May 1993). This concession is adjacent to Wan'an Bei and falls within China's historical line, as do nearby Vietnamese concessions to Australia's Broken Hill Proprietary, Japan's Arabian Energy Development, and British Gas. Meanwhile Vietnam was planning to award a rival concession in the Wan'an Bei area to CONOCO. And Crestone, with China's concurrence, formally offered joint development to PetroVietnam for the Wan'an Bei area, which Vietnam rejected.

Vietnam and China also have a dispute over the maritime boundary in the Gulf of Tonkin; China has used similar tactics there. For example, in June 1992 China sent a drill ship to drill in Vietnamese territorial waters (*Japan Times*, 6 June 1993; *FEER*, 20 Aug. 1992, p. 6; Hiebert, 1992b). Then China agreed to negotiate the issue. But in January 1993, one day after China's negotiating team left Hanoi, China prohibited all maritime activities in a rectangular area extending to within 20 nautical miles of Vietnam's coast, so that China could carry out seismic activities in areas claimed by Vietnam.

Chinese President Jiang Zemin and Vietnamese Communist Party Chief Do Muoi met in November 1994 and promised to resolve their dispute peacefully. Nevertheless the dispute had threatened to edge into violence already the previous summer, when Vietnam began drilling in the Crestone concession. Chinese ships blocked the drilling rig during a tense face-off in July. The informal multilateral talks held in October 1994 in Bukittinggi, Indonesia, were marked by sharp exchanges, particularly between Vietnam and China. China and Taiwan declined to reaffirm the 1991 confidence-building measures, and some feared violence was imminent. The meeting of the Chinese and Vietnamese leaders in November may thus have headed off a clash. Meanwhile conflict flared on another location.

The China-Philippines Mischief Reef/Panganiban/Meijijiao Flap

In September 1994 the Philippine armed forces detained some fifty-five fishermen from the People's Republic of China who tried to set up homes on one of the islands claimed by the Philippines. They were charged with illegal entry and illegal possession of explosives (*China News Digest*, 24 Jan. 1995; FBIS, 21 Feb. 1995; FBIS, 1 March 1995). Then in what may have been a tit-for-tat, in late January 1995 China detained 35 Filipino fisherman for a week in an area of the Spratlys claimed by Manila and called Kalayaan (*Japan Times*, 9 Feb. 1995; *China News Digest*, 10 Feb. 1995, p. 13; Voice of America, 15 Feb. 1995; *FEER*, 23 Feb. 1995, p. 14). On 8 February 1995, the Philippines accused China of breaking international law by stationing armed vessels at, and building structures on, its Panganiban (or Mischief) Reef.

Mischief Reef is a barely submerged coral reef and spit extending over 15 square nautical miles (nm) some 135 nm west of Palawan (*Honolulu Advertiser*, 11 Feb. 1995, p. A8). The Philippines had failed to monitor the Chinese construction because it lacks proper air, naval and radar equipment. And its ally by virtue of the 1951 Manila Mutual Defence Treaty, the United States, does not fly P3 Orion marine reconnaissance nor collect and analyse satellite surveillance over the area because there is said to be no threat to US forces there, and because there have been cutbacks in its surveillance capabilities. Moreover, the United States says that the Treaty does not apply to the disputed area because it covers only the 'metropolitan' areas of the Philippines as stipulated in the 1899 Paris Treaty and the 1935 Philippine Constitution, and because the Philippines claimed this area subsequent to the Treaty (FBIS-EAS-95-031, 15 Feb. 1995).

After the discovery at Mischief Reef, the Philippine Department of Foreign Affairs sent a very firm *aide memoir* to China's Manila Embassy. But China denied that the Chinese Navy had set up a base or detained Filipinos in the disputed area and said that the structures on what it calls Meijijiao were shelters for fishermen and were placed there by a department of the Chinese fisheries administration. It also said the occupation of the reef was ordered by low-level functionaries without the knowledge or consent of the Chinese government (*AWSJ*, 10–11 March 1995). But experts who have seen photographs say the structures are typical guard posts set on concrete pillars and include a satellite dish for communications, as well as the PRC flag fluttering from each structure. Their purpose certainly seems to be to demark territory and establish control.

In a nationally televised press interview Philippine President Fidel Ramos charged that China's actions were inconsistent with the spirit of the 1992 Manila ASEAN Declaration on the South China Sea which among others called for the peaceful settlement of the dispute and cooperation in the exploration and exploitation of the area. The Philippines claims that China, although not a signatory, nevertheless pledged to respect its provisions (FBIS-EAS-95-033, 17 Feb. 1995). Even though Malaysia, Taiwan and Vietnam also occupy features claimed by the Philippines, the Philippine Foreign Ministry argues that these occupations occurred well before the Manila Declaration. Thus – according to this argument – China should not be able to use the presence of other countries' forces as leverage to remain on the atoll.

Although President Ramos ordered reinforcement of Filipino defence forces in the area, it was thought unlikely that the incident would lead to violence, primarily because the Philippines does not have the capacity to project power. However, the Philippines did send a squadron of five aging fighter planes and twenty-nine patrol ships to surveille the reef occupied by China (*Japan Times*, 15 Feb. 1995, p. 4; 18 Feb. 1995, p. 4). In a minor conciliatory gesture China withdrew seven of its nine vessels to a location outside the Philippines' 200-nm exclusive economic zone, but left the structures in place. President Ramos told his National Security Council that the Chinese moves were incursions into Philippine territory and that the structures were new outposts and a possible naval support installation built in the middle of the Philippines' 200-nm EEZ (*Japan Times*, 16 Feb. 1995). Ramos asked 'foreign' intruders to leave the Philippines in peace and vowed not to allow a slackening of the country's defence capabilities (*Japan Times*, 20 Feb. 1995, p. 3). Partially motivated by the incident, the Philippine Senate passed a long-awaited bill to modernize the country's armed forces (FBIS-EAS-95-032, 16 Feb. 1995).

China clearly did not anticipate the degree of outcry from the Philippines. Instead of threatening to use military force, the Philippines was primarily trying to elicit the sympathy and support of ASEAN and the international community. It has warned that it may take the issue to the United Nations Security Council and to the World Court (the International Court of Justice) (*Japan Times*, 14 Feb. 1995, p. 45). However, China is a member of the Security Council and can veto any of its proposed resolutions, and the World Court cannot adjudicate if China does not accept its jurisdiction. The Philippines' appeal to ASEAN to form a solid front on this issue confronts obstacles because not all its members are claimants and because most do not want to collectively provoke China. The appeal of the Speaker of the House of Representatives, Jose de Venecia, for an early meeting of claimant country ambassadors, fell mostly on deaf ears.

However, the Philippines' strategy to depict this as a multilateral – not bilateral – issue has had some success. Vietnam condemned the Chinese action. The United States urged a peaceful resolution of the problem and reiterated that it would oppose the use of force to solve the dispute (FBIS-EAS-95-036, 23 Feb. 1995). And Japan and New Zealand expressed concern about Chinese activity in the area (Ching, 1995). Singapore's President Ong Teng Cheong said that ASEAN should present a united front and file a protest against such aggression (FBIS-EAS-95-028, 10 Feb. 1995; FBIS-EAS-95-032, 16 Feb. 1995; FBIS-EAS-95-033, 17 Feb. 1995). ASEAN did present a somewhat united front at the ASEAN–China forum on political and security issues (April 2–4) in Hangzhou, China (*FEER*, 20 April 1995, p. 12). The ASEAN foreign ministers also issued a statement expressing 'serious concern over recent developments which affect peace and stability in the South China Sea'. The statement also reminded the Spratly claimants to abide by the Manila Declaration of 1992, which calls for a peaceful settlement of the dispute (*Japan Times*, 20 March 1995, p. 3). The ASEAN Regional Forum (ARF) meeting in Brunei in July (Pereira 1995) discussed the issue as well, where China took a more conciliatory line.

Meanwhile, the Philippines proposed that the area be demilitarized, and that as an interim measure each disputed island should be placed under the stewardship of the claimant country closest to it geographically. The steward would accommodate the other claimants' needs for shelter, anchorage and other peaceful pursuits (FBIS-EAS-95-031, 15 Feb. 1995). This proposal was rejected out of hand by China. Undeterred, the Philippines also tried to convince the other claimants and the ARF that the waters around the islands should be declared a marine reserve (FBIS-EAS-95-041, 2 March 1995).

The Philippines and China did agree to talks. China repeated its offer of bilateral joint development (*Japan Times*, 24 March 1995). But the Philippines is opposed to bilateral negotiations for joint development of their overlapping areas because it does not want to be bullied by China, and because it would leave the sovereignty questions unsettled. To make matters worse, it was also discovered, just a day before the bilateral talks were to begin, that China had built new facilities on the Philippines-claimed Jackson Atoll and Half Moon Reef. Philippine Foreign Affairs Secretary Romulo confirmed the presence of Chinese markers but said they were removed by Philippine naval patrols, immediately after the talks concluded (FBIS-EAS-95-041, 2 March 1995; Butler, 1995). China commented that such destruction of Chinese survey markers would not help settle the dispute nor detract from China's sovereignty over the area (*Japan Times*, 26 March 1995, p. 1). The Philippines subsequently announced that it was building lighthouses on its claimed features and running naval patrols close to the Chinese-held reef (FBIS-EAS-95-036, 23 Feb. 1995). Meanwhile, it released the fifty-five fishermen detained in September of 1994.

Not surprisingly, the Sino-Philippine talks did not produce an agreement, although they supposedly set the groundwork for agreed future discussions. But the Philippine military complained that Chinese nationals were still occupying the platforms on Mischief Reef (*Honolulu Advertiser*, 29 March 1995, p. A7). And on 25 March Filipino troops seized four Chinese fishing boats and some fifty PRC citizens near Alicia Annie in the disputed area (*Honolulu Advertiser*, 27 March 1995, p. A5); China quickly demanded the release of the boats and their crew (*China News Digest*, 30 March 1995). Further antagonizing China, the Philippines arranged a visit to the disputed area by a group of foreign journalists. But by August, as a sign of some de-escalation of the conflict, President Ramos pardoned 58 of the 62 fishermen detained.

Given these recent incidents, pessimists wonder whether the Indonesian-sponsored multilateral process has become just a diversion – a 'talking club' holding out a false promise of cooperation while some nations strengthen their bargaining or military positions. A more optimistic view is that the informal workshops can still help to cool tensions and constrain parties from taking unilateral action. But further fruitless talks combined with unilateral military and economic initiatives may well erode rather than build confidence.

China's actions have some disturbing implications. For the first time in two decades, China has seized control of a disputed territory from a non-communist Southeast Asian neighbour. The conventional wisdom that China would leave ASEAN countries alone and focus on islands occupied by Vietnam has been shattered. Thus the idea that ASEAN countries could resolve the issue with China bilaterally – championed primarily by Malaysia – is now in some doubt. China seems to be saying 'negotiate with us on our terms or we will simply occupy the islands and create a *fait accompli*'.

THE PARACELS

The Sino-Vietnamese dispute in the Paracels is a separate but related issue because of its strategic location (Valencia 1985). On 19 to 20 January 1974, a People's Liberation Army-Navy (PLA-N) fleet consisting of four Hainan-class fast attack craft, two mine sweepers and two fishing boats defeated a South Vietnamese force of three destroyers and a corvette, and then seized three islands in the Crescent Group (Garver 1992). The motives for this action lay in geostrategic thinking. Beijing-Hanoi relations had become tense because of China's growing rapprochement with the United States during 1972, a year which saw renewed and intense U.S. bombing of North Vietnam. Chinese leaders were concerned about the growing closeness of North Vietnam and the USSR, and thus possible Soviet use of the islands and a tightening of its encirclement of China. The US/North Vietnam 'peace agreement' of January 1973 meant that the United States was disengaging from Indochina and China calculated that the United States would not get involved. Moreover, Soviet naval strength in the South China Sea was growing rapidly and if the islands were under China's control, the Soviet naval threat to China's vital southeast coast could be kept several hundred miles to the south.

Since January 1974 the entire Paracel archipelago has been firmly in the hands of China. The archipelago comprises 15 islets, covering a total land area of about 3 km^2 (1.2 miles^2). The largest island, Woody (Yongxing), is also the main Chinese garrison in the Paracels and is reported to have the largest civilian population. Photographs published by China of the life of Chinese residents in the Paracels show numerous buildings on the islands. In addition, several of the islands are said to have harbors that serve as bases for naval and fishing activities, as well as canals, dams, meteorologic observatories, and multi-storied buildings.

However, Sino-Vietnamese tension over the Paracels has resulted in a number of skirmishes, including the Chinese capture of twenty-four Vietnamese troops near the Paracels. On 10 April 1979, immediately following its leasing of a concession to Amoco in the disputed area in the Gulf of Tonkin, China declared four areas in the vicinity of Hainan and the Paracels to be 'danger zones' and forbade overflights at altitudes between 1,000 and 20,000 m (3,280 and 65,600 ft). The 'danger zones', one of which covered North Reef in the Paracels, were the sites of Chinese naval and air exercises. In spite of protests from Vietnam and the International Civil Aviation Organization (because the declaration necessitated the closing of a major commercial air corridor), the 'danger zone' warning stayed in effect from October 1979 to February 1980.

Early in 1984, then Chinese Army Chief of Staff Yang Dezhi visited the Paracels and placed soil from Zhongnanhai – the compound in Beijing revered as the seat of the Chinese government – around coconut saplings, thus symbolically renewing China's claim to the islands (*Honolulu Advertiser*, 12 Feb. 1982, p. C1). Both claimants maintain that the Paracels have been their territory since ancient times, and their positions are too rigid to facilitate a negotiated settlement (La Grange, 1980, pp. 15–18).

The Sino-Vietnamese conflict in the Spratlys has sharply increased the strategic importance of the Paracel Islands. China needs the islands for effective control and reconnaissance on its southern flank and for sustaining pressure on Vietnam. After the departure of the US Navy from Vietnam, China sought to build a southern wall of defence by extending a string of island bases onto the mainland and reinforcing its southern fleet with landing craft to defend territorial claims in the South China Sea. The Paracels could also be used to mount a strike at the Spratlys (Breeze, 1982). Given China's 1982 seizure of Vietnamese cargo vessels bound for Vietnam from Hong Kong (*Asiaweek*, 18 Sept. 1992, p. 35), Vietnam may be concerned about a possible future blockade by China (Samuels, 1982, p. 139; Tack, p. 1992). The Paracel Islands occupy a position central to the shipping lanes connecting Hong Kong with Hanoi and Ho Chi Minh City and could be used as a base for a blockade. It is thus understandable that Vietnam continues to claim the Paracels.

GEOPOLITICS AND THE SPRATLYS

The Spratly Islands in the South China Sea have long been known to mariners as the "Dangerous Ground," because of their numerous shoals. However they have also long borne the seeds of international conflict (Valencia, 1988). Control of the Spratlys by an adversary could have implications for the national security interests of Japan, the United States and even Russia. All concerned are aware that Japan used Tai Ping Dao as a submarine base and staging area for its invasion of the Philippines, the then Dutch East Indies and Malaya in the Second World War II. And the Imperial Navy cut off Allied shipping in the South China Sea during the War. Major international shipping lanes pass through the South China Sea near the Spratlys, and two of the world's great ports – Singapore and Hong Kong – are situated close to its southern and northern approaches. More than 70 percent of Japan's oil passes through this area. In times of hostilities, the United States might have to convoy seaborne oil headed for Japan and the United States.

Free navigation through, under and over the straits, and sealanes of Southeast Asia is also critical to the war-fighting strategy of the United States. Its Seventh Fleet plies this area on missions and transits between the Pacific and Indian Oceans. Four of 16 strategic straits in the world which are important to the mobility of the US fleet are in Southeast Asia – Malacca, Lombok, Sunda, and Ombai-Wetar. The Spratly Islands could be used as bases for surveillance and monitoring of the fleet. Furthermore, in order to attack or defend against a submarine, its location must be known. Indeed, the United States maintains that the invulnerability of its SSBNs (the Trident fleet) and hence their indispensable deterrent role as a second-strike depends on their ability to pass through straits and sealanes submerged, unannounced, and undetected. Without secure submerged passage in Southeast Asia, the routes available to the submarines would be severely limited increasing the chance of their detection and targeting. The outcome of the dispute over the Spratlys thus should be of particular interest to the United States since the controller of the islands could control the major sea lines of communication. While the end of the Cold War has lessened their strategic significance, US defense planners must still consider the worst scenario of their control by a hostile power.

During the Cold War, the US/Soviet rivalry in the region actually served as a stabilizer to the dispute. The United States was intent on keeping the sealanes free from threat and thus neither China nor Vietnam, a Soviet ally, dared to press an advantage there. The China-Soviet struggle also influenced the dispute. For example, the frequency and intensity of belligerent statements and incidents between China and Vietnam in the Spratlys ebbed and flowed with progress on a Cambodian solution. When China perceived Vietnam as being obstinate in Cambodia, it stepped up pressure in the Spratlys. When the Cold War began to wane and the Soviet Union disengaged from Vietnam, both Vietnam and China began to expand the number of features occupied as well as the number of troops thereon. In the late 1980s, with Vietnam isolated by the collapse of the Soviet Union and the American-led embargo, China began to press home its power advantage in earnest, occupying eight features, and in March 1988 attacking and defeating Vietnamese forces there. This produced a tense temporary military stalemate.

Post-Cold War Southeast Asia – like other regions – is in a state of geopolitical flux. There is a widespread perception that as the United States focuses more on domestic problems, it will inevitably withdraw from the region, undermining the Pax Americana in the Pacific. Thus there is a growing feeling that the region can no longer rely on the United States as a guarantor of regional stability. Further, US relations with both China and Japan are deteriorating (Zagoria 1993), and there is concern that one or both will replace the United States as the dominant power in the region. Japan is already dominant there economically and is very tentatively considering expanding its defense presence in the region, particularly the protection of the sealanes which carry its vital trade and oil. In partial response, ASEAN has begun to consider security cooperation, Indonesia is attempting to assert leadership in Southeast Asia, and Vietnam, isolated and vulnerable, is joining ASEAN.

The significance of the Spratly dispute is that it has broad geopolitical implications reaching far beyond ownership of the scattered fly specks. Indeed the results can be considered a test or indicator of trends in regional relationships in the post-Cold War era. First, what are China's intentions towards the region? Can China be internationally 'socialized'? Some of the smaller nations believe China will eventually 'democratize' and either relent or settle its claims peacefully. But China's growing economic and military power may also enable it to win complete control or the lion's share in any settlement. Will China be a cooperative, benign neighbor or will it seek to dominate? If so, what will be the policies and reactions of Japan and the United States – albeit behind the scenes? Will Japan and/or the United States get involved? If so, how and in what fashion? Can ASEAN maintain solidarity in the face of an aggressive China? And could ASEAN solidarity on this issue persuade China to mitigate its aggressive stance? Will Vietnam and the rest of ASEAN form a united front against China on what is essentially a security issue? And will Indonesia emerge as a subregional leader by successfully brokering a solution to the imbroglio? These are not trivial questions for the future of the region.

VIETNAM'S PERSPECTIVE

Vietnam feels that in the long term, China desires hegemony over the South China Sea and that it will do or say whatever will help achieve this goal. From Vietnam's perspective, if the United States does not support the small countries, or does not somehow serve as a stabilizer, Vietnam may have no choice but to accommodate China. Already there are pro-China elements in Vietnam which are arguing for this option. If Vietnam is dominated by China, the South China Sea and its sealanes will also be dominated. This would not be in the interests of Japan or the United States.

Vietnam is thus attempting to force the issue for the United States by offering concessions near the Crestone area to American oil companies. During the embargo US oil companies could sign contracts, but could not produce (Chanda, 1993). And Mobil has farmed in to the Japanese-held Arabian Oil Company concession in an area encompassed by China's historic claim line. The China/Vietnam conflict may be coming to a head because oil has been discovered adjacent to the Crestone area, Crestone may be about to be joined by a company with the financial and technical capability to drill, and Vietnam is offering the Crestone area to potential concessionaires. At this stage, for US oil companies to become active in such a disputed area would presumably require the tacit approval of the US government.

Vietnam has so far eschewed the options of military build up, confrontation or the seeking of overt military alliances against China, all difficult in any case. Its strategy appears to be to enmesh Sino-Vietnamese relations within a much larger regional network of interlocking economic and political interests. In this situation, an attack by China on Vietnam in the Spratlys area would be seen as a threat to others' interests as well. But China understands this strategy well and at one point anyway seemed determined by 'carrot-and-stick' to separate its relations with Vietnam in the South China Sea from those with other claimants.

Vietnam prefers third party arbitration of the issues. But China has refused. Vietnam is thus facing a dilemma. If it believes China's 'carrot-and-stick' approach is only a tactic designed to bring Vietnam to the bargaining table and to persuade it to accept joint development, then it will probably continue to reject the offer. Agreeing would be tantamount to recognizing the validity of China's historic claim, its ownership of the Spratly Islands and other features, and more importantly for its precedent in international law, the ability of these islands to generate an EEZ and a continental shelf. This would, in turn, have implications for other claimants. However, if Vietnam believes, as do some other observers[4] that China's actions are part of an overall plan to dominate the South China Sea, then it may consider accepting the joint development proposal, thus ensuring that it will retain a share of any resources there, since the alternative may be the loss of the entire area to superior force as well as severe damage to its fragile relationship with China.

WHY IS CHINA ACTING THE WAY IT IS?

On the one hand China seems to maintain its traditional claim of sovereignty over the entire South China Sea, but refuses to specify or justify this claim. On the other hand, China acknowledges that other countries also claim sovereignty to parts of the area and continues to propose joint development. But it gives mixed signals as to what it means by joint development, i.e., whether it means joint development of the Spratly area only, or of the entire South China Sea, including areas that rival claimants consider well within their continental shelves, like that granted to Crestone.

China's sincerity in participating in a peaceful cooperative solution to the disputes is now in some doubt. Indeed, there has been speculation that China has reverted to its previous hardline position, that is, that other claimants must first recognize its sovereignty before joint development is possible. Furthermore, although its joint development offer was initially taken to mean multilateral joint development, China has since shown a strong preference for quiet bilateral negotiations on these issues, and for awhile tried to play some ASEAN claimants off against Vietnam. China is certainly opposed to 'internationalization' of the issue.

Many hypotheses have been offered to explain why China is acting the way it is. Perhaps China is simply responding to other claimants' actions, or, by demonstrating its authority and possession, seeking a tactical and negotiating advantage ahead of negotiations (Chanda, 1992a; Lee, 1992; Awanohara, 1992). In this context, some analysts believe that Li Peng and Yang Shangkun's offers of joint development in 1990 were premature and that the relevant ministries and, more importantly, the Peoples Liberation Army (PLA) were not consulted (Kreisberg, 1992). This view also suggests that eventually a consensus will emerge that will be generally conciliatory and include as its major elements joint development of resources and avoidance of conflict. If this is correct, the ASEAN Declaration may reinforce a coordination of policy among the different interests in China.

Other observers are less sanguine about China's intentions. They argue that China's foreign policy is based on its sense of vulnerability as a continental power surrounded by hostile nations, that it has no buffers, and thus finds it difficult to project power. In this view, China is bent on reestablishing the 'greater China' and regaining its ancient role as the dominant power in Asia – in short, forging a Pax Sinica. Others attribute this drive more to China's very long-term view of its strategic resource and economic interests rather than to geostrategic concerns (Garver, 1992). In both scenarios, China has embarked on an aggressive campaign to acquire and develop conventional weapons that will allow it to assert control over the islands and the South China Sea as a whole. They point to China's August 1992 detention of Vietnamese ships near Hong Kong as evidence that China views the South China Sea as an 'internal passageway' (Balman, 1992; Hamzah, 1992; *Asiaweek*, 18 Sept. 1992, p. 35).

China or its military may well have viewed the reduction of the US military presence in the region as an opportunity to advance its cause with relative impunity. Russia's withdrawal from Vietnam and global power projection may have also encouraged China's initiative. A Chinese military leader has publicly stated that China wishes to develop an oceangoing fleet to bolster its claim to the Spratly Islands (*Honolulu Star Bulletin*, 11 Jan. 1993). The much vaunted effort of China to acquire an aircraft carrier may be viewed in this context. But some analysts suggest that China's naval build-up is really stimulated by a potential threat from Japan and that the Spratly Islands problem provides a convenient smokescreen for its real concerns and intentions, as well as an opportunity for the PLA Navy to enhance its budget.

Others think that China already has a sufficient amphibious force to effect multiple landings against Vietnamese, Philippine, and Malaysian garrisons with a sure guarantee of success. These analysts also note that PLA ships and naval aircraft have the tactical missile capabilities to destroy artillery and electronic installations on the islands they would attack prior to marine landings (N. Lee, 1990, p. 7; Jacobs, 1990; Cheung, 1992a; Balman, 1992). Still others downplay this supposed buildup arguing that it will be some time before China will be capable of seizing and holding islands occupied by others, and that anyway China has long needed to modernize its antiquated weapons systems and is simply taking advantage of bargain basement prices. This school argues that China is too calculating and preoccupied with domestic economic development to divert resources to such a regional conflict. However, for similar reasons, others suggest that China is deliberately trying to provoke Vietnam into a conflict to scare away its investors and retard its competitive economic growth (Scalapino, 1992; Awanohara, 1992).

Other explanations invoke domestic politics as the underlying cause of China's confusing actions. One view holds that Beijing simply wants to demonstrate to its increasingly assertive provinces, as well as to the democracy movement in China and Hong Kong and the independence movement on Taiwan, that China's government is firmly in control of national policy. China is also particularly sensitive to criticism from the Kuomingtang on Taiwan that it did not adequately safeguard China's territorial integrity (Pan, 1993). Another theory holds that China's actions are the result of a rising tide of nationalism which seems to be replacing socialism as the new preferred societal glue. In this view, the economic reforms pushed by Deng Xiaoping have put China's conservatives on the defensive, and they are using nationalistic issues, such as sovereignty over the Spratlys, as a way to reassert themselves. Others see the behavior as a result of a trade-off between the two factions – a more assertive policy in the South China Sea in exchange for the 'Coca Cola-isation' of China's economy (Greenburger, 1992; Terrill, 1992; Findlay, 1992).

The contradictions between China's statements and its actions probably reflect a real dialectic of goals, as well as contradictory positions of the Ministry of Foreign Affairs (MFA) and the People's Liberation Army (PLA) (Bert, 1993; Glaser, 1993; Chen, 1993; Garver, 1992). On the one hand, the MFA desires a peaceful and stable Southeast Asia which can complement and aid China's economic modernization. On the other, the PLA has long-term territorial, security, and economic goals that require domination of the South China Sea islands and their attendant maritime space. The Chinese government is attempting to balance these conflicting goals and viewpoints. What we are witnessing is the manifestation of these contradictions.

EMERGING PROBLEMS AND PROGNOSIS

Regardless of the reasons, China's actions have rattled ASEAN governments as well as Vietnam and have drawn the attention of Japan, the United States and even Russia (Bowring, 1992; Awanohara, 1992; Giacomo, 1992), which is still concerned about the security of sealanes on which it depends for communication between its European and Asian parts (Bogaturov, 1992). For the first time since the 1970s the notion of China as a threat to the region is gaining currency. A mini-arms race in the region is in the offing. The Philippines plans to arm its three new fast patrol boats with Exocet missiles (*New Straits Times*,

21 June 1992, p. 11; *The Star*, 6 July 1992, p. 22) and Malaysia is also considering buying Exocet missiles, as well as up to thirty MiG-29 fighter aircraft from Russia. The worst scenario is one of an increased frequency and scale of violent incidents endangering freedom of navigation along strategic sealanes and eventually involving the United States or Japan in the imbroglio (Bowring 1992; *The Economist*, 25 July 1992; Awanohara, 1992; *FEER*, 13 Aug. 1992, pp. 14–16).

China's drive to project power, its development of a blue-water navy, and its assertiveness in the South China Sea make it a potential enemy of the United States. Indeed, there are reports that the United States is casting China as the adversary in planning joint naval exercises with allies in the region (Hiebert, 1992a; Cheung, 1992b; Awanohara and Kaye, 1992; Giacomo, 1992; Tasker, 1992). On the other hand, military ties with China have been renewed.

The presence of US ships and aircraft in the South China Sea is generally believed to be a stabilizing influence. ASEAN countries thus fear that without the US presence, disputants may feel less restrained to assert and enforce their claims (Tefft, 1992). Some Southeast Asian countries have reportedly asked the United States to mediate the disputes in an effort to avoid being bullied by China. US involvement in the Spratly disputes could even encourage a new geopolitical alignment in Asia – a Southeast Asia with implicit US and perhaps Japanese backing united against China. As an indication that China has begun to realize the dangers of its actions, it recently warned outside powers to stay out of the conflict. Meanwhile, the *People's Daily* raised the spectre of a new Western conspiracy similar to that which followed the Boxer rebellion (Awanohara 1992; Baum, Chung, and Kaye 1992). At the very least, China's policies toward the South China Sea will strongly influence its relations with Southeast Asia. (*International Herald Tribune*, 24 April 1995). Continued Chinese expansion in the South China Sea, particularly if accompanied by violence, could ultimately risk China's international isolation.

The March 1994 agreement between Taiwan's China Petroleum Corporation (CPC), the China National Offshore Oil Corporation, and Chevron to form a joint venture for oil exploration in the East and South China Seas raises the possibility of a China–Taiwan 'united front' on the Spratly issues (Valencia and Zha, 1994; *World Journal*, 13 March 1994; 25 April 1994, p. 6.). The first sign that China and Taiwan might form common ground on these issues surfaced during the March 1988 clash in the South China Sea between China and Vietnam, when Taiwan's Defence Minister stated that Taiwan would help China defend

the island group from a third party if asked to do so (Shim, 1988). At
the 1991 round of Indonesian-sponsored talks it became apparent that
China and Taiwan had the same sweeping claim to most of the South
China Sea, with the same historical rationale. This claim is often accompanied by a map showing a historic claim line which encompasses much of the continental shelf and even subsequently discovered
oil fields of ASEAN nations, including those of Indonesia.

Taiwan has recently reiterated its claim to most of the South China
Sea, and, supported by China, argues that multilateral cooperation should
be pursued throughout the entire area (Asian Legal Studies Center,
1993). Taiwan has even initiated an effort to formulate a joint China–
Taiwan legal position to support its sweeping claim. And although joint
hydrocarbon exploration in the disputed areas of the South China Sea
will be inhibited by the claims of others, there are ongoing discussions for a joint China–Taiwan oceanographic expedition to the Spratlys
(*World Journal*, 17 Jan. 1994, p. 1).

Such a united front could mute the competition between the two to
be the most visible defender of Chinese sovereignty, and could also
simplify the ongoing consultation process among the claimants, because other claimants would no longer have to weigh the political costs
of choosing between China and Taiwan. But although a united China–
Taiwan front *could* bode well for a solution to the disputes, there is
also the possibility that China and Taiwan may push each other to
take a stronger stance than either would by itself. A strident and intransigent Chinese united front would bring the negotiations to a stand-
still and help confirm Southeast Asia's worst fears of a resurgent,
aggressive China.

A POSSIBLE SOLUTION?

A cooperative solution is needed now to reduce tension and possible
regional instability. There should be apparent a convergence of interests
in such a solution. If Beijing were to throw its weight behind a plan,
it could allay Southeast Asian fears about possible Chinese hegemony
and prevent further common ground emerging between Vietnam and
the other ASEAN countries in their opposition to Chinese claims. For
Vietnam, it would be an opportunity to improve relations with China
and to demonstrate to other ASEAN members its sincerity in avoiding
conflict. And joint development would offer the Philippines and Malaysia
a way of sharing in any resources that might be found in the Spratlys

while avoiding a costly defence build-up and a military position they could not possibly defend.

A negotiated solution would most appropriately allow all the contending powers to share jointly in exploiting the area's resources, while putting the sovereignty question on hold indefinitely. All claimants would set aside their claims and establish a multilateral Spratly Management Authority. The SMA would administer the contested area. This scenario would require China and Taiwan to set aside their 'historic' claim to most of the Sea. In return, they could be rewarded with a combined 51 per cent of the shares in the SMA. (They would have to settle between themselves how to manage their stake). Of course, this would mean Vietnam setting aside its own expansive claims to the South China Sea. But it might well be prepared to do so in return for a favourable settlement from China on the disputed Gulf of Tonkin and Vanguard Bank issues, which the 'experts' are already working on. If so, Vietnam, Malaysia and the Philippines would share most of the remaining 49 per cent of the SMA. Brunei would get only a very small share, since its claims in the core Spratlys area are small.

Such a solution would leave the sovereignty question officially unresolved. In any case, nobody would have much incentive to push the matter far, since they would all be sharing in the proceeds of developing the disputed waters, and continuing conflict would scare off investors. Indeed, the various claimants would be working together to pursue exploration, develop resources, manage fisheries and maintain environmental quality. Such cooperation could greatly lessen, if not eliminate altogether, the chance of miscalculation and dangerous confrontations. Other powers not party to the Spratlys dispute – like the United States and Japan – would be highly supportive, since safety and freedom of navigation would be assured.

The ASEAN Declaration on the South China Sea and the ASEAN Treaty on Amity and Cooperation in Southeast Asia could serve as the basis and framework for negotiations. First might be a formal pact not to threaten or use force. Then the level of military activity could be limited by agreement and the size of forces frozen. A multinational joint development arrangement is not ideal. It would be difficult, complex and cumbersome. But it may be the only way to avoid armed conflict.

The Indonesian-sponsored, Canadian-funded workshops have helped form a potential climate for negotiations. The new political balance in the region created by Vietnam's joining ASEAN may provide the opportunity for a breakthrough. But the window of opportunity is closing as nationalism becomes a growing influence.

Notes

1. The research for this chapter was partially supported by the US Institute of Peace.
2. See, for example, Valencia (1985, pp. 80–83), Valencia and Marsh (1986), *Energy Asia* (August 1987), Yuan (1989), Wu (1991), Yahaya (1988, p. 29), Valencia (1992, pp. 67–84), and Shirley (1992).
3. China has acquired aerial-refuelling kits and when operational this will significantly alter the military balance in the Spratly Islands (*FEER*, 4 Oct. 1990; Valencia, 1992a; Chanda, *AWSJ* 1992; *AWSJ Weekly*, 23 March 1992; Balman, 1992).
4. See, for example, Garver (1992).

References

Asian Legal Studies Center, University of British Columbia (1993), *Managing Potential Conflicts in the South China Sea: Reports and Final Statements*.

Awanohara, Susumu (1992) 'Washington's Priorities', *Far Eastern Economic Review*, 13 August, pp. 18–19.

Awanohara, Susumu and Lincoln Kaye (1992) 'The China finale', *Far Eastern Economic Review*, 10 December, p. 11.

Balman, Sid, Jr (1992) 'China Seeks to Seize the Spratly Islands Forcibly', *Korea Herald*, 22 September.

Baum, Julian, Tai Ming Cheung and Lincoln Kaye (1992) 'Ancient Fears', *Far Eastern Economic Review*, 3 December, pp. 8–10.

Bert, Wayne (1993) 'Chinese Policies and US Interests in Southeast Asia', *Asian Survey*, vol. XXIII, no. 3 (March), pp. 317–32.

Bogaturov, Alexei (1992) 'Russian Perceptions of Real Threat in the Pacific', paper prepared for a Workshop on Real Threat Perceptions in Asian States, East–West Center, 24–25 August.

Bowring, Philip (1992) 'In South China Sea, Worrying Noises from Beijing', *International Herald Tribune*, 21 July, p. 4.

Breeze, R. (1982) 'A New Gulf Flash Point', *Far Eastern Economic Review*, 11 June, pp. 26–8.

Butler, Gil (1995) 'Philippines Spratly's Action', 24 March, Voice of America.

Chanda, Nayan (1992a) *Asian Wall Street Journal Weekly*, 23 March, pp. 1–3.

Chanda, Nayan (1992b) 'China Acquires Sensitive Military Gear', *Asian Wall Street Journal*, 23 March, p. 2.

Chanda, Nayan (1993) 'Stampede for Oil', *Far Eastern Economic Review*, 25 February, p. 48.

Chanda, Nayan and Tai Ming Cheung (1990) 'Reef Knots', *Far Eastern Economic Review*, 30 August, p. 11.

Chen, Qimao (1993) 'New approaches in China's foreign policy', *Asian Survey*, vol. XXIII, no. 3 (March), pp. 237–51.

Cheung, Tai Ming (1992a) 'Fangs of the Dragon', *Far Eastern Economic Review*, 13 August, p. 21.

Cheung, Tai Ming (1992b) 'Real threat perceptions in Asia: the perspective from Beijing', paper prepared for a workshop on Real Threat Perceptions in Asian States, East–West Center, 24–25 August.

Ching, Frank (1995) 'Manila Looks for a Slingshot', *Far Eastern Review*, 9 March, p. 40.

Christ, Janice M., Regional Coordinator, Asia Pacific Advance Exploration Organization, CONOCO, Inc. (1992) personal communication.

Crestone Energy Corporation (1992) personal communication.

Findlay, Trevor (1992) 'South China Sea Scramble', *Pacific Research*, November, pp. 10–11.

Gao Anming (1992) 'Li urges speedy end to Viet Nam disputes', *China Daily*, 2 December, p. 1

Garver, John W. (1992) 'China's push through the South China Sea: The Interaction of Bureaucratic and National Interests', *China Quarterly*, vol. 132 (December), pp. 999–1028.

Giacomo, Carol (1992) 'US Says It Could Mediate in Spratlys Dispute', *Reuters*, 25 July.

Glaser, Bonnie W. (1993) 'China's Security Perceptions', *Asian Survey*, vol. 23, no. 3 (March), pp. 252–70.

Greenburger, Robert S. (1992) 'Dispute Underscores Necessity in Asia for US Presence', *Asian Wall Street Journal*, 3 August.

Hadipranowo, M. Singgih, Ian Townsend-Gault and Hasjim Djalal (1991) Draft Report of the Bandung Conference, (28 October).

Hamzah, B.A. (1992) 'China's Strategy', *Far Eastern Economic Review*, 13 August, p. 22.

Hiebert, Murray (1992a) 'Unhealed Wounds', *Far Eastern Economic Review*, 16 July, pp. 20–21.

Hiebert, Murray (1992b) 'Ruffled Waters', *Far Eastern Economic Review*, 24 September, p. 22.

Jacob, Paul (1992) 'Call to Boost Cooperation Among Claimants to Isles in S. China Sea', *Strait Times*, 3 July.

Jacobs, G. (1990) 'China's Amphibious Capabilities', *Asian Defence Journal*, January, p. 68.

Kanwerayotin, Supapohn (1992) 'China, Vietnam Fail to Resolve Territorial Rows', *Bangkok Post*, 3 December, p. 6.

Kreisberg, Paul, Fellow, East–West Center (1992) personal communication.

La Grange, C. (1980) *South China Sea Disputes: China, Vietnam, Taiwan and the Philippines*, East–West Environment and Policy Institute Working Paper No. 1 (Honolulu, Hawaii: East–West Center).

'Law on the Territorial Seas and Their Contiguous Waters of the People's Republic of China' (1992). Approved by the 24th Session of the Standing Committee of the Seventh National People's Congress on February 25.

Lee Kuan Yew (1992) 'The Battle is Economic', *Newsweek*, 21 September, p. 60.

Lee, Ngok (1990) 'Chinese Maritime Power', paper presented to the 31st annual convention of the International Studies Association, Washington, DC, March.

MacDonald, Lawrence (1992) 'ASEAN to Tackle Regional Security Issues', *Asian Wall Street Journal Weekly*, 20 July, pp. 1, 4.

McDorman, Ted L. (1993) 'The South China Sea Islands Dispute in the 1990s: A New Multilateral Process and Continuing Function', *International Journal of Marine and Coastal Law*, vol. 8, no. 2, pp. 263–85.

Pan, Senior Colonel Zhen Qiang, Deputy Director, Strategic Research Institute, National Defence University, People's Liberation Army (1993), Seminar, East–West Center, 5 March.

Pereira, Derwin (1995) 'ASEAN ministers concerned over developments in Spratlys,' *Strait Times* (Singapore), 19 March.

Pura, Raphael (1992a), 'China Seeks Closer Security Ties to ASEAN', *Asian Wall Street Journal*, 22 July, pp. 1, 7.

Pura, Raphael (1992b) 'ASEAN Proposes Guidelines for South China Sea', *Asian Wall Street Journal*, 23 July, p. 1.

Samuels, M. (1982) *Contest for the South China Sea* (New York: Methuen).

Scalapino, Robert, Institute of East Asian Studies, University of California, Berkeley (1992) personal communication, October.

Shenon, Philip (1992) 'Asian Nations Hope to Settle Dispute Over Islands Peacefully', *New York Times*, 23 July.

Shim Jae Hoon (1988) 'Blood Thicker than Politics', *Fast Eastern Economic Review*, 5 May, p. 26.

Shirley, Kathy (1992) 'Oil Potential Overshadows Risks', *AAPG Explorer*, December, pp. 8–9.

Smith, Charles and Suhaini Aznam (1992) 'Reason and Rhetoric', *Far Eastern Economic Review*, 17 September, pp. 10–11.

Statement of the Ministry of Foreign Affairs of the Socialist Republic of Vietnam on the Agreement Between Chinese and US Oil Companies for the Exploration and Exploitation of Oil and Gas on the Continental Shelf of Vietnam, 16 May 1992.

Tack, Nguyen Hong (1992) 'Vietnam-China Ties; A New But Not Easy Era', *Business Times*, 31 December.

Tasker, Rodney (1992) 'End of the Sentry', *Far Eastern Economic Review*, 26 November, pp. 18–20.

Tefft, Sheila (1992) 'Southeast Asians Build Up Navies to Protect Territorial Interests', *Christian Science Monitor*, 6 July, pp. 1, 4.

Terrill, Ross (1992) Seminar at the East–West Center, Honolulu, Hawaii, 14 December.

Third Workshop on Managing Potential Conflicts in the South China Sea, Jogjakarta, Indonesia, 29 June–2 July 1992, Center for Asian Legal Studies, University of British Columbia.

Valencia, Mark J. (1985) *South–East Asian Seas: Oil Under Troubled Waters* (Oxford: Oxford University Press).

Valencia, Mark J. (1988) 'The Spratly Islands: Dangerous Ground in the South China Sea', *Pacific Review*, vol. I, no. 4, pp. 382–95.

Valencia, Mark J. (1992a) 'The South China Sea: Potential Conflict and Cooperation', Proceedings of the VI Institute for Strategic and International Studies Malaysia Round Table, Kuala Lumpur, Confidence Building and Conflict Reduction in the Pacific, 21–25 June.

Valencia, Mark J. (1992b) 'The Regional Imperative', *Far Eastern Economic Review*, 13 August, p. 20.

Valencia, Mark J. (1992c) *Malaysia and the Law of the Sea* (Kuala Lumpur: ISIS).

Valencia, Mark J. (1993) 'Spratly Solution Still at Sea', *Pacific Review*, vol. 6, no. 2, pp. 155–70.

Valencia, Mark J. (1995) 'How to End the Spratly Spats', *Asian Wall Street Journal*, 17–18 February, p. 6.

Valencia, Mark J. and James Barney Marsh (1986) 'Southeast Asia: Marine Resource, Extended Maritime Jurisdiction and Development', *Marine Resource Economics*, vol. III, no. 1, pp. 3–27.

Valencia, Mark J. and Zha Daojiong (1994), 'The South China Sea Disputes: Recent Developments', *Ocean and Coastal Management*, vol. XXIV, pp. 199–204.

Walsh, James (1992) 'The Great Stone Wall', *Time*, 6 July, p. 20.

Wu Jinmin (1991) 'The Geological and Strucutral Features of Nansha Islands and their Prospect for Hydrocarbon Potential', *Geological Research of South China Sea* (Series 3) (Guangzhou: South China Sea Institute of Oceanology), pp. 24–38.

Yahaya, Jahara (1988) 'The Contributions of the Marine Sector to the Malaysian Economy', paper presented at seminar on Marine Environment: Challenges and Opportunities, sponsored by the Institute for Strategic and International Studies (ISIS), Kuala Lumpur, 31 March.

Yuan, Xia Kan (1989) 'The Comparison of Geophysics and Geology between Northern and Southern Continental Margins of the South China Sea', paper presented at the International Symposium on Geology and Geophysics of South China Sea, Guangzhou, 9–13 January.

Zagoria, Donald (1993) 'The United States and East Asia in the Post-Cold War Era: Time for New Thinking', paper presented at conference on Asia in Transition: Toward a New Regional Order, East–West Center, 4–7 January.

Part V
Conclusion

14 The 'New World Order' in Southeast Asia: Some Analytical Explorations

David Wurfel

CONCLUSIONS

The authors of this volume have described and analysed a regional political economy which has experienced some of the great changes occurring in the world system since 1989. Though there is some variation of explanation about world system change, it would appear to have been largely the result of the gradual collapse of the Soviet economy – derived from the structural inadequacies of the economy itself as well as from the pressure of the arms race – and the more rapid collapse of the Soviet state when it tried to reform itself and its economic policies. Less often noted as a cause of the 'end of the Cold War' was the fact that the US economy was also suffering severely from the costs of the arms race and thus US policy was itself considering military retrenchment. As we have explained earlier, there were other important underlying trends, the economic surge in Eastern Asia and the growing strength of international civil society – focusing particularly on the environment and human rights, which have made crucial contributions to the shaping of the 'New World Order'. But their importance was greatly enhanced by the disappearance of superpower confrontation.

To summarize subsequent developments, we may note that relations among the great powers of the Asia Pacific, the most crucial context for the Southeast Asian political economy, were at first little affected by the end of the Cold War. The US and Japan declared the enduring importance of their alliance, while the growth in economic cooperation by both Japan and the US continued with the Peoples' Republic of China. And the changes in the influence of great powers since 1989 – the sharp decline of the USSR/Russia, and to a much lesser degree of the US; the rapid growth of China's economic as well as military power, and the slow but steady expansion of Japanese economic influence, combined with cautious political initiatives – show evidence of trends dating from the early 1980s as much as they do the end of the Cold War.

Yet the removal of the Soviet strategic threat has allowed certain controversies to surface and gain prominence that would have been subordinated to the requirements of grand strategy earlier. US demands for Japan to open its markets more widely, subtle promotion of Taiwan's status by both the US and Japan, and US efforts to link human rights, arms sales and other issues with trade concessions to China have exacerbated relations among the three. This contentious process has been further fed by China's new confidence derived from the greater bargaining power bestowed by its expanding market. Thus, while Soviet-American nuclear confrontation has little significance in the 'New World Order', great power competition, even conflict, has not disappeared, though the purpose and means of conflict are for the foreseeable future much more likely to be economic than strategic – yet the Spratlys could prove to be an exception to that rule. And as an expanding ASEAN represents an ever larger percentage of world trade, the stakes of economic competition in the region will increase. Furthermore, China acts as a magnet for Japanese and other foreign capital, thus depriving a capital hungry Southeast Asia.

In the meantime globalized culture and communications, the power of IFIs and transnational corporations, and other market forces, as well as the growing influence of NGOs continue to erode the autonomy of state actors – though without overwhelming them. So the international environment for the SE Asian political economy contains elements of both abrupt change and continuing trends – despite the fact that it is sudden change which is most noticeable.

Within SE Asia itself we must also recognize both change and continuity. Change since 1989 has been greatest for those countries which had closest ties to the two superpowers, namely the Philippines and the three in Indochina. They experienced withdrawal of military bases and drastic aid cutbacks. While such tendencies existed in Indochina even before the collapse of the Soviet Union, they became much more rapid and more drastic as a result of that collapse. In the Philippines 'divine intervention' at Mt Pinatubo and the nationalist backbone of the Senate may have had more to do with a change in US policy than did Washington decision-makers themselves. In any case, the change in the relationship with a superpower was less drastic than for the Indochina states.

For other parts of SE Asia changes concomitant with the end of the Cold War were minor, when compared to those in other regions of the world. Just as in Northern Asia, certain issues have emerged into prominence which had been muffled by Cold War tensions. But in large part the increased role in world affairs which SE Asia, especially ASEAN, has exhibited has resulted from the economic dynamic internal to the region which, while accelerated in the early 1990s, had been evident for some years earlier. Economic dynamism was, of course, aided by the massive inflow of capital from Japan, Korea and Taiwan after the 1985 Plaza Accord. But to a degree seldom given adequate recognition, that dynamism was also a result of accelerating rapaciousness in the extraction of natural resources. The wealth of the forests especially – the legacy of millenia – is being exhausted in a few decades. Thus no particular economic policy can claim full credit for rapid ASEAN growth.

It is obvious that SE Asia, without the superpower intervention characteristic of the Cold War, has not become a 'power vacuum', as once predicted. SE Asia, particularly ASEAN, has set out quite deliberately to try to shape its own international political and economic environments.

These changes which have taken place in recent years at both the world and regional level, whether strategic or economic, have sometimes raised questions about our stock of analytical tools. Now it is appropriate to examine those questions in light of data presented in this volume about SE Asia in its broader Asia Pacific setting. Exploring these analytical questions not only will help throw new light on changes within the region, but will reveal how useful SE Asia is for testing worldwide generalizations.

We will begin by examining the concept of region and its applicability in Asia, followed by an assessment of the role of world organizations in the area. Next we will look at the nature of markets, a key construct in political economy. A longer section then discusses the state, both as actor and as unit of analysis, in the new international political economy, succeeded by a comment on democracy and the 'New World Order' in SE Asia. We conclude with a review of the character of SE Asian dynamism.

DEFINING 'REGION'

The question of what *is* this creature called 'region' can hardly be avoided in a discussion of SE Asia or the Asia Pacific. Evans emphasizes the importance of regionalism by asserting that we are seeing the emergence of a 'world of regions'. Crone calls it a 'more regionalized world order'.

There seems to be no doubt that ASEAN, even SE Asia (which in a few years may be coterminous with ASEAN), fits the definition of a 'region' in this new order, though some authors would relegate it to a 'subregion' of the 'Pacific Basin', or, inaccurately, 'East Asia'. (Gilpin, 1993, p. 32). A recently articulated definition of a region is quite serviceable. Stubbs and Underhill (1994, pp. 331–2) specify that a true region has three dimensions: a distinct geographic area with common historical experience; internal cultural, political and/or economic linkages; and organizations to regulate interactions and/or manage common affairs.[1] For ASEAN there were three major experiences, World War II Japanese occupation, the struggle for independence against colonialism, which even Thailand assisted, and the sense of threat from the People's Republic of China. By the 1950s there began to emerge a number of both private and public regional organizations to promote interchange and mutual understanding, so that when ASEAN was formed in the 1970s there was already a pattern of ongoing cultural and economic interactions. After ASEAN was established the sense of common interest was stimulated by the Vietnamese occupation of Cambodia, and more recently by the perceived threat of economic regionalism in Europe and North America. The ethnic, religious and political disparities within ASEAN at its founding have gradually been overlain by a growing sense of regional identity.

Neither 'Asia Pacific' nor 'Eastern Asia' would seem to fit the definition above. The broadest of these categories, which stretches from Canada to Korea to Australia – and for some even includes Peru and Chile – has none of these three qualifications. APEC, its organizational expression, neither regulates interactions nor manages common affairs, but merely discusses potential relationships. It has been argued elsewhere that APEC is an 'international regime', albeit a weak one (Crone, 1993, p. 524). If one accepts Krasner's definition of a regime as 'sets of implicit or explicit principles, norms, rules and decision-making procedures around which actors' expectations converge' (Krasner, 1982, p. 186), then it is apparent that a regime is something both less institutionialized and less territorially defined than a 'region', as we have used the term.

Even Eastern Asia, which includes the close linkages provided by Japanese firms to SE Asia, lacks the minimal cohesion of a region. The stormy fate of Prime Minister Mahathir's proposal for an East

Asian Economic Grouping is ample evidence of this fact. What is notable is that while some Japanese, it is reported, had initially given quiet encouragement to Mahathir, the Japanese government refused to back the plan publicly; but China quickly did. (However, a Chinese commentator noted realistically, 'Economic cooperation at the regional level cannot be expected to develop quickly in the Asia-Pacific.' Jin, 1991, p. 5) China saw a chance to legitimize her penetration of SE Asia while Japan, still relying primarily on the North American market, reacted to American pressure. The area of the proposed EAEG did not coincide with the area of tightest economic linkages, Japan and SE Asia (Machado, 1992; Arase, 1991). Yet Japan feared, on both economic and political grounds, that it would exclude the US – even after it was downgraded to a 'caucus' by ASEAN foreign ministers. And the clearly different Chinese agenda was also an obstacle to cooperation (Yoo, 1993, p. 318). Only protectionist regionalism in Europe and North America, requiring strong defensive action, could bring Eastern Asia together in a meaningful regional organization. The World Bank endorsement of trade liberalization in Eastern Asia, even without an organizational framework (*International Herald Tribune*, 9 August 1994), may not have a major impact.

While the end of the Cold War diminished strategic conflict, a new emphasis on economic relations still embodies great power competition as well as cooperation. This is not to endorse the farfetched scenario of US–Japan war (see Huntington, 1991), but neither is it to imagine that the alliance of the 1980s is to survive unscathed. If one can argue that Australian and Canadian policy-makers were 'liberated . . . to pursue more autonomous policies' at the end of the Cold War, as Nossal does, then why not expect Japan to behave likewise? (Taiwan and South Korea are still faced with strategic threats practically unchanged by the Cold War's end.) A study for the US Congress states judiciously, 'There is no guarantee that the oft-proclaimed mutuality of US and Japanese interests will indefinitely sustain the US–Japan alliance' (Cronin, 1990). As noted by Donnelly and Stubbs, 'a younger generation of Japanese politicians, bureaucrats and managers, who want their country to play a larger regional and world role are gaining power'. And to their right is an increasingly influential nationalist current in the Liberal Democratic Party, a potentially dangerous force (Bello, 1992, p. 106).

With the collapse of the USSR, China too is largely freed from the need to court the US as a strategic balancer, though it welcomes US military presence as a balance to Japan, as noted by Ross. For China has a darker view of Japanese intentions than does the West, or even many SE Asian leaders (Jin, 1991). The stage is also being set for future Japan–China economic conflict. China, according to some recent economic reanalysis, already has greater total national output than Japan, and will surpass that of the US within a decade (Cable and Ferdinand, 1994; p. 224). While total foreign trade is still less than half that of Japan, Chinese trade is growing at a much faster rate. As a possible harbinger of things to come, Japan has already initiated anti-dumping action against over 100 Chinese companies. But on the whole the Japanese economy as yet is essentially complementary to that of China and in 1992 Japanese investment there doubled. (Cable and Ferdinand, 1994, p. 260). Still, the future path of these two great powers may involve at least as much conflict as cooperation – a view held by many in both Tokyo and Beijing – again dimming the prospect of Eastern Asian or Asia-Pacific regionalism.

Yet while a wider Asian regionalism faces many obstacles, ASEAN continues to grow – what we have called the 'ASEANization' of SE Asia. Vietnam and Laos acceded to the Treaty of Amity and Cooperation in June 1992 (see Crone), and Burma and Papua New Guinea more recently. Full membership for Vietnam was finalized in July 1995. Within the decade Burma, Laos and Cambodia are likely to join as well. ASEAN's 'solution' to gross human rights violations in Burma has already been 'constructive engagement' – followed by a ferocious offensive against ethnic rebels. Since the historical experiences of these prospective members have been largely in common with the rest of ASEAN and since they are rapidly being enveloped by the same economic linkages, their incorporation in the regional organization is logical.

Yet an expansion of membership could bring sharper factionalism, clearer subregional groupings. An important dimension of alignment within ASEAN is the degree to which China is perceived as the major threat to the region. It produced divisions on policy toward the process of settlement in Cambodia, and may again as a result of the flare-up in the Spratlys. The level of economic development is also a factor, perhaps countervailing. Pro-China, high wage Singapore, the major trading partner of Vietnam, with capital for export, will have economic reasons for Vietnam's closer incorporation into the region, greater, in fact, than those of Vietnam's old friend, Indonesia.

Nevertheless, even if there were some more evident political distinctions within ASEAN as a result of expanded membership, progress toward greater economic integration would probably offset this tendency. As Lim notes, integration is furthered more by private corporate strategies than by government policy, and thus is less affected by shifts in political leadership, more influenced by world market forces.

The dynamism of ASEAN as a regional organization is not only evidenced by greater economic integration and prospects of expanding membership, but by the assumption of new functions. As Crone noted, security cooperation was originally excluded from ASEAN's purview, even though there were bilateral military and intelligence connections. As the Cold War ended, the causes for ASEAN's earlier inhibitions also melted. Though a process modelled on CSCE was rejected, an ASEAN Regional Forum was created in 1993 which, by inviting powers beyond ASEAN, began to serve as the centre for security dialogue for all of the Asia Pacific. Its efficacy will be sorely tested by trying to deal with China's aggressiveness in the Spratlys.

Thus while the euphoria for the Asia Pacific may be, at least, premature, SE Asia-cum-ASEAN is becoming a region expressing its interests with increasing clarity and strengthening the organizations to pursue them. Definitions of regional integration which originated in the 1950s may now need some amendment. But if we veer too far from well-established concepts, current enthusiasms may becloud our vision of the future.

MULTILATERALISM

Multilateral cooperation at the world level is sometimes taken as an essential characteristic of the 'New World Order'. There is no question that the disappearance of Soviet–American nuclear confrontation makes it much easier. But does the experience in SE Asia justify liberal optimism about a steadily strengthened UN? Certainly the structural impediments within the UN itself will have some effect on the answer, as would any steps toward Charter reform, while the specific political and economic contexts in which the UN is called to intervene will also be important.

In post-Cold War SE Asia the UN has played a major role. In fact, even before the Cold War ended the UNHCR was dressing a festering wound, the dispersion of Indochina refugees. There would have been more human suffering and more interstate conflict arising from the refugee flow without the UN. But the great breakthrough was in Cambodia, a UN intervention of unprecedented size and legal status, as Lizée describes. The unanimity of the permanent members of the Security Council which made this intervention possible was a celebration of the end of the Cold War. The support of ASEAN greatly facilitated the UN's efforts, but the resources, and legitimacy which the UN could offer were much beyond the capabilities of ASEAN. In any case, ASEAN was seen by pro-Vietnamese parties as more an antagonist than a mediator. So that even with the growing strength of regionalism in the 'New World Order', Cambodia dramatized the need for the UN.

When examining SE Asia's major strategic controversy, control of the Spratlys, one is reminded, however, of the severe limits on the UN's own capacity. The UN has not shown ability in the past to settle disputes that involved the declared 'essential interests' of those Security Council members with a veto. China is adamant about its territorial claims in the Spratlys, despite counter-claims of SE Asian powers (see Chapter 13). In this case, economic pressure, political bargaining and military manoevres by regional states – in the context of the ASEAN Regional Forum – may be more effective than the UN. But China still holds influential cards: besides a Security Council veto, profitable economic links between China and ASEAN are growing, US policy itself is more and more driven by visions of gain in the huge China market, and Japan, having the same economic constraints, is also disinclined to upset China while the Japanese bid for permanent membership in the Security Council is pending. So the will to stand up to China in early 1995 was not strong, either within ASEAN or beyond.

In 1992 circumstances converged to allow the UN to break new barriers and establish a 'transitional authority' in Cambodia. But it has not succeeded in implementing General Assembly resolutions on East Timor, though blocked only by a regional power, Indonesia, and its friends, and the prospects are not good of its playing a useful role in the Spratlys dispute. Thus optimism about the UN's role in the 'New World Order' was first confirmed in Cambodia, but then brought into doubt by the fate of other disputes in the region. (Any optimism will, of course, shrink if the UN's budgetary crisis is deepened by actions of the US Congress.)

In effect, UN assistance is sought by regional governments only to deal with problems that they cannot solve themselves. One of the most prominent is the nearly 20,000 Vietnamese boatpeople who remain in refugee camps in Thailand, Indonesia, Malaysia and the Philippines. The UNHCR is still providing millions of dollars every year for their care and maintenance and at the same time urgently trying to arrange their repatriation to Vietnam. Only the UNHCR is capable of doing this, since the problem is one with worldwide implications. And though much diminished from a few years ago, the problem is not likely to be solved in the next year, as hoped. So UNHCR services and funding are still eagerly sought, even as demands on their capacities are severely strained by crises elsewhere. In the 'New World Order' we cannot be overly optimistic about the growth of UN authority and institutional strength, but its functions will expand when the demand for them is great enough.

TYPES OF MARKETS

The key concept in international political economy is 'market', which is certainly global, and also national, and may be regional as well. As we shall see, there are also other possible configurations. The market may be controlled by the state, or – a more recent trend – overwhelm state mechanisms. Some would regard the market itself as a 'political institution' (Underhill, in Stubbs and Underhill, 1994, p. 19), which 'plays a crucial role in structuring society and international politics'. Perhaps a more modest formulation, that the 'market is a power relationship' (Cox, in Stubbs and Underhill, 1994, p. 45) is more frequently and easily defensible. Developments in the SE Asian political economy since the end of the Cold War demonstrate both the state's ability to control the market and cases of the market's overpowering presence.

The most prominent case of the market as creature of the state is AFTA, which is indeed becoming institutionalized, though rather slowly (see Chapter 2). Nor would this creation have had any meaning without the continuing attempt of ASEAN states – with different levels of success – to regulate national markets through customs duties and other mechanisms.

Another market, determined by political priorities to a much greater degree, was a child of the Cold War. The COMECON, centered in the Soviet Union, counted Vietnam among its members from 1978, despite sparse economic rationale. Thus the virtual collapse of COMECON in 1990 and Vietnam's reorientation to trading partners in Asia and the West was the most dramatic example of the ability of the global market to overwhelm smaller enclaves that were not based on sound economic principles.

The subsequent intrusion of both global financial and commodity markets into Vietnam was but one example of another dimension of globalization. While the global market has 'no explicit political or authority structure' (Cox, in Stubbs and Underhill, 1994, pp. 48–9) there is a 'transnational process of consensus formation among the official caretakers of the global economy'. It generates its own ideology which is transmitted through universities, business conferences, or policy-making channels of IFIs linked to national governments. The Pacific Economic Cooperation Council is an example in Asia of one institution which 'tighten[s] the transnational networks'. This is, at one level, the growing international civil society, but cooperating with the state. The IMF and World Bank also contribute mightily to the new ideology. So that the state becomes 'an agency for adjusting national economic . . . policies to the perceived exigencies of the global economy'. The Philippines, reluctantly, and Vietnam, more enthusiastically, adapted to IMF/ World Bank guidelines in the 1980s and '90s. Indonesia had already been pressed into this pattern from the late 1960s. Thus, except for the case of Vietnam, this is not a phenomenon particular to the end of the Cold War. But the downgrading of strategic considerations, and the demonstrable errors of command economies, have created the context in which a free market global ideology has gained even greater ascendancy. International trade union cooperation, another aspect of civil society, has suffered as a result; in fact, it has often been specifically restricted by NIC, or aspiring NIC, governments.

There are other clearly defined supranational markets which have emerged in SE Asia either with or without state approval. Lim has spelled out how 'growth triangles' have begun to spring up within ASEAN, some with considerable success. They are the result of substantial private initiative and capital, but with the cooperation of state agencies.

There is considerably less state involvement in international labour markets, even though, as the 1995 crisis in the Philippine–Singapore relation demonstrates, labour migrations are capable of producing major political consequences. As Lim notes in Chapter 2, Malaysia and Singapore – and Brunei too – are net importers of labour. While all other countries in the region are labour exporters, Thailand, as well as Malaysia, exports the more skilled and imports less skilled workers. In large part labour migrations are fuelled by purely market forces, the desire for better wages. But in some countries, especially the Philippines and Vietnam, labour exportation has become state policy, producing many hundreds of millions of dollars in foreign exchange earnings each year. Many workers have gone abroad as a result of government to government contracts. Since growth rates at recent levels are likely to expand rather than to narrow wage differentials between the richer core (Singapore, Malaysia and Thailand) and the poorer periphery, the movement of wage seekers across boundaries, legal or illegal, is likely to increase in coming years. And that could produce more inter-nation friction.

Another older market has survived for years in SE Asia, despite considerable effort by states large and small to suppress it: the production and trading of heroin. Its curious mixture of ethnic rebellion, CIA machinations, political corruption and extraordinary profitability have endowed it with considerable staying power.

Two markets which have gained notoriety in post-Cold War SE Asia are also very unfortunate examples of the weakening of the state. The lucrative and fiercely protected trade in gems and timber between Khmer Rouge-controlled areas of Cambodia and the Thai military had already emerged by the mid-1980s. But when China – by most accounts – cut off military aid to Pol Pot's guerrillas in order to facilitate a political settlement (see Lizée), this trade became even more crucial to Khmer Rouge survival and thus to Cambodian political outcomes. While there probably was a desire by the Thai prime minister, Chuan Leekpai, to curb this trade – and he was partially successful, the memory of the dismissal of his predecessor by the military and the precarious balance of power in his own regime apparently makes it impossible for his cabinet to clamp down completely on profiteers among the military brass – who often have tie ups with parliamentarians. And so the Khmer Rouge continues to be financed – and militarily bold – while the Cambodian forests are increasingly denuded of tropical hardwoods.

The next case, the smuggling of Chinese goods into Vietnam, is proof of the maxim that state capacity to suppress the political opposition does not ensure the capacity to regulate the market. By 1989 aggressive salesmen in the booming economy of South China were given a new opportunity by the thawing of relations between their government and that of Vietnam. Restrictions on cross border trade began to be lifted, having already been considerably eroded. The Vietnamese military who guarded the border were beset by inflation on the one hand and budget cuts on the other, and thus soon learned about new sources of income provided by the market economy. While the government in Hanoi tried to rationalize the tariff structure, customs duties went uncollected. Soon Vietnamese consumer goods industries began to suffer from the low cost Chinese competition. The textile and bicycle industries in particular have been devastated, pushing up the already high unemployment. But though civilian leaders were well aware of the seriousness of the problem, they were unable to stem the flow of smuggled Chinese goods, abetted by their own military. The illegal sale of Vietnamese rice to China, even by state firms, has also become a problem. Vietnam, *de facto*, is becoming part of the Chinese market. The intrusion of the Chinese market into Upper Burma is a similar case. It is clear that the state is often not strong enough to stop a burgeoning market boosted by powerful economic incentives. And the size of the Chinese market is simply overwhelming.

THE STATE AS ACTOR? AS UNIT OF ANALYSIS? CHALLENGED OR REVIVING?

If state capacities are sometimes overwhelmed by runaway markets, if institutions of the global economy sometimes determine state policies, and if 'global consensus' often sets the agenda of state policy-makers, how can we continue to focus on the state as *the* actor in international relations? Of course, we cannot. The most sophisticated treatments of world politics and world economy have for some time recognized the presence of other actors. But if there are other actors, can we still speak of the state as 'sovereign'? Sovereignty as the ability of the state to exercise absolute power and authority in a given territory is indeed passing (Camillieri and Falk, 1992, p. 18). But that does not rule out the persistence of the state as the preeminent actor in the world political economy. As Halliday puts it, 'the state ... retains a central role within and between societies' (in Leaver and Richardson, 1993, p. 24). There are instances of both the state's eroding autonomy and of its continued vigour in the emergence of the SE Asian political economy in recent years.

Paradoxically, at the same time that economists in the region have increasingly adopted a free market ideology, propagated by the IMF/ World Bank, it is actually state guidance of the economy, somewhat in the Japanese or Korean manner, that has led to remarkable economic growth. The successful economies of Singapore, Malaysia and Thailand have been guided by states which have augmented their capacities in recent years. In sharpest contrast is the tragic case of Cambodia. With the collapse of a state that once tried to control the minutest detail of life for every individual, there was almost no state at all. It lacked resources, a bureaucracy or legitimacy and could not effectively control large areas of the countryside. Ultimately to try to bring peace and preserve at the least the legal territorial integrity of the state, Cambodia's leaders accepted a brief abandonment of sovereignty to the UN. In effect, the sovereign state of Cambodia disappeared temporarily to be endowed with new unity and legitimacy through UN administered elections – a process which achieved only partial success. But this is a precedent of tremendous significance for the future of UN peace-keeping and peace-making functions.

Between these two extremes of ASEAN NICs and Cambodia is evidence of the pulling and tugging between the state and non-state actors. While the IMF has seemed to dominate state policy-making in the Philippines, and now, to a lesser extent in Vietnam, its autonomous role can be sharply restricted by a great power. While France, Australia and others, apparently with the quiet support of the secretariat, were pushing as early as 1990 for the reopening of IMF lending to Vietnam, the US was able to block such efforts until its own policy switch in mid-1993. And when the switch did come, it appeared to be a result of domestic considerations, not direct international pressure.

The end of the Cold War caused the demise of what was once thought to be a very important non-state actor, the international communist movement. And even where national Communist parties survive, as in Vietnam or the Philippines, the inter-party network is gone. The influence of the oldest of non-state actors, the Roman Catholic church, has also waned in recent years. Filipinos largely disregard the pope's moral guidance in sexual matters, despite the enthusiastic welcome given him, and the Philippine state's direct challenge to the church on population policy seems successful. In the meantime many believe that fundamentalist Islam has now displaced in importance the two previous ideological movements. In SE Asia as well as in the Middle East economic development often undermines traditional values, the process that triggers Islamic fundamentalism. Muslim clerics have brought down Middle Eastern governments, and some leaders have rushed to try to meet their demands. More recently in Malaysia, however, the state has taken a firm restrictive, and so far successful, stand, indicating that in SE Asia, at least, states may be able to contain the surge of worldwide religious movements. (Though in Malaysia the saga is far from finished.)

National and international NGOs, especially in the fields of human rights and the environment, have become the latest challengers to the state, from within and without, a dimension of international civil society very different from that of conferences of economists, noted above. When the agenda in important fields of state policy is set from outside, it is hard any longer to speak of 'sovereignty'. Yet in the pulling and tugging the state has not always been the loser. As Clad and Siy have pointed out (Chapter 4), pressure from international NGOs for tropical forest preservation – working, by the way, primarily through their home governments – produced an angry retort from Prime Minister Mahathir. The immediate goals of NGO campaigns were resisted. In Indonesia as well, NGO-engendered aid suspensions by Canada and the Netherlands after the Dili massacre in East Timor seemed to be counterproductive in the short run (see Chapters 1, 5 and 11). Yet international NGO pressure, with domestic support, continued and some mildly responsive steps have been taken, indicating at least that it is no longer good foreign policy to 'stonewall' well-intended NGO requests backed by major governments. The first round of verbal pyrotechnics by embattled regimes may not be the best indicator of the long term impact. But whether anything more than the facade is altered remains to be seen. In any case, the ultimate defence of states in the past, 'domestic jurisdiction', is no longer effective. The most valid question now about non-state actors is how effective are they in influencing states' policies? They seldom seem able to achieve their goals except by acting *through* state policies. The 'central role' of the state remains.

Yet the state as level of analysis, as well as the state as actor, has been downgraded by some scholars. Underhill reassures us that a premise of international political economy is the 'intimate connection', even the 'two-way relationship', between domestic and international levels of analysis (Underhill, in Stubbs and Underhill, 1994, p. 20). His is a healthy corrective to the tendency of some in the field to focus overwhelmingly on the international level.

As one looks at the way the Cold War itself ended, the importance – one could almost say the preeminence – of political economy *within* the state can hardly be ignored. While the economic impact of the arms race was also very influential, the deciding event was the collapse of the inefficient Soviet economy and the consequent failure of the Soviet state to reform itself. Thus perhaps the most dramatic and fundamental change in the world political economy in the last half century came about primarily as a result of interaction between a state and its society. In thinking about the future of SE Asia within an Asia-Pacific setting, we must also recognize that change in the regional system is most likely to come from changes within a particular society and state.

Within SE Asia Vietnam is the state whose instability could most easily trigger regional change, since it has land borders with three neighbours. Most commentators are presently quite sanguine about prospects for Vietnamese stability, but one of the most knowledgeable observers (Fforde, 1993) doubts that such confidence is wise beyond the next few years. Social change has been rapid, with sharpening income disparities and a growing gap between north and south, and between rich and poor. At the same time political change has been very limited. Rapid shifts in Party policy, leadership struggles, a spectacular corruption case, or increased centre/periphery tensions could trigger unexpected responses.

Succession struggles could also produce increased instability in Indonesia, as they already did in 1994. But the frustrations or adventurism of a hardline military faction would most likely be turned against hapless protestors in Jakarta or rebels in Aceh, East Timor or West Irian rather than outward. Still, domestic preoccupation by an unstable regime in Jakarta would change the make-up of ASEANs leadership and thus also its policies.

It is China, because of its size and power and history of involvement in SE Asia, that could have the greatest impact on regional affairs. And signs of instability are already present. American participants in the 1992 Williamsburg Conference suggested that 'China was potentially the most destabilizing factor in the region'. One speaker went so far as to maintain that 'the implications outweighed those of the collapse of the Soviet empire' (Williamsburg, 1992, pp. 12ff). While that is probably an exaggeration, the consequences of the outbreak of inter-regional conflict within China, or the consequent emergence of a military regime would be incalculable. Thus no balanced assessments of future trends through the Asia Pacific could omit consideration of the prospects of a dramatic regime change in China. Its impact could be immediate for SE Asia, such as in the Spratlys – one interpretation of the most recent military moves by China is related to intra-elite competition (see Chapter 13) – or indirect, by way of heightened policy conflict with Japan or Taiwan. Conversely, regime change in Taiwan, producing a 'declaration of independence', could trigger Chinese actions having an indirect impact on Southeast Asia.

Even Japan, the rock of stability until recently, could undergo significant political change in coming years. While differences between major parties are not of much import, the undermining of bureaucratic control of foreign policy could produce unpredictability. And differences within parties and coalitions remain wide, producing in the same month prime ministerial apologies for World War II and cabinet level denials that in the war Japan did anything wrong. Though the prospect of heightened US–Japan trade conflict has certainly been overplayed by some American analysts, it may indeed emerge, and would certainly spill over into SE Asia, mediated in part through changes it helped to bring about in Japanese domestic politics. Increasingly critical views of the US are gaining credence among both political and economic elites (*International Herald Tribune*, 12 Dec. 1994). As this comment admits, domestic political change could be triggered by shifts at the international level. But changes in the international system originating in national upheavals have been more important in the past and are likely to be in the future.

If political economy looks at domestic state–society interaction as a cause of change in the international system, then it must also examine the more persistent and less dramatic role of those interactions in explaining national foreign policy. Sometimes the interests of state institutions are dominant, and other times socio-economic forces bring effective pressure on the state. In all cases the state leaders presume to speak on behalf of *both* state and society. This is a particular problem in the new issue areas of environment and human rights, when particular societal interests (e.g. timber producers) or state institutions (e.g. the military) have often been able to see their goals voiced through state leaders. Some observers have uncritically accepted those statements at face value, without examining the political process which produced them. Accurately disaggregating the interests represented in the policy process is often a necessary preliminary to an adequate understanding of its outcome.

DEMOCRACY AND THE 'NEW WORLD ORDER'

If instability in state or society, or changes of regime type can have a profound impact on the international system, then it is no wonder that many are asking whether democracy should be regarded as an essential component of the 'New World Order'. For insofar as democracy is a political system with institutions widely regarded as legitimate, it is conducive to a stable international system. But if the 'New World Order' is simply a synonym for the existing international arrangements, as we suggest, then it is obvious that in Asia there are as many undemocratic regimes as before 1989.

Nevertheless, without the frequent toppling of dictatorships, as in Eastern Europe, there have been movements toward greater democracy. In Thailand, as in the Asia Pacific states of South Korea and Taiwan, authoritarianism is slowly being displaced as a result of the political consequences of economic growth. As the middle class expands, it demands a larger voice. This process has had little connection to the end of the Cold War, though the popular rejection of the 1992 Thai coup may have had something to do with a worldwide mood that encouraged a greater voice for freedom. The end of the Marcos martial law regime in the Philippines, the toppling of a dictator, predated the collapse of the Soviet empire and was also primarily the result of domestic forces and initiatives, even though the negative impact of the halt in IMF credits, and the American support for some anti-regime elements also played a role.

While the bold popular initiatives for democracy in Burma at the end of the 1980s were a response to intolerable local conditions, economic as well as political, many of the popular leaders must have been aware of the worldwide mood for freedom mentioned above. But in Burma, unlike Thailand, the military was tenacious in clinging to power and vicious in its exercise. Despite the increasingly vocal human rights NGOs (see Chapter 5) and their ability to find supporters in some Western legislatures (see Chapters 6 and 11), international community pressure was far from emptying Rangoon's overcrowded political prisons. Even though some Western aid and trade sanctions were applied to the repressive military regime in Burma, China came to its aid, massively, while Singapore and Thailand expanded lucrative investment and trade, and Japan, the region's dominant economic power has, as Robinson notes, been reluctant to press very hard for protection of human rights. 'Given the experience of the past, Japan will remain reluctant to pursue policies that can be construed as direct interference in the domestic affairs of Asian countries', in fear of attacks against a 'new imperialism' (Tamamoto, 1991). The global consensus in the 'New World Order' is much wider on matters of economic policy than it is on 'democracy'.

The gradual disappearance of Communist parties in ASEAN countries, which began before the end of the Cold War, but was speeded by it, has lessened one earlier justification for authoritarianism, 'the fight against communism'. At the same time there may also be a tendency in certain circumstances for authoritarian regimes to seek new sources of legitimacy through expanding political participation. But rapid economic growth itself may provide regime legitimacy, as in Singapore, obviating the necessity to seek it in other ways. And if expanding participation should activate groups which appear to challenge the position of the dominant class, as did the environmental movement in Malaysia in the 1980s or the independent labour movement in Indonesia in 1994, the participation will be restricted.

Elite fragmentation provides opportunity for a more articulate opposition, but if that fragmentation involves no conflict of economic interest, it is easily healed when the opposition is perceived as a threat. The fact that both Chinese and indigenous business interests in Indonesia still depend heavily on regime favours makes them an unlikely basis of a democratization process (Robison in Hewison *et al.*, 1993, pp. 58ff). The presence of more independent bourgeoisie, along with expanding middle classes, in Thailand and the Philippines create more favourable conditions for continued democratization there. Yet the very sizable resources – augmented by foreign aid and investment – controlled and distributed by central leaders in SE Asia still pose obstacles to peaceful regime change, since they are resources not easily surrendered.

Thus SE Asia's dynamic economic growth, creating a larger middle class in each country, does not automatically lead to democratization, even though it may improve its chances. The prospects are also tied to cultural and social factors, as well as to political institutions and the vagaries of leadership. Nor is the worldwide popularity of democratic ideas in the post-Cold War world sufficient to produce more democratic regimes in SE Asia. Such regimes will emerge only when those ideas coincide with the interests of democratic political forces which gain sufficient strength to change national political directions. Democracy is a consequence of national political struggle, often little affected by the positive encouragement of any particular 'world order'. But its chances are greater after the removal of such Cold War obstacles as the posing of strategic threats or super-power foreign assistance for military regimes. Only in Cambodia was democratization a direct consequence of the end of the Cold War, and without strong domestic forces supporting it, it is very fragile.

SOUTHEAST ASIAN DYNAMISM

The focus of this book has been a region more dynamic than any other in the non-Western world during the 1990s. It has been dynamic both in terms of economic growth and in terms of cooperative efforts to shape its international environment. SE Asia today is a far cry from the 'row of falling dominoes' that some Western analysts – incorrectly – imagined it to be in the 1960s. To be sure, SE Asian states in the past were most often simply reacting to probes and initiatives by external powers, but no longer.

The causes of this dynamism have been both internal and external to the region. Rapid economic growth was largely internally generated, by political stability, high savings rates, appropriate economic policies and rapid resource extraction – though massive foreign investment, as mentioned above, and favourable world market conditions were also important. Political dynamism itself derives in large part from the self-confidence and resource base provided by economic growth. The cooperative dimension of this dynamism also springs from within the region – the gradual emergence of a strong regional organization long before 1989. Yet ASEAN's vigour has also been fed by the threats and opportunities of the 'New World Order'. The major opportunity was the opening for settlement in Cambodia made by the end of the Cold War, facilitating efforts already underway by ASEAN, Australia and Japan, and augmenting ASEAN diplomatic experience and sense of accomplishment. On the other hand, ASEAN as an economic region felt threatened by emergence of European and North American integration in the 1990s, thus accelerating its efforts to form a free trade area.

In part the appearance of dynamism in SE Asia is simply a result of the greater freedom of manoeuvre inherent in the shift from a bi-polar to a multi-polar world. In regard to economic autonomy, Lee Kuan Yew sees SE Asian interests protected in the context of tripolarity. At a conference in Singapore (*International Herald Tribune*, 14 Oct. 1994), while encouraging European economic engagement, he said, 'A tripod is better than bipod. If we have only predominance of Americans and Japanese, there isn't the same comfort as when you have three major sources of capital, technology, expertise and markets.' Europeans have, of course, attempted to exploit this attitude (see Chapter 11). And Lee might have noted that if Korean and Taiwanese trade and investment continues to grow at recent rates, they will soon provide a fourth pillar to support SE Asian economic autonomy, and thus its dynamism. From a very low ranking in 1985 Taiwan moved to become the world's seventh largest exporter of capital in 1990, most of which was directed to SE Asia. In fact, Taiwan became the top investor in both Malaysia and Vietnam. And trade with the ASEAN countries nearly doubled from 1989 to 1993, reaching $15.6 billion in the latter year (Ho, 1993; Republic of China, External Trade Development Council).

But, while SE Asian dynamism is readily apparent, it is not a phenomenon as uniform across the region or as entirely benign in its consequences as is sometimes suggested. Neither Burma, nor, even within ASEAN, the Philippines – nor, until recently, Vietnam – have shared the rapid economic growth mentioned above. Laos is just climbing on the economic bandwagon and Cambodia, though experiencing improvement in 1993–5, still faces serious threats to economic growth, and even to stability. The population of these less fortunate countries constitutes 42 per cent of that of the entire region. So far the pull of prosperity in the more successful five has been stronger than any contrary drag effect. But not all SE Asian economies are dragons rampant. Neither, however, can SE Asia be included in the generalization that the Third World has suffered economically from the end of the Cold War (Korany, 1994, p. 11).

Furthermore, among the most successful countries in the region there is a tendency to spend increasing percentages of national budgets on arms. This is not, as most official spokesmen are happy to point out, an arms race aimed against anyone, but merely a push for 'military modernization' (Panitan and Ball, 1995). More realistically, it is often an effort by the military establishments to acquire 'their share' of expanding resources, as well as bargain-hunting in the arms bazaars of formerly Communist states in Europe. Even with official assurances, however, neighbours may not all be satisfied that new arms pose no potential threat. And where regional rebellions persist, as in Burma and Indonesia, or the Philippines, it is likely that at least some of the new arms *will* be used, internally.

Though strategic conflict among SE Asian states has clearly diminished in the 'New World Order', it has not disappeared. Cambodia, despite the initial success of a UN-brokered settlement, continues to be the major hotspot, particularly because of some Thai military support for the Khmer Rouge, and Phnom Penh's reaction thereto. Other conflicts are localized border disputes, not likely to escalate. But arms build-ups could increase that danger.

The main strategic task of a dynamic SE Asia is to balance the power of the US and Japan against the presence of China, both nearby and in recent times willing to use military force. Despite its history of interventions in the region, the US presence is now viewed as the most benign, and highly desired, though perhaps not entirely reliable. Japan is not only reluctant to project military force into the region, but SE Asian states are, for the most part, reluctant to invite it. Russia is not now a factor, despite its unwillingness to give up a toehold in Camranh Bay.

In this configuration it must be noted that at the same time the US is expanding military cooperation *with* China, to the extent of planning joint exercises (*International Herald Tribune*, 4 Oct. 1994), it has been unwilling to offer any assistance to its traditional ally, the Philippines, even in the case of an attack against its forces stationed in the Spratlys, let alone to the long-time enemy, Vietnam, whose outposts have actually been attacked. Apparently the hope is that the best way to restrain China's adventurism is to have close contact with its military, an approach fraught with difficulty.

ASEAN has also placed its faith in consultation as the first line of defence, a faith embodied in the ASEAN Regional Forum, to which the great powers in the Asia Pacific are invited. Dialogue, leading to confidence building, is indeed the best road to genuine collective security. Vietnam was especially eager to join ASEAN in order to share fully the benefits of dialogue as a partner with other ASEAN states. But dialogue alone cannot contain Chinese ambitions.

The economic objectives of a dynamic region, increasingly ASEAN-ized, are to acquire capital and technology and to expand and protect markets. (Only a minority of elites place any importance on the environment.) All of these goals are being pursued through the creation of the ASEAN Free Trade Area, which, if realized according to plan, will enhance bargaining power with other economic blocs, even while maintaining the principle of open regionalism. The more controversial step was that promoted by Prime Minister Mahathir, the EAEG, designed to further greater integration in Eastern Asia faster than in the Asia Pacific. The proposal is explainable in part by the fact that Malaysia within ASEAN has a particularly high percentage of its exports going to Asia. For the time being differences have been avoided by greatly diluting the original Malaysian proposal, which is now called simply East Asian Economic Caucus. This would give more chance for the strengthening of AFTA in the meantime. But unless Japan finally agrees to join the EAEC, it may never function.

In the longer run, however, controversy over the establishment of a trading zone in Eastern Asia is likely to be greater among great powers outside ASEAN than in the region. The basic fact is that China has only 23 per cent of its trade outside Asia while Japan's exceeds 60 per cent, and China seems to have a desire to eventually displace Japan's economic leadership in Asia. In the meantime there is concentration on expanding the functions of APEC. But APEC is approached by different countries with very different motivations, sometimes with conflicting intentions; the 1994 declaration from Bogor, proclaiming vague goals for more than a generation hence, attempted for the time being to conceal those conflicts.

In sum, Southeast Asia is a politically and economically dynamic region within the context of the broader dynamism of the Asia Pacific. In fact, the growth rate in most SE Asian economies is closing the gap with industrialized states. While ASEAN is gaining institutional strength, broadening membership and promoting closer integration, the emergence of genuine regionalism in Eastern Asia or Asia Pacific is fraught with difficulties. As former Thai Prime Minister Anand Panyarachun has said, 'The Asia Pacific is a concept, not a reality.' But he added that it was a concept with potential (*International Herald Tribune*, 10 Nov. 1994).

The 'New World Order', disorderly in spots, characterized by elements of continuity as well as change, marked by large variation among world regions, and hardly just a tool of the US, has come to Southeast Asia. The early optimism about the import of its arrival – aroused in part by the sharp deescalation of conflict in Cambodia and by the accompanying unprecedented UN intervention – was questioned by those who warned that all would not necessarily be sweetness and light in the post-Cold War multipolar world. Their pessimism was in large measure justified. Multipolarity, like bipolarity, has its downside. Regional balances can be destabilized if an overly ambitious great power is not effectively countered in a multipolar system. Yet, as we have already asserted, Southeast Asia is no 'power vacuum', and is by no means a passive participant in the global political economy. More than any other part of the Third World, the region possesses the organizational, economic and diplomatic capabilities needed to take advantage of multipolarity – and any other challenge the 'New World Order' might pose. Nevertheless, in the 'New World Order', as throughout history, Southeast Asia cannot alone thwart the ambitions of an ascendent China.

Note

1. A much less demanding definition is given to 'regional subsystem' by William R. Thompson, requiring only interaction, but neither common experience nor organization, thus accomodating the possibility of mutually hostile members of a subsystem (see W. R. Thompson, 'The Regional Subsystem . . .', *International Studies Quarterly*, vol. 17, no. 1 (March 1973), pp. 89–117).

References

Arase, David (1991) 'US and ASEAN Perceptions of Japan's Role in the Asian–Pacific Region', in Harry Kendall and Clara Joewono (eds) *Japan, ASEAN and the US* (Berkeley: University of California, Institute of East Asian Studies).

Bello, Walden (1992) *People and Power in the Pacific: The Struggle for the Post-Cold War Order* (San Francisco: Pluto Press).

Cable, Vincent and Peter Ferdinand (1994) 'China as an economic giant: threat or opportunity?' *International Affairs*, vol. 70, no. 2, pp. 243–61.

Camilleri, Joseph and Jim Falk (1992) *The End of Sovereignty? The Politics of a Shrinking and Fragmenting World* (Aldershot: Edward Elgar).
Colbert, Evelyn (1992) 'Southeast Asian Regional Politics: Toward a Regional Order', in H. Howard Wriggins (ed.) *Dynamics of Regional Politics* (New York: Columbia University Press).
Crone, Donald (1993) 'Does Hegemony Matter? The Reorganization of the Pacific Political Economy', *World Politics*, vol. 45, no. 4 (July), pp. 501–25.
Cronin, Richard P. (1990) 'Japan's Expanding Role and Influence in the Asia–Pacific Region: Implications for US Interests and Policy', *CRS Report for Congress* (Washington: Library of Congress, Congressional Research Service).
Fforde, Adam (1993) *Vietnam: Economic Commentary and Analysis* (Canberra: ADUKI), no. 3 (April 1993), no. 4 (December 1993).
Gilpin, Robert (1993) 'The Debate about the New World Economic Order', in Danny Unger and Paul Blackburn (eds) *Japan's Emerging Global Role* (Boulder: Lynn Rienner).
Hewison, Kevin, Richard Robison and Garry Rodan (eds) (1993) *Southeast Asia in the 1990s* (St Leonards, NSW: Allen & Unwin).
Ho Khai Leong (1993) *The Changing Political Economy of Taiwan-Southeast Asia Relations*, JIIA Fellowship Paper no. 1 (Tokyo: Japan Institute of International Affairs).
Huntington, Samuel (1991) 'America's Changing Strategic Interests', *Survival*, vol. 33, no. 1 (January/February).
Jin Dexiang (1991) 'China and Southeast Asia in a Changing Security Environment', paper delivered at 'ASEAN and the Asia–Pacific Region: Prospects for Security Cooperation in the 1990s', June, Manila, Philippines.
Korany, Bahgat (1994) 'End of history, or its continuation and accentuation? The global South and the "new transformation" literature', *Third World Quarterly*, vol. 15, no. 1, pp. 7–15.
Krasner, Stephen (1982) 'Structural Causes and Regime Consequences: Regimes as Intervening Variables', *International Organization*, vol. 36 (Spring).
Leaver, Richard and James Richardson (1993) *Charting the Post-Cold War World* (Boulder: Westview Press).
Machado, Kit (1992) 'ASEAN State Industrial Policies and Japanese Regional Production Strategies: The Case of Malaysia's Motor Vehicle Industry', in Cal Clark and Steve Chan (eds) *The Evolving Pacific Basin in the Global Political Economy* (Boulder: Lynne Rienner).
Palat, Ravi Arvind (1993) *Pacific-Asia and the Future of the World-System* (Westport: Greenwood Press).
Panitan, Wattanayagorn and Desmond Ball (1994) 'A Regional Arms Race?' *Journal of Strategic Studies*, vol. 16, no. 4 (December).
Stubbs, Richard and Geoffrey Underhill (1994) *The Political Economy of the Changing Global Order* (Toronto: McClelland & Stewart).
Tamamoto, Masaru (1991) 'Japan's Uncertain Role', *World Policy Journal*, vol. VII, no. 4 (Fall).
Williamsburg Conference (1992), *Report* (New York: Asia Society).
Yoo, Se Hee (1993) 'Sino-Japanese Relations in a Changing East Asia', in Gerald Curtis (ed.) *Japan's Foreign Policy: After the Cold War, Coping with Change* (Armonk, NY: M. E. Sharpe).

Appendix: Tables

Table A1 Basic demographic and economic indicators in Southeast Asia

	POPULATION		GROSS DOMESTIC PRODUCT						
	Total 1991 (thousands)	Average annual growth rate (1970–91) %	Total 1991 (millions of dollars)	Average annual growth rates of total real GDP at market prices %		Per capita 1991 (US$)	Average annual growth rates of per capita real GDP at market prices %		
		1980–91		1960–70	1970–80		1960–70	1970–80	1980–91
Brunei Darussalam	264	3.4	3,816	–	–	14,455	–	–	–
Cambodia	8,553	1.0	1,964	–	–	230	–	–	–
Indonesia	187,724	2.1	115,876	3.4	7.8	617	1.1	5.4	3.1
Laos	4,335	2.3	1,027	4.3	-0.1	237	2.0	-1.7	1.6
Malaysia	18,342	2.5	47,105	5.9	7.9	2,568	2.9	5.3	2.5
Myanmar	42,738	2.2	27,983	2.4	4.6	655	0.2	2.3	-1.5
Philippines	63,819	2.6	45,297	5.2	6.3	710	2.0	3.6	-1.6
Singapore	2,739	1.3	40,203	9.4	8.4	14,678	6.9	6.8	5.2
Thailand	55,393	2.1	93,311	8.3	7.1	1,685	5.1	4.3	5.9
Vietnam	68,082	2.2	–	–	–	–	–	–	–

Source: UNCTAD, *Handbook of International Trade and Development Statistics,* 1992, 1993.

Table A2 Basic social indicators in Southeast Asia

	Life expectancy at birth (years)		Infant mortality (per 1,000 live births)		Adult literacy rate %		Combined primary and secondary enrolment ratio	
	1960	1992	1960	1992	1970	1992	1970	1987–1990
Brunei Darussalam	62.3	74.0	63	8	–	86.0	–	–
Cambodia	42.4	50.4	146	117	–	37.8	–	–
Indonesia	41.2	62.0	139	66	54	84.4	49	81
Laos	40.4	50.3	155	98	–	55.0	29	65
Malaysia	53.9	70.4	73	14	60	80.0	62	75
Myanmar	43.8	56.9	158	83	71	81.5	54	62
Philippines	52.8	64.6	80	40	83	90.4	85	97
Singapore	64.5	74.2	36	8	–	92.0	77	87
Thailand	52.3	68.7	103	26	79	93.8	58	59
Vietnam	44.2	63.4	147	37	–	88.6	69	69

Source: United Nations Development Programme, *Human Development Report*, 1993, 1994.

Table A3 Military and social expenditures in Southeast Asia

	Population	HUMAN RESOURCES Armed forces (thousands)	Teachers	Physicians	PUBLIC EXPENDITURES Military % of GNP		Education % of GNP		Health % of GNP	
	1990	1990	1990	1990	1960	1990	1960	1990	1960	1990
Brunei Darussalam	256	4	4	0.2	–	9.0	–	5.0	–	0.8
Cambodia	8,469	112	54	0.6	5.4	–	3.5	–	1.3	–
Indonesia	178,232	283	2,039	23.2	5.8	1.7	6.3	2.8	0.3	0.5
Laos	4,140	55	30	0.6	–	–	–	1.0	0.5	–
Malaysia	17,861	130	192	6.8	1.9	3.7	2.7	5.5	1.1	1.3
Myanmar	41,609	230	272	12.4	7.0	4.9	2.2	2.2	0.7	1.0
Philippines	61,480	108	385	9.0	1.2	2.2	2.3	3.0	0.4	0.8
Singapore	3,003	56	19	3.6	0.4	5.3	2.8	3.8	1.0	1.2
Thailand	55,801	283	473	11.3	2.4	2.6	2.1	3.8	0.4	1.0
Vietnam	66,312	1,052	469	22.3	–	–	–	–	–	–

Source: Ruth Leger Sivard, World Military and Social Expenditures, 1993.

Table A4   Southeast Asian long-term debt

	Debt outstanding (millions of dollars)			Debt service (millions of dollars)			Debt outstanding as a percentage of GNP			Debt service as a percentage of exports of goods and services		
	1980	1987	1991	1980	1987	1991	1980	1987	1991	1980	1987	1991
Brunei Darussalam	62	27	0	7	2	1	1.4	0.8	0.0	0.1	0.1	0.0
Cambodia	251	960	1,563	1	10	15	–	–	–	4.0	46.0	45.3
Indonesia	16,670	45,855	56,272	2,080	8,244	9,494	22.3	63.5	51.0	9.4	31.5	28.9
Laos	75	1,390	1,668	2	12	7	–	127.9	161.9	11.0	13.2	5.6
Malaysia	3,923	19,851	18,552	506	3,478	2,457	16.6	67.0	41.3	3.4	16.6	6.2
Myanmar	1,524	4,344	4,737	112	206	85	26.5	41.5	16.8	22.8	60.0	21.3
Philippines	8,721	24,308	22,993	1,220	3,127	3,113	24.8	74.3	50.2	15.3	34.1	21.5
Singapore	1,698	3,783	3,913	331	888	494	15.3	18.1	9.6	1.3	2.3	0.6
Thailand	5,239	19,826	25,393	984	3,201	3,515	16.4	41.4	26.2	11.5	20.3	9.3
Vietnam	–	–	–	–	–	–	–	–	–	–	–	–

Source: UNCTAD, *Handbook of International Trade and Development Statistics*, 1992, 1993.

Table A5   Direction of Southeast Asian trade

Country	Region	1980 Imports %	Exports	1985 Imports %	Exports	1991 Imports %	Exports
Brunei Darussalam	South & Southeast Asia	29.2	13.2	38.7	30.4	47.2[1]	32.4
	Europe	21.0	–	18.3	–	21.2[1]	9.3
	USA & Canada	20.4	8.7	15.8	7.4	12.9[1]	1.2
	Japan	23.6	71.9	19.9	62.1	14.8[1]	52.1
Indonesia	South & Southeast Asia	20.9	16.7	15.2	18.7	28.1	29.8
	Europe	15.2	6.7	19.8	6.4	23.0	14.7
	USA & Canada	13.9	19.8	18.7	22.0	15.7	13.9
	Japan	31.5	49.3	25.8	46.2	22.0	31.8
Malaysia	South & Southeast Asia	23.4	31.7	30.2	39.8	26.9	42.6
	Europe	17.8	18.6	17.0	15.1	15.3	15.6
	USA & Canada	16.1	16.8	16.4	13.7	16.5	19.5
	Japan	23.0	22.8	23.2	23.8	–	13.3
Myanmar	South & Southeast Asia	29.0[2]	52.7	–	52.8	10.8[1]	49.2
	Europe	28.2[2]	11.7	–	15.0	26.5[1]	8.9
	USA & Canada	5.2[2]	1.6	–	2.7	6.3[1]	1.2
	Japan	26.5[2]	14.8	–	11.1	39.0[1]	5.8
Philippines	South & Southeast Asia	13.6	15.7	25.8	19.5	26.1	15.0
	Europe	12.3	18.4	10.1	17.0	12.6	19.4
	USA & Canada	24.6	28.8	25.9	37.5	19.7	40.9
	Japan	19.9	26.5	14.4	19.0	21.2	17.8

continued on page 304

Table A5   continued

Country	Region	1980 Imports % Exports		1985 Imports % Exports		1991 Imports % Exports	
Singapore	South & Southeast Asia	23.7	39.4	26.4	37.4	31.2	40.7
	Europe	13.3	14.1	13.3	11.5	14.9	16.6
	USA & Canada	14.6	13.4	15.5	21.9	16.9	21.9
	Japan	17.8	8.1	17.0	9.4	21.0	7.6
Thailand	South & Southeast Asia	17.7	24.8	25.9	25.0	20.0	21.4
	Europe	16.2	29.2	17.9	21.0	17.4	23.1
	USA & Canada	18.0	13.2	12.6	21.0	12.7	22.8
	Japan	20.7	15.3	26.5	13.4	29.3	18.1

[1]1989 [2]1977

Source: UNCTAD, Handbook of International Trade and Development Statistics, 1992, 1993.

Table A6   Official Development Assistance in Southeast Asia

| Country | NET DISBURSEMENT OF ODA FROM ALL SOURCES | | | | | |
| | *Per capita ($US)* | | | *As a % of GNP* | | |
	1985	*1990*	*1991*	*1985*	*1990*	*1991*
Cambodia	–	4.9	–	–	–	–
Indonesia	3.7	9.7	10.2	0.7	1.6	1.6
Laos	10.3	36.6	30.8	2.7	17.5	12.7
Malaysia	14.7	26.3	15.9	0.8	1.1	0.6
Myanmar	9.6	4.1	–	5.1	0.8	–
Philippines	8.9	20.8	16.7	1.5	2.9	2.3
Singapore	9.3	–1.0	2.8	0.1	0.0	0.0
Thailand	9.3	14.4	12.6	1.3	1.0	0.7
Vietnam	1.8	2.9	–	–	2.1	–

Source: World Bank, *World Development Report*, 1987, 1992, 1993, 1994.

Index

Abdulgaffar Peang Meth, 236
Aceh, 85, 90, 287
Afghanistan, 129, 205
Alatas, Ali, 69, 86, 91, 198
Amnesty International, 80, 85, 89, 95
Amoco, 255
Anand Panyarachun, 293
anti-communism, 74, 133
Aquino, Corazon 37, 41, 79
Arabian Energy Development, 250
Arabian Oil Company, 259
arms race, 166, 244, 262, 273, 286, 292
arms sales, 78, 115, 120, 146, 174
Asia Pacific xiv, xvi, xvii, 4–9, 12–14, 103, 109, 129, 134, 135, 138, 165 166, 168, 174, 175, 181, 184, 187, 190, 199, 215, 216, 226, 273, 275, 276, 279, 287, 293
Asia Pacific, economic integration, 165, 174, 181
Asia-Pacific Conference on Human Rights, Jakarta, 89
Asia-Pacific Economic Cooperation (APEC), 4, 13, 21, 46–8, 91, 107, 113, 121, 138, 157, 182, 198, 199, 215, 276, 293; secretariat, 21; summit, 120, 199
Asia-Pacific Roundtable, 13
Asia Regional Meeting of the World Coference on Human Rights, Bangkok, 12, 77, 89
Asian Development Bank (ADB), 58, 62, 66, 196
Asian Non-Governmental Organization Coalition (ANGOC), 66
Asiawatch, 89
Association of South East Asian Nations (ASEAN), xiv, xvi, xvii, 3–7, 11–14, 19–51, 61, 67, 76, 78, 85, 88, 90, 91, 104, 109–11, 129–131, 133, 134, 137–40, 143, 145, 155, 169, 172, 186, 189, 204–10, 213, 216, 224, 244, 249, 252, 253, 258, 260, 262–4, 274–6, 278–80, 282, 291–3
ASEAN Chambers of Commerce and Industry (ASEAN-CCI), 23
ASEAN Declaration on the South China Sea, 249, 252, 260, 265
ASEAN Foreign Ministers' meeting, 137, 159, 182, 247, 248, 277
ASEAN Free Trade Area (AFTA), 7, 20–2, 24, 25, 28, 33, 34, 41, 208, 281, 293
ASEAN Industrial Complementation (AIC), 23
ASEAN Industrial Joint Venture (AIJV), 23, 207
ASEAN Post-Ministerial Conference (PMC), 19, 44, 45, 47, 48, 109, 137, 157, 176, 209, 214–16, 247
ASEAN Preferential Trading Arrangements, 24, 32
ASEAN Regional Forum (ARF), 10, 13, 45, 49, 112, 216, 253, 279, 280, 293
ASEAN Secretariat, 23, 41, 48, 63
ASEAN states, 32, 33, 37, 39, 40, 42–6, 49, 52, 90, 109, 112–15, 118, 121, 124, 138, 143, 146, 147, 150, 152–5, 158, 168–74, 181–3, 187, 193–6, 199, 205–7, 214, 224, 254, 281, 289, 291
ASEAN Treaty of Amity and Cooperation, 11, 36, 44, 49, 265, 278
ASEAN, dialogue partners, 47, 176 *see also* security dialogue

ASEAN, economic integration, *see* regional economic integration
ASEAN, economic development of, 153, 159, 169
ASEAN, factionalism, 147, 278
ASEAN, human rights position, 90 *see also* human rights
ASEAN, nuclear free zone, 43, 138
ASEAN, security role, 45, 46, 49
ASEAN, summits, 19, 21, 40, 48
ASEAN, trade, 24–26; with China, 156; with Japan 25, 172; with Russia 136, 138, 156; with South Korea 156; with Taiwan, 156; with US, 25
ASEAN-ization, xiv, 14, 278
Aung San Suu Kyi, 117, 214
Australia, 5, 11, 13, 19, 21, 42, 44–7, 79, 94, 131, 187–90, 193, 194, 196–201, 211, 212, 215, 228, 230, 276, 277, 285, 291
    Department of Foreign Affairs and Trade, 79
    Parliament, 188
    economic assistance by, 186, 188, 193, 196
    investment by, 186, 188
    military, 79, 189, 197; military aid, 190
    security concerns, 188–90
    trade, 186, 188; with ASEAN countries, 193, 194
Australian Country Party, 189
Australian Labour Party, 196, 198
authoritarianism, 288, 289

balance of power, 13, 39, 109
Bali, 19
Bandung principles, 133
Bangkok, 32, 44, 64, 74, 89, 133
Bangladesh, 214
Bank of America, 58
Batam, 27, 32
Batamindo Management, 27
bayanihan, 59
Beazley, Kim, 190
Beijing Declaration, 68
Berlin Wall, xvi

bipolar system, xv, xvi, 110, 187, 291, 294
Borneo, 66
Bosnia, 88, 90, 106, 123
Boxer Rebellion, 263
Brahmanism, 235
Britain, 42, 78, 84, 90, 188, 189, 194, 205, 208–13
British Aerospace (BAE), 79
British Gas, 250
British Petroleum, 250
Broken Hill Proprietary, 250
Brunei, 24, 134, 154, 208, 253, 244
Buddhism, 235
Burma (Myanmar), xiv, 26, 54, 67, 68, 74–7, 84, 85, 90–2, 117, 118, 165, 192, 205, 214, 278, 289, 292
Bush, George, xv, 104, 105, 109, 113
Bush administration, 117, 168
'Buy Australia Last', 199
'Buy British Last', 206

Cairns Group, 40
Cam Ranh Bay, 144
Cambodia, xiv, 41, 42, 44, 49, 67, 75, 83, 85, 90, 93, 95, 121, 122, 124, 129–32, 136, 144, 145, 165, 169, 175, 178, 179, 183, 189, 195, 196, 204, 205, 208, 210–13, 215, 221–3, 225, 226, 230, 232, 235–7, 239, 257, 278–80, 283–5, 291, 292
    Supreme National Council (SNC), 82, 132, 143, 144, 149, 237
    elections, 221, 223, 224, 231, 238, 284
    peace process, 41, 132
    Phnom Penh government, 122, 227–232, 237; *see also* State of Cambodia
    Vietnamese invasion of, 142, 145, 146, 168, 189, 192, 210, 224, 276
    Vietnamese withdrawal from, 132, 144, 148, 196, 211, 228
    war, 9, 143, 157, 225, 226
Cambodia: An Australian Peace Proposal, 197

Canada, 11–13, 19, 21, 44–7, 80,
    84, 187, 190–201, 265, 276,
    277, 285
  Department of External Affairs,
    198
  economic assistance, 186, 188,
    191, 193
  human rights policies, 192
  investment by, 186, 188
  security interests, 191
  trade, 186, 188; with ASEAN
    countries, 193, 195
Canada–ASEAN Centre, 195
Canadian International Development
  Agency (CIDA), 195
Casey, Richard G., 188
Central Intelligence Agency (CIA),
  89, 283
Chaeron Pokphand, 6
Chatichai Choonhaven, 42, 43, 183
Chico River, 55
Chile, 47, 276
China, xv, 6, 9, 10–13, 30, 38, 43,
    44–7, 50, 84, 85, 90, 108–10,
    112, 118, 120, 121, 128–31,
    142–64, 174, 183, 187, 190,
    192, 196, 210, 215, 224–31,
    240, 244–69, 273, 274, 277,
    278, 280, 283, 284, 287, 289,
    292–4
  Ministry of Foreign Affairs, 148,
    262
  Ministry of Geology, 250
  People's Liberation Army–Navy
    (PLA–N), 251, 255, 260–2
  diplomacy, 10, 152, 155, 161
  economic relations with Southeast
    Asia, 30, 155, 156, 158
  human rights issues, 12, 85, 90,
    118
  military, 146, 159, 160; military
    capabilities, 45, 148, 151, 158,
    160, 161
  regime change, 287
  relations with Cambodia, 149,
    150; with Indonesia, 147,
    152–5; with Laos, 149; with
    Singapore, 147, 154; with
    Soviet Union, 129–31, 143,

    227, 257; with Taiwan, 9;
    with Thailand 6, 145, 146;
    with US, *see* US, relations
    with China; with Vietnam,
    130, 143, 144, 148, 158, 160,
    159, 229, 244, 248–50, 253,
    255–6, 258–60, 261–2, 265,
    283
  strategic objectives, 143; Asian
    security concerns over, 159,
    161, 262, 276, 278
  trade, 278; with Japan 156; with
    Russia 156; with South Korea,
    156
Chinese territorial claims, 44, 160,
    161, 280
Chinese, overseas, *see* Overseas
  Chinese
Christopher, Warren, 76, 103, 120
Chuan Leekpai, 283
civil society, xv, 282, 285
Clark Field, 109, 110, 114, 115
Clark, Joe, 195
Clinton, Bill, 103, 105, 107, 108,
    111–14, 120–2, 124, 174,
    199
Clinton administration, 45, 80, 105,
    106, 113, 115, 116, 118, 120,
    121
Clinton Doctrine, 125
Coalition Government of
  Democratic Kampuchea
    (CGDK), 190, 210, 211, 224,
    225, 227, 228, 230, 232
'Coca Cola-isalation', 262
Cold War, xv, xvi, 3, 4, 8, 12, 37,
    39, 104, 105, 108, 114, 122,
    125, 157, 161, 167, 168, 187,
    189, 191–3, 195, 197, 200,
    204, 208, 221, 244, 257, 275,
    277
  end of, 39, 43, 52, 70, 71, 74,
    78, 81, 82, 95, 122, 187, 197,
    199, 201, 216, 257, 273–5,
    277, 279, 281, 282, 285, 288,
    289, 291, 292
collective security, *see* security
  arrangements
Colombo Plan, 192

colonial administrations, 60, 204, 205
Common Effective Preferential Tariff, (CEPT), 32
Commonwealth, 187, 189, 191
Commonwealth of Independent States, 138
communism, 74, 108, 123, 129, 152, 168, 169, 174, 188, 191, 192, 204, 205
Communist parties, 153, 155, 285, 289
Communist Party of Indonesia (CPI), 139, 152
Communist Party of the Soviet Union, 229
Communist Party of Thailand, 146
Communist Party of Vietnam, 112, 226, 286
comparative advantage, 26, 27, 29–31, 33, 34
comprehensive national security, 38, 58
Comprehensive Political Settlement (Cambodia), 132, 143, 144, 149, 197, 230, 231
Conference on Security and Cooperation in Asia (CSCA), proposed, 44
Conference on Security and Cooperation in Europe (CSCE), 10, 44, 216, 279
Confucian, 5
Conoco, 250
constructive engagement, 91, 214, 278
Consultative Group on Indonesia, 209
Council for Mutual Economic Cooperation (COMECON), 281
Crestone Energy Corporation, 248–50, 259, 260

de Venecia, Jose, 253
deforestation, 54, 60, 66, 68, 210, 283
democracy, 12, 74, 84, 103, 108, 110, 112, 115–19, 122–5, 168, 275, 288–90

democratization, 79, 93, 105, 106, 124, 223, 237, 239, 290
Deng, Xiaoping, 262
Dili Massacre, *see* Santa Cruz Massacre
Do Muoi, 133, 148
domestic jurisdiction, *see* sovereignty
Dutch East Indies, 256

Earth Summit (Rio de Janeiro, 1992), 210
East Asia, xiv, 6, 12, 34, 181, 276
East Asia Economic Caucus (EAEC), 4, 21, 26, 47, 49, 181, 182, 215, 293
East Asia Economic Grouping (EAEG), 21, 47, 181, 276, 293
East Asia Security Initiative (EASI), 109–111, 119, 123
East Timor, 74, 75, 77, 78, 81, 82, 90, 95, 115, 119, 120, 123, 189, 197, 205, 209, 280, 285, 287
Eastern Asia, 5, 6, 8, 11–13, 26, 39–41, 177, 181, 273, 276–8, 293
Eastern Europe, 204, 208, 216, 229, 288
ecology, *see* environment
economic assistance (ODA), 20, 36, 38, 76, 77, 80, 115, 128, 180, 193, 195
economic assistance, conditionality, 12, 76, 88, 90
   see also environmental advocacy, external pressures
economic assistance, donors, 21, 77, 80
economic assistance, sanctions, 80, 192, 198
economic development, 124, 167, 169, 174
   see also economic growth
economic dynamism, of Southeast Asia, 172, 186, 190, 200, 208, 275, 290, 291, 293
   see also ASEAN, economic development

economic growth, 8, 12, 20, 38, 103, 108, 112, 115, 120, 166, 205
economic issues, 40, 157
economic liberalization, 22, 31, 33, 37
economic policy, 113, 151
economic priorities, 40, 46, 142
economic security, *see* economic priorities
education, 193
elections, 232, 237
elites, 52, 53, 62, 63, 67–69, 94
'emerging "world order"', 4, 8, 41
environment, 273, 285, 288
environmental advocacy, 58, 59, 62, 65; external pressures, 66, 67
environmental awareness, 52, 61, 64, 70
environmental degradation, 9, 108
environmental issues, 53, 54, 62, 65, 208, 210
environmental security, 64, 65, 129
Environmental Defence Fund, 67
Environmental Policy Institute, 67
Epifanio de los Santos Avenue (EDSA) revolution, 94
ethnic conflicts, 135
Europe, 76, 205, 216, 291
Europe, regional integration, *see* regional integration
European attitudes toward SE Asia, 204
European Community (EC), 19, 20, 34, 40, 45, 76, 78, 82, 88, 90, 181, 195, 204, 205, 207, 208, 210, 211, 213–216
EC–ASEAN Cooperation Agreement, 88, 205, 209
EC–ASEAN Economic Ministers Meeting, 207, 209, 211
EC–ASEAN relations, 206, 214, 215
EC, economic assistance, 208, 210, 213
EC, trade with SE Asia, 205, 206, 213
EC member states, 65, 66, 204, 209, 210

European Free Trade Area (EFTA), 20
European Parliament, 76, 88, 214
European Union (EU), 11, 204, 207, 215
Evans, Gareth, 190, 230
exclusive economic zone (EEZ), 24, 31, 121, 248, 252, 259, 291
Exocet missiles, 262
export processing zones, *see* exclusive economic zones

'falling dominoes', 290
Feingold, Russell, 119, 120, 123
Five-Power Defence Arrangement (FPDA), 189, 215
foreign direct investment, 7, 21, 28, 29, 30, 31, 38, 39, 69, 78, 90, 110, 113–16, 170, 193, 207, 208, 274, 290
see also under investment in individual counties
Fortress Europe, 207
Framework Agreement on Comprehensive Political Settlement in Cambodia, *see* Comprehensive Political Settlement (Cambodia)
Framework Agreement on Enhancing ASEAN Economic Cooperation, 41
France, 31, 78, 90, 122, 132, 205, 208, 210–13, 227, 285
Free Legal Assistance Group (FLAG), 93
free trade zones, *see* exclusive economic zones
Free World, 105
Fretilin, 197
Front Uni National Pour un Cambodge Indépendant, Neutre, Pacifique et Coopératif (FUNCINPEC), 222, 223, 238
Fukuda Doctrine, 169, 174

G-7 Summit, 179
General Agreement on Tariffs and Trade (GATT), 49, 107, 117, 121, 181, 207

Generalized System of Preferences (GSP), 81, 117, 120, 170
genocide, 132
Germany, 31, 78, 79, 84, 90, 105, 208, 212
Giddens, Anthony, 235
glasnost, 228
global economy, 39, 165, 182, 186, 193, 294
Goh Chok Tong, 26, 33, 181, 183
Gorbachev, Mikhail S., xv, 44, 128, 129, 133, 190, 226
gotong-royong, 59
great power competition, 274, 277
Great Society, 104
Green Forum, 64
'green imperialism', 69
growth triangles, 7, 26–9, 33, 34, 282
Gulf of Tonkin, 250, 255
Gulf War, 178, 212, 217
Gusmao, Xanana, 197

Hainan, 255
Haiti, 123
Half Moon Reef, 253
Halperin, Morton, 116–18
Haribon Foundation, 64
Hatfield, Mark, 119
Hawke, Bob, 190, 196
Hawke government, 197
hegemony, 37, 39, 110
Helsinki, 133
heroin, 283
Hong Kong, 21, 39, 46, 47, 63, 181, 213, 256, 257, 261, 262
Hosokawa, Morihiro, 105, 166, 174, 175
human rights, 12, 44, 74, 75, 119, 121, 124, 125, 187, 197–200, 204, 208, 209, 214, 273, 274, 278, 285, 288
human rights advocates, 75, 89, 93, 94, 118–20, 289
human rights policies, 77, 79, 83, 84, 93, 95
human rights practices, 95, 96
human rights standards, Asian, 85–87, 124

human rights violations, 9, 74, 78, 83, 85, 87, 88, 93, 106, 115, 120 123
human rights, external pressure for, 13, 75, 83, 84, 88–90, 92, 95, 106, 122, 210, 286
human rights, respect for, 112, 120
Hun Sen, 131, 149, 150, 211
Hurd, Douglas, 215

International Committee of the Red Cross (ICRC), 95
India, 43–6, 192, 250
Indo-China, 3, 26, 131, 136, 142, 148, 150, 161, 174, 181, 183, 188, 189, 192, 205, 206, 216, 274, 279
Indonesia, 21, 22, 26, 42, 43, 48, 54, 110, 112, 114, 122, 123, 131–3, 138, 170, 182, 183, 189, 191, 192, 197, 198, 200, 206–7, 209–11, 247–9, 254, 258, 265, 278, 280, 282, 285, 287, 292
National Commission on Human Rights, 92
armed forces, 43, 79, 80
economy, 5, 6, 22, 30, 114, 170, 206
environmental issues, 54, 61, 64–6, 68, 69, 71, 210
human rights issues, 12, 74, 75, 78, 80–2, 84–6, 88–92, 94, 115, 118–20, 197, 198, 200, 209, 285
relations with China, 147, 153, 154; with Russia, 139
Institute of Southeast Asian Studies, 63
Intergovernmental Group on Indonesia (IGGI), 209
International Civil Aviation Organization (ICAO), 255
international civil society, 70, 96, 274, 285
International Commission of Supervision and Control (ICSC), 190, 191
International Covenant on Civil and Political Rights (ICCPR), 85

international financial institutions, 13, 66

International Military Education and Training (IMET), *see US*, military assistance

International Monetary Fund (IMF), 211, 213, 282, 284, 285, 289

international political economy, 180, 193, 281, 286
see also political economy

international regime analysis, 47, 71, 276

International Rice Research Institute (IRRI), 62

International Tropical Timber Organization, 67

Iraq, 106

Ireland, 210

Islam, 138, 285

Israel, 88, 113

Jackson Atoll, 253

Jakarta, 44, 54, 124, 133

Jakarta Informal Meeting, 226, 227

Japan, xv, 5, 10, 13, 19–21, 31, 36–9, 44–7, 69, 77, 78, 84, 90, 104–6, 109, 110, 113, 114, 118, 121, 128, 151, 158, 165–8, 172, 181, 195, 205, 207, 211, 215, 246, 250, 253, 256–9, 262, 263, 273–5, 277, 287, 289, 291–3

Constitution, 176–178, 238

Ministry of International Trade and Industry (MITI), 182

Overseas Economic Cooperation Fund (OECF), 58

Peace-Keeping Operations Law, 175, 178

Self Defence Agency, 175–177, 183

attitudes towards militarism, 178, 182

economic assistance (ODA), 78, 114, 169, 170, 180, 208

economic presence in Southeast Asia, 121, 151, 161, 169, 172, 215, 258

foreign economic policy, 179, 182

human rights policy, 77, 78, 84, 90, 118, 289

investment by, 39, 169, 278; in Southeast Asia, 6, 31, 38, 90, 113, 157, 158, 165, 170, 172, 180, 182, 250, 259, 275, 291

military, 41, 43, 175, 178, 188

military aid, 78

military capability, 151, 168, 176

naval operations, 157, 256

policy-making, 166, 179

relations with China, 131, 151, 158, 159, 259, 273, 278, 280, 287; with US, *see* US, relations with Japan

role in Southeast Asia, 11, 19, 38, 39, 170, 174, 175, 181, 183, 205, 291

role in the Asia Pacific, 5, 13, 21, 36, 38, 46, 277, 293

security role, 44–46, 64, 109, 110, 167, 182, 183, 246, 256, 258, 262, 263, 292

trade with Southeast Asia, 6, 69, 172

Japan, Inc., 180

Japan-ASEAN Investment Corporation, 169

Java, 60, 64

Johnson, Lyndon, 104

Johnston Reef, 248

Johor, 26–8, 32

Jurong Environmental Engineering, 27

Kaifu Toshiki, 174

Kalimantan, 27, 63

Kampuchea, 205, 210
see also Cambodia

Kantor, Mickey, 121

Kaysone Phomivane, 149

Keating, Paul, 199

Kedung Omo dam, 55

Khin Nyunt, 85

Khmer People's National Liberation Front, (KPNLF), 224, 228, 231

Khmer Rouge, 67, 122, 131, 144, 145, 150, 189, 190, 210–12, 221, 224, 225, 228–31, 236, 237, 283, 292
Koh, Tommy, 227
konfrontasi, 191
Korea, 9, 21, 275, 191
    see also South Korea
Kuala Lumpur, 44, 54, 124
Kuala Lumpur Declaration on Human Rights, 89
Kuomintang, 262

labour-importing countries, 25, 282
labour unions, 120, 282, 289
labour-intensive operations, 31, 32
Lake, Anthony, 106
Laos, xiv, 45, 67, 114, 129, 131, 136, 137, 149, 180, 189, 278
Latin America, 93
Law of the Sea Convention, 249
Lee Kuan Yew, 147, 291
Leifer, Michael, 225, 226
Lembaga Bantuan Hukum (LBH), 93
levels of analysis, 286
Leyte, 54
Li Peng, 149, 155, 159, 249, 260
Liberal Democratic Party (LDP), 166, 175, 176, 180, 277
Liberal Party (Australia), 189
logging firms, 53, 61, 62, 64, 67–9, 71
Lombok, straits of, 257
Lord, Winston, 104, 109
Loridon, Michel, 212
Luzon, 59

Madura, 61
Mahathir bin Mohammed, Datuk Seri, 21, 34, 43, 63, 68, 69, 155, 181, 199, 210, 276, 285, 293
Malacca, straits of , 26, 67, 257
Malayan Communist Party (MCP), 152
Malayan Emergency, 189
Malaysia, xv, 26, 28, 42, 43, 133, 138, 139, 152–4, 158, 183, 188, 189, 191, 195, 199, 206, 207, 215, 244, 252, 254, 261, 263, 264, 285
    and EAEG/EAEC, 26, 49, 181, 182, 215, 293
    economy, 5, 6, 25, 29, 32, 39, 170, 284, 291
    environmental issues, 54, 61, 65, 69, 210
    human rights issues, 75, 85, 87, 88, 90, 91, 93, 115, 119, 209, 214
Manglapus, Raul, 42
Manila, 44, 54
Marcos regime, 288
markets, xv, 106, 275, 281–4
McDougall, Barbara, 198
Medan, 26
Mekong, 7
Mexico, 47
middle class, 61, 93, 94, 112
Middle East, 159
middle powers, 191, 195, 200
MiG, 263
migration, 9, 193
military aggression, *see* security threats
military conflict, 9
military issues, 115, 128, 129, 172
    see also security issues
military spending, 9
    see also arms race
Mindanao, 66
Mischief Reef, 251, 254
missing in action (MIA), 112, 119
Mitterrand, François, 212
Miyazawa Kiichi, 174, 175, 177
Mobil, 259
Mongolia, 129
moralpolitik, 116, 118, 120, 124
Most Favored Nation (MFN), 12
Moynihan, Daniel, 117
Mulroney, Brian, 195
multilateralism, 9, 253, 254, 275, 279–81
multinational corporations, 25, 27, 30–34, 39, 71, 115, 121, 274
multipolarity, 13, 294
Myanmar, *see* Burma (Myanmar)

National Resources Defence Council, 67
national security, 105, 107
see also security; comprehensive national security
National Security Council, 252
national sovereignty, *see* sovereignty
nationalism, 262, 265
Netherlands, 66, 78, 80, 84, 205, 208–210, 212, 285
Netherlands, economic assistance, 94, 208, 209
'New Pacific Order', 49
'New World Order', xv, xvi, 4, 14, 37, 41, 43, 46, 50, 142, 201, 221, 223, 273–5, 279, 280, 288, 289, 291, 292, 294
New Zealand, 19, 21, 42, 45–7, 189, 215, 253
Newly Industrialized Countries (NICs), 34, 282, 285
Newly Industrialized Economies (NIEs), 30, 38, 39, 158
Nguyen Van Linh, 133
Non-Aligned Movement (NAM), 43, 69, 88, 91, 133, 249
non-governmental organizations (NGOs), xv, 12, 55, 58, 59, 61, 65, 68, 87, 95, 115, 200, 274, 285, 286
see also human rights advocates, environmental advocacy
international, 53, 59, 65, 67, 68, 70, 89, 92
local, 58, 64, 67, 70, 83
regional, 64, 65, 68
non-state acts, 285, 286
Norodom Chakrapong, 238
Norodom Ranariddh, 238
Norodom Sihanouk, 131, 143, 145, 149, 211, 212, 222–4, 228, 231, 237, 238
North American Free Trade Agreement (NAFTA), 20, 34, 107, 215
see also regional economic integration
North Korea, 106, 129, 165
North–South issues, 47, 68

Northeast Asia, 275
Northern Asia, 6, 9, 14, 159, 168
nuclear free zone, *see* ASEAN, nuclear free zone
nuclear proliferation, 9

off-shore drilling, 159
see also Crestone Energy Corporation
Official Development Assistance (ODA) Charter, 77
Ohira Masayoshi, 174
Ohira Report, 38
oil, 258
Ombai-Wetar, 257
Oñate, Burton, 62
Ong Teng Cheong, 253
Organization for Economic Cooperation and Development (OECD), 74, 77, 187
Overseas Chinese, 11, 30, 67, 152–5

P-5 peace plan, for Cambodia, 211, 212
Pacific Basin, 46, 276
Pacific Community, 103, 106
Pacific Economic Cooperation Council (PECC), 13, 46, 47, 282
'Pacific international system', 36, 37, 39
Papua New Guinea (PNG), 44, 45, 67, 278
Paracels, 9, 248, 255, 256
Paris Conference on Cambodia (August 1989), 131, 197, 227
Paris Peace Agreements on Cambodia (October, 1991), 76, 82, 83, 221–4, 232, 236, 238, 299
Pathet Lao, 189
Pax Americana, 258
Pax Nipponica, 44
Pax Sinica, 261
Pell, Claiborne, 119
pembangunan, 65
Penang, 26
Penang Consumers' Association, 93
People's Daily, 263

People's Republic of Kampuchea (PRK), 211
People's Republic of China, *see* China
Perak, 55
perestroika, 228
Perry, William, 104
Peru, 47, 276
Petro Vietnam, 250
Philippine Assistance Plan, 38
Philippines, 6, 27, 42, 80, 85, 89–91, 108, 133, 140, 244, 251–4, 264, 282, 285, 288, 292
  Department of Foreign Affairs, 251, 252, 253
  Human Rights Commission, 80
  Senate, 109, 252, 274
  economy, 22, 165, 172, 282, 285, 291
  environment, 54, 60, 61, 67, 68
  human rights situation, 75, 80, 84, 93, 94, 192, 290
  military, 251–4
  relations with China, 153, 154, 158, 251–4, 261, 262; with Japan, 170; with US, 42, 109, 110, 114, 115, 183, 274, 292
Phuket, 27
Pinatubo, Mt, 274
Plaza Accord, 3, 6, 165, 170, 181, 275
Pol Pot, 122, 131, 192, 283
political economy, xv, 3, 13, 19, 53
  of Southeast Asia, 186, 187
  of the Asia Pacific, 193
Portugal, 82, 90, 119, 205, 208, 209
post-Cold War, xv, xvi, 4, 10, 42, 111, 123, 150, 151, 158, 167, 177, 178, 198, 258, 290
power vacuum, 275
Praphat Kritsanachan, Admiral, 146
prosperity, 103, 104, 106, 108, 110, 116, 121–123, 125, 182
PT Batamindo Investment Corp, 27
Putting People First, 113

Qian Qichen, 149, 152, 159
Qin Jiwei, 146

Rainforest Action Network, 67
Ramos, Fidel, 91, 252
Rare Earth Ltd, 55
Reagan, Ronald, 105
Reagan administration, 41
refugees, 115, 119, 213
regime, 47, 71, 276, 289
region, 4, 275, 276, 279
  sub-region, 7
regional economic integration, 4, 6, 7, 19, 20–2, 24, 26, 28–34, 40, 41, 49, 129, 156; 157, 180, 182, 216;
  in North America, 21
  in Southeast Asia, 28, 33, 276, 278
regional identity, xiv, 47
regional institutions, 7, 12–14, 156, 157
regional integration, 22, 28, 31
  Europe, 6, 174, 181, 204, 207, 208
Regional Meeting for the World Conference on Human Rights, Bangkok, 86
regional security, 8, 19, 110, 176, 190
  see also security
regional security dialogue, 10, 45
regionalism, 11, 71, 207, 278, 280, 293
'regionalized world order', 36
Riau, 26, 27
Rogachev, Igor, 130
Roman Catholic church, 285
Rowley, Kelvin, 231
Russia, xvi, 8, 10, 19, 36, 44, 45, 90, 106, 139, 140, 174, 247, 256, 261, 262, 273
  relations with Cambodia, 136; with Indonesia, 139; with Malaysia, 139; with the Philippines, 140; with Singapore, 140; with Thailand, 139; with Vietnam, 136, 137
Russia–Vietnamese Joint Commission on Economic, Scientific and Technological Cooperation, 137
Ryzhkov, Nicholay, 133

Sabah, 27, 60
Sahabat Alam, 64
Sakharov Prize, 214
Salim, Emil, 63
Santa Cruz Massacre, 12, 76, 79,
    80, 84, 92–4, 119, 197, 198,
    200, 209, 285
Sarawak, 55, 60, 61
Saudi Arabia, 175
Scott Paper Company, 61, 64
security, 103, 106, 108, 110, 111,
    116, 121–5
  see also comprehensive national
    security
security arrangements, 42, 44–6, 77,
    116, 123, 166, 174, 177
security concerns, 36, 71, 137, 142,
    157, 168
security dialogue, 14, 44–6
security issues, xv, 9, 39–41, 44,
    49, 52, 253
security threats, 8, 177, 188
Shevardnadze, Eduard, 129, 131,
    133, 134
Sierra Club, 67
Singapore, 5, 21, 24–9, 31, 32, 42,
    43, 45, 48, 54, 69, 75, 85, 87,
    90, 93, 109, 114, 121, 124,
    133, 146, 147, 153–6, 170,
    181, 182 188, 189, 207, 209,
    215, 253, 257, 278, 284, 289
Singapore Declaration of 1992, 40
Singapore Technologies Industrial
    Corp., 27
Sino-Soviet relations, *see* Soviet-
    Chinese relations
smuggling, 283
social class, 53, 93, 94
socialist countries, 128, 139
Somalia, 123
South China Growth Triangle, 7
South China Sea, 44, 45, 55, 159,
    160, 244, 248, 249, 253, 256,
    258–64
South China Sea, joint development,
    248, 249, 259, 260, 264, 265
South Korea, 6, 13, 19, 45–7, 90,
    103, 129, 170, 181, 276, 277,
    288

South Vietnam, 189, 255
Southeast Asia Treaty Organization
    (SEATO), 43
sovereignty, 63, 69, 88, 110, 116,
    159, 248, 254, 260, 265, 284–6
Soviet Union, xv, xvi, 20, 37, 38,
    41, 43, 44, 105, 108, 110,
    128–40, 148, 160, 167, 187,
    192, 215, 228, 229, 232, 273,
    274, 281, 287,
  collapse of, 20 36, 105, 174,
    187, 195, 204, 273, 277, 286,
    289
  economic assistance by, 128, 136
  foreign policy, 128, 131
  former states of, 156
  military presence, 128, 130, 144
Soviet threat, 41, 189
  absence of, 147, 274
Soviet–American relations, 4, 37,
    71, 129, 130, 131, 257, 274,
    279
Soviet–Chinese relations, 129–31,
    192, 224, 226, 229, 255
Soviet–Japanese relations, 128, 129,
    130
Soviet–Vietnamese relations, 129,
    130–3, 136, 142, 145, 147,
    150, 158
Spratly Islands, 9, 45, 143, 158–60,
    190, 244, 248, 249, 251, 253
    256–61, 263, 278, 280, 287, 292
Spratly Management Authority, 265
state, xv, 53, 60, 87, 88 120, 180,
    235, 275, 281, 283–6
state capacity, 283
state intervention, 27
state–society interaction, 286, 288
State Law and Order Restoration
    Council (SLORC), 76, 77, 85,
    91, 117, 118
State of Cambodia (SOC), 222,
    223, 225, 238
Statoil, 250
strategic concerns, 120, 142, 167,
    177, 192, 200
  see also security concerns
SU-27 military aircraft, 160
Subic Bay, 109, 110, 114, 115

Suez Canal, 60
Suharto, 27, 30, 43, 63, 88, 91,
     133, 154, 139
Sukarno, 152, 191
Sulawesi, 27
Sunda straits, 257
Survivor International, 68

Taiwan, 6, 21, 28, 39, 46, 47, 63,
     158, 170, 181, 244, 247, 252,
     262, 275, 277, 287, 288, 291;
     investments, 6, 156
     status of, 274
Takeshita Noburo, 174
tariffs, 22, 24, 208
     see also ASEAN Free Trade Area
Tarnoff Doctrine, 107, 116, 121,
     122, 125
Tarnoff, Peter, 106, 107
Thailand, xv, 6, 26, 42, 68, 76, 85,
     89–91, 114, 131, 133, 139,
     157, 182, 183, 188, 224, 235,
     240, 276, 283, 288–90
     arms sales, 140, 283
     economy, 5, 22, 24, 39, 170
     environment, 54, 59, 62, 66, 68
     human rights, 75, 89, 93, 94, 290
     military, 42, 67, 77, 145, 146,
          283, 289, 292
     relations with great powers, 114,
          139–40, 145–7, 153, 157, 169,
          170, 183
Than Shwe, 85, 88
Third World, 292
Tiananmen Square, 121, 197
tourism, 193
Toyota, 6
trade, 77, 115, 121, 122, 124, 139,
     166, 180, 182, 187, 193
trade liberalization, 23, 24
     see also AFTA
trade sanctions, 84
trade unions, *see* labour unions
Trudeau, Pierre Elliot, 192
Tumen River project, 7

Ukraine, 160, 248
United Nations, 48, 80, 82, 96,
     107, 122, 132, 143, 144, 167,

175, 178, 183, 197, 198,
     209–12, 222, 224, 230, 232,
     237, 279, 280, 284, 292
UN Advance Mission in Cambodia
     (UNAMIC), 197
UN Charter, 279
UN Commission on Human Rights
     (UNCHR), 76, 79, 81, 91, 209,
     279
UN Conference on Environment
     and Development (UNCED)
     (Rio de Janeiro) 67–69, 210
UN Conference on the
     Environment, Stockholm, 61
UN Development Programme
     (UNDP), 65
UN General Assembly, 76, 133
UN Security Council, 42, 122, 132,
     151, 211, 252, 279, 280
UN Security Council Framework
     Document on Cambodia, *see*
     Framework Agreement
UN Special Rapporteur for
     Myanmar, 76
UN Transitional Authority in
     Cambodia (UNTAC), 76, 82,
     83, 95, 143, 197, 212, 215,
     221–4, 237–9
UN World Conference on Human
     Rights in Vienna, 12, 86, 89,
     92, 103
UN, peacekeeping activities, 143,
     151, 217, 284
United Kingdom, *see* Britian
United States (US), 8, 10, 13, 19,
     21, 36–47, 49, 65, 66, 103–25,
     148, 181, 187, 188, 194, 195,
     199, 210–15, 224, 228, 231,
     232, 246, 251, 253, 256, 263,
     277, 285, 289, 294
     Agency for International
          Development (USAID), 115
     Trade Representative (USTR),
          114, 124
     Congress, 80, 111–15, 118, 124,
          277, 280
     Department of Commerce, 114
     Department of Defence (DOD),
          109, 119, 123, 124

Foreign Aid Appropriations Bill, 81
Navy, 256, 257
Peace Corps, 64
State Department, 113, 114, 119, 120
departure from Vietnam, 168, 189
economic assistance, 21, 114, 208; *see also* economic assistance
economic decline, 38, 40, 105, 113, 273
foreign policy, 78, 103–125
human rights policy, 78, 80–82, 87, 90, 274; *see also* prodemocracy policy *below*
investment by, 21, 31, 38, 207, 259
military, 44, 46, 108, 109, 169
military assistance, 80, 81, 82, 118, 119
military presence, 41, 42, 43, 44, 46, 109, 110, 168, 256, 257, 261, 263, 292
policy leverage, 104, 111, 114, 118, 119, 205
prodemocracy policy, 115, 117, 121, 124, 231
relations with China, 120, 151, 196, 228, 231; 255, 258, 262–3, 273–4, 280; with Japan, 104, 105, 113, 121, 167, 176, 183, 184, 258, 273, 277, 287; with USSR, *see* Soviet–American relations
trade, 120, 172; with Japan, 8, 104, 287, with Southeast Asia 8, 119, 291
US–ASEAN Alliance for Mutual Growth, 114
US–Asia Environmental Partnership, 108
US–Japan Mutual Security Treaty, 168, 176
USSR, *see* Soviet Union
Universal Declaration of Human Rights (UDHR), 86
Uruguay Round, 40
Uzbekistan, 138

Vietnam, xiv, 30, 54, 61, 65, 66, 75, 149, 157, 158, 189, 191, 192, 195, 196, 210, 215, 224, 250, 252, 254, 257, 264, 286, 293
Foreign Ministry, 148
and ASEAN, 44, 45, 196, 225, 244, 258, 278, 293
debt, 133, 211
economy, 30, 213, 225, 281–3, 291
embargo on, 30, 112, 169, 200, 211, 213, 226
emigration, 213, 214
investment in, 30, 158, 183, 250, 291
military, 160, 283
relations with Cambodia, 42, 131, 132, 144, 145, 149, 192, 205, 210, 211, 213, 224, 225, 226, 227, 228, 229, 235; with China, *see* China, relations with Vietnam; with US, 112, 119, 124, 189, 259, 292; with USSR, *see* Soviet–Vietnamese relations
Vietnam War, 19, 104, 107, 191
Vietnamese Communist Party, *see* Communist Party of Vietnam
Vladivostok-Krasnoyarsk platform, 129
Vo Van Kiet, 148, 249
Voice of Malayan Democracy, 152

Wang Hai, 146
Wang Shu, 156
Wan Bei, 248, 250
West Irian, 61, 63, 66, 287
Western Europe, 187, 204, 211
Williamsburg Conference, 287
World Bank, 20, 55, 58, 66–8, 114, 209, 277, 282, 284
World Conference on Human Rights (Vienna), *see* UN World Conference
World Court, 252
world political economy, 284, 286
see also international political economy
World Resources Institute, 62

World Trade Organization (WTO), 121
World War II, 167, 175, 189, 204, 256, 276
World Wildlife Fund, 67

Yang Dezhi, 256
Yang Shangkun, 152, 160

Yao Yilin, 152
Yeltsin, Boris, 44
Yugoslavia, 216

Zhongnanhai, 256
Zone of Peace, Freedom and Neutrality (ZOPFAN), 11, 43, 46, 130, 136